1984
YEAR BOOK OF
ORTHOPEDICS

THE 1984 YEAR BOOKS

The YEAR BOOK series provides in condensed form the essence of the best of the recent international medical literature. The material is selected by distinguished editors who critically review more than 500,000 journal articles each year.

Anesthesia: *Drs. Kirby, Miller, Ostheimer, Saidman, and Stoelting.*

Cancer: *Drs. Clark, Cumley, and Hickey.*

Cardiology: *Drs. Harvey, Kirkendall, Kirklin, Nadas, Resnekov, and Sonnenblick.*

Critical Care Medicine: *Drs. Rogers, Booth, Dean, Gioia, McPherson, Michael, and Traystman.*

Dentistry: *Drs. Cohen, Hendler, Johnson, Jordan, Moyers, Robinson, and Silverman.*

Dermatology: *Drs. Sober and Fitzpatrick.*

Diagnostic Radiology: *Drs. Bragg, Keats, Kieffer, Kirkpatrick, Koehler, Sorenson, and White.*

Digestive Diseases: *Drs. Greenberger and Moody.*

Drug Therapy: *Drs. Hollister and Lasagna.*

Emergency Medicine: *Dr. Wagner.*

Endocrinology: *Drs. Schwartz and Ryan.*

Family Practice: *Dr. Rakel.*

Medicine: *Drs. Rogers, Des Prez, Cline, Braunwald, Greenberger, Bondy, Epstein, and Malawista.*

Neurology and Neurosurgery: *Drs. De Jong, Sugar, and Currier.*

Nuclear Medicine: *Drs. Hoffer, Gottschalk, and Zaret.*

Obstetrics and Gynecology: *Drs. Pitkin and Zlatnik.*

Ophthalmology: *Dr. Ernest.*

Orthopedics: *Dr. Coventry.*

Otolaryngology: *Drs. Paparella and Bailey.*

Pathology and Clinical Pathology: *Dr. Brinkhous.*

Pediatrics: *Drs. Oski and Stockman.*

Plastic and Reconstructive Surgery: *Drs. McCoy, Brauer, Haynes, Hoehn, Miller, and Whitaker.*

Psychiatry and Applied Mental Health: *Drs. Freedman, Lourie, Meltzer, Nemiah, Talbott, and Weiner.*

Sports Medicine: *Drs. Krakauer, Shephard, and Torg, Col. Anderson, and Mr. George.*

Surgery: *Drs. Schwartz, Najarian, Peacock, Shires, Silen, and Spencer.*

Urology: *Drs. Gillenwater and Howards.*

The YEAR BOOK of

Orthopedics

1984

Edited by

MARK B. COVENTRY, M.D., M.S.

*Emeritus Consultant, Department of Orthopedics
Mayo Clinic, and Emeritus Professor of Orthopedic
Surgery, Mayo Medical School*

YEAR BOOK MEDICAL PUBLISHERS, INC.
CHICAGO

The editor for this book was Jane Toomey, and the production manager was H. E. Nielsen.

Table of Contents

The material covered in this volume represents literature reviewed up to February 1984.

Journals Represented

Acta Orthopaedica Scandinavica
Acta Radiologica (Diagnosis)
American Family Physician
American Journal of Clinical Pathology
American Journal of Medicine
American Journal of Nursing
American Journal of Roentgenology
American Journal of Sports Medicine
American Journal of Surgery
Annales Chirurgiae et Gynaecologiae
Annales Orthopediques de l'Ouest
Annals of Emergency Medicine
Annals of Neurology
Annals of Plastic Surgery
Annals of Rheumatic Diseases
Annals of the Royal College of Surgeons of England
Annals of Surgery
Archives of Disease in Childhood
Arthritis and Rheumatism
British Journal of Radiology
British Journal of Surgery
British Medical Journal
Canadian Journal of Psychiatry
Canadian Journal of Surgery
Canadian Medical Association Journal
Cancer
Chinese Journal of Orthopedics
Chirurg
Cleveland Clinic Quarterly
Clinical Radiology
Clinical Science
Dermatologica
Diagnostic Imaging
Foot and Ankle
Injury
International Orthopaedics
Israel Journal of Medical Sciences
Journal of the American Medical Association
Journal of Bone and Joint Surgery (American Volume)
Journal of Bone and Joint Surgery (British Volume)
Journal of the Canadian Association of Radiologists
Journal de Chirurgie

Journal of Hand Surgery
Journal of the Japanese Orthopaedic Association
Journal of Laboratory and Clinical Medicine
Journal of Neurological and Orthopaedic Surgery
Journal of Neurosurgery
Journal of Nuclear Medicine
Journal of Orthopedic Research
Journal of Pediatric Orthopedics
Journal de Radiologie
Journal of the Royal College of Surgeons of Edinburgh
Journal of Surgical Research
Journal of Trauma
Journal of the Western Pacific Orthopedic Association
Lancet
Mayo Clinic Proceedings
Medical Imaging
Neuroradiology
Neurosurgery
Orthopaedic Review
Pathology
Pediatric Infectious Diseases
Pediatric Radiology
Pediatrics
Physician and Sportsmedicine
Plastic and Reconstructive Surgery
Radiology
Revue de Chirurgie Orthopedique et Reparatrice de l'Appareil Moteur
Scandinavian Journal of Plastic and Reconstructive Surgery
Scandinavian Journal of Rheumatology
Skeletal Radiology
South African Medical Journal
Southern Medical Journal
Spine
Surgery
Surgical Neurology
Virchows Archive A: Pathological Anatomy and Histology

Introduction

The number of readers of the YEAR BOOK OF ORTHOPEDICS is steadily increasing. There is also an increasing number of publications today that have orthopedic pertinence. Yet, ironically, the number of published papers your editor feels are of significant value to the reader has slightly diminished this year, and the consistent reader of the YEAR BOOK will notice I have selected fewer articles for this 1984 edition. We make a determined effort to select only those papers which are of excellent quality, and the reader will notice that there are no less of these. Substance is our main measure of quality; but we also wish to bring you new and innovative ideas from the world's literature.

The new size and shape of the bound volume is now consistent with our other Year Book publications. The 1984 YEAR BOOK OF ORTHOPEDICS has been published in a larger size to present illustrations in more suitable dimensions as well as to match the size of all of the other 1984 YEAR BOOKS. We hope this will enhance its readability.

We have added a few new journals to our list of those we review, including the Chinese Journal of Orthopedics.

Your editor, with the considerable help of his colleagues at Mayo, which I gratefully acknowledge, continues to find his endeavors regarding the YEAR BOOK OF ORTHOPEDICS a learning experience, and one which is exciting and pleasurable. We hope the reader shares these feelings.

MARK B. COVENTRY, M.D. M.S.

1. Miscellaneous

1–1 **Pulmonary Fat and Bone Marrow Embolism in Aircraft Accident Victims.** Anthony R. Bierre and T. D. Koelmeyer (Univ. of Auckland) reviewed the autopsy findings after an airplane crash in Antarctica in 1979 in which 257 people died. Lung tissue was available in 205 of the 231 autopsy cases. Pulmonary fat emboli were discovered in 65% of autopsies, pulmonary bone marrow emboli in 29%, and pulmonary edema in 37%. Marrow emboli were not found without fat emboli, and the extent of marrow embolism increased with that of fat embolism. Pulmonary edema increased with the severity of fat embolism and was present in nearly three fourths of victims with marrow embolism. Marrow embolism was much less prevalent in persons with lacerations of the heart and aorta. The extent of both fat embolism and marrow embolism varied inversely with the severity of the injuries that were present. The most severely injured victims were those seated in the rear cabin, suggesting that this was the site of impact.

Fat and bone marrow emboli are found in the lungs of severely injured persons thought to have been killed instantly. The extent of fat and marrow embolism is clearly related to both the presence of pulmonary edema and the presence or absence of cardiovascular damage. Embolism certainly occurs within a few seconds of severe injury. The production of emboli is time dependent. The extent of pulmonary fat embolism and marrow embolism can be used as an objective indicator of the severity of injury where a large number of persons have been subjected to the same force. Such information may be particularly useful in assessing aircraft accidents in which the flight data recorder is unavailable.

▶ [This is a rather interesting postmortem account of 231 airline crash victims. It concentrates on the documentation of the presence or absence of fat embolism and bone marrow embolism, and their relationship to pulmonary edema.

The fact that fat emboli were present in 65% of the cases, pulmonary bone emboli in 29%, and pulmonary edema in 37%, is quite startling, particularly in light of recent literature which has tended to downplay this phenomenon. This article serves as a stimulus to examine the relationship of bone marrow embolism in posttraumatic insufficiency following extensive soft tissue trauma, particularly of the extremities.—P. Mucha, Jr.] ◀

1–2 **Making the Most of Gastrocnemius Muscles.** The gastrocnemius muscles are among the most dependable units in the lower ex-

(1–1) Pathology 15:131–135, April 1983.
(1–2) Plast. Reconstr. Surg. 72:38–48, July 1983.

tremity for use as muscle and musculocutaneous flaps, but the muscle heads are not always as long or as wide as is desired. Phillip G. Arnold and Roger C. Mixter (Mayo Clinic and Found.) describe several measures that provide more versatility with the medial and lateral gastrocnemius segments. When more length is needed with either muscle head, the neurovascular leash is isolated and the femoral bony attachment divided. The fascia over the muscle can be scored or excised to gain length or width. The separate muscle head can be split, or half the muscle used. Both muscle heads can be transposed, or adjacent muscles utilized. The muscle may be passed directly through the bone and into the defect where the knee has been fused or replaced with a prosthesis. A V-Y advancement can be used to obtain length distally for coverage. Mobilization of both muscle heads through a "stocking seam" incision permits them to be advanced medially to close a long anterior defect.

No marked functional disorders have resulted from using both the muscle heads. If a leg has been revascularized secondary to trauma below the popliteal space, the gastrocnemius muscle flap should not be used unless an adequate blood supply is confirmed. When the lateral gastrocnemius head is used, care is needed to avoid injuring the peroneal nerve. The V-Y advancement musculocutaneous flap using one or both gastrocnemius heads appears to be the most promising of the musculocutaneous flap methods. It is useful for covering the lower third of the leg and in revising short amputation stumps. The "stocking seam" incision and mobilization of bilateral muscle flaps along with the entire skin of the leg can be helpful when other muscles are unavailable and only skin and subcutaneous tissue are available for use over the exposed bone.

▶ [With their extensive experience in dealing with soft tissue coverage problems in the lower extremities, the authors are qualified to relate to us in a technical paper their experience with the gastrocnemius muscle flap. With the versatility gained by the seven modifications reported by the authors and substantiated by case reports, this flap becomes even more of an essential part of the reconstructive effort of severely injured lower limbs. The authors delineate a number of pitfalls and, more importantly, point the way out. They provide clear evidence that they are masters of the technique of muscle transfer for the lower limb reconstruction.—W.P. Cooney] ◀

1–3 **Posttraumatic Dystrophy of the Extremities: Clinical Review and Trial of Treatment.** Sudeck's posttraumatic dystrophy is characterized by refractory pain, swelling, and limited extremity motion after limb trauma, typically associated with vasomotor instability, trophic skin changes, and patchy demineralization of bone. Disability is much greater than that expected from disuse alone. The pathology remains obscure. Z. J. Poplawski, A. M. Wiley, and J. F. Murray (Toronto) evaluated a new treatment method in some of a series of patients with posttraumatic dystrophy of the hand and foot, most of

(1–3)   J. Bone Joint Surg. [Am.] 65-A:642–655, June 1983.

them followed for 5 years and longer. Fifty-six of the 126 patients in the review series were still under observation or treatment. Thirty-six of these patients and 26 others were examined. Pain was by far the most disabling symptom, and most patients reported loss of motion and stiffness. Vascular instability was noted in a majority of affected extremities. Most patients had patchy demineralization or generalized osteoporosis in the extremity. Twenty-five of 55 patients had been unable to return to work, and 7 others had changed to lighter work.

Regional intravenous block with lidocaine, with methylprednisolone added, was tried in 27 other patients referred with posttraumatic dystrophy of the hand or foot. A total of 64 blocks were administered. All patients had failed to respond adequately to physiotherapy for at least 3 weeks. Each block generally lasted 30 minutes. Manipulation was carried out if indicated. Active and passive joint mobilization and deep friction massage followed each block. Dynamic splints were used where indicated. Twenty-one of 28 affected extremities improved significantly after treatment, and 11 were graded excellent. All 7 poor results were in patients who had developed dystrophy 9 months or longer before treatment, while patients with fair or better results usually were treated within 6 months of the onset. Many patients required 2 or 3 blocks. No serious or lasting complications occurred.

Intravenous regional block with steroid added is an effective treatment of established posttraumatic dystrophy of the hand or foot in many cases, permitting rehabilitation by conventional physical therapy. Treatment is best instituted within 6 months of the onset, and certainly within a year. Significant complications have not occurred.

▶ [Although this study was conducted without double-blind design, it was done in such a way that the results would stimulate the readers to investigate further in a large number of patients.

Among many modalities, intravenous blocks using steroids, guanethidine, reserpine, and other agents have been shown to be effective in managing sympathetic dystrophy of the extremities. Unfortunately, in a large patient population, they are not nearly as successful as they have been reported to be.

Further studies are required to clarify the etiology of the syndrome and to define the specific modality for the individual patient.—J.K. Wang] ◀

1–4 **How Effective Is TENS for Acute Pain?** Ann Gill Taylor, Betty Anne West, Bunny Simon, James Skelton, and John C. Rowlingson discuss the use of transcutaneous electric nerve stimulation (TENS) as a noninvasive alternative to narcotic analgesia for the management of acute postoperative pain. The method appears to be simple and safe, and does not cause systemic side effects. How TENS produces analgesia is uncertain, but both prevention of the passage of painful stimuli to the spinal cord and release of endorphins have been proposed as mechanisms. Most previous studies showing TENS to be

(1–4)   Am. J. Nursing 83:1171–1174, August 1983.

effective in the treatment of postoperative pain have not included appropriate controls.

A functional TENS unit was used by 30 of 77 patients after abdominal surgery and 22 others used a sham unit; 25 patients received standard narcotic analgesia. The TENS unit was used every 4 hours as needed for an hour at a time. Medication could be requested if relief did not occur after 30 minutes of stimulation. Both the functional and sham TENS groups had significantly less pain than reported by patients given narcotic analgesics in the first 3 postoperative days, and both the TENS and sham TENS groups required significantly less narcotic analgesia on all postoperative days. Physiologic depression was most evident in the group given narcotic analgesia. Bowel sounds returned most rapidly in the patients using TENS.

A placebo effect may be important in the use of TENS postoperatively. Placebos may stimulate endogenous opiate release, and a feeling of being able to do something to control pain may be helpful. Reported discrepancies in the efficacy of TENS in relieving pain may result from differences in the amount of electric current delivered. The treatment appears to be a useful option in postoperative pain control. Future efforts should focus on identifying those patients who can be expected to benefit more from TENS than from pharmacotherapy.

▶ [We utilized TENS in patients undergoing bilateral total knee arthroplasty, utilizing a sham on one side and a functioning unit on the other side. Patients received narcotics on request in the usual dosage. We were unable to detect any statistically significant difference in pain relief between the sham and the functioning TENS. Some patients, however, experienced almost complete relief of pain with the TENS units and required almost no narcotics. Our impression is that this may indeed be a placebo, but a useful one in the postoperative patient, especially if a preoperative trial of the device focuses the patient's attention on the desired response.—R.S. Bryan] ◀

1–5 **Metal Hypersensitivity in Total Joint Replacement: Review of the Literature and Practical Guidelines for Evaluating Prospective Recipients.** Prem Kumar, Christopher E. Bryan, Stephen H. Leech, Ronnie Mathews, James Bowler, and Robert D. D'Ambrosia (Louisiana State Univ.) point out that some failure of total joint replacement arthroplasty may be related to hypersensitivity to a metal component of the implant. The incidence of contact sensitivity to various metals in the general population is unknown. Both genetic and exogenous factors may be involved. The diagnosis of cutaneous metal sensitivity is based primarily on the history and physical findings. The tissues surrounding an implant must be exposed to the metal for a hypersensitivity reaction to occur. Metal debris deposited in tissues surrounding an implant apparently can produce a tissue reaction.

(1–5) Orthopedics 6:1455–1458, November 1983.

The released metal must be able to stimulate an immune response. Deeper metal implants apparently can produce cutaneous hypersensitivity reactions and lead to prosthetic failure. Some studies have argued against metal hypersensitivity as a cause of prosthetic failure, but many of these have been retrospective, and others have used different types of prostheses; also, some studies have included only a few patients and no appropriate controls.

At present, close attention should be given to historical and clinical manifestations of metal sensitivity in all prospective joint replacement patients and in candidates for revision. Patients with a history of metal sensitivity should have patch testing, human leukocyte antigen phenotyping, and in vitro studies of lymphocyte transformation by metal salts. If metal sensitivity is diagnosed, a prosthesis lacking the metals implicated should be used. All patients whose first prosthesis fails should undergo extensive immunologic evaluation for metal sensitivity. Metal-to-metal prostheses should be avoided. Metal-to-plastic prostheses presently are preferred.

▶ [Among patients with chronic dermatitis, nickel and chromium sensitivity are among the most frequently identified allergens (approximately 10%). Thus, it makes sense to establish the presence of a history of a dermatitis in patients who will carry a prosthesis, as well as a more specific relationship of this sensitivity to metal objects. However, the most frequent source of allergy to chromium is cement and tanned leather. The rare but definite sensitivity to metal orthopedic prostheses cannot only be recognized, but anticipated. Patch testing with the metal salts of patients with a history of dermatitis may predict the problem. The use of a patch test with a portion of the prosthesis for 3 to 7 days may be important confirmation. The composition of available prostheses makes selection of non-nickel and nonchromium containing prostheses possible in those rare cases for which it seems indicated. Such questions should be a mandatory part of the history of patients who are to undergo joint replacement surgery.—R.K. Winkelmann] ◀

1–6 **Juxta-Articular Adiposis Dolorosa—A Neglected Disease.** A. M. Nahir, D. Schapira, and Y. Scharf (Haifa) report the findings in 6 women with painful fatty deposits about the knee, i.e., juxta-articular adiposis dolorosa (JAAD). All were postmenopausal and described continuous pain in the knees, aggravated by all movements and not relieved by bed rest. Deposits of fatty tissue were observed along the thighs and knees (Fig 1–1). The fatty tissue on the medial side of the knee was tender and painful but not inflamed. The knees were stable and had full movement, although flexion was limited by the fatty tissue deposits. Nonsteroid anti-inflammatory drug therapy gave inconsistent results, and neither physiotherapy nor local corticosteroid injection into the anserine bursa was effective. Pain was temporarily relieved by injecting lidocaine into the deposits medial to the knee. Two of the 4 patients who lost 15 to 20 kg experienced partial long-term pain relief.

The cause of the fatty deposits in patients with JAAD is unknown,

(1–6) Isr. J. Med. Sci. 19:858–859, September 1983.

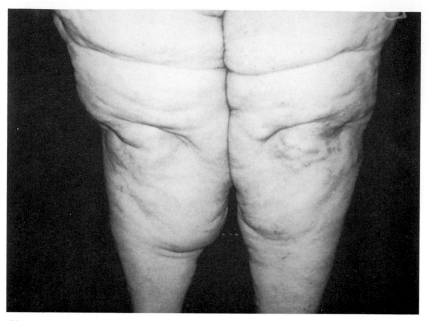

Fig 1–1.—Bilateral fatty tissue deposits in thighs, especially around knees. Note absence of fatty deposits in lower portions of legs. (Courtesy of Nahir, A.M., et al.: Isr. J. Med. Sci. 19:858–859, September 1983.)

and the pathogenesis of the pain is unclear. Most patients are obese postmenopausal women. The general symptoms include malaise, fatigability, and weakness. Emotional instability, depression, and mental confusion also occur. Occasionally the elbows, hips, and ankles are affected. Current treatment for JAAD is unsatisfactory. Adequate long-term results from the surgical removal of fatty deposits remains to be documented. A low-salt diet and diuretics have not been helpful. Substantial weight loss may, but does not always, lead to relief from pain associated with the fatty deposits. A correct diagnosis is important so that unnecessary treatment may be avoided.

1–7 **Pneumatic Tourniquet and Deep Venous Thrombosis.** The pneumatic tourniquet is widely used to obtain a bloodless field during extremity operations, but its effect if any on the development of deep venous thrombosis is uncertain. Peter D. Angus, R. Nakielny, and D. T. Goodrum used radionuclide venography to detect deep vein thrombosis in consecutive patients undergoing elective foot operations. Thirty-five patients with no history of deep vein thrombosis or varicose vein operations participated in the study. Twenty-two had operations on both feet. The limb was exsanguinated before inflation of

(1–7)   J. Bone Joint Surg. [Br.] 65-B:336–339, May 1983.

TABLE 1.—AGE AND SEX DISTRIBUTION IN LEG GROUPS

Leg groups	Number of legs	Average age (years)	M:F ratio
Group 1	29	48.3	6:23
Group 2	28	48.6	5:22
Group 3	13	50.9	3:10

(Courtesy of Angus, P.D., et al.: J. Bone Joint Surg. [Br.] 65-B:336–339, May 1983.)

TABLE 2.—RESULTS OF RADIONUCLIDE VENOGRAPHY IN 69 LEGS

Leg group	Venogram positive n	per cent	Venogram negative n	per cent	Standard error of percentage
Group 1	10	34.5	19	65.5	8.82
Group 2	9	33.3	18	66.7	9.06
Group 3	6	46.2	7	53.8	13.80

(Courtesy of Angus, P.D., et al.: J. Bone Joint Surg. [Br.] 65-B:336–339, May 1983.)

the tourniquet to 350 mm Hg. Bilateral radionuclide venography was carried out with ^{99m}Tc-labeled macroaggregated human albumin 7 to 10 days after operation. Dynamic rapid-sequence images were recorded, and perfusion lung scan imaging was then carried out before delayed imaging of the calves, thighs, and pelvis after calf exercise for 1 minute.

Twenty-nine extremities (group 1) operated on with a tourniquet applied were compared with 28 not having a tourniquet (group 2) and 13 that were not operated on (group 3). The groups are compared in Table 1. The durations of operation were similar in groups 1 and 2. The incidence of thrombosis was comparable in all groups (Table 2). All but 1 of the abnormal venograms showed thrombus in the calf veins. The exception was femoral vein thrombosis in a patient operated on with a tourniquet in place; the thrombus occurred in the leg that was not operated on.

A pneumatic tourniquet did not influence thrombus formation either systemically or locally in this study of patients undergoing operations on the foot. No effect of the tourniquet on thrombus formation mediated by changes in the circulating concentrations of thrombotic or thrombolytic factors was apparent.

► [This paper reports an effort to determine whether tourniquet use alters the incidence of deep venous thrombosis. In the particular case of patients undergoing foot surgery with a tourniquet on the leg, no difference in the incidence of deep venous thrombosis was observed in patients who were operated on with the tourniquet as compared with those operated on without the tourniquet. Although these findings are reassuring, caution should be exercised when applying them to other situations. It is difficult to know whether similar results would be obtained in operations in which the tourniquet is placed more proximally, or in operations which are performed more proximally on the limb, or in operations that are more extensive, or whether these findings would apply to patients who have a history of venous thrombosis.—D.C. Campbell, II] ◀

1–8 **Detection of Retained Surgical Sponges.** George Revesz, Tariq S. Siddiqi, William A. Buchheit, and Michael Bonitatibus (Temple Univ.) undertook to determine the accuracy of roentgenographic detection of laminectomy sponges in a study in which surgical sponges were inserted paravertebrally in the lumbar, thoracic, and cervical regions in a cadaver of a man, aged 60. The sponges were x-rayed several times. Films were obtained with Cronex-4 film, a par-speed screen, and an 8:1 linear grid, and the images were scanned by a laser densitometer. Four neurosurgeons and 4 radiologists viewed the 144 roentgenograms singly in three sessions.

All observers had 3% to 20% false negative findings, and the false positive rates also varied. Mean true positive and false positive rates for the 8 observers were 91% and 10.5%, respectively. The false negative and false positive errors were compensatory; all responses were located along the same receiver operating characteristic (ROC) curve. False negative rates varied with the different types of commercially available neurosurgical sponges used. Detection appeared to be compromised below a marker length of about 10 to 12 mm.

Whether present neurosurgical sponges are optimally detectable roentgenographically is questionable. Further work is needed to determine the best marker sizes and patterns for detection. It seems that sponges should have radiopaque markers well over 10 mm long, with highly artificial patterns such as parallel lines or grid patterns. The specifications of sponges should include an illustration of their roentgenographic appearances.

▶ [The authors have made a good case for technical improvement in some surgical sponges used for laminectomy surgery. In this era of crises in professional liability, it behooves all physicians to obtain x-rays of the surgical wound in which radiopaque surgical sponges have been used before the patient leaves the surgical theater.—D.C. Utz] ◀

1–9 **Separation of Sutured Tendon Ends When Different Suture Techniques and Different Suture Materials Are Used: An Experimental Study in Rabbits.** Many different suture materials and techniques have been used for tendon anastomosis, and tensiometric studies have shown that suture holding capacity varies significantly with the suture material and technique used. Bengt Nyström and Dan

---

(1–8) Radiology 149:411–413, November 1983.
(1–9) Scand. J. Plast. Reconstr. Surg. 17:19–23, 1983.

Holmlund (Univ. of Umeå, Sweden) sutured the divided calcaneal tendons of rabbits with various materials and methods and determined separation of the tendon ends radiographically, using thin steel wires as markers. Suturing was performed using 3–0 Prolene, Ethiflex, and stainless steel wire sutures. Suturing was by Bunnell's crisscross technique or "near" suturing with either a single small loop or ligatures of Dexon placed around the tendon ends inside the suture loop.

Biphasic separation of the tendon ends was recorded separate from the suture material and technique used, 4–5 days and 20–24 days after suturing. Steel wire appeared to be ideal for Bunnell suturing. The single short loop method gave good results with all the suture materials. The use of Dexon ligatures around the tendon ends to prevent the suture strands from cutting the tissue did not reduce initial separation of the tendon ends.

The properties of suture material must be taken into account when using a complex tendon suture method, such as the Bunnell technique, because the results will be affected. With a simple technique, however, such as a single short loop, good results can be achieved using any suture material. Steel wire sutures are appropriate for use with Bunnell suturing. The use of Dexon rings around the tendon ends did not improve the results of tendon suture in this study.

▶ [This paper is important because it applies basic unbiased research methods to tendon suturing techniques. Marketing pressures for commercially available suture materials often result in a confusing picture of physical properties of suture material and inappropriate clinical indications. Further basic research along these same lines is necessary to place various suture "claims" in proper perspective.—M.B. Wood] ◀

1–10 **Permeability of Surgeons' Gloves to Methyl Methacrylate.** Contact sensitization to methyl methacrylate, used in operating rooms as a bone cement in orthopedic surgery, has been described, and long-lasting sensory neuritis of the hands can occur. T. H. J. M. Waegemaekers, E. Seutter, J. A. C. J. den Arend, and K. E. Malten (Univ. of Nijmegen, The Netherlands) quantified the passage of methyl methacrylate through 7 different surgical glove materials at 21 C and 35 C in a diffusion chamber, using a gas chromatographic analytic method. Material from examination gloves and a household glove also was assessed. Studies were done with 4.7 M methyl methacrylate in ethanol to prevent dissolution of material from reversible expansion; even then, however, the time during which methyl methacrylate permeated the membrane was too short for adequate protection. Among the nonsurgical glove materials, vinyl was inferior to latex. A very thin polyethylene copolymer was more resistant to diffusion, but was insufficiently elastic and perforated easily.

Orthopedic surgeons who fix endoprostheses in place using bone cement are undoubtedly exposed to methyl and other methacrylates,

(1–10) Acta Orthop. Scand. 54:790–795, December 1983.

benzoyl peroxide, rubber additives, and other materials. A better protective glove material is urgently needed. It should be possible to produce a material having the diffusion characteristics of polyethylene copolymer while being thicker, mechanically stronger, and somewhat more elastic, and lacking sensitizing agents.

▶ [It has been almost 15 years since the first orthopedic surgeon with contact dermatitis to methyl methacrylate was identified in England. Subsequent cases have been identified in New York. Scaling dermatitis of the fingers and positive patch tests to methyl methacrylate are important to the diagnosis.

It has now been shown that methyl methacrylate will dissolve all forms of surgical gloves, and that even double layers of gloves offer no complete protection. What is remarkable is that there have been so few additional cases of orthopedic surgeons who develop methacrylate dermatitis. We have not identified any cases in our experience at the Mayo Clinic with intense exposure to methacrylate.

It is necessary to worry about the ultimate evolution of dermatitis. Surgeons should remove all gloves and replace them following the use of methacrylate. It is hoped that manufacturers will provide polyethylene gloves to protect surgeons during the use of methacrylate cement.—R.K. Winkelmann] ◀

1–11 **Vascular Accidents During Orthopedic Surgery: Report of 55 Cases.** Within the framework of iatrogenic vascular pathology, lesions of orthopedic origin occupy second place after trauma related to catheterizations. P. Jue-Denis, E. Kieffer, H. LeThoai, M. Benhamou, and J. Natali (Paris) collected data on 55 vascular injuries observed in 40 patients during a 10-year period (1970 to 1980), involving 40 arterial and 15 venous lesions. These vascular injuries occurred during spinal operations in 9 cases and during shoulder operations in 7. Nine cases involved hip surgery and 15 cases involved operations of the lower extremities. The most common iatrogenic vascular accidents of orthopedic origin are those secondary to hip surgery and interventions on the femur and on disk hernias.

In the present series, emergency operation was necessary in 18 cases because of an hemorrhagic or ischemic incident. All other cases, except 3, required secondary surgery for false aneurysm, arteriovenous fistula, or residual ischemia. Four patients (10%) died; complications arose in 8 (20%). About 70% of patients who had such accidents had no sequelae of the vascular trauma.

The risk of vascular injury during orthopedic surgery can be explained by the proximity of skeletal structures and vasculoneural axes. This is all the more true for repeat interventions after tissues have lost their flexibility. The mechanism of these lesions is not uniform, although it frequently involves the utilization of instruments, and cement used in total hip replacement may cause mechanical ulcerations. The heat released during the course of polymerization of methylmetocylate may cause arterial or venous thromboses. The use of badly placed or poorly monitored retractors poses a danger of pressure on vasculoneural axes, causing a hemorrhage when removed.

(1–11) J. Chir. (Paris) 120:437–441, Aug.–Sept. 1983.

The diagnosis of a vascular lesion is not always easy, and any delay affects prognosis. In fact, it is sometimes difficult to attribute pain in a just operated-on lower extremity to ischemia, and the slightest doubt should require a Doppler examination. A hemorrhagic syndrome is generally more evident, although in certain cases the hemorrhage occurs at a distance from the surgical site and will be detected only postoperatively. Aims of treatment are to stop bleeding and ensure vascular continuity. A simple ligature will generally not suffice; a lateral suture or resection and bridging may be required.

▶ [There are several lessons for the orthopedic surgeons in this very important paper. No one knows the true incidence of intraoperative iatrogenic vascular accidents. This paper points out the severity of their consequences (10% mortality and 20% sequelae). Hip surgery, particularly revision surgery for failure of total hip replacement, appears to have the gravest risk of intraoperative vascular complications. What is more important is that at least half of the lesions had the potential to be missed initially; thus, a high index of suspicion and a careful postoperative evaluation (including Doppler exam) is advisable, particularly when pain patterns are unusual.—M.E. Cabanela] ◀

1–12 **Malpractice as a Contract Law Proceeding** is discussed by Richard S. Goodman (Smithtown, N.Y.). Orthopedic surgeons in particular have had a long and unfortunate experience with the legal system in the area of negligence. Richard Epstein, in his book, *Medical Malpractice: The Case for Contract,* raises the question of whether the medical malpractice and liability crisis has arisen because of a failure to distinguish between contract law and tort law. Tort law is civil proceedings in negligence between strangers, while contract law is civil proceedings when an agreement between 2 parties known to one another is not fulfilled or is broken. Epstein suggested that medical liability might best be subsumed under contract law, on the basis of the use of contracts between the physician and patient with disclaimer clauses rather than consents.

All physicians could profit from reading Epstein's book and from considering his views on present faults in the area of negligence and what could be done to correct them. Excessive malpractice judgments can be viewed as resulting from a failure of society to recognize the contractual relationship between the patient and physician and from the failure to limit liability, as is inherent in most contracts. Epstein deplores the practice of courts and juries deciding both what risks should be disclosed and what degree of disclosure is adequate, with customary medical standards being weighed as only one piece of evidence. Physicians should not be encouraged to make disclosures that are intended not to advance their patients' best interests, but to insulate themselves from liability.

▶ [Mr. Benjamin R. Hippe, from the Legal department, Mayo Clinic and Foundation, Rochester, Minnesota comments:

(1–12) Orthopedics 6:1354–1364, October 1983.

"There may be some basis to use contract language to limit liability. The Minnesota Supreme Court has just upheld such a provision in a contract."] ◄

1–13   **Comparison of Bone Scan and Radiograph Sensitivity in Detection of Steroid-Induced Ischemic Necrosis of Bone.** Ischemic necrosis of bone (INB) is a known complication of corticosteroid therapy in patients with systemic lupus erythematosus (SLE). James J. Conklin, Philip O. Alderson, Thomas M. Zizic, David S. Hungerford, Jean Y. Densereaux, Anita Gober, and Henry N. Wagner (Baltimore) compared bone scanning with roentgenography in detecting INB in a prospective study of 36 patients at risk because of SLE and treatment with prednisone in daily doses of 40 to 200 mg. All but 3% of patients were females; age range was 16 to 36 years. Images of the hips, knees, and shoulders were obtained after injection of 20 mCi of ^{99m}Tc-methylene diphosphonate. All patients had joint roentgenography, and 10 had intraosseous pressure measurements in affected joints.

Ischemic necrosis of bone was present in 45% of the 216 major joints evaluated. Shoulders were involved in nearly half the cases and knees in over a third. The abnormalities were bilateral in nearly 80% of affected patients. No disagreement with marrow pressure measurements was observed. Visual determinations detected all but 3 of 27 joints with increased marrow pressure. Only 11 of these joints were roentgenographically abnormal. All patients with x-ray abnormalities had abnormal scintigraphic findings. Scanning was 89% sensitive in demonstrating INB in comparison with marrow pressure measurements. Two of four joints with normal pressures had abnormal scan findings. The positive predictive value of scanning was 92%. All 7 hips scanned showed a photon-deficient area, and only 1 of these hips was roentgenographically abnormal.

Subjectively interpreted bone scans are a sensitive means of diagnosing INB in patients receiving corticosteroid therapy for SLE. An earlier stage of disease is detected by scanning than by roentgenography. The use of semiquantitative scintigraphic ratios has not improved the results, but quantitation may provide a more objective means of interpreting serial examinations.

► [This study is carefully designed to evaluate bone scintigraphy for the detection of steroid-induced ischemic necrosis of bone (INB). In this often bilateral and multijoint disease, which requires an examination of multiple joints, bone marrow imaging as an alternative procedure is not indicated because bone marrow scanning interpretation of scans depends on comparison of normal and abnormal joints. With the exception of the hip, bone marrow imaging has not yet been evaluated for the detection of INB in other joints.

Using intraosseous pressure determinations and venography after intraosseous injection of contrast medium as reference standards, the authors demonstrate quite convincingly that the bone scan is significantly more sensitive than the radiograph in detecting INB. This increased sensitivity will depend somewhat on the age of the INB, since radiographs are known not to show changes for the first few months while the

(1–13)   Radiology 147:221–226, April 1983.

bone scintigram is positive after 48 hours. Sensitivity in this population was 89% for scintigraphy and the positive predictive value was 92%. Radiographs had a sensitivity of 41%. Quantitative evaluations of uptake on scintigram did not improve the diagnostic value of the test over subjective scan interpretation.

Bone scintigraphy is the best nontraumatic method presently available to evaluate the multiple joints likely to be affected in SLE under steroid treatment when early recognition of INB is the issue. A careful study of the typical imaging patterns, however, is necessary to avoid false positive scans in case of degenerative or SLE-related joint disease.—H.W. Wahner] ◄

1–14 **Femoral Head Blood Flow in Long-Term Steroid Therapy: Study of Rabbit Model.** Evidence of avascular necrosis in renal transplantation has raised interest in the use of long-term steroid therapy in this setting. Previous studies in rabbits showed that steroid administration induced hyperlipidemia with subsequent fatty embolization of the subchondral arteries, hypertrophy of the marrow fat cells, and elevation of femoral head pressure. Gwo-Jaw Wang, Sandra L. Hubbard, Steven I. Reger, Edward D. Miller, and Warren G. Stamp (Univ. of Virginia) determined femoral head blood flow using the radioactive microsphere method in rabbits after treatment with 12.5 mg of methylprednisolone weekly for 6, 8, and 10 weeks. Blood flow decreased in steroid-treated animals at 10 weeks, averaging 0.163 ml/minute/gm on the 2 sides, compared with a control average of 0.292 ml/minute/gm (Fig 1–2). The difference between steroid-treated and control animals was significant after 8 weeks of treatment.

Although actual avascular necrosis did not develop in animals in this study, Gold et al. demonstrated osteonecrosis in rabbits given

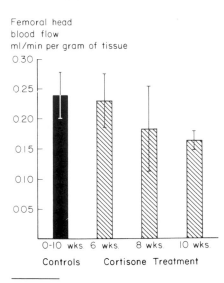

Femoral head
blood flow
ml/min per gram of tissue

Fig 1–2.—Femoral head blood flow in control and steroid-treated rabbits pretreatment through 10 weeks. (Courtesy of Wang, G.-J., et al.: South. Med. J. 76:1530–1532, December 1983. Reprinted by permission of the Southern Medical Journal.)

(1–14)   South. Med. J. 76:1530–1532, December 1983.

long-term steroid therapy. A substantial decrease in femoral head blood flow was documented in association with long-term steroid administration. The side differences in femoral head blood flow observed in treated rabbits may parallel the unpredictable extent of avascular necrosis of the human hip.

▶ [This interesting study suggests that steroid therapy has some effect on femoral head blood flow. It should be noted in the discussion section, however, that differences are not statistically significant.—P.J. Kelly] ◀

1–15 **Bone Blood Flow in Conscious Dogs at Rest and During Exercise.** Most body tissues can regulate their perfusion so as to insure optimal nutrition, but the extent to which bone can increase its perfusion during muscle activity and normal limb use is not known. Erik Tøndevold and Jens Bülow (Univ. of Copenhagen) used the microsphere method to estimate bone blood flow in different regions of the long bones of conscious dogs. Studies were done with the use of labeled microspheres after 1 and 2 hours of treadmill exercise and after 1 hour of rest. Perfusion rates increased 50% in the femur and tibia during exercise when measured in cortical bone. A greater increase was seen in the cancellous bone of the femoral head. Comparable flow responses were noted in the fat-filled tibial condylar and femoral supracondylar bone. Increased perfusion was significant after 2 hours of treadmill running but not after 1 hour.

These findings suggest that bone is capable of vasodilatation during muscular work, but the increase in perfusion occurs slowly. It seems likely that the vasodilatation is mediated by a metabolically induced stimulus. Hyperemia was maintained at a high level for at least 1 hour after cessation of work in this study. It is not clear whether this is due to repayment or redistribution of the blood in the extremities after exercise.

▶ [This is a timely article. It may be that evaluation of blood flow and other morphological parameters might be useful objective methods to determine whether graduated exercise has any effect on osteoporosis. Such methods should be conducted on a dog model.—P.J. Kelly] ◀

1–16 **Isotopic Bone Mineralization Rates in Maintenance Dialysis Patients.** Malcolm Cochran and Elisabeth Stephens (Adelaide, Australia) used the expanding pool model of radiocalcium kinetics to measure bone mineralization rates in 13 patients receiving maintenance hemodialysis, aged 29–67 years, from whom bone samples were obtained at the time of the isotope study. Studies were done with an intravenous dose of 10 μCi of ^{47}Ca. Hemodialysis ordinarily was for 4 hours 3 times a week, with the use of conventional single-pass systems and dialysate prepared from water treated by reverse osmosis. Dialysis was withheld until 48 hours after isotope injection, and then was carried out for 1 hour, and 1-hour dialyses were carried

(1–15)   Acta Orthop. Scand. 54:53–57, February 1983.
(1–16)   J. Lab. Clin. Med. 102:324–331, September 1983.

out daily for the 6 days of the study. Bone samples were taken from the iliac crest.

The mean plasma calcium concentration was 2.4 mmole/L initially and at the end of the study. The plasma phosphate level increased by a third in 10 patients and fell by a third in the other 3 patients. The blood pH remained close to normal in all cases. Parathyroid hormone levels rose by 28% in the 11 patients studied. Four patients had inactive-appearing osteomalacic bone, and the rest had varying degrees of osteitis fibrosa. Bone mineralization rates ranged from 0 to 2.0 mmole/kg of calcium daily. The rate correlated with the degree of secondary hyperparathyroidism, low rates being associated with atypical osteomalacia or inactive-appearing bone. Both the plasma alkaline phosphatase concentration and the immunoassayable parathyroid hormone level correlated significantly with the bone mineralization rate. The size of the exchangeable calcium pool was not related to the plasma calcium concentration, the parathyroid hormone level, or the histologic findings.

The isotopic method for measuring the bone mineralization rate is applicable to patients receiving hemodialysis. The findings support the concept of a low mineralization rate in histologically inactive bone, and help explain why the plasma calcium is unstable over time in these patients. The method may prove useful in quantitating skeletal responses to therapeutic agents.

▶ [I believe this paper is important because it gives a noninvasive means of attempting to predict bone histomorphometry. Unfortunately, it is a rather complex procedure and may be of limited benefit to physicians without access to a large referral center.

The major shortcoming of the paper is that it does not validate the current technique using a concurrent method of measuring bone formation rate. The standard means of measuring this parameter would be the use of bone biopsies with double tetracycline labeling. Their method of evaluating bone histology is also prone to some subjective error since histomorphometry was not objectively quantitated.—J.T. McCarthy] ◀

1–17 **Quantitative Assessment of Bone Density on X-Ray Picture.** Tetsuo Inoue, Kazuhiro Kusida, Shigehito Miyamoto, Yoshihiko Sumi, Hajime Orimo, and Gentaro Yamashita used a densitometer to measure bone density at the middle of the second metacarpal on x-ray films of the hands taken from the rear alongside an aluminum step-wedge. The densitometric pattern was recorded at 10 times magnification, and the optical density of each step of the aluminum wedge was measured simultaneously. Measurements were made of bone width, marrow width, cortical widths on the radial and ulnar sides, peak of the cortex on the radial and ulnar sides, and peak of the middle of the bone marrow. The metacarpal index was calculated. Both normal persons and patients with osteoporosis were studied.

(1–17) J. Jpn. Orthop. Assoc. 57:1923–1936, December 1983.

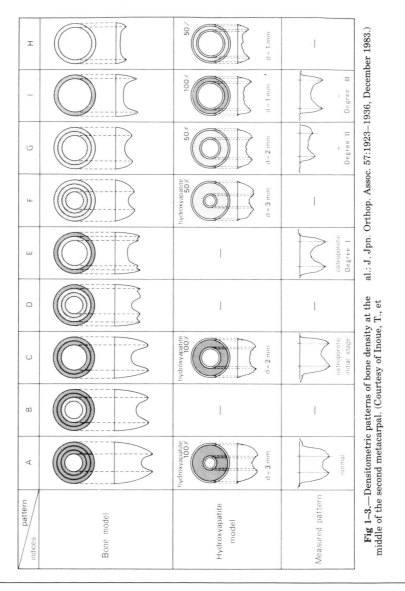

Fig 1–3.—Densitometric patterns of bone density at the middle of the second metacarpal. (Courtesy of Inoue, T., et al.: J. Jpn. Orthop. Assoc. 57:1923–1936, December 1983.)

Various densitometric patterns are shown in Figure 1–3. In normal persons, changes in the indices were more marked in females after age 30 years, particularly those changes indicating a reduction in bone weight. In osteoporosis the densitometric pattern was abnormal, with a small metacarpal index and a large marrow width. The findings correlated closely with those obtained by the Jikei method. The indices related closely to bone mineral content, except for marrow width. Assessments of the degree of bone atrophy in osteoporotic patients agreed closely with those obtained using the Jikei method. Increased indices corresponded to increases in bone area and bone weight in the 62 patients having iliac bone biopsy.

This method appears to be satisfactory for assessing bone density in patients with metabolic bone disease, for making comparisons between individuals, and for following changes in bone mass in these patients.

▶ [The authors describe a reproducible yet simple technique for assessment of bone density. Previous techniques have been either extremely complex or simple and inaccurate. The technique described in this paper is well documented and reproducible and does not require expensive equipment.—T. Berquist] ◄

1–18 **Studies on Antigenicity of Bone: Donor-Specific Anti-HLA Antibodies in Human Recipients of Freeze-Dried Allografts.** Little is known of whether immune responses directed against bone graft-related antigens occur in patients, and, if so, what the clinical sequelae might be. Gary E. Friedlaender, Douglas M. Strong, and Kenneth W. Sell attempted to determine whether donor-specific anti-human leukocyte antigen (HLA) antibodies develop in recipients of freeze-dried bone allografts. The series included 43 patients, aged 1–63 years, having 44 allograft procedures for benign skeletal lesions. The allografts consisted of crushed cortical bone, ground cancellous bone, or a segment of cortical bone with or without crushed cortical bone added. No attempt was made to match the cadaver donor and recipient for histocompatibility.

Allografting evoked donor-specific anti-HLA antibodies in 9 of the 43 patients. Eight of the 9 sensitized patients were followed radiographically for an average of 23 months and had a satisfactory clinical outcome. The ninth patient was doing well when lost to follow-up 4 months after allografting. Sensitization could not be related to graft volume or to use of cortical rather than cancellous bone. Only 2 sensitized patients received a blood transfusion during or after surgery. Three of the patients were women at or past childbearing age.

Clinically successful bone allografting is not impeded by the development of donor-specific anti-HLA antibodies after placement of a freeze-dried graft. Relatively small amounts of bone were used in this study, however, and different biologic responses could occur with the use of larger allografts. Other antigens (e.g., HLA-Dr and those for matrix components) should be studied.

▶ [This is an important contribution to our understanding of the immune responses to bone allografts. It tells us rather definitely that donor-specific anti-HLA antibodies were not detected in patients who had undergone transplantation of freeze-dried bone. Thus, this study suggests that even though donor-specific anti-HLA antibodies evoked by the freeze-dried bone grafts appear, they do not preclude the success of

(1–18)   J. Bone Joint Surg. [Am.] 66-A:107–112, January 1984.

freeze-dried allografting. It would certainly also suggest that tissue typing is probably unimportant.—Ed.] ◄

1–19 **Free Physeal Transplantation in the Rabbit: Experimental Approach to Focal Lesions.** Focal lesions of the physis continue to cause considerable morbidity from angular deformity and shortening. Osteotomy must be repeated frequently if growth difficulty occurs several years before maturity. Antonio Olin, Charles Creasman, and Frederick Shapiro (Harvard Med. School) developed a method of transplanting free autogenous iliac-crest physeal grafts into defects made in the lateral aspect of the distal femoral physis in rabbits. The resectional procedure led to formation of a bone bridge, growth arrest, and valgus deformity, with no evidence of an attempt by the remaining physis to fill the defect. The graft, from the posterior iliac-crest apophysis, included the physis and some overlying epiphyseal cartilage, with the outermost fibrocartilaginous layer and the surrounding perichondrium removed. Separation was at the lower hypertrophic-chondrocyte zone. Grafting was performed in 39 rabbits aged 3–4 months (Fig 1–4) after the procedure was optimized.

Fig 1–4.—Photograph showing an iliac physeal graft in position in the lateral femoral physeal defect. The distal end of the femur was sectioned in the coronal plane after decalcification. (Courtesy of Olin, A., et al.: J. Bone Joint Surg. [Am.] 66-A:7–20, January 1984.)

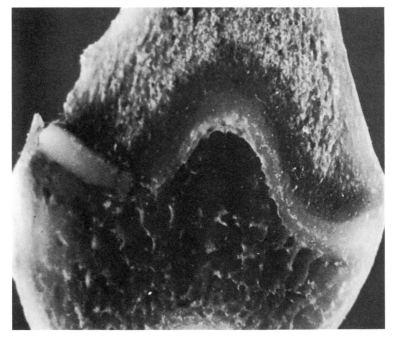

The morphology and organization of the physis were retained in the grafts. Union by cartilage at the graft-host junction was noted as early as 2 weeks. Metaphyseal bone formation, maintenance of cytologic organization, and the absence of vascular infusion indicated viability of the growth plate. Good to excellent results were obtained by grafting in most cases. Bone bridge formation, growth arrest, and valgus deformity were minimized or prevented in most graft recipients.

Free physeal transplantation to femoral physis defects in the rabbit is followed by maintenance of the morphology, viability, and normal function of the transplant. A narrow graft is important. This approach is suited to well-localized, focal lesions of the physis. Full physeal, and certainly epiphyseal grafts would be most successful if transplanted with an associated vascular supply, and the use of vascularized iliac-crest apophyseal transplants is under study. Free iliac-crest physis transplants may prove useful in managing focal physeal arrest due to trauma or Blount's disease, where the epiphyseal and metaphyseal bone is intact and well-vascularized.

▶ [Transplanting an autogenous iliac crest apophysis into defects created in the distal femoral physis in rabbits is a logical extension of previous similar animal experiments, and utilizes a variety of materials all designed to prevent physeal bar formation. The iliac crest apophysis is the largest readily available similar biologic material which might be transplanted without harm to the animal. There are very few clinical situations in human beings for which this principle might be applied. One possibly applicable situation might be a compound fracture with loss of physis. Iliac crest cartilage apophyses might be inserted to replace the missing physis at the time of injury to prevent an anticipated bar from forming. The next logical step in a series of experimentations would be to create a bar in an animal and later resect the bar, transplanting the iliac crest apophysis to see if normal physeal growth would resume. This procedure would have many applications to human beings, since physeal bars form after trauma, tumor, infection, and iatrogenic placement of metal across the physis. Most physeal bars are larger than one piece of iliac crest apophysis. Several pieces of iliac crest apophysis would need to be placed side by side to fill the defect and act effectively as an interposition material.—H.A. Peterson] ◀

1–20 **Early Development of Articular Cartilage After Perichondrial Grafting.** Standard perichondrial grafting involves suturing of the graft onto the cancellous bone surface in order to promote vascular proliferation from the spongiosa. An alternative is to use Tisseal, a fibrin glue of highly concentrated human fibrinogen cryoprecipitate that provides tissue adhesion on a biologic basis. Lennart Ohlsén and Bertil Widenfalk (Uppsala, Sweden) examined the effects of Tisseal in rabbits in which the articular cartilage of the femoral condyles was resected, and the defect covered by a perichondrial graft of rib cartilage which was fixed to the bony surface using the fibrin glue. The chondral side of the perichondrium was turned to face the joint space in 33 animals, while in 6 others the chondral side faced the bone

(1–20) Scand. J. Plast. Reconstr. Surg. 17:163–177, 1983.

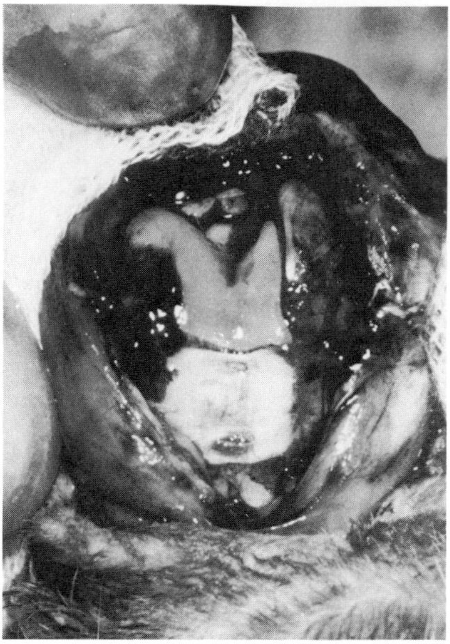

Fig 1–5.—When the K-wire used for immobilizing the joint was removed on the 13th day, the joint was opened and the graft examined. Ninety percent of the grafts were found in the original place where they had been positioned. (Courtesy of Ohlsén, L., and Widenfalk, B.: Scand. J. Plast. Reconstr. Surg. 17:163–177, 1983.)

surface. The joint was immobilized with a K-wire for 2 weeks.

Nearly all grafts were found in the original site where they had been positioned (Fig 1–5). The early appearances are shown in Figure 1–6. A cartilage matrix was evident in the transitional cell layer after 7–9 days. At 11–13 days, only remnants of the fibrin glue were present. No foreign body reaction or inflammation was noted in the area of the glue fragments. After 6 weeks, the entire graft was transformed into tissue that nearly had the appearance of normal cartilage. At 3 months, the newly formed cartilage was very similar to normal cartilage (Figs 1–7 and 1–8). Similar changes were noted where the graft had been placed with the transitional layer turned to the bone surface rather than facing the joint space.

Neochondrogenesis occurred in the median and fibrous layers of perichondrial grafts in this study, in which Tisseal was used to join the graft with the cancellous bone surface. No vascular proliferation penetrated the fibrin glue, indicating that the graft is nourished by synovial fluid only. It is not necessary to place the graft with the fibrous layer facing the recipient site. The chondroblasts can be expected to form cartilage independent of the local environment.

▶ [This very interesting paper details a histomorphological examination of the development of a cartilagenous matrix after grafting a perichondrial graft to resected rabbit femoral condyles. However, the technique is deficient because a cartilagenous union fails to form between the graft and the surrounding normal cartilage. After 3 months only fibrous tissue bridged this gap in all of the 39 rabbits studied.—J.P. Gorski] ◀

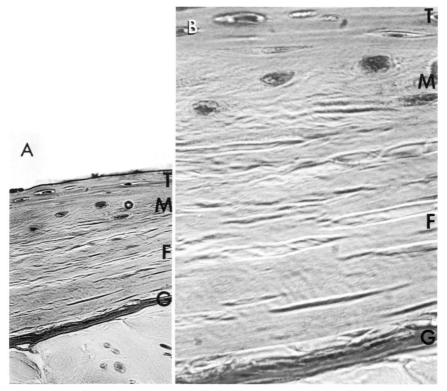

Fig 1–6.—A, 1 day after the operation the graft is seen well fixed to and separated from the cancellous bone by the fribin glue layer *(g)*. Hematoxylin-eosin; ×180. **B,** when stripped from the cartilage, the perichondrium under high magnification is seen to consist of the three described layers. The line of separation between the cartilage and the perichondrium is just where the cells in the transition layer appear in pairs. Hematoxylin-eosin; ×470. (Courtesy of Ohlsén, L., and Widenfalk, B.: Scand. J. Plast. Reconstr. Surg. 17:163–177, 1983.)

1–21 **Evidence for Two Distinct Syndromes of Involutional Osteoporosis** is reviewed by B. Lawrence Riggs and L. Joseph Melton, III (Mayo Clin. and Found.). Involutional osteoporosis is the occurrence of vertebral or hip fracture resulting from age-associated bone loss. Type I osteoporosis, with an excess of type A fractures of the vertebrae and distal forearm, is found in a relatively small group of postmenopausal women aged 51–65 years and less frequently in men of comparable age. Type II osteoporosis, with type B fractures of the proximal humerus, proximal tibia, and pelvis, as well as residual type A fractures, occurs in many women and men older than 75 years. A combination of the 2 types may occur in persons aged 66–75. Type C fractures of the shafts of the limb bones do not appear to occur more

(1–21) Am. J. Med. 75:899–901, December 1983.

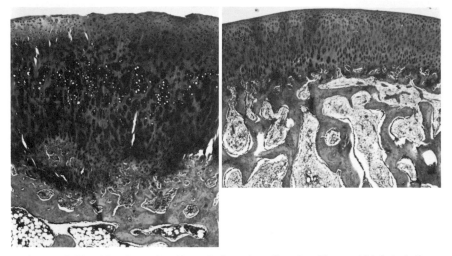

Fig 1–7 (left).—After 3 months, the newly formed cartilage is still very thick but similar to normal cartilage. Hematoxylin-eosin; ×30.

Fig 1–8 (right).—Normal cartilage from the femur condyle of a rabbit. Hematoxylin-eosin; ×30. (Courtesy of Ohlsén, L., and Widenfalk, B.: Scand J. Plast. Reconstr. Surg. 17:163–177, 1983.)

frequently in females or with age, and do not seem to be directly related to osteoporosis.

Type I osteoporosis is characterized by the accelerated, disproportionate loss of trabecular bone, whereas type II osteoporosis involves a proportionate loss of both cortical and trabecular bone at a rate similar to that occurring in the general population. Women with type I osteoporosis have relatively low serum immunoreactive parathyroid hormone levels. Also, estrogen deficiency has been implicated in type I osteoporosis, and accelerated bone loss has been documented after oophorectomy. The authors, however, found no differences in serum sex steroid levels in postmenopausal women and in those without osteoporosis. Type II osteoporosis may be related to both impaired bone formation and secondary hyperparathyroidism. Increased bone turnover from hyperparathyroidism with reduced bone formation would result in increased bone loss.

The heterogeneity of involutional osteoporosis has obvious implications for developing effective means of prevention and treatment.

▶ [The orthopedist must be aware of the current thinking regarding involutional osteoporosis. This article clarifies it and brings it up-to-date. The authors believe that there are two syndromes of osteoporosis: Type I, which occurs in postmenopausal women 51–65 years of age, though occasionally in men as well; and Type II, which occurs in a large proportion of women and men who are older than 75 years. Type I is characterized by an accelerated and disproportionate loss of trabecular bone whereas Type II is characterized by a proportionate loss of both cortical and trabecular bone and a rate of loss similar to that of the general population. The authors have evaluated the incidences of Colles' fractures and femoral neck fractures in a large captive population in Rochester, Minnesota. They have shown the exponential increase in femoral neck fractures after age 74. They believe the Type I osteoporosis does indeed relate to estrogen deficiency. The Type II osteoporosis is probably caused by two major factors: impaired bone formation and secondary hyperparathyroidism.—Ed.] ◄

1–22 **Physical Exercise as Prophylaxis Against Involutional Vertebral Bone Loss: Controlled Trial.** Since physical activity is a major determinant of bone remodeling and bone mass, exercise has been suggested as a prophylactic measure where involutional bone loss and osteoporosis are risks. Bjørn Krølner, Birte Toft, Stig Pors Nielsen, and Erik Tøndevold (Hillerød, Denmark) evaluated physical exercise in preventing involutional bone loss from the lumbar vertebrae in 31 otherwise healthy women, aged 50 to 73 years, who had Colles' fractures. They were studied 9 to 21 months after the injury. Sixteen women exercised for 1 hour twice weekly over 8 months under supervision at a moderate training load. Walking and running were complemented by exercises in standing, sitting, lying and all fours and by ball games. The exercise and control groups were comparable in age, duration of menopause, performance capacity, and mineral metabolism.

The exercise group showed an 11% reduction in the blood pressure-pulse rate product at submaximal work after 8 months. A mean increase of 3.5% in lumbar bone mineral content, as measured by dual-photon absorptiometry, was observed in the exercise group and a decrease of 2.7% in the control group; the difference was highly significant. Forearm bone mineral content was practically unchanged in the exercise group, but it decreased by 1.8% in controls. Biochemical variables were unchanged during the study. Comparable results were obtained when premenopausal women and women receiving estrogens were excluded.

Physical exercise can inhibit or reverse involutional bone loss from the lumbar vertebrae in normal women, and it may prevent spinal osteoporosis. Motivation for long-term prophylaxis is necessary for successful prevention of spinal osteoporosis. The social aspects of group exercise can be used in encouraging middle-aged women to exercise so as to reduce their risk of vertebral fractures.

► [It has long been believed that exercise is good for bone density and immobilization is bad for it. This well-controlled study shows impressive results on the effect of exercise on bone density. As yet it remains to be shown that exercise will result in a continued increase in bone mass beyond that observed in the first 6 months. Indeed, it appears that most of the increases in bone mass occurred during the first 3 months. Nevertheless, the exercise was relatively mild and would be possible for most middle-aged women who are at great risk for osteoporosis.—B.L. Riggs] ◄

1–23 **Arthritis of Hemochromatosis: Clinical Spectrum, Relation to Histocompatibility Antigens, and Effectiveness of Early Phlebotomy.** Arthritis has been described in nearly half of patients with

(1–22) Clin. Sci. 64:541–546, May 1983.
(1–23) Am. J. Med. 75:957–965, December 1983.

hereditary hemochromatosis. Ali D. Askari, W. Angus Muir, Itzhak A. Rosner, Roland W. Moskowitz, Gordon D. McLaren, and William E. Braun (Case Western Reserve Univ.) describe five patients with arthritis as the only manifestation of hemochromatosis.

Man, 54, had had chronic arthritis in the hands and feet for 15 years and had been treated for gout, rheumatoid arthritis, and osteoarthritis. Both second and third metacarpophalangeal (MCP) joints (Fig 1–9) were enlarged,

Fig 1–9 (top).—Bilateral enlargement of second and third MCP joints *(arrowheads)*.

Fig 1–10 (bottom left).—Joint space narrowing, subchondral cysts, and osteophytes involving second and third MCP joints *(arrowheads)*.

Fig 1–11 (bottom right).—Lateral view showing joint space narrowing and large osteophytes of second and third MCP joints *(arrowheads)*.

(Courtesy of Askari, A.D., et al.: Am. J. Med. 75:957–965, December 1983.)

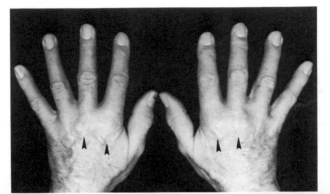

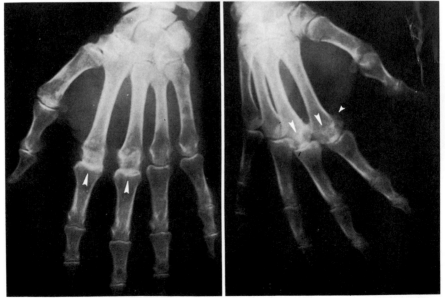

red, and painful on motion. The sedimentation rate was normal, and no rheumatoid or antinuclear factor was identified. A remote inferior myocardial infarction was found on ECG study. Roentgenography showed joint space narrowing, subchondral cysts, and bone sclerosis in the affected joints (Figs 1–10 and 1–11). The serum iron concentration was 216 mg/dl, with a transferrin saturation of 95%. The serum ferritin concentration was 1,105 mg/L. The patient excreted 3.6 mg of iron in the urine 24 hours after injection of 1 gm of deferoxamine. Liver biopsy showed a marked increase in parenchymal hepatocytic iron with relatively little iron in the Kupffer cells. The patient failed to improve with nonsteroid anti-inflammatory drug therapy and weekly phlebotomy. Swanson arthroplasties were then performed on the affected joints of both hands and showed severe degeneration of the metacarpal heads and degenerative cartilage changes on histologic study, without apparent hemosiderin deposits or synovitis. Pain was reduced postoperatively, but functional improvement was not notable.

One of the 5 patients had only unilateral involvement. One had bilateral metatarsophalangeal swelling as well as MCP joint involvement. In only 1 of the 4 patients in whom it was measured was the serum ferritin concentration elevated. Arthritis was found in 45% of 18 family members with strongly suspected or confirmed hereditary hemochromatosis. Phlebotomy usually was not helpful, although it lessened musculoskeletal symptoms in 1 patient.

The classic triad of diabetes, hepatic dysfunction, and hyperpigmentation is not always necessary for a diagnosis of hereditary hemochromatosis. Unilateral arthritis may be present, and roentgenographic abnormalities need not be present for the diagnosis. Phlebotomy, resection osteotomies, and nonsteroid anti-inflammatory agents may be helpful in some cases.

1–24 **Joint Involvement in Psoriasis: Scintigraphic, Radiologic, and Clinical Findings.** Psoriasis vulgaris is not infrequently accompanied by arthritis. Elisabeth Bachmann, Ole J. Clemmensen, Martin Dyrbye, and Kim Larsen (Univ. of Copenhagen) compared the scintigraphic and radiographic findings in matched groups of psoriatic patients with and without past or present arthritis, and assessed the effects of zinc treatment. Sixteen patients with active nummular, plaque-type psoriasis or both, for at least a year and no evidence of arthritis were compared with 14 others who had arthralgias, arthritic signs or both, for at least 6 months. Nine control subjects had various minor skin disorders and no family or personal history of arthritis. Bone scintigraphy was performed with ^{99m}Tc-methyl diphosphonate. Zinc therapy was with 220 mg of zinc sulfate in tablet form, given 3 times daily for 8 weeks.

The duration and extent of psoriasis were comparable in the groups with and without arthritis. The mean duration of joint symptoms was 8 years. Finger joints were nearly exclusively involved. Scintigraphic

(1–24) *Dermatologica* 166:250–254, May 1983.

abnormalities were most frequent in the group with clinical arthritis, and scintigrams were abnormal more often than x-ray films. No overall change in symptoms occurred during zinc administration. No x-ray changes were noted, but 3 patients with arthritis had fewer scintigraphic abnormalities. Four patients in the other group had additional accumulations of activity during zinc administration. Total gamma globulin levels fell significantly during zinc therapy. No side effects were observed.

In this study, scintigraphy did not provide significant evidence of extracutaneous involvement in psoriatic patients without clinically evident arthritis. Zinc sulfate has proved effective in psoriatic arthritis, and nuclide accumulation decreased in some treated patients in the present study.

1–25 **Sacroiliitis in Women—Sequela to Acute Salpingitis: Follow-up Study.** Recent studies indicate an unexpectedly high incidence of sacroiliitis (SI) in women, especially those hospitalized for severe salpingitis. Erika Szanto and Kerstin Hagenfeldt (Sweden) reviewed the course of 37 women treated for severe acute salpingitis in 1974–1976 who had SI documented on evaluation 24–28 months after initial hospitalization. Sacroiliitis was demonstrated by pertechnetate scanning of the sacroiliac joints. Thirty-nine of 57 women treated for salpingitis had evidence of SI. Thirteen of them had HLA-B27 antigen. The 37 evaluable patients were followed up for 2–3 years after initial evaluation.

The mean age at follow-up was 27.5 years. Symptoms had developed in 5 of the 10 patients who were asymptomatic initially. Eight patients had considerable, persistent low back discomfort. Five of 10 patients who had conceived reported having worse low back pain and stiffness during pregnancy, but the progression of SI did not appear to have increased. Three of 6 patients reported worsening of symptoms in association with recurrent salpingitis. Two patients with definite SI had peripheral arthritis.

These findings strengthen the possibility that salpingitis is a pathogenic factor in SI. Symptomatic SI may be more frequent in women carrying the HLA-B27 antigen. The relation between salpingitis and SI in these women may be analogous to that presumed to be present between urogenital infection and SI in men. Treatment has been difficult to evaluate, but nonsteroidal anti-inflammatory drugs have been helpful in relieving symptoms. Patients with urinary tract infection have become asymptomatic after receiving long-term antibiotic therapy.

▶ [This cause of sacroiliitis is not widely recognized and it appears that previous reports on the subject are written primarily by the authors of this article. Several questions can be raised that are not satisfactorily answered in the paper. The main

(1–25) Scand. J. Rheumatol. 12:89–92, 1983.

questions relate to the method of diagnosis of the salpingitis initially: Could the pain have been sacroiliitis from onset?; Were the radiologic changes clearly distinguishable from osteitis condensans ilii? No radiographs are shown of sacroiliitic joints. It would be helpful to have this finding confirmed by others.—G.G. Hunder] ◄

1–26 **Prediction of Amputation Wound Healing: Role of Transcutaneous P$_{O_2}$ Assessment.** Below-knee amputations still fail in about 15% of patients, but present tests cannot accurately predict healing at a given level of amputation. D. A. Ratliff, C. A. C. Clyne, A. D. B. Chant, and J. H. H. Webster (Southampton, England) attempted to determine whether transcutaneous oxygen tension measurements accurately reflect limb ischemia and whether they can be used to predict amputation healing. Measurements were made in 59 patients having 62 amputations for severe occlusive vascular disease of the lower extremity. Nearly 40% of the patients were diabetic. Two patients had bilateral amputations, and 1 had 2 procedures on a lower extremity. The Roche transcutaneous partial pressure oxygen monitor was used to obtain P$_{O_2}$ readings within 24 hours of surgery at the midthigh level and 12–15 cm below the knee over the medial head of the gastrocnemius. Thirty-seven below-knee and 21 above-knee amputations were done.

Excluding the 6 perioperative deaths, 15% of the below-knee amputations and 16% of the above-knee amputations failed, as did a Syme amputation, for an overall failure rate of 16%. All below-knee amputations having a preoperative below-knee transcutaneous P$_{O_2}$ value of more than 35 mm Hg healed, whereas failures had values of 35 mm Hg or less. Nine patients who had above-knee amputations had preoperative below-knee transcutaneous P$_{O_2}$ values well above 35 mm Hg and might have been able to have below-knee amputation successfully. The mean above-knee transcutaneous P$_{O_2}$ value in failed above-knee amputations was significantly lower than in healed amputations (28 mm Hg vs. 53 mm Hg). Ankle systolic pressures did not correlate with amputation healing.

Transcutaneous P$_{O_2}$ measurements appear to reflect accurately the degree of lower limb ischemia. Significantly reduced values were present in both types of amputation failures. If the present findings are validated, some patients now subjected to above-knee amputation who have a below-knee transcutaneous P$_{O_2}$ value well above 35 mm Hg might be amenable to below-knee amputation. Amputation failures, however, often are the result of postoperative factors, and no single preoperative measure can be expected always to predict the outcome correctly.

▶ [While we have no experience with this method of evaluating ischemic legs, we have been unable so far to find an objective method that provides results which are better than can be obtained from clinical judgment. Perhaps this method will provide such an approach.

(1–26) Br. J. Surg. 71:219–222, March 1984.

We agree that technical factors and postoperative management also significantly affect the success of healing.—D.J. Pritchard] ◄

1–27 **The Fate of the Below-Knee Amputee.** In order to preserve the knee joint, Linda de Cossart, P. Randall, P. Turner, and R. W. Marcuson (Salford, England) perform below-knee amputations, when possible. A study was made of 47 patients having 51 below-knee amputations from 1974 to 1981. The 32 male and 15 female patients had a mean age of 62 years. A long posterior flap technique was used. Amputation was performed when reconstruction was not possible. Thirty-one other procedures preceeded amputation in 22 patients. Twenty-one patients had atherosclerosis, 18 had both atherosclerosis and diabetes, 3 had venous occlusive disease, 3 had arteritis, and 2 had neuropathy. Five amputations were done after artery grafts had failed. Follow-up ranged from 3 months to 6 years.

Wet gangrene was present at the time of amputation in 17 extremities, and dry gangrene, in 6. Seven patients had poor flap perfusion at the time of the operation, and 4 required conversion to an above-knee amputation. The overall success rate of below-knee amputation was 84%. Healing was delayed in 9 instances because of wound infection or dehiscence. Three of the 8 failed procedures that required conversion to above-knee amputation were done on diabetics. The 2-year mortality was 17%. Presently, 6 patients are permanently in a wheelchair, and 10 require a wheelchair when outside the home.

Below-knee amputation may be attempted if the Doppler ankle-brachial systolic ratio exceeds 0.5, the popliteal pulse is palpable, and the skin flap area is free of infection. Under different circumstances, the surgeon should be guided by his experience, but he should be guided by the better quality of life and greater chance of mobility assured the below-knee amputee.

► [Our experience is similar. The surgeon's judgement in selecting patients for below-knee amputation is the most important factor in determining the success or failure of this procedure.—D.J. Pritchard] ◄

(1–27) Ann. R. Coll. Surg. Engl. 65:228–232, July 1983.

2. Pediatrics

2–1 **Infantile Idiopathic Scoliosis: Can It Be Prevented?** Idiopathic scoliosis is a structural deformity of the spine with no evident clinical cause. A large proportion of infantile scoliotic curves resolve spontaneously, whereas adolescent curves nearly always progress. Michael J. McMaster (Edinburgh) reviewed the occurrence of the different types of idiopathic scoliosis in 672 patients seen between 1968 and 1982. There were 144 cases of infantile scoliosis, 51 of juvenile scoliosis, and 477 of adolescent scoliosis. Males were more numerous in the infantile group and females in the juvenile and adolescent groups.

Fig 2–1 (top).—Postural molding of skull producing left-sided plagiocephaly and contralateral bat ear. Note molding of thorax.

Fig 2–2 (bottom).—Postural molding of thorax when baby is laid supine and partly turned toward its side.

(Courtesy of McMaster, M.J.: J. Bone Joint Surg. [Br.] 65-B:612–617, November 1983.)

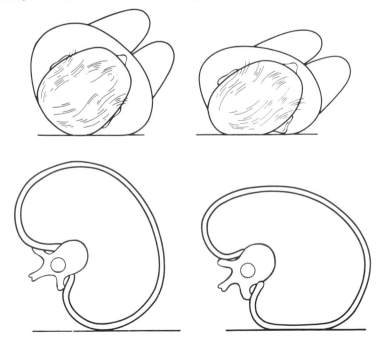

(2–1) J. Bone Joint Surg. [Br.] 65-B:612–617, November 1983.

The number of cases of infantile scoliosis declined steadily after 1971. Both progressive and resolving infantile scoliotic curves decreased in occurrence during the review period. Yearly incidence of juvenile scoliosis was fairly constant, whereas that of adolescent idiopathic scoliosis increased. Nearly three fourths of all patients with infantile scoliosis had curves that resolved spontaneously, including 83% of those who developed curves in the first 6 months of life. All 6 infants with double structural scoliosis had a progressive course. Plagiocephaly was present in 86% of the infants. All those without this condition had resolving curves. In cases of progression, the "recessed" side of the plagiocephaly always corresponded with the convex side of the thoracic or thoracolumbar curve. The recessed side of the head corresponded with the convex side of the curve in most patients who had resolving curves.

The relative frequency of both progressive and resolving infantile idiopathic scoliosis has declined. There is a close association between plagiocephaly and both resolving and progressive infantile idiopathic scoliosis (Fig 2–1). When an immobile infant is laid supine and turned partly toward the right, the immature thorax may undergo plastic deformity from the effect of gravity, causing the thoracic vertebrae to rotate backward on their long axes (Fig 2–2). The uppermost hemithorax, like the skull, tends to flow backward. Use of the prone position could explain a lower incidence of infantile scoliosis in North America. In recent years, mothers in Britain have been increasingly advised to lay their infants prone.

▶ [The increased incidence of infantile idiopathic scoliosis in Europe as compared to North America has always been an enigma.

Infantile idiopathic scoliosis (onset, from birth to 3 years) continues to be very rare in the United States; in fact, it is almost a medical curiosity. Most infantile curves resolve spontaneously, but some don't, and they prove to be very difficult problems for management.

This paper and papers like it in the German literature, suggest that the decreasing incidence in Europe is due to the increasing tendency to position infants in the prone position, a position which has always been popular in North America. This explanation seems almost too simple to be true, particularly since the author admits that in Edinburgh, at least, 75% of infants are still positioned in the supine position. A controlled study is obviously needed to answer this question.—A.J. Bianco, Jr.] ◀

2–2 **Progression in Idiopathic Scoliosis After Conservative Treatment.** The average result of conservative treatment of adolescent idiopathic scoliosis by brace or plaster jacket is a curve of the same magnitude as was present initially, but a wide range of results is obtained. Ibrahim Hassan and Ingjald Bjerkreim (Univ. of Oslo) examined the progress of curves in 100 patients (92 females) conservatively treated for idiopathic scoliosis in 1943–1978. Sixty-nine patients were treated by a correcting plaster jacket and 41 by a plaster

(2–2) Acta Orthop. Scand. 54:88–90, February 1983.

TABLE 1.—CURVE SIZE AT DIFFERENT
OBSERVATION TIMES IN CONSERVATIVELY TREATED
IDIOPATHIC SCOLIOSIS

Mean curve size (range)

	Single (n=84)	Double (n=16)	
		Upper	Lower
Start of treatment	43°	51°	49°
	(17–82)	(31–102)	(17–80)
End of treatment	41°	54°	52°
	(7–99)	(19–99)	(20–88)
16 years of age	44°	53°	49°
	(15–152)	(19–103)	(20–92)
20 years of age	54°	66°	60°
	(18–165)	(27–110)	(32–99)

(Courtesy of Hassan, I., and Bjerkreim, I.: Acta Orthop. Scand. 54:88–90, February 1983.)

TABLE 2.—CURVE PROGRESSION IN CONSERVATIVELY TREATED IDIOPATHIC SCOLIOSIS

Review period	Follow-up mean, years	Single curves (n=84)		Double curves (n=16)			
				Upper		Lower	
		Curves increased n	Progression mean (range)	Curves increased n	Progression mean (range)	Curves increased n	Progression mean (range)
16 years to last X-ray	10.6	58	15° (−12–55)	11	15° (−5–39)	10	13° (−4–46)
16–20 years old	3.8	60	10° (−5–52)	12	12° (−1–23)	12	10° (−6–36)
20 years to last X-ray	6.2	50	5° (−10–30)	9	3° (−7–20)	8	3° (−6–20)

(Courtesy of Hassan, I., and Bjerkreim, I.: Acta Orthop. Scand. 54:88–90, February 1983.)

jacket, Milwaukee brace, or both. Mean follow-up after treatment was completed was 10½ years.

Treatment ended at a mean age of 15.8 years, after an average of about 2½ years. The mean curve reduction was 0.4 degrees; for single curves it was 1.7 degrees. Single curves progressed by 3 degrees from the end of treatment to age 16 years, whereas double curves decreased slightly (Table 1). About two thirds of all curves increased from ages 16–20 years and about 60% increased after age 20 (Table 2). During the entire follow-up period, single curves increased 1.3 degrees a year and double curves 1 degree per year (Table 3). All types of curve progressed most before age 20 years. Curves of less than 40 degrees increased significantly less than curves of other sizes; curves

TABLE 3.—MEAN PROGRESSION PER YEAR IN
DIFFERENT CURVE TYPES AND PERIODS AFTER
CONSERVATIVE TREATMENT

		Mean progression per year		
	n	16 years to last X-ray	16–20 years of age	After 20 years of age
Single curves				
All	84	1.3°	3°	0.9°
Below 40°	32	.0.6°	1.4°	0.3°
40–60°	30	1.6°	3.1°	0.8°
60–80°	19	1.7°	3.4°	0.9°
Above 80°	3	1.4°	2.9°	0.7°
Thoracic	45	1.5°	3.1°	0.9°
Thoraco-lumbar	36	1°	3.1°	0.5°
Lumbar	3	1°	0.9°	0.5°
Double curves				
All	32	1°	2.1°	0.6°
Upper curves	16	1.1°	2.5°	0.7°
Lower curves	16	0.9°	1.7°	0.5°
Below 40°	10	0.7°	0.9°	0.3°
40–60°	9	1.5°	1.9°	0.7°
60–80°	8	1.7°	2.7°	0.9°
Above 80°	5	0.9°	1.9°	0.2°
All female curves	108	1.3°	2.7°	0.8°
All male curves	8	2°	4.4°	0.6°

(Courtesy of Hassan, I., and Bjerkreim, I.: Acta Orthop.
Scand. 54:88–90, February 1983.)

of 60–80 degrees increased most. Thoracic curves progressed more than lumbar ones and single more than double curves.

Idiopathic scoliosis increases significantly after the end of conservative treatment, especially at ages 16–20 years. Curves greater than 40 degrees often progress significantly after the end of treatment. Patients with these curves, particularly if single and thoracic, should be operated on in adolescence. Those with smaller curves can be managed in a brace until about age 20 and then followed during early adult life.

▶ [This brief article makes the point that idiopathic scoliosis is not only a disease of adolescence but requires surveillance on a long-term basis as well. This is a point that must be made with every afflicted patient, with the parents, and with the observing physician. Studies by Lonstein et al. have delineated the risk factors for progression in better detail.—R.A. Klassen] ◀

2–3 **Curve Progression in Idiopathic Scoliosis.** Appropriate treatment of idiopathic scoliosis is based on an understanding of the natural course of the disorder. Stuart L. Weinstein and I. V. Ponseti

(2–3) J. Bone Joint Surg. [Am.] 65-A:447–455, April 1983.

(Univ. of Iowa) followed 102 patients having a total of 133 curves for an average of 40.5 years to quantitate progression of the curves after skeletal maturity and to identify factors associated with curve progression. Thirty-one patients had a thoracic curve, 30 had a lumbar curve, 10 had a thoracolumbar curve, and 31 had combined or double primary curves.

The average curve at skeletal maturity measured 50 degrees and at final follow-up, 64 degrees. About two thirds of the curves progressed more than 5 degrees during follow-up. Curves less than 30 degrees at skeletal maturity tended not to progress. Important prognostic factors for thoracic curves were the degrees of the Cobb angle, apical vertebral rotation, and the Mehta or rib-vertebra angle. In lumbar curves the degrees of apical vertebral rotation and the Cobb angle, the direction of the curve, and the relationship between the fifth lumbar vertebra and the intercrest line were of prognostic significance. Curves measuring 50–75 degrees at skeletal maturity, especially those in the thoracic region, progressed the most.

Patients with adolescent idiopathic scoliosis whose curves measure less than 30 degrees at skeletal maturity tend not to have progression regardless of the curve pattern. Progression of more pronounced curves appears to be related to the amount of vertebral rotation. Thoracic curves of 50–75 degrees progress most rapidly. The course of lumbar curves is related to vertebral rotation, the direction of the curve, and the position of the fifth lumbar vertebra relative to the intercrest line. The course of thoracolumbar curves is affected by vertebral rotation and the magnitude of the curve. Combined curves tend to balance with advancing age.

▶ [This paper, which documents the natural history of curve progression in untreated scoliosis, is required reading for those orthopedists who care for patients with scoliosis. The study is especially valuable because of the large number of patients and the long duration of follow-up.—H.A. Peterson] ◀

2–4 **Costodesis and Contralateral Rib Release in the Management of Progressive Scoliosis.** Scoliosis in infants and children is less amenable to treatment by fusion than adolescent involvement. An alternative is to prevent growth on the convex side of the spine by unilateral curettage of the apical growth plates. J. F. Taylor, R. Roaf, R. Owen, G. Bentley, R. Calver, R. S. Jones, and M. Thorneloe (Liverpool, England) performed convex costodesis in 41 immature patients with progressive scoliosis in 1971–1974. Either the curve was deteriorating at a rate of more than 10 degrees annually or the rib-vertebra angle difference exceeded 20 degrees. Thirteen patients had congenital scoliosis, neurologic disorder, or Marfan's syndrome, and 4 had adolescent scoliosis. In 24 cases, no etiologic factor was apparent; 21 of these patients had infantile scoliosis, and 3 had juvenile sco-

(2–4) Acta Orthop. Scand. 54:603–612, August 1983.

liosis. At surgery, performed with the patient under general anesthesia without hypotension, the posterior ends of 2 ribs were excised at the apex of the curve. The bone was laid down on the laminae and transverse processes for posterior fusion in 5 cases. The ribs near the apex were depressed toward the pleura to derotate the scoliotic curve. Release was done on the concave side in all but 4 cases.

Pneumothorax developed postoperatively in 2 cases, and hemothorax in 1. Three patients had pulmonary consolidation. Another required oxygenation for 3 days for respiratory insufficiency. One patient had long-lasting effort dyspnea. Ten of the 24 patients with infantile idiopathic scoliosis maintained the improvement obtained at surgery 5 years later. In almost 80% of all patients, the mean rate of curve progression was decreased after the operation. Instrumentation and fusion were necessary in 15 instances. Only 6 patients were free of a brace at 5 years. The cosmetic results were satisfactory in most patients with infantile and juvenile idiopathic scoliosis. A favorable result was more likely with an initial rib-vertebra angle difference of less than 30 degrees and with successful convex rib fusion. Patients with congenital and adolescent scoliosis did less well than those with infantile idiopathic scoliosis.

Concave release is no longer recommended to accompany costodesis in the treatment of scoliosis. The operation is contraindicated in patients with compromised respiratory function.

▶ [It is to be noted that this procedure is best applied to the condition of infantile idiopathic scoliosis, a condition not frequently seen in North America. The authors also concluded that this procedure should not be used in congenital or adolescent idiopathic scoliosis.—H.A. Peterson] ◀

2–5 **System for Electrophysiologic Monitoring of the Spinal Cord During Operations for Scoliosis.** The correction of spinal deformities with distraction force, as with Harrington instrumentation, carries a significant risk of neurologic complications from cord lesions. S. J. Jones, M. A. Edgar, A. O. Ransford, and N. P. Thomas (London) evaluated an epidural electrophysiologic monitoring technique in 138 patients who underwent Harrington instrumentation for correction of scoliosis. Mean age was 15 years. Stimulating electrodes were placed on each leg over the posterior tibial nerve in the popliteal fossa, and cord potentials were recorded cortically or from the posterior spinal elements cephalad to the area to be fused in early cases. In most cases, spinal somatosensory evoked potentials (SEPs) were recorded from the epidural space at the low cervical or upper thoracic level.

The epidural SEP-recording electrode was easily inserted, and the leads did not obstruct operation. The current rate of technical failure is about 5%. Most of the records showed less than 10% change in amplitude on limb stimulation. No response was obtained in 1 of the

3 patients with mild neurologic symptoms after operation. The other 2 patients had transient SEP changes.

It appears to be warranted to record the epidural SEP through any operation in which there is a significant risk of neuron damage. It is hoped that this method will be widely adopted in the operative treatment of scoliosis. The spinal SEPs are sensitive to minor spinal cord impairment, possibly because of ischemia, and any changes can be rapidly reversed in the course of operation. The SEP monitoring system interferes minimally with anesthetic and surgical procedures.

▶ [Spinal cord evoked potential monitoring has become the standard method of treatment for patients undergoing reconstructive surgery of the spine. Techniques vary according to instrumentation availability. The authors of this article prefer using epidural electrodes. Pitfalls are mostly technical; however, there are some limitations in the diagnosis of neurogenic deficit. Root lesions may be entirely missed. We have tried to overcome some of these problems by using multiple electrodes in the areas of the skull, cervical, bilateral buttocks, and ankle.—R.A. Klassen] ◀

2–6 **Spinal Cord Monitoring** is discussed by Wilton H. Bunch, Timothy B. Scarff, and John Trimble (Loyola Univ.). Maintenance of spinal cord integrity is a concern in all spinal operations. The use of cortical somatosensory evoked potentials for monitoring is complicated by their great sensitivity to anesthetic agents. Spinal evoked potentials can be recorded epidurally or by using bipolar or monopolar bone recordings. In bipolar recordings, the electrodes are placed in the posterior spinous processes of two adjacent vertebrae. These recordings yield potentials that are as reproducible as those given by epidural recordings, and appear to be the most consistent means of recording spinal responses. A distal nerve generally is stimulated, but dermatomal stimulation is useful where nerve root function is of prime importance. The usual stimulation site for most spinal surgery is the posterior tibial nerve or the peroneal nerve. If more rostral dissection is planned, cortical leads can be placed and halothane or enflurane anesthesia avoided.

The current clinical use of evoked response recording is more limited than most clinicians would wish. Sets of summed potentials are quite reproducible under closely controlled conditions, but the requisite stability is not always present in the operating room because anesthesia changes the latency and amplitude of waveforms. The problem of what constitutes a real change rather than an apparent one persists. The physiologic changes underlying the observations remain to be elucidated. Major changes in latency or waveform can, however, reasonably be taken to indicate damage. The site or cause of injury cannot be inferred from the contour of the evoked response.

▶ [This review of spinal cord monitoring places its use in proper perspective. The technology presents many problems and requires a dedicated team to make it work. It is also very expensive. We have used a system for the past 3 years and have found

(2–6)   J. Bone Joint Surg. [Am.] 65-A:707–710, June 1983.

it very useful in defining intraoperative problems. A major advantage over the wake-up test is the constant monitoring that is possible. It is because of this that we have detected and resolved several problems of spinal cord dysfunction.

As the authors noted here, cord and root lesions must be separately monitored. To do both simultaneously adds significantly to the complexity of the system. We have noted that several root lesions were created intraoperatively and could not be documented until the postoperative period.—R.A. Klassen] ◄

2–7 **Recurrences of Transient Synovitis of the Hip.** Transient synovitis of the hip occurs in children, particularly boys aged 5–6 years, often after respiratory tract infection. C. M. Illingworth (Sheffield, England) assessed recurrences in a series of 54 children seen in 1977–1982 with transient synovitis of the hip. All 44 boys and 10 girls had hip pain or limited motion, and many had referred pain in the knee. Children with evidence of Perthes' disease were excluded. The mean age at the time of the first attack was 6½ years. Upper respiratory tract infection was a factor in 42% of the total of 134 episodes, and a high antistreptolysin O titer or positive culture was found in another 16% of episodes. A few children had mild diarrhea or vomiting at the time of the attack, but none was markedly febrile. Virologic studies were negative in all 11 patients studied. Two of 30 evaluable children had positive results on rheumatoid factor testing, but findings were negative at follow-up.

The 54 children had a total of 134 episodes of synovitis of the hip. Thirty-six children had a total of 80 recurrences, 69 of which were observed by 1 of the authors. Eighteen patients have not yet had recurrences. Recurrences were especially frequent within 6 months of the first attack. The same hip was affected in nearly half the children with recurrences. In 7 children, joints other than the hip were also affected.

Transient synovitis of the hip can recur after many years without symptoms. The prognosis is difficult to determine because of a lack of specificity of the clinical and laboratory findings. Careful record keeping can help avoid unnecessary pelvic irradiation from repeated radiographic examinations.

► [In addition to attempting to document recurrences of transient synovitis of the hip, this article is also an excellent basic review of the subject. In the absence of positive physical findings and radiograms, blood tests were of no help in determining the diagnosis or prognosis.—H.A. Peterson] ◄

2–8 **Bone Scintigraphy of Hip Joint Effusions in Children.** Impaired uptake of radionuclide would be expected when effusion compresses vessels leading to the femoral head. Reinhard Kloiber, William Pavlosky, Oliver Portner, and Kathleen Gartke (Ottawa, Ontario) reviewed the bone scintigraphic findings in 22 boys and 16 girls, aged 1–14 years, evaluated for an irritable hip within a 1-year period. Patients with x-ray evidence of Legg-Perthes disease or focal

(2–7) Arch. Dis. Child. 58:620–623, August 1983.
(2–8) AJR 140:995–999, May 1983.

destructive bone lesions were excluded. Twelve children underwent aspiration of the affected hip within 24 hours of nuclide imaging. Intra-articular pressure was recorded in 8 instances. Scanning was done with 250 μCi/kg of ^{99m}Tc-methylene diphosphonate.

Four children had septic arthritis and 19 were believed to have transient synovitis. Of the 9 children with reduced nuclide activity in the entire proximal femoral ossification center, joint aspiration results in 8 confirmed effusion. In 5 children followed up after aspiration, femoral head uptake became normal in all but 1, who proved to have infarction. A photopenic zone was seen on blood pool imaging in 10 patients, many of whom also had fluid aspirated. Six of the 19 patients with a diagnosis of transient synovitis had entirely normal scintigraphic findings. In all 6 with uniformly reduced femoral head activity, the epiphysis still could be identified.

Bone scintigraphy can help diagnose hip effusions and can provide information on the state of perfusion of the femoral head. Follow-up studies after aspiration of the joint can distinguish infarction from reversible ischemia. Most of the children who had a well-defined blood pool defect also had decreased femoral head uptake on delayed imaging without reduction of activity in the intra-articular part of the femoral neck. The blood pool defect is considered to be related to the actual volume of fluid present.

▶ [It is hoped that advances in equipment and technique will improve the diagnostic capabilities of scintigraphy, and allow differentiation of a variety of hip problems in children in the future. This article describes the state-of-the-art, and outlines the capabilities and deficiencies.—H.A. Peterson] ◀

2–9 **Idiopathic Chondrolysis of the Hip.** Eugene E. Bleck (Stanford Univ.) reviewed the findings in 4 boys and 5 girls seen between 1973 and 1978 with 11 hips affected by idiopathic chondrolysis. Mean age at onset of symptoms was 11½ years, and the children when first seen, had a mean age of 14½ years. All had decreased passive hip motion. Radiography showed regional osteoporosis, premature closure of the femoral capital epiphysis, joint space narrowing, and lateral overgrowth of the femoral head on the neck. The results of laboratory studies for infection and rheumatoid disease were negative. Seven children underwent arthrotomy. Synovial tissue specimens were sterile on culture, and histologic studies showed only minimal inflammation. The articular cartilage appeared normal.

Acetylsalicylic acid was given to maintain blood salicylate levels of 15–25 mg/dl. Active nonloading hip exercises were prescribed, with protected weight-bearing on crutches. Traction was used over the short term to relieve contractures developing after biopsy. Three children had iliopsoas tenotomy or lengthening, and 1 had an adductor myotomy. Six had no significant symptoms on follow-up after a mean

(2–9) J. Bone Joint Surg. [Am.] 65-A:1266–1275, December 1983.

of 6 years. Radiographs of these children showed restoration of the joint space, but lateral overgrowth of the femoral head and overgrowth of the lateral acetabular margin. Joint deterioration was seen in the 3 children who had disabling pain at follow-up; 1 of whom underwent resurfacing arthroplasty to relieve pain.

Idiopathic chondrolysis of the hip is usually managed conservatively except for diagnostic arthrotomy. Biopsy does not seem to carry a significant risk of further chondrolysis. The cause of the disorder remains unknown. Follow-up radiographic findings may suggest what might represent early osteoarthritis. Patients are cautioned against overusing and overloading the hip, although regular exercise such as swimming and bicycling is encouraged.

▶ [The etiology of both idiopathic chondrolysis and of acute chondrolysis secondary to other conditions such as slipped capital femoral epiphysis and trauma is still unknown. For some reason, many, if not most, of these patients recover in time, regaining most of their hip motion and eventually finding significant relief from their pain. However, some patients never recover, but go on to develop degenerative arthritis or fibrous ankylosis of the hip, often in a severely flexed adducted position.

In the acute phase, control of pain, preservation of joint motion, and prevention of flexion adduction contracture are formidable problems. The author advocates the use of aspirin, traction, and, in some patients, surgical releases of the contractures. This appears to be sound advice.

My only criticism of this paper is that most of these patients were not seen by the author in the acute phase of their disease (mean age at onset of symptoms, 11.5 years; mean age of when first seen by the author, 14.5 years).

It is possible that some of these patients had already started to recover. Nevertheless, the paper is valuable particularly for the long follow-up of these hips and for the detailed analysis of the final results.—A.J. Bianco, Jr.] ◀

2–10   **Sonography of the Neonatal and Infant Hip.** Treatment of congenital hip dislocation in neonates is necessary to prevent serious deformity, but arthrography is technically difficult in young infants and carries risks of vascular compromise and infection, as well as heavy radiation exposure. Gary Novick, Bernard Ghelman, and Morton Schneider (New York) used real-time high-resolution sonography to examine the hips of 20 normal infants aged 1 year and younger; 4 infants suspected of having hip dysplasia who had physical abnormalities but who were normal radiographically, 5 with known congenital hip dislocation, 3 with conditions predisposing to hip dislocation, and 1 suspected of having a septic dislocation. Studies were done without sedation. A 7.5-MHz sector transducer was used. The hip was evaluated in about 5 minutes unless the joint was abnormal. A postmortem study indicated that joint fluid can be detected sonographically (Fig 2–3).

All control infants had normal sonograms. Seven of the 16 studies done in the 13 clinically suspect or abnormal patients were normal. Three patients had sonographic dislocations that were confirmed by

(2–10)   AJR 141:639–645, October 1983.

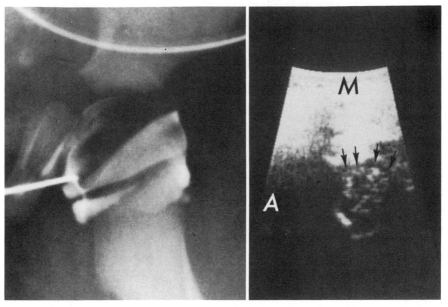

Fig 2–3.—**Left,** postmortem anteroposterior arthrogram made with 1 ml of contrast. **Right,** postarthrogram medial *(M)* transverse sonogram. Anechoic halo of fluid *(arrows)* surrounds femoral head. *A,* anterior. (Courtesy of Novick, G., et al.: AJR 141:639–645, October 1983.)

computed tomography or arthrography. In 1 instance the sonographic findings may have been misleading when fluid was suspected in the joint but was not aspirated. Two patients could not be adequately assessed sonographically, 1 because of contracture deformities and 1 because of large femoral head ossification centers. Four studies were done in infants in a cast or splint and were of diagnostic quality.

Congenital hip dislocation can be diagnosed sonographically in young infants. The cartilaginous femoral head is directly visualized by real-time high-resolution sonography. The lateral transverse view shows the triradiate cartilage. The medial transverse view is especially helpful in splinted and casted patients.

▶ [Recently, real-time ultrasonography in infants has become a very useful tool, but up to now had been rarely used in orthopedics. The technique is more easily performed than arthrography. Though experience is limited, the technique described appears to provide a noninvasive method for detection and follow-up of congenital hip dislocation.—T.H. Berquist] ◀

2–11 **Treatment of Congenital Dislocation of the Hip by the Pavlik Harness: Mechanism of Reduction and Usage.** Congenital hip dislocation generally is treated on an outpatient basis when the Pavlik harness is used, but a question of how well the device is used often

(2–11)   J. Bone Joint Surg. [Am.] 65-A:760–767, July 1983.

arises. Katsuro Iwasaki (Nagasaki Univ., Japan) reviewed the results of outpatient treatment of hip dislocation in 1966–1976. The occurrence of avascular necrosis of the femoral head was determined in 193 hips of 164 patients followed for over 1 year, and the rate of anatomical healing was assessed in 153 hips of 131 patients followed for over 5 years. Forty-four patients with 50 dislocated hips were treated in 1976–1979 with the Pavlik harness as inpatients.

Reduction was achieved in 84% of the outpatients, but in only 58% of those older than 6 months. Avascular necrosis developed in 7% of the hips followed. Anatomical healing was observed in 83% of evaluable hips. Deformity of the femoral head or acetabular dysplasia, or both, persisted in 17% of hips. Three fourths of the hips of inpatients were reduced within 7 days of application of the harness, and all these patients had successful reduction; 10 required traction as well. Avascular necrosis developed in 28% of hips in hospitalized patients. Anatomical healing occurred in 56% of patients after 3 years of follow-up. Femoral head deformity persisted in 12 of 14 hips with avascular necrosis, and acetabular dysplasia persisted in 10 of 13 hips.

The Pavlik harness is a simple device that is comfortable for the child with hip dislocation. Control during its application is necessary to achieve successful healing without complications. The harness should be used in the outpatient clinic initially. If successful reduction is not achieved, traction is indicated, followed by application of the harness in hospital if necessary.

▶ [One suspects that the higher incidence of avascular necrosis in hospitalized patients as compared to outpatients was the result of too forceful abduction in the Pavlik harness in an attempt to obtain a reduction as rapidly as possible.

The authors recognized the value of preliminary traction in those patients for whom reduction could not be easily obtained, and one wonders if the incidence of avascular necrosis was less in this group.

Reduction of the dislocated hip in the infant using the Pavlik harness is a well accepted method of treatment. To avoid avascular necrosis, the leg must be brought out into abduction gradually and gently by carefully adjusting the harness every few days.—A.J. Bianco, Jr.] ◀

2–12 **Congenital Dislocation of the Hip in Children: Comparison of the Effects of Femoral Shortening and of Skeletal Traction in Treatment.** Preoperative skeletal traction has been associated with a high rate of avascular necrosis and redislocation in older children with congenital hip dislocation, while femoral shortening has had a high rate of very satisfactory results in such cases. Perry L. Schoenecker and William B. Strecker (St. Louis) compared the results of these 2 approaches in children aged 3 and older who had not been treated when first seen. Seventeen children with 26 affected hips (group 1) underwent preoperative skeletal traction in 1961–1975. Eight patients with 13 affected hips (group 2) had primary femoral

(2–12) J. Bone Joint Surg. [Am.] 66-A:21–27, January 1984.

diaphyseal shortening at the time of open reduction in 1976–1980. The respective average ages were 4 years, 8 months; and 5 years, 11 months. All but 1 of the group 1 patients underwent open reduction of the dislocated hip. The average duration of skeletal traction was 4 weeks. Percutaneous adductor tenotomy usually was done at the time of open reduction. A Salter innominate osteotomy was done at the time of open reduction in 6 cases in group 2 and a Gill acetabuloplasty in 1 case.

Cumulative range of motion was much better in group 2 cases. Radiographic assessment also indicated a better outcome in group 2 than in group 1 cases. Limb-length discrepancy was present in 8 patients in group 1, all but 1 of whom had associated avascular necrosis of the hip. Two patients required epiphyseodesis, and another refused limb-length equalization. Four group 2 patients had limb-length discrepancy. Avascular necrosis was not observed in group 2 patients. Redislocation occurred in 8 hips in group 1 and in 1 hip in group 2. Two group 1 patients had ankylosed hips, and 2 had wound infections, 1 requiring debridement.

Primary femoral diaphyseal shortening has yielded much better results in older children with congenital hip dislocation than preoperative skeletal traction. Pelvic osteotomy now is deferred, and time is allowed for maximum spontaneous acetabular remodeling after concentric reduction of the femoral head. Quite stable reduction is produced by femoral shortening and redirectional osteotomy, and the period of postoperative immobilization is minimized.

▶ [This paper concludes that preoperative traction before reduction of the dislocated hip is associated with a much higher incidence of avascular necrosis than femoral shortening. This appears to be valid. However, one wonders if the 2 groups are really comparable. The group in which skeletal traction preceded open reduction is an older heterogeneous group, performed by many surgeons. The second group in which femoral shortening preceded open reduction was performed by only one surgeon and was a carefully controlled group of patients. In spite of these obvious variables, one cannot help but conclude that femoral shortening and varus osteotomy is a much safer procedure in preventing avascular necrosis of the femoral head, even though the surgery involved is much more extensive. Femoral shortening and varus osteotomy appears to be much more likely to result in concentric reduction of the femoral head in relation to the acetabulum with less pressure on the vascular supply to the femoral head.

I would recommend this procedure. The indications for innominate osteotomy in addition to femoral shortening and varus osteotomy are not well outlined in this paper.—A.J. Bianco, Jr.] ◀

2–13 **Reasons for Late Detection of Hip Dislocation in Childhood.** Newborn infants are routinely examined at birth for hip instability or dislocation, but the comprehensiveness of such screening varies. T. J. David, M. Ruhiyyih Parris, Margaret U. Poynor, Jane M. Hawnaur, Susan A. Simm, Elizabeth A. Rigg, and Fiona C. McCrae (Man-

(2–13) Lancet 2:147–148, July 16, 1983.

chester, England) reviewed findings in 56 children seen with hip dislocation after age 6 months. The mean age at which the parents first noticed that something was wrong, including 10 infants in whom abnormalities were noted at birth, was 11 months; however, the mean age at diagnosis was 25 months. Thirteen infants did not have their hips examined at birth. In 7 other cases, abnormalities were not followed up, and in 36 instances the parents noted abnormal symptoms but failed to alert a health care professional to the possibility of a dislocated hip. Also, 27 infants were not checked routinely after 3 months, and in 28 cases the parents failed to note the significance of abnormalities and to act on them. In 2 infants diagnostic delay occurred despite x-ray studies.

Serious delay between onset of initial symptoms of hip dislocation and diagnosis was apparent in these children. Controversy over the efficacy of neonatal hip screening may have diverted attention from assessment of late-presenting symptoms. In addition, neonatal screening can lead to a false sense of security. Hip screening should continue beyond the neonatal period to include routine checks of all children until they walk normally. Greater awareness by health care professionals of the features of hip dislocation also is necessary, as is further health education for parents. However, it is generally agreed that hip dislocation or potential hip dislocation in some infants is not detectable at birth.

▶ [This article confirms that examination and re-examination of hips is the single most important feature of the neonatal detection of hip subluxation and dislocation. The responsibility for performing these examinations must be clearly defined in each delivery unit. Abnormalities found must be carefully evaluated and followed closely.—H.A. Peterson] ◀

2–14 **Treatment of Perthes' Disease in Older Children.** Predrag J. Klisić (Belgrade, Yugoslavia) managed 181 consecutive hips with Perthes' disease in children aged 7–16 years by either containment or simple observation in 1963–1978. A total of 148 hips in 135 children were evaluated 2 years or more after presentation. The average age at the onset of treatment was 9 years. Most of the patients were boys. Containment was by femoral osteotomy in 86 hips, cheilectomy in 25, innominate osteotomy in 6, and nonoperative measures in 22. Nine hips were untreated. Eighty-eight hips had prolonged postoperative treatment until epiphyseal restitution was demonstrated. The average follow-up was about 6 years.

Patients aged 7–9 years at the time of treatment who had initially contained epiphyses did better with prolonged nonoperative treatment than with femoral osteotomy. The same was true where a slightly subluxated epiphysis was present, but femoral osteotomy gave good results in patients with initially severely subluxated epi-

(2–14)   J. Bone Joint Surg. [Br.] 65-B:419–427, August 1983.

physes. Older patients with initially contained epiphyses did not do well with any form of management. Those with slightly subluxated epiphyses did best with femoral osteotomy and prolonged postoperative treatment. Cheilectomy was useful in those with severely subluxated epiphyses, and patients with crushed epiphyses did well only after cheilectomy. Untreated hips did poorly regardless of the extent of involvement. Of 46 hips followed radiographically for an average of 3½ years, 6 showed improvement over time while 4 became worse.

Prolonged containment is much superior to short-term treatment in older children with Perthes' disease. All older children should be treated. Nonoperative measures are preferred for children aged 7–9 years with contained or slightly subluxated epiphyses, and femoral osteotomy is preferred for those with severely subluxated epiphyses. Femoral osteotomy also is used for older children with slightly subluxated epiphyses, and the Salter osteotomy is used for those with contained epiphyses. The Chiari osteotomy is used for patients with crushed but smooth epiphyses and also for those children 10 or older with severely subluxated epiphyses. Children with crushed and saddle-shaped epiphyses in the regenerative phase are managed by cheilectomy.

▶ [This is an interesting paper in that it attempts to develop an orderly plan for the treatment of the older child with Perthes' disease. Unfortunately, the number of patients in some of the treatment groups is so small that expressing the results as a percentage is open to question. The authors do point out the importance of long-term treatment even after containment has been achieved surgically.

The rationale for Chiari osteotomy in this disease is not brought out in this paper. It would have been helpful to have seen some of their postoperative results.

I also question the need for Salter innominate osteotomy if the femoral head is well contained by nonoperative methods, even if the child is over age 10 years.—A.J. Bianco, Jr.] ◀

2–15 **Perthes' Disease of the Hip in Liverpool.** A. J. Hall, D. J. P. Barker, P. H. Dangerfield, and J. F. Taylor reviewed the occurrence of Perthes' disease of the hip between 1976 and 1981 in the Liverpool region, where a relatively high incidence had been observed. A total of 157 new cases were registered during the review period, for an average annual incidence of 15.6 cases per 100,000 children aged 14 and younger. The male-female ratio was 5.3:1. The peak ages at diagnosis were 5 years for boys and 4 years for girls. A steep gradient with social class was found, ranging from 7.7 cases per 100,000 children in the higher classes to 26.3 cases per 100,000 in social class V. An underprivileged area of Liverpool had an incidence of 21.1 cases per 100,000 children aged 14 and younger. The distribution of incidence rates by ward correlated with population density and overcrowding.

These findings imply that some factors in the cause of Perthes' dis-

(2–15) Br. Med. J. 287:1757–1759, Dec. 10, 1983.

ease are associated with poverty. The high incidence in the most socially deprived part of the study area, the higher rate in the lower social classes, and the higher urban than rural incidence of Perthes' disease all support the hypothesis that undernutrition is a causal factor. Recent anthropometric studies suggest that children with Perthes' disease are shorter than control subjects, even after allowance for parental stature. The findings do not support a causal role for infection in the etiology of Perthes' disease.

▶ [The authors of this paper have found an increased prevalence of Perthes' disease among families associated with poverty, as manifested by unemployment and poor housing. They have made the assumption, but have in no way documented, that these patients have less adequate nutrition than patients found in other areas known to be more affluent. The hypothesis that undernutrition is a causative factor of Perthes' disease is interesting and deserves more definitive study.—H.A. Peterson] ◀

2-16 **Femur Lengthening Using the Wagner Technique.** Wagner, in 1971, described an apparatus for leg lengthening that provides effective stability of the osteotomy and permits the patient to ambulate. Ingjald Bjerkreim and Cato Hellum (Univ. of Oslo) used the Wagner technique in 10 female and 7 male patients, aged 10½–26 years at the time of surgery, who were followed up for at least a year after the osteosynthesis. Most patients had limb length discrepancy due to bone or joint sepsis in infancy or poliomyelitis. Patients who were not severely paretic were ambulatory on crutches 1–2 days after the procedure. A distraction of 0.75 mm was exerted twice a day. When desired lengthening had been achieved, an osteosynthesis was done using plate fixation and bone grafting.

The average limb length discrepancy at the outset was 6.8 cm, and the mean femoral lengthening was 5.8 cm. Distraction lasted an average of 6 weeks. Two AO plates were used in 10 cases; 1 plate was used in 7 cases. Cancellous bone from the iliac crest was used in 16 procedures. Homologous bone only was used in 1 patient; additional homologous bone was used in 4 cases. Equal leg lengths were achieved in 9 patients on follow-up 1–5 years after the operations. Three others had a residual discrepancy of less than 1 cm. In 3 cases, full equalization was not desired because of a need for orthotic devices. The 2 oldest patients were left with greater discrepancies, 1 because of peroneal nerve paresis and 1 because of major discomfort. The mean hospital stay was 9 weeks. Full weight-bearing was allowed an average of 10 months after the osteosynthesis. Complications were frequent, but there were no deep infections. Refractures occurred in 5 instances, necessitating reosteosynthesis in 3 patients. One patient without healing had a reosteosynthesis with autologous bone grafting.

The Wagner leg lengthening procedure is an effective and fairly

(2–16) Acta Orthop. Scand. 54:263–266, April 1983.

safe method, but complications are frequent, and great caution is necessary in using this method. The procedure is best performed at ages 10–16 years. If the predictable discrepancy at completion of growth is estimated at under 4 cm, epiphysiodesis or leg shortening is preferable.

▶ [The high percentage of satisfactory results recorded in this paper appears to result from close attention to the multiple details of this procedure. Sharing this information between institutions is essential in order to gather enough cases for these details to be properly recognized.—H.A. Peterson] ◀

2–17 **The Reduction of Supracondylar Fractures of the Humerus in Children Treated by Traction-In-Extension: A Review of 18 Cases.** The displaced supracondylar fracture of the humerus in a child remains a difficullt clinical problem. John S. Bosanquet and R. W. Middleton (Sydney) reviewed the records of 182 children seen between 1965 and 1979 with displaced supracondylar humeral fractures. Eighteen patients had gross swelling, neurovascular damage, or instability or had suffered a delay in hospitalization that made them unsuitable for closed reduction and collar-and-cuff immobilization. These fractures were managed with the elbow extended and the forearm supinated in traction, using a Thomas splint. This approach is contraindicated where skin lesions prevent the use of skin traction and where the circulation is impaired even with the elbow extended. The traction is adjusted regularly as swelling subsides. Immobilization in traction is continued for 2 to 3 weeks, until there is clinical and radiologic evidence of callus. A collar and cuff then are used, with the elbow flexed as much as possible. Exercising begins after 1 month.

Eight of the 14 evaluable patients showed excellent results, with a less than 5-degree change in the carrying angle, fewer than 10 degrees of restriction of motion in any plane, and no complaints. Four other patients had good results, while 2 had an unsatisfactory outcome. The average length of follow-up was 5½ months. One patient with an unsatisfactory result lacked full flexion. The other, treated by traction in extension for only 1 week, had a cubitus varus of 30 degrees that necessitated late osteotomy.

Most pediatric patients with supracondylar humeral fractures that are unsuitable for standard management do well with traction in extension. This is a simple, safe, and predictable method that reduces the risk of infection and ulnar nerve damage. The carrying angle can be seen. The position is ideal where the circulation is compromised after injury. It does not appear to be important to restore end-to-end apposition, since much of the posterior displacement of the distal fragment is overcome through remodeling. Most patients regain nearly full motion in the elbow joint.

(2–17) Injury 14:373–380, January 1983.

2–18 **Monteggia Lesion in Children: Fracture of Ulna and Dislocation of Radial Head.** John V. Fowles, Noureddine Sliman, and Mohamed T. Kassab reviewed the management of 15 children seen from 1966 to 1980 at the University of Tunis with a Monteggia lesion; all were followed up for a year or longer. Fourteen children had a fracture of the proximal or middle third of the ulnar shaft, 10 with anterior dislocation of the radial head and 4 with anterolateral dislocation. The remaining child had a greenstick fracture of the metaphysis of the proximal ulna and anterolateral dislocation of the radius. Two children had open wounds. Treatment was delayed for more than 6 weeks after injury in 5 instances. Two of the children given acute treatment had primary open reduction and intramedullary pin fixation of an open fracture; the other 8 had closed reduction initially, but 4 later required open reduction of an oblique fracture. A Kirschner wire was used in 3 children and a plate in 1. Two children with delayed treatment had osteotomy of the angulated ulna and stabilization with a 4-hole plate. The annular ligament was divided or excised in all 5 children, and fibrous tissue was removed from the joint space in order to reduce the radial head. In 3, the annular ligament was reconstructed with a fascial loop.

Five acutely treated patients had clinically normal elbows on follow-up at 1–8 years after injury. Two others had lost a little flexion, 2 lacked some pronation, and 4 had a slight change in the carrying angle. All but 2 children had normal findings radiographically. In those given delayed treatment, flexion was 50% improved at follow-up an average of 4 years after operation. Radiohumeral and radioulnar alignment and configuration of the radial neck were normal in all children having reconstruction of the annular ligament.

Transverse and metaphyseal ulnar fractures in children with the Monteggia injury are stable after closed reduction, but oblique ulnar shaft fractures require intramedullary pinning. Children treated more than 6 weeks after injury do well if the annular ligament is reconstructed or repaired. Radial reduction should be maintained by a humeroradial Kirschner wire while the new ligament heals. Malunion of the ulna may necessitate osteotomy and internal fixation.

▶ [Very few pediatric fractures require open reduction and internal fixation. The Monteggia lesion, with the oblique ulnar metaphyseal or shaft fracture, should be recognized as one that does, thus avoiding the futility of an attempted closed reduction. Annular ligament repair is an important adjunct in the treatment of the chronically dislocated radial head.—R.A. Klassen] ◀

2–19 **Growth Disturbances Following Distal Femoral Physeal Fracture Separations.** Fracture separation of the distal femoral physis can lead to lower limb length discrepancy, angular deformity, and decreased joint motion. Edward J. Riseborough, Ian R. Barrett,

(2–18)   J. Bone Joint Surg. [Am.] 65-A:1276–1283. December 1983.
(2–19)   Ibid., pp. 885–893, September 1983.

and Frederic Shapiro (Boston) reviewed the effects of such injuries on distal femoral growth in 47 boys and 19 girls who were followed for an average of 4 years after injury. The average time of roentgenographic follow-up was 25 months. Five children had birth fractures. The average age at injury in the others was 11 years for boys and 10 years for girls. Salter-Harris type II fractures predominated. Six injuries were open. Most type II and type III lesions were managed by closed reduction and cast immobilization. Three of the 6 type IV lesions were managed by open reduction and Kirschner wire fixation.

Only 16 children were first seen at the Children's Hospital Medical Center in Boston; many of the others seen secondarily already had growth problems. Lower limb length discrepancy exceeding 2.4 cm or leading to contralateral distal femoral physeal arrest occurred in 56% of the children. Also, 26% had an angular deformity of more than 5 degrees or one requiring osteotomy. Central arrest, noted radiographically in 20%, was closely associated with the development of limb length discrepancy. Growth problems correlated well with the severity of injury and occurred in all Salter-Harris injuries. More than 80% of injuries in children aged 2–11 years were followed by growth problems. Half of the adolescents, who generally had less severe injuries, had growth problems. None of the birth fractures or injuries sustained in the first 2 years of life caused serious growth problems.

The final outcome in these children might be improved by anatomical reduction and the greater use of internal fixation in types II, III, and IV injuries. Possible difficulties might be anticipated by evaluating physeal injuries using pathophysiologic criteria relating to the blood supply, continuity of the physis, and the presence or absence of vascular communication between the epiphyseal and metaphyseal segments.

▶ [This article clearly underscores the need to study this problem. It will be necessary to follow a large number of primary cases to maturity in order to determine the incidence of problems and the problem areas (age of patient, mechanism of injury, type of fracture, timing and nature of treatment, etc.). It will be difficult to accumulate sufficiently large numbers of primary cases because less than 2% of all physeal injuries occur in the distal femur.—H.A. Peterson] ◀

2–20 **Blount's Disease in the Antilles: Review of 26 Cases** is presented by Y. Catonne, H. Dintimille, S. Arfi, and A. Mouchet (Forte de France, Martinique), Blount's disease is characterized by a varus deformity of the tibia secondary to agenesis of the medial tibial plateau. Blount's disease may be distinguished in an infantile form, appearing in children between 1 and 3 years, and in an adolescent form, becoming manifest between 8 and 13 years of age. The present study involved 26 black natives of the Antilles (15 male and 11 female), 20

(2–20) Rev. Chir. Orthop. 69:131–140, 1983.

of whom had a diagnosis during the developmental years, and 6 when adults. Of the 26, 24 had Blount's infantile form.

The disease may be classified into 6 stages; stage IV is considered the most critical. Before this stage, corrective osteotomy will often lead to complete cure. After stage IV, lateral epiphysiodesis must be performed to avoid recurrence of deformity. Early signs include asymmetry of the epiphyseal core and the presence of an asymmetrical process primarily involving the tibial metaphysis. In doubtful cases, evolution will be decisive; constitutional genu varum regresses spontaneously around age 3.

In the present series the technique of osteotomy varied according to the age of the child and obliquity of the joint line. In young children, a subtraction closing wedge osteotomy is suitable. Figure 2–4

Fig 2–4.—Blount's disease in 6-year-old girl, in stage III *(left)*, and 3 years after external subtraction-type osteotomy *(right)*. (Courtesy of Catonne, Y., et al.: Rev. Chir. Orthop. 69:131–140, 1983.)

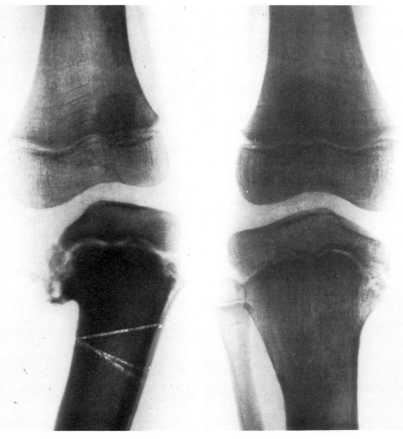

shows the results of intervention in a 6-year-old child. In older children a V-shaped osteotomy is recommended to lessen the amount of shortening. At the end of the growth period a medial opening wedge osteotomy is advisable. In adults, whose deformity may reach 50 degrees with considerable ligamentous laxity, reefing of the ligament must be included in the osteotomy.

▶ [This lesion has become quite rare in the central United States. The author has demonstrated the ability of the epiphysis to remodel itself after realignment has been achieved.—R.A. Klassen] ◀

2–21 **Fractures of the Distal Tibial Epiphysis in Adolescence.** Luciano S. Dias and Clare R. Giegerich (Chicago) studied the cases of 9 adolescents with a Salter-Harris type III fracture of the lateral part of the distal tibial epiphysis, or juvenile Tillaux fracture, and 8 with a triplane fracture of the distal tibial epiphysis. They represented about 10% of all patients with ankle fracture seen in an emergency room in a 20-month period. Both types of injury were postulated to be caused by external rotation of the foot on the leg.

The 9 patients with an isolated fracture of the lateral part of the epiphysis had an average age of 13½ years. The distal fragment constituted 20%–50% of the width of the epiphysis. Five patients were managed by closed methods, while 4 with more than 2 mm of displacement of the fragments underwent open reduction. All patients had full ankle motion without pain and roentgenographic evidence of a healed fracture with a closed physis on follow-up at 18–36 months. Six patients had a typical 3-fragment triplane fracture, and 3 of them also had a distal fibular fracture. The entire distal tibial physis appeared open in all these patients. The fragment comprised 40%–50% of the width of the epiphysis. Three patients were treated by closed methods; 3, by open reduction and internal fixation. The patients treated by closed methods were normal at follow-up, but the surgically treated patients, who had more severe injuries, reported occasional aching after athletic activities. Only 1 patient had slight loss of ankle motion. Both patients with a 2-part triplane fracture were treated by closed reduction, with no adverse sequelae.

External rotational force appears to produce isolated anterolateral fractures of the distal tibial epiphysis, as well as 2-fragment and 3-fragment triplane injuries. Reversing the mechanism of injury by gentle internal rotation usually leads to restitution of a congruent joint surface. Open reduction usually is necessary if there is wide separation or impaction of the fragments. Intraoperative internal rotation of the foot generally reduces the fracture.

▶ [The triplane fracture meets all the criteria of a Salter and Harris type IV fracture because it traverses articular cartilage, epiphysis, physis, and metaphysis. It may be therefore more anatomically correct to classify this as a variant of a type

(2–21) J. Bone Joint Surg. [Am.] 65-A:438–444, April 1983.

IV fracture rather than as a type III fracture, as suggested by the authors.—H.A. Peterson] ◀

2–22 **Salter-Harris Type IV Injuries of the Distal Tibial Epiphyseal Growth Plate, With Emphasis on Those Involving the Medial Malleolus.** Joseph R. Cass and Hamlet A. Peterson (Mayo Clinic and Found.) reviewed the records of 32 patients seen between 1975 and 1979 with Salter-Harris type IV distal tibial epiphyseal injuries, extending through the articular cartilage, epiphysis, physis, and metaphysis. They represented over one fourth of all injuries at this site. Average follow-up of patients treated initially at the Clinic was 39 months. Eighteen patients had a fracture involving the medial malleolus (Fig 2–5), 13 had a triplane fracture, and 1 had a fracture of the lateral part of the physis.

Among the 13 patients treated initially at the Clinic, 6 of the 11 with closed fractures had closed reduction and immobilization in a below-knee plaster, and the other 5 had open reduction and internal fixation. An attempt was made to achieve anatomical reduction in all instances. Kirschner wires were used in most operative cases. One of the 2 open injuries was reduced surgically. Two younger patients had leg length discrepancies after closed treatment. Two patients who were operated on had tibial shortening, and 1 had a physeal bar. Premature partial closure of the distal physis developed in 9 of all 18 tibias with a medial malleolar fracture and resulted in angular deformity or limb length discrepancy requiring operation. The findings in 1 case are shown in Figures 2–6 and 2–7. All the patients with triplane fracture or fracture of the lateral plafond were near maturity when injured, and none had growth arrest problems.

Fig 2–5.—Three variations of Salter-Harris type IV injuries of distal tibial physis seen in this series. **A,** medial malleolar fracture; **B,** triplane fracture (the three planes of fracture that are located in epiphysis, physis, and metaphysis are visible on the two views, but sometimes metaphyseal fracture can be seen only on appropriate oblique view); and **C,** fracture of lateral part of plafond. (Courtesy of Cass, J.R., and Peterson, H.A.: J. Bone Joint Surg. [Am.] 65-A:1059–1070, October 1983.)

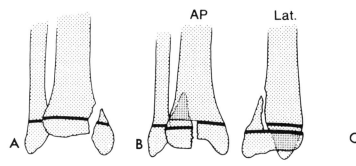
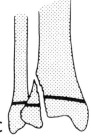

AP   Lat.

A   B   C

(2–22) J. Bone Joint Surg. [Am.] 65-A:1059–1070, October 1983.

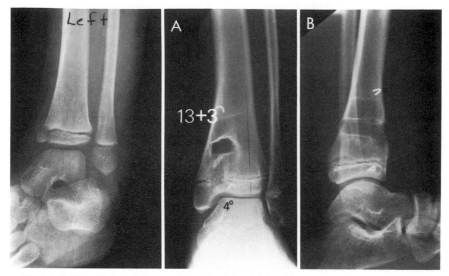

Fig 2–6 (left).—Girl, aged 7 years 5 months, injured left ankle in automobile accident. Oblique (mortise) roentgenogram made at time of injury, shows displaced type IV fracture of medial malleolus. This was treated by immobilization in plaster cast, leaving fracture fragments in displaced position.

Fig 2–7 (right).—Anteroposterior *(A)* and lateral *(B)* roentgenograms made at age 13 years 3 months. Patient was normally active and asymptomatic. Lateral roentgenogram shows 41 mm between the metal markers. Tibial length discrepancy had decreased from 12 to 10 mm.

(Courtesy of Cass, J.R., and Peterson, H.A.: J. Bone Joint Surg. [Am.] 65-A:1059–1070, October 1983.)

Anatomical reduction of Salter-Harris type IV fractures of the medial malleolus usually requires open reduction and internal fixation, preferably with smooth Kirschner wires that do not cross the physis. Follow-up to skeletal maturity is desirable. If premature partial growth arrest occurs, excision of the physeal bar is an acceptable alternative to repeated osteotomies or tibial lengthening. This procedure permits resumption of longitudinal growth, and angular deformity may also be reduced or corrected.

▶ [This series of patients again points out the frequency with which epiphyseal injuries and late complications are associated with this often innocuously appearing fracture. Premature partial closure of the physis was a common complication. It should also be noted that radiographic analysis is important since some of the fractures are not seen on routine anteroposterior and lateral films. These are best shown on oblique films. The authors, however, do not note if any of the associated injuries, such as a fracture of the lateral malleolus, did occur or whether other fractures in the area had any bearing on the outcome of these fractures.—R.A. Klassen] ◀

2–23 **Lateral Talocalcaneal Angle in Assessment of Subtalar Valgus: Follow-Up of Seventy Grice-Green Arthrodeses.** James

---

(2–23) Foot Ankle 4:56–63, Sept.–Oct. 1983.

Aronson, James Nunley, and Karl Frankovitch reviewed 70 extra-articular subtalar arthrodeses done by Grice's method by 5 different surgeons between 1972 and 1980 at Shriner's Hospital for Crippled Children in Erie, Pennsylvania, to determine whether definitive radiographic criteria can be established for the procedure. Most of the children had cerebral palsy, usually in the form of spastic diplegia. Cortical slots were made in the talus and calcaneus perpendicular to the axis of the subtalar joint, engaging the anterosuperior lip of the calcaneus, and a contoured bicortical tibial graft was wedged in place. Determination of the talocalcaneal angle on the standing lateral radiograph is shown in Figure 2–8 and the postoperative evaluation in Figure 2–9.

The 22 boys and 16 girls had an average age of 5½ years at the time of surgery. The average follow-up was 59 months. Immediate operative improvement of 19 degrees in the standing lateral talocalcaneal angle was observed. A shift into 5 degrees more valgus occurred within 5 years after operation, producing a final angle of 34 degrees. The 9 "nonunions" had a mean angle of 39 degrees at late follow-up. The "valgus" failures were more deformed initially and had a mean angle of 51 degrees at follow-up. The 11 feet reported to be painful at follow-up could not be distinguished radiographically. The 31 patients evaluated were pleased with their feet. The clinical out-

Fig 2–8.—To determine the talocalcaneal angle on the standing lateral radiograph, (1) draw the longitudinal axis of the calcaneus through midpoint A at the posterior tuberosity and midpoint B at the sustentaculum; (2) draw the longitudinal axis of the talus through midpoint C at the body and midpoint D at the neck; (3) measure the angle formed by the intersection of these axes. Normal range = 25–45 degrees (mean, 33 degrees); valgus hindfoot more than 45 degrees; varus hindfoot less than 25 degrees; variation ± 2 degrees through 40-degree arc of x-ray beam; variation ± 8 degrees with active supination and pronation. (Courtesy of Aronson, J., et al.: Foot Ankle 4:56–63, Sept.–Oct. 1983.)

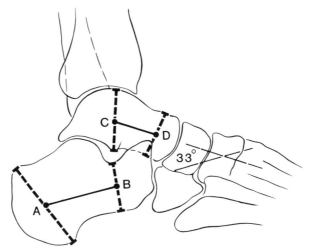

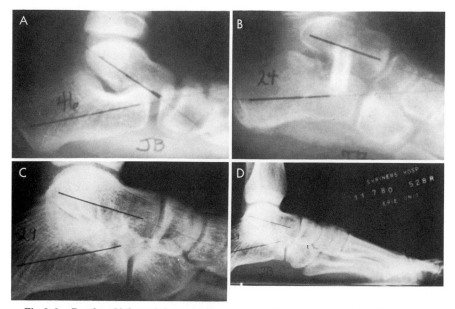

Fig 2–9.—Results of bilateral Grice procedures using tibial autograft and lengthening of heel cords in child with spastic diplegia. **A,** preoperative standing lateral talocalcaneal angle of 55 degrees shows significant talar tilt. Because of their radiodensity, the ossific nuclei of the talus and calcaneus are easily measured for longitudinal axes. Posterior subluxation of the calcaneus is not reliably demonstrated. **B,** immediate perioperative correction was 30 degrees. Note anterior angulation of the slotted bicortical strut graft abutting the anterosuperior lip of the calcaneus in the sinus tarsi; this prevents posterior subluxation and eversion of the calcaneus. **C,** after 7½ years, the talocalcaneal alignment remains stable; trabeculations of the extra-articular graft are seen on the x-ray film; **D,** overall foot alignment on standing lateral x-ray view is satisfactory. (Courtesy of Aronson, J., et al.: Foot Ankle 4:56–63, Sept.–Oct. 1983.)

come was better than the radiographic outcome: only 25% of 16 feet judged radiographically to be failures were considered to be clinical failures. Only 4 procedures failed in both respects. Genuvalgus resulted from tibial overgrowth near the medial graft site in 2 patients.

The standing lateral talocalcaneal angle is the most useful criterion for patient selection for the Grice-Green arthrodesis and for evaluating the results of surgery. Hindfoot valgus is corrected in more than 90% of patients. Good results can be obtained even in obese children. The graft must be angled anteriorly in order to maintain a solid strut between the calcaneus and talus.

▶ [The Grice operation appears to be standing the test of time successfully. The authors have effectively used the standing lateral talocalcaneal angle as the most accurate measure of preoperative hindfoot valgus and postoperative correction. This is a useful, relatively simple and objective method.

As the authors stress, over correction of the hindfoot into a permanent varus position results in a painful, disabled foot and should be avoided at all cost.—A.J. Bianco, Jr.] ◀

2–24 **Sprained Ankle in Children: Clinical Follow-Up Study of 90 Children Treated Conservatively and by Surgery.** V. Vahvanen, M. Westerlund, and M. Kajanti (Helsinki) reviewed the outcome in 90 children with lateral ankle sprains. In 1978, a consecutive series of 25 boys and 25 girls aged 5–14 years had their injured ankles immobilized for 1–5 weeks, usually by an elastic bandage; all were reassessed at a mean of 18 months after injury. From 1979 to 1980, 28 boys and 12 girls of the same ages were operated on for acute inversion injury of the ankle. The latter groups represented 7.2% of all children seen with acute ankle sprain in this period. Indications for surgery included severe swelling, severe lateral pain, presence of a limp, clinical ligamentous instability, and a displaced avulsion fragment below the fibular apex. The mean follow-up after operation was 9 months. A fragment was removed in 5 instances.

At initial follow-up, 21 conservatively treated children had symptoms of disability, and 4 of them required surgical treatment for functional instability and pain. Five others continued to have functional instability 4 years after injury. The surgically treated ankles healed well, and the children were asymptomatic at follow-up. All of these ankles were roentgenographically stable at follow-up. An isolated rupture of the anterior talofibular ligament was present in 17 operated-on ankles.

Lesions of the anterior talofibular ligament are surprisingly frequent in children with acute inversion injury of the ankle. Primary repair of the ligament ensures a symptom-free and stable ankle. Disability was not uncommon in conservatively treated children. A displaced fibular or talar avulsion fragment should be fixed surgically or removed at the time of repair of the damaged ligament. Considerable instability of the ankle also is an indication for operative treatment.

▶ [The authors correctly stress that the 2 groups of patients reported in this paper cannot be objectively compared. I also agree with their conclusions that the manual stress test is painful and unreliable in children and that more objective methods are needed to measure ankle instability. In addition, arthrography in 3 cases who were subsequently operated on resulted in false negative diagnoses in 2. A study of cases with conclusive documentation of rupture of the anterior tibiofibular ligament complex treated nonoperatively is needed before approving the suggestion that most severe sprains (pain, tenderness, swelling, hematoma, etc.) should be subjected to surgery, especially in young children.—H.A. Peterson] ◀

2–25 **Development of the Menisci of the Human Knee Joint: Morphological Changes and Their Potential Role in Childhood Meniscal Injury.** Meniscal injuries are unusual in children but become increasingly common in adolescence. Current emphasis on the repair of meniscal tears raises the question whether the structure of the immature meniscus can enhance the chances of reparative procedures succeeding in skeletally immature patients. Charles R. Clark

(2–24) Ann. Chir. Gynaecol. 72:71–75, 1983.
(2–25) J. Bone Joint Surg. [Am.] 65-A:538–547, April 1983.

and John A. Ogden (Yale Univ.) examined 548 menisci from prenatal and postnatal cadaver knees in order to elucidate the developmental changes that occur before skeletal maturity. The medial and lateral menisci were taken from 109 fetuses aged 14–34 weeks' gestation and from 28 cadavers aged 3 months to 14 years. The fetal material was obtained from therapeutic abortions and stillbirths. Most of the postnatal patients had died of general medical disorders or accidents.

Both the medial and lateral menisci assumed their characteristic shapes early in prenatal life, but the fetal menisci were very cellular and had numerous intrameniscal vessels. Gradual postnatal changes included decreasing vascularity, starting centrally, and growth commensurate with enlargement of the femur and tibia. The lateral meniscus tended to vary more developmentally, but at no stage was it discoid. The ratio of the area of each meniscus to the area of the corresponding tibial plateau and the ratio of the areas of the medial and lateral menisci remained fairly constant throughout growth. The collagen fiber arrangement within the menisci appeared to change in response to biomechanical function.

The developing menisci, because of their vascularity and physical properties, may have greater reparative ability than those of adolescents or adults. The findings suggest that all possible efforts should be made to preserve at least some of an injured meniscus in children and adolescents and to reattach peripherally detached menisci rather than removing them. The biomechanical properties of a discoid meniscus may, however, be improved if it is partially excised to permit more normal growth and development, especially if this is done at an early age.

2–26 **Meniscectomy in Children: Long-Term Follow-Up Study.** Reported success rates from meniscectomy in children and adolescents have ranged from 40% to 90%. Marc Manzione, Peter D. Pizzutillo, Alan B. Peoples, and Paul A. Schweizer (Alfred I. duPont Inst., Wilmington, Del.) reviewed the results of meniscectomy in 20 children with isolated meniscal tears who were operated on before skeletal maturity and were followed up at an average of 5½ years after operation. None had evidence of ligament damage or instability, or bilateral knee pathology.

Five children had excellent and 3 had good results on the basis of subjective and objective parameters. Eleven had fair results, and 1 had a poor outcome. The results could not be related to age at operation or to the type or site of injury. The average time from injury to meniscectomy was 12 months, and was shorter in patients who had satisfactory results. Half of the children had bucket-handle meniscal tears. Fifteen underwent total and 5 had partial meniscectomies. The roentgenographic findings were comparable in the groups with satis-

(2–26)   Am. J. Sports Med. 11:111–115, May–June 1983.

factory and unsatisfactory results. The most evident difference between these groups was in hip abductor testing; children with unsatisfactory results had an average decrease of 37% in hip abductor function on the side of meniscectomy.

Meniscectomy is not a benign procedure in children and adolescents. Significant and possibly progressive long-term morbidity is associated with it, and a more conservative approach is suggested. Every attempt should be made to determine the extent of the lesion preoperatively. Meniscoplasty may be indicated in selected patients. Only when meniscal damage is extensive or totally within the body of the structure should total meniscectomy be considered in children. Restoration of a functional lower limb after meniscectomy requires complete rehabilitation of all weakened muscle groups, especially the hip abductors.

▶ [Analysis of this article is enhanced by the commentary by Dr. Kenneth DeHaven that follows. It is unlikely that a meniscus can be significantly torn without some injury to the supporting ligaments and articular cartilage. In addition, since neither the type nor the site of the original injury correlated with the overall late results, and since there was no correlation between radiographic findings (80% of cases demonstrated degenerative changes) and clinical results, could factors other than the removed meniscus be related to the late findings? These factors might include varying surgical indications, techniques, and postoperative care by the surgeons, the presence of genu valgum or varum, undiagnosed small tears in the other meniscus, and, in the partial meniscectomies, the possibility of double or triple tears in the retained portion of the meniscus. In this series, the proportion of satisfactory and unsatisfactory results was similar for complete and partial meniscectomies and for medial and lateral meniscectomies.—H.A. Peterson] ◀

2–27 **Split Posterior Tibial Tendon Transfer in Spastic Cerebral Palsy.** Varus and equinovarus deformities of the hindfoot are relatively frequent in children with spastic hemiplegia secondary to cerebral injury in the neonatal period. Kaufer described a split posterior tibial tendon transfer in 1977. Neil E. Green, Paul P. Griffin, and Richard Shiavi (Vanderbilt Univ.) performed such an operation on 16 children in 1976 to 1980. Average age was 6.2 years. None had had previous surgery on the leg that had this operation. All but 1 of the patients also underwent lengthening of the tendo achillis. All but 1 had an equinovarus gait.

Electromyographic study and video gait analysis were performed in all cases. The dynamic deformity always was more marked than the static deformity, and the equinus position during gait was greater than expected from the rest examination. The operation is illustrated in Figures 2–10 and 2–11.

All the varus deformities were corrected on follow-up for 2 years or more after operation, although 2 patients required osteotomy of the calcaneus because of fixed varus deformity. In all cases the posterior tibial muscle was active during the swing phase of gait after opera-

(2–27) J. Bone Joint Surg. [Am.] 65-A:748–754, July 1983.

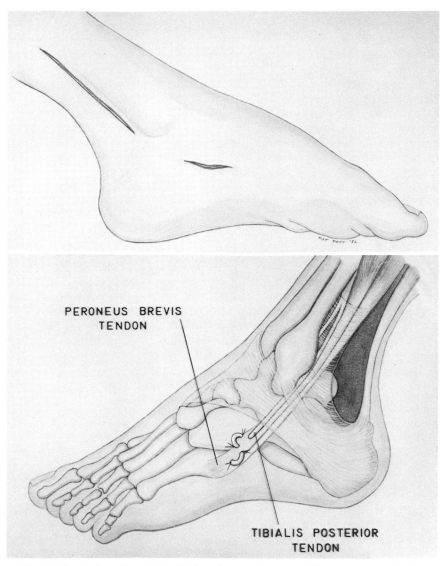

PERONEUS BREVIS TENDON

TIBIALIS POSTERIOR TENDON

Fig 2–10 (top).—In split posterior tibial tendon transfer two medial incisions are made. First is 2 cm long and is placed over distal portion of posterior tibial tendon and over insertion on navicular bone. Second is 6 cm long and begins at level of medial malleolus and is carried proximally. It is placed approximately halfway between posterior border of tibia and tendo achillis. If heel cord lengthening is not performed, incision may be placed slightly closer to tibia, as shown here.

Fig 2–11 (bottom).—Split half of posterior tibial tendon is delivered in distal lateral incision. Sheath of peroneus brevis tendon is opened, and split tendon is passed in and out of peroneus brevis. Tension on split transfer is adjusted so foot will rest in neutral position when it is suspended. Split tendon is then sutured in place with nonabsorbable suture material.

(Courtesy of Green, N.E., et al.: J. Bone Joint Surg. [Am.] 65-A:748–754, July 1983.)

tion. Twelve feet were rated as excellent, with a plantigrade posture, no postural or fixed deformity, and no need for a brace. The other 4 feet were rated as good. There were no recurrences of varus deformity, and no valgus or calcaneal deformities were produced by the surgery.

The split posterior tibial tendon transfer, along with tendo achillis lengthening when indicated, has given good results in patients with spastic varus deformity of the hindfoot. The equinovarus deformity is corrected, and recurrent varus deformity is prevented. The posterior tibial muscle cannot function independently as an inverter or everter of the hindfoot, but rather it stabilizes the hindfoot after the operation.

▶ [The authors have presented a reasonable solution for a difficult problem. The operation appears to prevent the major complication of all surgery of this type; namely, balance (or imbalance) of muscle groups. Our experience is limited to judicious lengthening of the posterior tibial tendon, which is a simpler procedure with minimal complications.—R.A. Klassen] ◀

2–28 **Supramalleolar Derotation Osteotomy for Lateral Tibial Torsion and Associated Equinovarus Deformity of the Foot.** Lateral torsion of the tibia in children with paralysis is most often associated with a varus or equinovarus deformity of the hindfoot, resulting from unbalanced muscle action about the ankle. David McNicol, J. C. Y. Leong, and L. C. S. Hsu developed a derotation osteotomy on the basis of an association of a varus or equinovarus position of the hindfoot with forefoot supination and lateral rotation of the tibia.

TECHNIQUE.—A fibular osteotomy is first done in the lower third for complete derotation of the ankle mortise, followed by a small oblique incision over the anteromedial aspect of the distal tibia (Fig 2–12). The periosteum is lifted off the bone circumferentially, and a transverse osteotomy is outlined in the supramalleolar region (Fig 2–13); 2 Kirschner wires may be used as guides. After the osteotomy has been made and lateral torsion has been eliminated, a single staple is placed across the osteotomy (Fig 2–14). An above-knee plaster is applied, which is maintained for 6 weeks.

Twenty operations were done in 18 patients with lateral tibial torsion. The age range was 7–26 years. Thirteen patients, including the 2 with bilateral torsion deformities, had had poliomyelitis. Most of the poliomyelitis limbs had an associated equinovarus deformity of the hindfoot. Lateral tibial torsion was corrected in all 7 patients with mobile hindfoot varus, who had 8 operations. There was 1 case of nonunion. Two patients have had subsequent surgery to help balance the foot, but all hindfeet have remained in satisfactory position without further surgery. All these patients are free of a brace. The 11 patients who had 12 operations for fixed hindfoot varus had sufficient correction of lateral tibial torsion to proceed with triple arthrodesis or bracing. One patient had premature fusion of the distal tibial epi-

(2–28) J. Bone Joint Surg. [Br.] 65-B:166–170, March 1983.

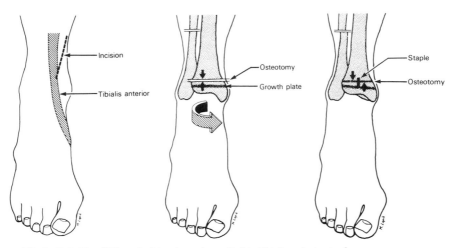

Fig 2–12 (left).—Oblique incision is made medial to tibialis anterior tendon.

Fig 2–13 (center).—Transverse osteotomy in supramalleolar region of tibia is completed above level of tibiofibular syndesmosis. Care is taken to avoid damage to growth plate. Osteotomy of fibula is made in its lower third, so that ankle mortise can be rotated as a unit.

Fig 2–14 (right).—On completion of derotation, position achieved is held with single staple. Care must be taken to avoid damage to growth plate.

(Courtesy of McNicol, D., et al.: J. Bone Joint Surg. [Br.] 65-B:166–170, March 1983.)

physis because the osteotomy was made too close to the growth plate. All patients are free of a brace except the 1 who did not have triple arthrodesis. Another patient also had fusions of the talonavicular and calcaneocuboid joints. In all 11 patients, the normal radiographic malleolar relationship was restored after supramalleolar derotation osteotomy.

Supramalleolar derotation osteotomy of the tibia is a technically simple, effective procedure for correction of lateral tibial torsion due to paralysis. The operation is done to correct hindfoot varus and help balance the foot in patients with mobile hindfoot varus deformity and to realign the ankle mortise in those with fixed hindfoot varus deformity.

▶ [This is an innovative approach. The level of this osteotomy should successfully avoid the complication of compartment syndrome which sometimes occurs following osteotomy at a more proximal level. The level of the osteotomy and insertion of the staple must be carefully chosen to avoid damage to the physis.—H.A. Peterson] ◀

2–29 **Emotional Aspects of Arm or Leg Amputation in Children** are discussed by Atilla Turgay and Birsen Sonuvar. Amputation in a child is one of the most traumatic of medical experiences. Information on 7 children younger than age 15 years who had had amputation of a leg or arm or were being readied for such an operation were reviewed. At least three personal and two family sessions were held in

(2–29) Can. J. Psychiatry 28:294–297, June 1983.

each case. Play material and story-telling techniques were used with the younger children.

Some children interpreted the accident and amputation as punishment for not being good. All were motivated to share their feelings about the amputation; denial was common but not extremely rigid. Each child had a unique approach to preparing himself or herself to accept the reality of the situation. All maintained some degree of resentment and protest; complete adjustment to the loss was impossible. Family members showed similar stages of loss and mourning. Guilt feelings in relatives can become intolerable. The hardest tasks were to acknowledge to the child the necessity for amputation and to visit the child for the first time after amputation. Parental anger and frustration with medicine and doctors were readily expressed.

The emotional response of members of the treatment team ranged from indifference to extreme sympathy with the child and family. The reactions resembled those of the patients and relatives to some degree, but emotional involvement was less. The team members generally attempted to suppress their feelings, but given the opportunity, they expressed depression, guilt, anger, disappointment, and feelings of failure. Some of the emotional trauma associated with the ordeal was alleviated through the discussions.

▶ [The things that everyone knows, such as the guilt, denial, and misconceptions that accompany amputation, seldom are investigated. Sometimes though, when they are examined, these feelings that everyone has experienced are understood and confronted for the first time. Reading this article will help our patients only after it helps us understand ourselves.—J.H. Dobyns] ◀

2–30 **Hypermobility Syndrome** has been recognized as a definite diagnostic entity among children referred with musculoskeletal symptoms to a pediatric arthritis clinic. Frank Biro, Harry L. Gewanter, and John Baum (Univ. of Rochester) diagnosed hypermobility in 15 (5.7%) of 262 clinic patients seen in a 2½-year period. The diagnosis was made when patients met at least three of five criteria, including extension of the wrists and metacarpal phalanges with the fingers paralleling the dorsum of the forearm; passive apposition of the thumbs to the flexor aspect of the forearm; hyperextension of the elbows to 10 degrees or more; hyperextension of the knees to 10 degrees or more; and flexion of the trunk with the knees extended and the palms resting on the floor.

Three of the 15 hypermobile children had juvenile arthritis, as did 42% of all 262 clinic patients. The usual presenting symptoms were pain and swelling of various joints, most often affecting the knees and then the fingers and hands. Most patients had symptoms in more than one joint. Effusions were seen in only 4 patients, including those with juvenile arthritis. Crepitus was heard in 5 patients. Several pa-

(2–30) Pediatrics 72:701–706, November 1983.

tients responded to salicylates, besides to rest and physical therapy. Four patients had a family history of hypermobility. Nearly half had relatives younger than age 60 years with degenerative joint symptoms. Most patients developed symptoms of hypermobility at ages 10 to 15 years.

Hypermobility syndrome is found in about 5% of the general population and is a not infrequent source of musculoskeletal symptoms. Any joint may be affected. Patients most often are seen with arthralgias in the knees, fingers, and hands. Patients usually respond well to analgesics, physical therapy, and reassurance. Where hypermobility syndrome is associated with other rheumatic disorders, it does not appear to influence their course.

▶ [The hypermobility syndrome, sometimes called generalized ligamentous laxity, is frequently seen by the pediatric orthopedist particularly as the underlying cause of hypermobile pronated flatfeet. Complaints and physical findings other than the joint hypermobility, particularly pain and swelling as mentioned in this article, are rare. Abnormal shoe wear may occur with significant foot pronation. Though no good longitudinal long-term studies are available, most pediatric patients do not appear to have permanent sequelae. The condition can usually be managed satisfactorily by explanation to the family, reassurance, reduction of activities if symptoms are present, and, occasionally, exercises.—H.A. Peterson] ◀

2–31 **Muscular Torticollis: Modified Surgical Approach.** Richard D. Ferkel, G. Wilbur Westin, Edgar G. Dawson, and William L. Oppenheim (Los Angeles) reviewed the results of a modified bipolar sternocleidomastoid muscle release procedure in 12 children operated on since 1967 for muscular torticollis. The results were compared with those obtained by conservative treatment or other operations in 22 different patients seen between 1952 and 1981. There were 22 girls and 12 boys overall. Torticollis was first seen at an average age of 10 weeks, and the average age at presentation was 28 months. Average follow-up was 9 years. Twenty patients in all were operated on because of an increase in tumor size, increasing or persistent deformity, or developing facial hemihypoplasia. The most common operation among patients who did not have the bipolar release procedure was simple division of the sternal and clavicular origins of the sternocleidomastoid muscle. Some patients were managed by exercises alone after operation; others were also immobilized.

Excellent or good reults were obtained with exercises alone in 86% of cases. A total of 25 operations were carried out on 20 patients. Excellent or good results were obtained with the bipolar release procedure in 92% of cases; the only fair result was due to an unsightly scar. None of these patients had loss of the normal neck contour or significant restriction of neck motion. Only 1 had a slight head tilt. Other procedures led to 2 good and 7 fair results and 1 poor result. Four of these patients required reoperation, whereas none of those

(2–31) J. Bone Joint Surg. [Am.] 65-A:894–900, September 1983.

who underwent bipolar release had to be reoperated on. In no group was there a correlatino between age at treatment and resolution of facial asymmetry.

Nonoperative treatment of muscular torticollis is suggested for children younger than age 1 year. If operation is indicated, a bipolar release procedure is recommended. Total muscle excision is rarely, if ever, indicated. A bipolar release of the mastoid part and the sternal and clavicular heads of the muscle in combination with a Z-plasty of the medial sternal head of the sternocleidomastoid muscle provides good correction of the contracture, minimal scarring, and maintenance of the normal contour of the neck.

▶ [This appears to be an excellent method of correcting the torticollis deformity that results from a contracted sternocleidomastoid muscle. It is particularly attractive as the Z-plasty of the sternal head appears to prevent the noticeable asymmetry of the neck muscles which frequently occurs after open tenotomy of the sternal and clavicular heads of the muscle.

Routine tenotomy of the mastoid attachment has not been necessary in our practice. It should be considered, however, if release of the sternal and clavicular heads does not produce full correction.

It has also been our experience that surgical correction in infancy (under 1 year) is not indicated, as approximately 80% of infants will correct spontaneously in infancy.

It has also been our experience that preoperative and postoperative exercises have been of no value in this condition, and we would agree that postoperative casting or bracing in a position of overcorrection for 4 to 6 weeks is important to prevent recurrence.—A.J. Bianco, Jr.] ◄

2-32 **Congenital Undescended Scapula: Surgical Correction by the Woodward Procedure.** Sprengel deformity is more accurately viewed as an undescended than as an elevated scapula. The Woodward procedure of detachment of the muscles at their midline origin and their transplantation distally to lower the scapula is the preferred procedure at most centers. Dennis P. Grogan, Earl A. Stanley, and Walter P. Bobechko (Hosp. for Sick Children, Toronto) reviewed the results of 21 Woodward operations performed on 20 patients with congenitally undescended scapula between 1964 and 1982. Thirteen patients were available for follow-up an average of 8½ years after operation. Average age at operation was 6½ years. Only 1 patient had a concomitant clavicular osteotomy.

The average increase in glenohumeral abduction after the Woodward operation was 37 degrees, and the average scapular lowering was 2 cm. Cosmetic results were excellent or good in four fifths of the evaluable patients, and nearly all patients were satisfied with the outcome. The findings and outcome in 1 patient are shown in Figures 2–15 through 2–18. Few complications occurred. One patient had temporary partial palsy of the brachial plexus. One patient had an exaggeration of scapular winging, and 1 had apparent reconstitution

(2–32) J. Bone Joint Surg. [Br.] 65-B:598–605, November 1983.

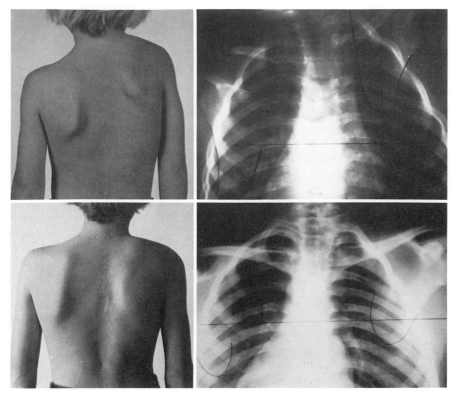

Fig 2–15 (top left).—Patient at age 5 years 5 months showing right undescended scapula and associated grade 3 deformity.

Fig 2–16 (top right).—Preoperative posteroanterior roentgenogram, made at same age, showing method of measurement of relative scapular positions by using centrum of each scapula; there was difference of 5.7 cm.

Fig 2–17 (bottom left).—Patient at age 12 years 9 months (7 years 4 months after operation) showing Cavendish grade 1 deformity. Surgical scar is acceptable. Lower lumbar scar is from resection of diastematomyelia.

Fig 2–18 (bottom right).—Postoperative posteroanterior roentgenogram showing residual difference of 2.3 cm, but scapula has been lowered by 3.4 cm.

(Courtesy of Grogan, D.P., et al.: J. Bone Joint Surg. [Br.] 65-B:598–605, November 1983.)

of the superior pole of the scapula and possibly of an omovertebral bar.

The Woodward procedure appears to be the best operation available for correcting congenital undescended scapula. It is a safe and relatively simple means of obtaining good functional and cosmetic results. Clavicular osteotomy may be added to gain more correction with less risk of neurovascular compression, but it is not recommended as a routine part of the procedure.

▶ [The Woodward operation is now generally accepted as the best surgical procedure for reducing the deformity associated with congenital undescended scapula.

The fact that there have been so many surgical procedures developed for this deformity in the past suggests that no one procedure completely corrects the deformity. In addition, the authors correctly point out that the patient may still have significant deformity related to the congenital anomalies of the cervical spine, the webbed neck, and associated scoliosis, even if the scapula is brought down to a more normal position.

The authors emphasize the importance of screening for other anomalies of the spine and genitourinary tract before surgery is contemplated.

This is a technically demanding surgical procedure. The reader is referred to Woodward's paper, *J. Bone Joint Surg.* [Am.] 43-A:219, March 1961, for a detailed description of the operation.—A.J. Bianco, Jr.] ◄

2–33 **Deltoid Contracture in Children of Central Calcutta.** P. Chatterjee and S. K. Gupta (Calcutta) describe 17 Muslim children from a lower middle class group in central Calcutta in whom deltoid contractures developed after they were given intramuscular injections in early childhood. The 13 boys and 4 girls had a median age of 9.3 years at presentation. Fourteen children had bilateral deltoid contractures. A clear history of multiple deltoid injections was obtained in 11 children, all of whom had such childhood disorders as recurrent tonsillitis and bronchitis, and had seen a physician who administered antibiotics. Only 1 child had a deltoid abscess. The syringes and needles were sterilized by boiling. The interval from injections to development of contracture ranged from 3 to 7 years. The chidren had winging of the scapulae and were unable to bring their arms along the side of the body (Fig 2–19). A thick cord usually was palpated in the intermedi-

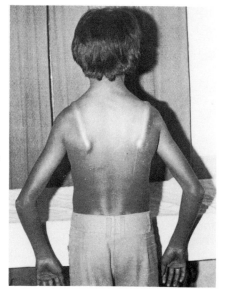

Fig 2–19.—Patient is unable to bring his arms to his sides and has winging of the scapulae. The shoulders are held in internal rotation. (Courtesy of Chatterjee, P., and Gupta, S.K.: J. Pediatr. Orthop. 3:380–383, 1983.)

(2–33) J. Pediatr. Orthop. 3:380–383, 1983.

ate acromial fibers, with thinner cords noted in the posterior fibers. Histologic studies showed dense fibrosis with atrophy of the surrounding muscle fibers.

The main fibrous cord was totally excised and secondary fibrous bands were incised or removed. Full correction was achieved in all but 2 of 31 affected shoulders on follow-up for 5–27 months after operation. One patient could not be operated on because all of the remaining muscle fibers were shortened. Hypertrophic scars developed in 2 patients. Scapular winging persisted for several months after operation despite full correction of the contracture. It tended to resolve with improvement in strength of the serratus anterior. None of the children were impaired in play activities.

Genetic or congenital factors may have had a role in the development of contractures in these children. The fibrosis probably resulted from aseptic necrosis, because violent inflammatory reactions were not the rule. The injections included both crystalline and long-acting penicillin, streptomycin, and tetracycline. Correction was obtained and persisted after excision of the main fibrosed band and incision of the secondary bands.

▶ [Repeated injections into the deltoid muscles of children are rarely performed in North America. Therefore, contractures of deltoid muscles in children of North America are rare. This article reminds us of this potential complication and offers a reasonable method of management.—H.A. Peterson] ◀

3. Fractures

3-1 **Closed Medullary Nailing of Fractures of the Femoral Shaft Using the AO Method.** G. Srirama Murti and P. A. Ring (Surrey, England) reviewed the results of treatment of 61 femoral shaft fractures by closed medullary nailing with the use of AO/ASIF techniques in 59 patients. The procedures were carried out under image-intensifier control. After the upper femoral canal was reamed to 12 mm, the fracture was reduced by longitudinal traction and insertion of a nail into the upper fragment. A guide wire also was used if necessary. The entire femur then was reamed, and the appropriate nail positioned. No attempt was made to repair butterfly or loose fragments. Movement was permitted as soon as the patient regained active control of the extremity.

Most injuries were midshaft fractures. Fourteen fractures were comminuted, and 8 were open. Most patients were operated on within a week after admission; the mean interval after injury was 8 days. Four patients were treated more than 3 weeks after injury. The outcome in 1 case is shown in Figures 3–1 and 3–2. The mean hospital stay for patients with uncomplicated fractures was 13 days. The average time to full weight-bearing was 42 days in the series as a whole. Most patients achieved 150 degrees of knee flexion, and only 3 had less than 70 degrees of flexion. No patient had nonunion or residual clinical deformity. Two wound infections occurred, and 1 patient had fat embolism.

Closed medullary nailing is a relatively simple means of treating femoral shaft fractures. Extensive soft tissue stripping is not necessary, and the risk of infection is minimized. Internal fixation is provided without the hazards of major open surgery. A grossly comminuted fracture involving the entire distal femur is readily managed in this way. The formation of callus at the fracture site is stimulated. Patients can ambulate and return home soon, which promotes their recovery.

▶ [Over the last few years, closed intramedullary nailing has become the most popular method for treating fractures of the femoral shaft. As the authors state, it reduces the hospital stay, has few risks of complications, a very low chance of infection or nonunion, and is quick to produce recovery of function and fracture healing. However, as is also stated in the paper, it requires a properly equipped center and a surgeon well trained in the technique.

A technical point worth mentioning is the entry point of the nail. Kuntscher, as well

(3–1) Injury 14:318–323, January 1983.

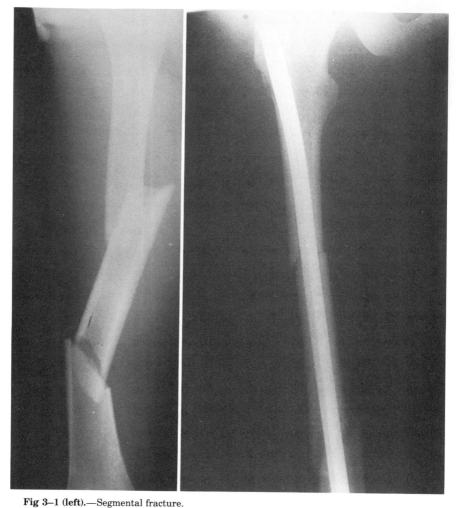

Fig 3–1 (left).—Segmental fracture.
Fig 3–2 (right).—Segmental fracture after nailing.
(Courtesy of Murti, G.S., and Ring, P.A.: Injury 14:318–323, January 1983.)

as the AO group, have advised inserting the nail at the tip of the greater trochanter. Although this minimizes the chance of perforating the hip joint capsule and, therefore, the possibility of a potential infection spreading into the hip joint as well as the possible damage to the blood supply of the femoral head (posterior retinacular vessels), it often causes the proximal medullary canal to be reamed from lateral to medial in an oblique manner and at the time of insertion of the nail might cause increased comminution at the fracture site. A more medial entry point at the level of the obturator fossa, as practiced by most surgeons in the United States, provides a straight "shot" at the medullary canal and facilitates reduction maneuvers, straight reaming, and anatomical insertion of the nail.

It is also worth emphasizing that "conservative" treatment with traction followed by early cast-bracing produces excellent results when attention is paid to details. This may be the treatment of choice in certain milieus.—M.E. Cabanela] ◄

3–2 **Early Intramedullary Nailing of Femoral Shaft Fractures: Cause of Fat Embolism Syndrome.** Mobilization is important in preventing pulmonary complications in severely injured patients. Raymond C. Talucci, James Manning, Simon Lampard, Alan Bach, and C. James Carrico (Univ. of Washington) reviewed 100 consecutive cases of intramedullary nailing of femoral shaft fractures to determine whether early nailing can be done safely to permit early mobilization. A total of 108 nails were placed by the modified Küntscher method. Fifty-seven patients had nailing within 24 hours of admission, while in 43 cases the procedure was delayed for 5–24 days. The age and sex distribution and general health of patients were similar in the 2 groups.

More blood was transfused to the immediate fixation patients, who had more fractures and more severe injuries than the patients who had delayed nailing (Table 1). Fat embolism syndrome occurred only with delayed nailing (Table 2). In 4 cases, the syndrome was diagnosed preoperatively. Another patient, in whom diagnosis was made in the immediate postoperative period, had evidence of respiratory dysfunction before nailing. Adult respiratory distress syndrome was comparably frequent in the 2 groups. Critical hypoxemia occurred in both groups but was more frequent in the immediate nailing group.

Intramedullary nailing of femoral shaft fractures can be done early in severely injured patients without an increased risk of fat embolism syndrome. The trend toward more pulmonary complications in the early nailing group in this study is attributed to the greater severity of injuries in these patients. The frequency of critical hypoxemia was

TABLE 1.—PATIENT DATA

	Immediate Nailing Group (n = 57)	Delayed Nailing Group (n = 43)	Significance (p value)
Transfusions (ml)	2,245	625	<0.001
Fractures per patient	3.01	1.16	<0.001
Average injury severity score	23.2	12.4	<0.001
Average age	30	32.8	NS
Men to women	48:9	36:7	· · ·

NS, not significant
(Courtesy of Talucci, R.C., et al.: Am. J. Surg. 146:107–111, July 1983.)

(3–2) Am. J. Surg. 146:107–111, July 1983.

TABLE 2.—Pulmonary Complications

	Immediate Nailing Group (n = 57)	Delayed Nailing Group (n = 43)
Fat embolism syndrome	0 (0%)	5 (11%)
Critical hypoxemia	13 (23%)	6 (14%)
Adult respiratory distress syndrome	4 (7%)	2 (5%)

(Courtesy of Talucci, R.C., et al.: Am. J. Surg. 146:107–111, July 1983.)

comparable to that in a group of patients with injuries that were of similar severity but were not fractures.

▶ [The comments by C. J. Carrico, which follow this article, are worth careful review. He points out the extreme difficulty of conducting clinical research in such a setting as the present study. The discussion is almost more valuable than the paper.—P.J. Kelly] ◀

3–3   **Incidence of Nonunion After Closed Intramedullary Nailing and Reaming: Results of 1,059 Kuntscher Procedures.** S. R. Babin, P. Graf, P. Vidal, N. Sur, and E. Schvingt (Strasbourg, France) report data involving 503 fractures of the tibia, 440 of the femur, and 116 of the humerus in both adolescent and adult patients. Nonunion was defined as failure to consolidate after 3 months or more, with necessary intervention.

The tibial lesions comprised 347 (69%) closed and 156 (31%) open fractures. Failures essentially involved type I open fractures caused by direct impact. Osteosynthesis was completed by a crural-pedal cast to reduce the risk of rotation of the distal fragment. These failures were characterized by 3 types of technical imperfection: poor centering of the nail in the tibial shaft, insufficient length, or insufficient caliber of the nail. A comparison with methods that do not use reaming shows that in the case of open fractures the rate of septic pseudarthroses is 3 times higher, whereas with Kuntscher's technique sepsis and "dry" pseudarthroses are more frequent. Nevertheless, the latter method is preferred since the rate of infection is less than 1% and reaming contributes to the immobilization of the fracture site. The failures in the femoral fractures all involved lesions within the median diaphyseal zone. The fractures of the humerus were all of the closed type, including 32 metastatic fractures.

The incidence of aseptic nonunion was considered small. Nonunion occurred more readily when the skin was damaged and when influenced by topographic factors. Most failures could be attributed to incorrect technique or excessive delay in weight-bearing. In comparison

(3–3)   Int. Orthop. 7:133–143, 1983.

with other techniques, Kuntscher's procedure is the most reliable treatment for routine use on an acute fracture service. The risk of aseptic nonunion is about 1%, of septic nonunion less than 0.5%, and of early sepsis and eventual union less than 1.5%.

▶ [The results shown here point out the unquestionable advantage of closed intramedullary nailing with reaming in fractures of the femur. Not so clear, however, are the advantages of this technique over nailing without reaming as far as the tibia is concerned. In the United States, nailing with reaming of fresh fractures of the tibia is not particularly popular, perhaps because the results reported using nailing without reaming (using, for example, the Lottes nail) are very satisfactory. There is no question, however, that in the lower extremity, the use of a weight sharing device in fracture treatment, such as the IM nail, especially when the closed technique is utilized, offers significant advantages over plating as far as speed and rate of union, as well as the incidence of infection.

Over the last few years, technological advances have led to a resurgence in the use of IM nailing of diaphyseal fractures.—M.E. Cabanela] ◀

3–4 **Increasing Incidence of Fractures of the Proximal Femur: An Orthopedic Epidemic.** W. A. Wallace (Nottingham, England) reviewed experience with proximal femoral fractures in Nottingham, where 110 beds at two centers are allocated to adult orthopedic trauma victims. These hospitals serve a population of about 750,000 because trauma services are centralized. All fractures in the region of the femoral neck were included in this study.

The number of cases increased from 290 in 1971 to 612 in 1981. The rate of increase was about 6% per year in 1971 through 1977 and 10% per year since 1977. The elderly population of Nottingham increased by less than 2% per year in 1977 to 1981. Women older than age 75 years had a disproportionate increase in proximal femoral fractures, from 8 per 1,000 women in 1971 to 16 per 1,000 in 1981. Persons aged 80 to 84 years showed a 250% increase in hip fractures. Inpatient mortality has fallen substantially in the past 5 years, presumably in relation to earlier and more aggressive surgical treatment of the fractures. Surgery ideally is done within 48 hours of admission.

The cause of this increase in incidence of proximal femoral fractures is unclear. There is little evidence that postmenopausal osteoporosis is becoming more prevalent. Patients presently at the highest risk went through a time of dietary restriction during the war. Many of them lived on a fixed low income between 1971 and 1981, a period of high inflation, and may have had to reduce their diet as a result. The intake of milk by this elderly population definitely has declined. The elderly now are advised to take precautions at home that lead to much less mobility than in the past, and this may be a contributing factor.

▶ [It is intriguing to observe the increased incidence of a particular type of fracture without an obvious explanation. The authors have made an effort to evaluate the influence that factors such as the changing percentage of older patients in the gen-

(3–4) Lancet 1:1413–1414, June 25, 1983.

eral population, osteoporosis, and activity level may have on this increase, but no clear answer has emerged. Although the authors cite evidence that reduced mobility may play a role, this is a difficult factor to analyze. Possibly the opposite is true, that is, due to improved general health in the elderly population as a whole, some may be more active at an older age than their counterparts in the past, thus subjecting them to a greater risk of injury.—D.C. Campbell, II] ◀

3–5 **Fractures of the Femoral Neck: Follow-up Study After Nonoperative Treatment of Garden's Stage 1 and 2 Fractures.** Failure rates as high as 19% have been reported with nonoperative management of impacted femoral neck fractures. J. Jensen and J. Høgh (Aarhus, Denmark) investigated whether Garden's staging system and alignment index can guide treatment of these injuries. Conservative treatment was given 128 patients seen between 1972 and 1979 with impacted femoral neck fractures, 101 females and 27 males with a median age of 73 years. Patients with an undisplaced or valgus fracture were managed by weight relief and physiotherapy. Cooperative patients were allowed to bear weight when the position of the fracture did not worsen after 2 weeks. Average follow-up was 22 months.

About two thirds of the fractures were Garden stage 1 injuries, and most of them had a good alignment index. Thirty-five fractures (27%) became displaced later; 61% of stage 2 fractures and 11% of stage 1 injuries displaced. Fifteen fractures displaced into stage 3 and 20 into stage 4. Displacement was not related to the time of weight-bearing, but the rate was greater when weight-bearing was never permitted. Only 4 of the 93 patients without later displacement developed late segmental collapse. The rate of late segmental collapse in patients followed for longer than a year was 7%.

Garden's staging system is an effective means of predicting the risk of failure of conservative treatment of impacted femoral neck fractures. Late displacement is more frequent in patients with stage 2 than in those with stage 1 cases and in patients who are not allowed to bear weight after the initial injury. The rate of late segmental collapse in this series is lower than previously reported rates.

▶ [The controversy continues whether any discernible fracture of the femoral neck should be treated without internal fixation. Certainly we should be able to diagnose the impacted femoral neck fracture in good position and decide on a radiographic and a clinical basis whether that patient should have surgical internal fixation or whether the patient should be treated without surgery. It is not enough simply to look at the x-ray. The history with regard to weight-bearing after the injury, and the ability to raise the straight leg off the bed in a day or 2 also confirm the relative security of the fracture. I think the lateral view is important and if there is definite anterior displacement of the neck, i.e., posterior position of the head, then the fracture should be pinned. If the lateral view shows good alignment and the anteroposterior view shows either no displacement or very slight valgus, and if the patient can lift the leg off the bed readily in 24 hours and has had a history of having walked on it prior to fracture, then I personally prefer not to pin these fractures. It is a mistake to keep the

(3–5) Injury 14:339–342, January 1983.

patients in bed. Rather they should be gotten up the day of fracture or the day after, with foot touch and crutches, and the only admonition when sitting or lying is that they not allow the extremity to externally rotate. This is easily accomplished with a belt around the thighs while they are sitting, and a small, firm pillow under the greater trochanter to prevent external rotation when lying. A foot splint to prevent rotation is not effective.

Nothing is lost if the fracture displaces, for most of these patients are candidates for endoprosthesis replacement anyway and if it does displace, this can be done. After a week in hospital the patients should be followed very closely. If they are returning home, adequate care must be provided at home so that they don't slip and fall again. If they have no particular help at home to aid them with dressing their foot and walking with crutches, they should be kept under hospital supervision until evidence of healing has taken place.

In my own series of patients with impacted fractures meeting the above criteria (admittedly rather rigid), there has been only 1 displacement in 23 patients not operated on.—Ed.] ◄

3–6 **Moore Prosthesis in the Treatment of Fresh Femoral Neck Fractures: A Critical Review With Special Attention to Secondary Acetabular Degeneration.** Initially fresh femoral neck fractures were treated with a one-piece device where reduction was not possible or the patient could not cooperate with a postoperative weight relief program after nailing. Subsequently, the indications were widened to include debilitated old patients from nursing homes and older patients from their own homes. Hakon Kofoed and John Kofod (Copenhagen) reviewed 106 consecutively seen patients with displaced femoral neck fractures who were initially treated with a Moore prosthesis between 1977 and 1979. The 90 women and 16 men had a mean age of 82.5 years. All of the injuries had resulted from falls. Ninety-three patients were admitted from their own homes, and 13 from nursing homes. Most patients were in poor general condition apart from the injury, but more than 90% were operated on within 48 hours of admission. General anesthesia was used in all cases. Weight-bearing was allowed as soon as a walking aid could be managed.

The average hospital stay was 23 days. Primary general complications occurred in 30% of patients, the most common being pneumonia and urinary infection. Mortality was 11% at 1 month and 21% at 6 months. After 2 years, 31% of patients had died, significantly more than expected. The prosthesis was improperly placed in 9 instances. All 5 secondary femoral fractures were mild. One of the 2 patients with postoperative hip dislocation required open reduction. There were 6 superficial and 4 deep infections. One patient had peroneal palsy. Of the 71 patients examined, 13 had undergone secondary total hip replacement, and 13 others had indications for this procedure. Twenty-five of the remaining 45 patients had Harris hip-assessment scores of fair or better. The chief cause of pain reported at follow-up evaluation was acetabular degeneration.

(3–6) Injury 14:531–540, May 1983.

Moore arthroplasty should be restricted to patients who fulfill the original indications for the procedure. Patients who are active and living at home should not undergo hemiarthroplasty for femoral neck fracture, regardless of age. Total hip replacement may be considered primary treatment in these cases.

3–7 **Bilateral Fractures of Femoral Neck in Patients With Moderate Renal Failure Receiving Fluoride for Spinal Osteoporosis.** Although fluoride, combined with calcium and vitamin D, is effective in preventing new vertebral crush fractures in primary and steroid-induced osteoporosis, long bone fractures have been reported during fluoride treatment. J. C. Gerster, S. A. Charhon, P. Jaeger, G. Boivin, D. Briancon, A. Rostan, C. A. Baud, and P. J. Meunier report data on 2 patients with moderate renal insufficiency who sustained spontaneous bilateral hip fractures after treatment of osteoporosis with fluoride, calcium, and vitamin D. The patients were women aged 69 and 78 years, respectively, who had taken 40–60 mg of sodium fluoride daily for 11 and 21 months, respectively. Histologic study of a bone specimen showed severe fluorosis in 1 case, and quantitative analysis of bone showed osteomalacia and skeletal fluorosis in the other. The fluoride content of the surgical specimen in the first case was 0.51%, compared with a normal value of 0.1%.

Bilateral femur neck fractures are extremely rare, and these 2 cases suggest a causal relationship between the fractures and fluoride intake in patients with renal failure. The skeletal fluorosis was thought to be caused by excessive retention of fluoride, secondary to renal insufficiency. Urinary fluoride excretion is reduced when the creatinine clearance reaches about 25 ml/minute. Bone fluorosis can occur even in the absence of renal failure when sodium fluoride is ingested in amounts exceeding 60 mg daily. Bone fractures have been described in patients without renal failure who are treated with niflumic acid and have severe fluorosis as a result.

Fluoride therapy in generally prescribed doses can cause severe skeletal fluorosis in patients with impaired renal function. For such patients, fluoride should be withheld or, at least, given in a lower dosage.

▶ [The main importance of this paper is the emphasis on rapid fluoride accumulation in patients with mild renal insufficiency. Fluoride is eliminated from the body primarily by renal excretion. Fluoride-induced osteomalacia in patients with *severe* renal insufficiency or in *dialysis* patients has long been recognized by nephrologists. Recent reports regarding the efficacy of sodium fluoride in the treatment of postmenopausal osteoporosis might prompt many physicians to use this agent in the treatment of osteoporosis. They should be aware therefore that evaluation of renal function is important before beginning therapy.

Although I feel the above point is very important, there are several flaws in this paper that I consider to be of major importance.

(1) Patient 1 was said to have had osteoporosis, yet no data is offered to substan-

(3–7) Br. Med. J. 287:723–725, Sept. 10, 1983.

tiate this claim aside from the fact that the patient suffered two vertebral crush fractures. She also has multiple other contributing factors to her underlying bone disease including prolonged corticosteroid use, hyperparathyroidism, and low levels of 25-hydroxyvitamin D. No data is offered regarding the patient's estrogen status, e.g.: How many years after menopause is she?; Had oophorectomy ever been performed? This point is important because the two disorders of postmenopausal and osteoporosis probably have a different pathogenesis, and response to treatment may not be assumed to be identical. Also, serum fluoride levels are not offered.

(2) Patient 2 had a misleadingly low serum creatinine level (1.5 mg/dl) with one creatinine clearance of 31 ml/minute. One might argue with the use of calcium and vitamin D in this patient who initially already had evidence of arterial calcification. Evidence is offered that only one of the femoral neck fractures was spontaneous. It is not stated whether the fracture of the left femur (which had occurred 1 month later) was due to trauma or was spontaneous. This patient is important to the text in that serum fluoride levels and urine fluoride excretion (which was low due to renal failure) are offered, along with histomorphometric bone data.

The authors also make the assumption that fluoride therapy, when combined with calcium and vitamin D, is effective in both primary and corticosteroid-induced osteoporosis. Recent data from other laboratories would indicate that this program may not be effective in preventing trabecular bone loss in corticosteroid treated patients. The fact that the original contention of the authors is somewhat controversial together with the fact that the authors' use of vitamin D in patients with renal failure pose a major question: Should vitamin D or sodium fluoride, or both, be used in patients with renal insufficiency? I, personally, would use these agents only with very close direct medical supervision. The authors present their conclusions in such a way that suggests that this treatment is the treatment of choice, and, thus, I believe their conclusions are subject to misinterpretation.—J.T. McCarthy] ◄

3–8 **Preoperative and Postoperative Scintimetry After Femoral Neck Fracture.** Both nonunion and segmental collapse after femoral neck fracture are thought to be caused by injury to the blood supply of the femoral head; scintigraphic findings of deficient vascularity have regularly been associated with complications. Björn Strömqvist, Lars Ingvar Hansson, Peter Ljung, Per Ohlin, and Harald Roos compared the scintimetric findings before and after surgery in 15 women and 9 men, mean age 73, with intracapsular femoral neck fractures to determine whether additional vascular injury occurred after the initial trauma. Eighteen patients had displaced fractures. Scintimetry was done 3–4 hours after injection of ^{99m}Tc-methylene diphosphonate on the day of operation and within 5–15 days postoperatively. Seventeen patients were reevaluated 4 months after surgery. All but 2 patients were operated on within 2 days of hospital admission. Osteosynthesis was carried out using the Rydell 4-flanged nail. Weight-bearing was allowed from the first postoperative day.

Six patients with increased femoral head uptake before operation and 8 with decreased uptake had comparable findings on postoperative study. Of the 8 patients with intermediate uptake before operation, 6 had reduced femoral head uptake after operation, and 2 had

(3–8)   J. Bone Joint Surg. [Br.] 66-B:49–54, January 1984.

increased uptake. Fracture line uptake was elevated in all patients 4 months postoperatively, with no significant difference between undisplaced and displaced fractures. All patients had increased uptake in the trochanteric region, and all but 2 had increased femoral shaft uptake.

Further injury to the blood supply of the femoral head is apparent after the initial injury in some patients with intracapsular femoral neck fractures. Complications in these patients might be reduced by an operative technique that causes minimal damage to femoral head circulation.

▶ [Femoral neck fractures remain the "unsolved" fracture. All surgeons who treat patients with femoral neck fracture would like to be able to identify those preoperative patients with irreversible damage to the vascular supply of the femoral head. Scintigraphy has demonstrated that damage to the vascularity of the femoral head is rarely an all or nothing phenomena but rather it is a gradient. We have yet to identify the degree of damage to the femoral head which will lead to irreversible changes.

This interesting study is an attempt to identify the degree of vascular insult which precludes normal healing. The use of dedicated computer systems and regions of interest allows the nuclear radiologist to be more specific than was previously possible. The data generated in this clinical study certainly indicates: (1) certain patients have significant damage to the vascular supply to the femoral head at the time of injury; and (2) further damage to the vascular supply of the femoral head does, indeed, occur at the time internal fixation devices are implanted.

Before widespread use of these techniques can be advocated, the authors and other investigators must show a strong correlation between the abnormal scintigraphic findings and the ultimate clinical result, that is, a direct correlation between decreased uptake of ^{99m}Tc-methylene diphosphonate and the development of osteonecrosis or femoral neck nonunion.

With improvement in the technology, especially the use of computers, it may be possible to use dynamic ^{99m}Tc-methylene diphosphonate to accomplish the same information. This area is certainly ripe for future investigations and applications of new technologies.—R.H. Fitzgerald, Jr.] ◀

3–9 **Radiographic Five-Year Follow-Up of Femoral Neck Fractures.** Reiner Brümmer, Lars Ingvar Hansson, and Wigher Mortensson (Univ. of Lund) report a prospective 5-year follow-up study of 40 patients with intracapsular subcapital or transcervical femoral fractures seen from 1975 to 1976. The mean age was 73 years, and all but 6 patients were older than age 60. Most patients were operated on within 24–48 hours of injury using the Rydell 4-flanged nail. Patients were encouraged to walk with full weight-bearing on the day after surgery.

Thirteen patients had uncomplicated healing, 22 had necrosis, and 5 had nonunion. Sclerosis of the femoral head, and compression and displacement of the fracture, were compatible with eventual healing and clinical recovery. Compression in the femoral neck was more frequent in patients with necrosis than in patients with uncomplicated healing. Subchondral fracture and collapse of the load-bearing surface were noted in 7 necrotic patients at 1 year, and were seen only

(3–9)   Acta Orthop. Scand. 54:865–871, December 1983.

after 3–5 years in 3 patients. In 4 of 5 patients, however, nonunion was evident roentgenographically within 1 year. Nonunion occurred only in patients with major displacement.

These findings suggest that arthroplasty in patients with femoral neck fracture should be based on the clinical and nuclide scintimetric findings. Waiting for radiographic confirmation of necrosis in patients with pain increases the risks of physical and social impairment secondary to poor hip function. Definite radiographic evidence of femoral head collapse often is not present for 2 years or more after fracture. Radiography is most useful in preoperative diagnosis and classification, in guiding surgery, and in early postoperative control after weight-bearing to assess the mechanical solidity of the fracture. Routine radiographic follow-up is expensive and not necessary.

▶ [This valuable prospective study emphasizes the value of radiographic examination for diagnosis and preoperative and postoperative management of femoral neck fractures. Radionuclide techniques were shown to be highly predictive of success or failure as they relate to nonunion or necrosis. Fifty-five percent of patients developed osteonecrosis. I would feel more comfortable using the multiple pin technique for fixation rather than a four-flanged nail. It would be very helpful now to correlate the occurrence of osteonecrosis with the anatomy of the fracture to see whether the anatomy might not have the same predictive value as radionuclide studies.—L.F.A. Peterson] ◀

3–10 **Hip Fractures in Patients With Parkinson's Syndrome.** Parkinsonism is thought to add substantially to the difficulties of managing hip fractures in elderly patients. I. Eventov, M. Moreno, E. Geller, R. Tardiman, and R. Salama (Tel-Aviv, Israel) reviewed experience with 65 patients with Parkinson's disease who were admitted in 1965 through 1978 with fractures of the upper femur. Forty women and 22 men with an average age of 74 years were followed up. Thirty-nine patients had subcapital fractures and 23 had trochanteric fractures. Thirty-four patients with subcapital fractures had primary replacement with a hip prosthesis by a posterolateral approach. Eleven patients with trochanteric fractures had internal fixation with a nail plate, most of them within 48 hours of injury. Fifty-two patients were receiving antiparkinsonism drugs at the time of injury.

Six patients died in the hospital and 13 others died within 3 months after injury. Mortality could not be related to the type of fracture, the duration of parkinsonism, or surgery. Fourteen surviving patients had a total of 33 complications, which were especially frequent in patients who had surgery. The most common complications were pressure sores and urinary tract infections. Pulmonary complications also were frequent in the group that had surgery. In 43 patients who were evaluated an average of 3 years after injury, the functional results were definitely better after operation. Nearly 90% of those who had operation and fewer than 60% of those who were

(3–10) J. Trauma 23:98–101, February 1983.

treated conservatively were able to walk unaided. Progression of disability was less marked in the group that had surgery.

Surgery seems to be indicated for patients with Parkinson's disease who have hip fractures, despite a higher rate of complications. A better functional result is obtained, and the quality of life is improved by surgical treatment. Further deterioration may be minimized. Antiparkinsonism medication may have to be adjusted, and special care is needed in anesthetizing these patients and in administering postoperative analgesia. Meticulous nursing care is essential. Prophylactic antibiotics are used for a longer time than usual.

▶ [This paper is a valuable contribution to the literature regarding hip fractures in patients with Parkinson's syndrome. This study provides a more rational basis for treatment selection in this special group. Clearly, these patients suffer more following periods of inactivity. Therefore, efforts should be made for rapid mobilization. Although the authors recommend endoprosthetic replacement for intracapsular fractures and internal fixation for extracapsular fractures, it would seem reasonable in many cases of extracapsular fractures, particularly those with comminution, to more readily consider endoprosthetic replacement. This would reduce the incidence of complications requiring secondary surgery or prolonged immobilization.—D.C. Campbell, II] ◀

3–11　**CAT Scan Evaluation of Traumatic Hip Dislocations With Associated Posterior Acetabular Fractures.** Fracture-dislocation of the hip can be a difficult diagnostic and therapeutic problem in patients with multiple injuries. J. K. Burkus (Yale Univ.) used computed axial tomography (CAT) scanning as well as conventional plain radiography and tomography to evaluate 11 patients seen between 1980 and 1981 with traumatic hip dislocation and associated acetabular fracture. The 10 males and 1 female had an average age of 28 years, and all were injured in motor vehicle accidents. Eight had multiple injuries or other fractures. Ten hip dislocations were posterior and 1 was central. All patients had posterior acetabular fractures. Immediate closed reduction was carried out in all 11 patients, and CAT studies were done afterward. Four patients were treated in traction, 4 had arthrotomy for removal of osteochondral fracture fragments, and 3 had open reduction and internal fixation of the acetabular fracture fragments.

All hip dislocations were diagnosed from the clinical and plain radiographic findings. The CAT findings aided understanding of the fracture pattern and helped in planning treatment. The extent and configuration of the fractures were demonstrated, as were the degree of comminution and extent of reduction. Joint stability and joint space widening were verified by CAT. Sacroiliac involvement and soft tissue injuries were demonstrated. The CAT scan showed changes not apparent on plain radiographs or on conventional tomograms in 3 of 4 patients. Surgical decisions were strongly guided by the CAT find-

(3–11)　Orthopedics 6:1443–1452, November 1983.

ings. Surgery was avoided in 4 patients in whom CAT showed concentric reduction of the femoral head and restoration of the articular weight-bearing surfaces.

The CAT findings influenced both the open and closed management of fracture-dislocation of the hip in all patients in this series. The technique is now considered an essential adjunct to conventional radiographic methods in the management of patients with fracture-dislocation of the hip. The proper management of these injuries remains controversial.

▶ [While there is no question today that CAT scanning gives an additional evaluation of a fracture dislocation of the hip, I believe there is definite reason to question whether this additional information is of much value in evaluating *all* such patients. If we would keep in mind the normal radiographic architecture of the hip and compare the fracture dislocation appearance with this control, as recommended by Letournel, and if the oblique films of Judet and Letournel, and even occasionally the tomogram, are utilized as well, then I believe we can have, in the vast majority of patients, the necessary information available to us for the treatment of that patient. "Layering" of tests, i.e. CT scanning, must be looked at critically today in view of cost accounting.—Ed.] ◀

3–12 **Insufficiency Fractures of Tibial Plateau.** Lawrence G. Manco, Robert Schneider, and Helene Pavlov (New York Hosp.-Cornell Univ. Med. Coll.) observed a pattern of high nuclide uptake confined to the tibial plateau in 5 patients with knee pain who were found to have insufficiency fractures of the tibial plateau. These fractures occur when stress is applied to bone with less than normal elastic resistance, e.g., osteoporotic bone. The patients were among 165 seen in an 18-month period with knee pain of uncertain origin who underwent bone scanning with ^{99m}Tc-labeled methylene diphosphonate. The 4 women had a mean age of 68, and the man was aged 21. All 5 had underlying disorders that could produce osteoporosis. Knee pain had been present for 2–7 weeks; in 2 patients it was localized to the medial or lateral tibial plateau. The scans showed a broad area of intense uptake in the tibial plateau in all 5 patients. Plain radiographs showed a linear density in the tibial plateau, characteristic of a stress fracture.

Nuclide bone scanning is useful in diagnosing insufficiency fracture in a patient with nontraumatic knee pain. Initial radiograph findings were negative at the time that bone scan findings were positive in 4 of the 5 patients. Scanning is indicated in patients with disuse osteoporosis who have knee pain if initial radiograph results are negative. Other causes of increased nuclide uptake in the knee on bone scanning include degenerative joint disease, inflammatory arthritis, osteonecrosis, osteomyelitis, and metastatic disease, all of which usually can be distinguished by the location and intensity of nuclide uptake.

▶ [This is an important paper. That insufficiency fractures exist in the medial tibial plateau is now unquestioned. It is interesting that one of the first to bring this to our

(3–12) AJR 140:1211–1215, June 1983.

attention was Göran Bauer (Bauer, G., et al.: *Acta Radiol.* [*Diagn.*] 22:619–622, 1981) who spent his early days at the Hospital for Special Surgery, where this article originates.

In my own experience, the appearance on the plain roentgenogram of sclerosis indicating a fracture has developed much later than in the cases reported by the authors, but as they emphasize, it may not even show at all. Lotke and Ecker[2] (*Clin. Orthop.* 176: June 1983) discussed the appearance of microfractures in this same region with a somewhat similar history and described it as an osteonecrosis-like syndrome of the medial tibial plateau. Our differentiation is going to have to be between microfractures, osteonecrosis of the medial tibial plateau rather than the medial femoral plateau (as is the usual), and true insufficiency fractures, which will appear on the plain x-ray further distal to subchondral bone. Radionuclide imaging has truly revolutionized the diagnosis of these vague, but often disabling pains about the knee in the older patient.—Ed.] ◄

3–13 **Is Conservative Treatment of Displaced Tibial Shaft Fractures Justified?** Improvements in methods of rigid fixation have led some to favor the surgical management of all displaced tibial shaft fractures. J. F. Haines, E. A. Williams, E. J. Hargadon, and D. R. A. Davies (Manchester, England) undertook a prospective study of the conservative management of 91 displaced fractures seen in adult patients in 1976–1981. All tibial shaft fractures except those involving the knee or ankle joint were included. Road traffic accidents were the chief cause of injury. Stable fractures with little soft tissue damage were managed by closed reduction under general anesthesia and placement of a long-leg plaster. Unstable injuries were subjected to os calcis traction for 2–3 weeks before cast application. Compound fractures were explored immediately. A few patients had internal fixation using a compression plate, and were not included in the series. Traction was used initially to treat 39 of the 91 stable fractures.

All the fractures united, in an average of 21 weeks. Bone grafting was carried out in 22 cases in an average of 19 weeks after injury, and union occurred in an average of 35 weeks in these cases. Middle-third fractures took the longest to unite. Comminution and displacement clearly influenced the healing time. Only 2 patients with more than 1 inch of shortening required a shoe raise. Only 2 patients were aware of deformity from malunion, and none required a corrective osteotomy. Six patients had significantly limited knee motion; 2 were helped by quadricepsplasty. Three fracture-site infections occurred, but no patient had residual infection. There was 1 refracture. The average time away from work for 60 patients was 31 weeks. Five other fractures required open reduction and internal fixation, and 2 injuries that failed to unite with conservative management were treated by compression-plate fixation.

A conservative approach to displaced tibial shaft fractures in adults is warranted, with early bone grafting where required. Internal fixa-

(3–13) J. Bone Joint Surg. [Br.] 66-B:84–88, January 1984.

tion in all cases will result in a majority of patients being unnecessarily operated on.

▶ [This is a prospective study of all displaced tibial fractures at one institution over a 5-year period. The data demonstrate that careful nonoperative treatment of tibial fractures, along with autogenous bone grafting for impending nonunion, results in a satisfactory outcome. The point is not that nonoperative treatment is better or worse than operative treatment, but if carefully employed, nonoperative treatment will have an outcome at least equal to early operative intervention.—J.R. Cass] ◀

3–14   **Open Fractures of the Tibia Treated With the Lottes Nail.** A. Velazco, T. E. Whitesides, Jr., and L. L. Fleming (Emory Univ.) reviewed the results of Lottes nailing in 50 consecutive patients with open tibial fractures of the midshaft, treated between 1975 and 1980. Transverse or segmental fractures that would allow axial loading once stabilized were included in the series. Fixation was achieved after wound debridement, and the Hoffman apparatus was applied if there was enough comminution for axial loading to be impossible. The need for complex soft tissue reconstruction precluded Lottes nailing. Five patients required cerclage wiring of a butterfly fragment, screw fixation of a malleolar fracture, or both. Most patients had other long bone fractures. All but 4 patients underwent skin grafting 4 to 12 days after operation.

All but 1 of the 50 tibial fractures healed. Eight patients had delayed union; all had marked soft tissue injuries. Two superficial infections and 1 deep infection occurred. There were 2 malunions due to use of too short a nail. The 1 treatment failure was due to irreversible vascular damage. One refracture occurred with bending of the nail. Shortening of 1 cm or less occurred in most patients. There were no rotational deformities.

Lottes nailing of an open tibial fracture is a simple treatment that stabilizes the fragments, permits soft tissue healing to occur, and makes early weight-bearing possible. Morbidity is minimal, even in patients with acute open fractures and severe soft tissue damage. Some of the complications that have occurred could have been avoided with closer attention to technique.

▶ [The excellent results reported here are similar to those reported by Doctor Lottes, and they may be due in part to the minimal disruption of endosteal blood supply produced by this nail. Most trauma surgeons would have no quarrel with IM nailing of open fractures of types I and II. However, the use of this technique in compound type III fractures has to be approached with a great deal of caution. In general, we prefer to utilize external fixation for type III injuries, but woud agree that treatment has to be individualized as it was in the series by the authors. As shown here, proper treatment selection and proper technique yield very few complications.—M.E. Cabanela] ◀

3–15   **Repair of Soft Tissue Defects in the Lower Leg: A Comparison of Different Flap Techniques.** Fractures of the lower leg are

(3–14)   J. Bone Joint Surg. [Am.] 65-A:879–885, September 1983.
(3–15)   Acta Orthop. Scand. 54:772–776, October 1983.

associated often with deep soft tissue defects. P. Riegels-Nielsen, C. Krag, S. Medgyesi, and M. Pers (Copenhagen) compared various methods of soft tissue reconstruction in 76 male and 26 female patients with a mean age of 37 years. Reconstruction was performed 5 days to 10 years after injury. Nineteen patients had reconstruction with the use of a cross-leg flap, and 45 with a muscle flap covered with split-skin grafts. A composite flap from the dorsum of the foot, pedicled on the anterior tibial-dorsalis pedis vessels, was used for 17 patients. Twenty-four patients had reconstruction which involved the use of a free composite island flap and a microsurgical technique. Thoracodorsal and iliofemoral flaps were used for most of the cases in which a microsurgical technique was employed.

Cross-leg flap procedures had a fairly high rate of complication and caused more secondary operations with the use of general anesthesia than did the other procedures. The muscle flap and dorsalis pedis island flap procedures had lower complication rates and produced healing in a shorter time. The "operative" costs of free composite island flap reconstruction were higher, but the frequency of complications was low and the length of time for healing was relatively short, causing a shorter hospitalization.

The cross-leg flap procedure was the least dependable means of reconstructing soft tissue defects in the lower leg in this study. Muscle flap and dorsalis pedis island flap reconstructions are preferred for use in the proximal and distal parts of the lower leg, respectively. Free composite island flaps are advantageous if simpler procedures are not feasible or are expected to yield comparable results at a higher overall cost. Close cooperation between the orthopedic and plastic surgeons is helpful in these cases.

▶ [This manuscript should be added to the growing bibliography attesting to the superiority of local muscle flaps or free tissue transfers over conventional distant pedicle flaps for soft tissue coverage of the distal lower extremity.—M.B. Wood] ◀

3–16 **Results of 39 Fractures Complicated by Major Segmental Bone Loss and/or Leg Length Discrepancy.** The management of segmental bone defects remains a difficult problem. Gregg L. Goldstrohm, Dana C. Mears, and William M. Swartz (Univ. of Pittsburgh) attempted to develop a comprehensive treatment protocol for use in patients with segmental bone loss or limb length discrepancy, or both. Limb lengthening had been attempted on 28 patients, 18 of them for a bony defect or length discrepancy exceeding 5.5 cm. Two other patients had lengthening terminated before full equalization was achieved. Eleven patients presented with a segmental bone defect but no indication for lengthening. The femur and tibia were the most frequently involved bones. Younger patients had been injured in vehicular accidents, while older ones had fallen or had failed total joint

(3–16) J. Trauma 24:50–58, January 1984.

replacements. Nearly three fourths of the fractures were comminuted. Most patients underwent numerous prolonged hospitalizations and had a variety of reconstructive procedures. A bone graft was used in 88% of cases, and some type of soft-tissue coverage was necessary in 40% of cases.

Over 60% of cases with an initial defect exceeding 5.5 cm healed to within 10% of the length of the original defect, as did 80% of the patients with lesser initial defects. The average length of the defect in cases where no lengthening was attempted was 4.1 cm. Attempts to lengthen the tibia led to transient peroneal nerve palsy in 6 cases. Patients resumed full weight-bearing in an average of 49 weeks. They previously had been treated for an average of 142 weeks. Only 1 patient underwent above-knee amputation, following 38 reconstructive procedures. The prolonged healing time was due in part to severe osteoporosis and disuse atrophy of the extremity.

Bone and soft tissue healing have been achieved in most patients, with restoration of suitable limb length, despite the presence of segmental bone loss or limb length discrepancy, complicated by soft tissue loss or chronic deep wound infection. Salvage is possible in more than 95% of these cases with available methods of internal and external fixation, bone grafting, and soft-tissue reconstruction. Amputation can be considered for a patient who is physically or emotionally unable to undergo the many procedures and prolonged hospitalization that may be necessary.

▶ [This paper presents a logical state-of-the-art approach to the management of segmental bone loss, whether acute or chronic. One might have minor disagreements with the type of external fixation device preferred by the authors, but most would agree with the general philosophy presented here. The advent of vascularized free tissue transfers has allowed us to undertake reconstructions today where amputation would be the only sensible alternative in the past.

As the author mentioned, we prefer to utilize conventional autologous cancellous graft when the size of the defect does not exceed 4–5 cm and reserve vascularized bone transfer for defects beyond that size. However, we use only the posterior or anterior iliac crest as a source of cancellous bone since we have seen intertrochanteric fractures occurring after bone graft harvesting from this area of the femur.

It is worth emphasizing how important it is to discuss with the patient, before beginning treatment, the prolonged time and repeated hospitalization necessary to carry out one of these reconstructions to successful completion.—M.E. Cabanela] ◀

3–17 **Intra-Articular Fractures of the Distal Tibia: The Pillion Fracture** has been associated with a poor prognosis because of violent injury, articular incongruity, and tibial comminution. Its management remains controversial. R. B. Bourne, C. H. Rorabeck, and J. MacNab (Univ. of Western Ontario, London) reviewed results in 42 patients with pillion fracture who were followed up for at least 2 years after injury. There were 11 type I fractures (Fig 3–3), 12 type II fractures with significant articular incongruity (Fig 3–4), and 19

(3–17) J. Trauma 23:591–596, July 1983.

type III fractures with comminution of the distal tibia (Fig 3–5). The average age at injury was 40 years, and the most common mechanisms were falls from a height and motor vehicle accidents. Nine patients had open fractures and 2 had neurovascular compromise. The average follow-up was 53 months.

Two of 4 patients with type I fractures had a poor outcome after closed reduction and immobilization, and immobilization was prolonged. Anatomical reduction was achieved surgically in 6 of 7 patients, and 5 of these had good results. Both patients with type II injuries managed by closed reduction did poorly. Anatomical reduction and internal fixation were achieved in 7 of 10 patients treated surgically, and 5 had good results. The mean immobilization time was 3 weeks. The 3 patients with type III injuries treated by closed reduction had poor results. Anatomical reduction and stable fixation

Fig 3–3.—Type I pillion fractures include cleavage fractures of the distal tibia with no major displacement of articular cartilage. (Courtesy of Bourne, R.B., et al.: J. Trauma 23:591–596, July 1983.)

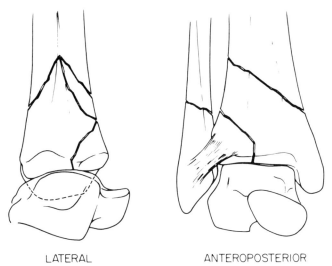

LATERAL   ANTEROPOSTERIOR

INFERIOR ASPECT

TYPE I

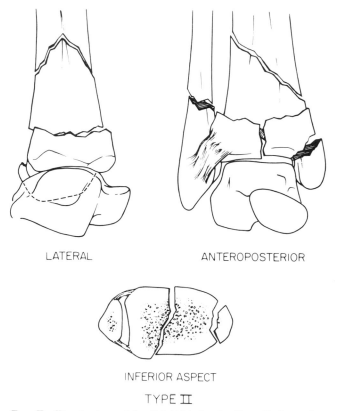

LATERAL   ANTEROPOSTERIOR

INFERIOR ASPECT

TYPE II

Fig 3–4.—Type II pillion fractures of the distal tibia involve the articular surface, causing significant articular incongruity. (Courtesy of Bourne, R.B., et al.: J. Trauma 23:591–596, July 1983.)

were achieved in only 2 of 16 patients treated surgically. One of these patients and 3 of those with nonanatomical reduction or unstable fixation had good results. Four nonunions developed, and 2 injuries became infected. Seven patients eventually underwent arthrodesis. All but 1 of them had type III fractures, and all had poor reduction or unstable fixation initially.

Types I and II pillion fractures are amenable to anatomical open reduction, stable internal fixation, and early movement. Type III injuries presently are managed by anatomical open reduction and internal fixation of the fibular if fractured, followed by reconstruction of the tibial plafond, bone grafting of defects, and medial or anterior buttress plating of the distal tibia to prevent angular deformity and allow early movement.

▶ [These are perhaps the most difficult of all tibial fractures to manage. Although no argument is taken with the recommendation for anatomical reduction, it is extremely

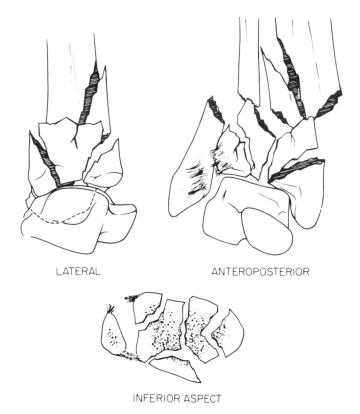

LATERAL   ANTEROPOSTERIOR

INFERIOR ASPECT

TYPE III

Fig 3–5.—Type III pillion fractures are compression fractures that disrupt the articular surface and cause comminution of the distal tibia. (Courtesy of Bourne, R.B., et al.: J. Trauma 23:591–596, July 1983.)

difficult to achieve in many of these fractures. As reduction with badly comminuted fractures proceeds, radiographs frequently provide information helpful in completing the procedure. The type III fractures remain the greatest challenge of all, and although a substantial proportion of these injuries result in ultimate arthrodesis, an attempt should be made to obtain anatomical reduction. This gives at least a chance of a functional ankle and will probably provide an improved anatomical basis for a more successful arthrodesis should it ultimately be required.—D.C. Campbell] ◄

3–18 **Importance of Anatomical Reduction for Subjective Recovery After Ankle Fracture.** Turkka Tunturi, Kari Kemppainen, Hannu Pätiälä, Markku Suokas, Olli Tamminen and Pentti Rokkanen (Univ. of Tampere, Finland) reviewed the results obtained in 237 patients treated for ankle fractures in 1977. The 128 men and 109

(3–18)   Acta Orthop. Scand. 54:641–647, August 1983.

women, were older than 16, and had a mean age of 46 years. Most fractures of the medial malleolus, large fractures of the posterior trigonum, and ruptured syndesmoses were operated on, while most plain fractures of the lateral malleolus and injuries of the posterior trigonum involving less than one fourth of the articular surface were managed conservatively. A screw was most often used to fix the malleoli and to repair the ruptured syndesmosis. Internal fixation usually was removed from patients younger than 50. Conservative treatment usually was by immobilization in a leg plaster for 4–6 weeks, with partial or full weight-bearing on the cast in the last 2–3 weeks.

A total of 206 patients were evaluated 1½–2½ years after injury. Surgery more often resulted in exact fracture reduction, despite the fact that the injuries that were operated on were considerably more severe. No deep infections followed surgical treatment, and no pulmonary emboli occurred. One patient who was operated on had a redislocation. Delayed union, nonunion, and refracture each occurred in 1 conservatively treated patient. Most respondents reported some sequelae, most often pain on exercise. Sequelae were less frequent in patients with better radiologic reduction at the end of treatment. The time away from work could not be related to the radiologic findings, the patient's age, the type of fracture, or the form of treatment.

Anatomical correction is the chief concern in treating ankle fractures. If it can be achieved nonoperatively, surgery may be avoided. Otherwise, operative reduction and fixation are indicated in the treatment of ankle injuries.

▶ [This interesting paper, which studied a large group of patients, indicates that the outcome of ankle fractures treatment depends almost entirely on the adequacy of the anatomical reduction of the fracture. The ankle is a very stable joint which bears tremendous compressive loads with relative ease, because of its large surface area. If the mechanics of the ankle, however, are disrupted even slightly by a less than perfect reduction of an ankle fracture, then subsequent degenerative changes are certain to occur. Age, sex, and type of treatment seemed to have no relevance to the subsequent outcome, as indicated by this paper. However, the period of follow-up of only 1½ to 2½ years seems inadequate to determine the ultimate outcome of these treatment methods. It is well known that a period of 3 to 5 years, and in some cases, even longer, is required before symptomatic degenerative changes in the ankle joint become apparent. It would seem, then, that a review of these same patients at 5 to 8 years follow-up would seem more informative.—R.N. Stauffer] ◀

3–19 **Displaced Ankle Fractures in Patients Over 50 Years of Age.** C. G. Beauchamp (Nottingham, England), N. R. Clay (Leeds, England), and P. W. Thexton (Sheffield, England) reviewed experience with 126 patients (92 women) older than age 50 who were seen in 1976–1979 with displaced fractures of the ankle. Fifty-five patients were treated in plaster, while 71 underwent open reduction and internal fixation. Severely displaced fractures were more likely to be treated operatively. General anesthesia was used in most of the con-

---

(3–19) J. Bone Joint Surg. [Br.] 65-B:329–332, May 1983.

servatively treated patients. Nine patients required a second manipulation. Casts were retained for an average of 7½ weeks. The technique and implants of the AO group were used in the surgically treated group. The average hospital stay was 15 days.

Six conservatively treated patients had complications, excluding deterioration in the original position. Twenty-six patients operated on had comminuted or porotic bone unsuitable for fixation. Thirty of 49 women and 6 of 22 men operated on had complications. Anatomical fracture position was achieved significantly more often after surgery. Anatomical, stable fixation was achieved in 38 cases after operation. Problems at follow-up 2 years or more after injury were comparably frequent in the 2 groups. Clinical examination showed little difference between the 2 groups with regard to the range of ankle joint and subtalar joint movements.

Internal fixation of displaced ankle fractures in women older than 50 carries a high rate of complications, and its benefits are limited. Men, however, usually have adequate bone stock for proper fixation unless they have been in plaster for 1–2 weeks after initially successful manipulation. Little difference in function was found after conservative and operative treatment in the present series. Most patients were satisfied with the outcome, although a considerable number had some pain or swelling.

▶ [The authors confirm that adequate reduction of an ankle fracture is of primary importance as far as long-term function and degenerative changes are concerned. It is not pertinent whether or not conservative or operative treatment is rendered. A marked increase in the incidence of complications, namely, loss of fixation or reduction, was found in elderly women over 70 years of age. This was presumably due to the more comminuted nature of the fractures and the presence of osteoporosis.— R.N. Stauffer] ◀

3–20 **Tarsal Navicular Stress Fractures: Radiographic Evaluation.** Tarsal navicular stress fractures are an underdiagnosed cause of prolonged, disabling foot pain in young athletes. Helene Pavlov, Joseph S. Torg, and Robert H. Freiberger reviewed the findings in 21 patients with 23 stress fractures of the tarsal navicular. Routine roentgenograms included anteroposterior (AP), oblique, and lateral views. "Coned AP" views were available in 13 cases and a direct magnification AP view for 1 foot. Bone scans were made with ^{99m}Tc-methylene diphosphonate (MDP) in 16 feet of 14 patients. Tomography was performed in 17 patients with 19 injuries. The methods of obtaining standard and anatomical AP tomograms are illustrated in Figures 3–6 and 3–7.

Ill-defined soreness or cramping of the foot and deep-seated pain on palpation were regular findings. Tenderness was present over the tarsal navicular in 17 feet. All but 3 fractures were in patients aged 27 and younger. All patients had participated in athletic activities, es-

(3–20) Radiology 148:641–645, September 1983.

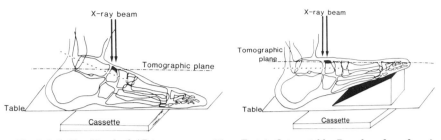

Fig 3–6 (left).—Standard AP tomogram position. Foot is flat on table. Dorsal surface of navicular *(shaded area)* and long axis of talus and navicular are oblique to tomographic plane.

Fig 3–7 (right).—Anatomical AP tomogram position. Forefoot is lifted off table with wedge so that dorsal surface of navicular *(shaded area)* and long axis of talus and navicular are parallel to tomographic plane.

(Courtesy of Pavlov, H., et al.: Radiology 148:641–645, September 1983.)

pecially basketball and running. The fractures were diagnosed on routine AP roentgenograms in 9 feet. The major findings were sclerosis of the proximal articular border of the tarsal navicular, metatarsus adductus, and hyperostosis or stress fractures of the second through fourth metatarsals. Bone scans showed increased uptake in all bones with stress fractures. Eleven of the fractures were complete. Seventeen fractures were diagnosed on anatomical AP tomograms, and 1 injury was diagnosed on a standard AP tomogram.

Bone scanning with ^{99m}Tc-MDP is a useful screening method for tarsal navicular stress fracture. Anatomical AP tomograms of the tarsal navicular are usually necessary for definitive diagnosis of this injury. The typical fracture is confined within the dorsal 5 mm of the central third of the bone and is not evident on a standard AP tomogram.

▶ [Certainly "anatomical" tomograms of the tarsal navicular demonstrate this stress fracture better than routine views. As mentioned by the authors, the technetium scan is probably the most useful detector of such an abnormality. When this indicates a navicular problem, the detailed tomograms should be obtained.—K.A. Johnson] ◀

3–21 **Spinal Fractures Complicating Ankylosing Spondylitis: A Long-term Follow-up Study.** Thomas Hunter and Hyman I. C. Dubo (Univ. of Manitoba, Winnipeg) reviewed data on 20 male patients treated between 1965 and 1982 for chronic ankylosing spondylitis and spinal fractures. The patients, had a total of 22 fractures of the ankylosed spine, 19 in the cervical spinal region. Fourteen injuries were caused by minor falls, 3 by falls down steps, 4 by motor vehicle accidents, and 1 by cardiopulmonary resuscitation.

Fifteen fractures in 14 patients were diagnosed immediately and treated conservatively. These patients had a mean age of 59 years and had had ankylosing spondylitis for a mean of 31 years. Three

(3–21) Arthritis Rheum. 26:751–759, June 1983.

patients died shortly after injury, 2 of pneumonia and pulmonary congestion and 1 of septicemia complicated by bradycardia and cardiac arrest. Nine patients were followed up for a mean of 3.2 years, and all had clinical and radiographic union after a mean of 13 weeks. No patient developed pseudarthrosis, and none had further neurologic deficit after the institution of conservative treatment.

Diagnosis of 7 fractures was delayed. These patients had a mean age of 56 years and had had ankylosing spondylitis for a mean of 27 years. Three of the 6 patients followed for a mean of 4.2 years had complete clinical and radiographic union with no neurologic deficit. Two patients developed pseudarthrosis and continued to have local tenderness and pain on motion. One patient presented with incomplete quadriplegia had major neurologic recovery after immobilization in a cervical collar.

Minor spinal trauma in patients with ankylosing spondylitis can lead to problems in diagnosis. Tomography of the spine is helpful in some cases. Careful immobilization is very important in these cases; patients have died while being turned. Even minor spinal trauma requires treatment as if a spinal fracture were present until this is ruled out. The use of halo traction and a body cast or vest may reduce the period of bed rest and hospitalization. Active attempts to avoid cardiorespiratory complications are necessary.

▶ [We agree with the authors that spinal fractures in patients with ankylosing spondylitis occur more often in the cervical spine and are difficult to diagnose and treat. A high index of suspicion does help and tomography and computed tomography scans usually confirm the diagnosis. Our attitude has, in general, been more aggressive than that of the authors. In cervical spine injuries, we utilize gentle reduction maneuvers with guided halo traction followed by early internal fixation (usually by wiring and bone grafting). In the thoracic and lumbar spine, the treatment of choice is usually postural reduction followed by Harrington compression rods. These operative procedures should be followed by prolonged postoperative support in a halo-thoracic device for cervical lesions or a molded brace for thoracic and lumbar lesions. Because of the deformities in these patients, it is often necessary to customize the immobilization devices.

We have had an instance in which a rapidly progressive neurologic deficit was relieved by laminectomy and evacuation of an epidural hematoma, a recognized complication of fractures in ankylosing spondylitis. Laminectomy was certainly cord-saving in this situation.—M.E. Cabanela] ◀

3–22 **The Disparate Diameter: Sign of Rotational Deformity in Fractures.** Allan Naimark, Judith Kossoff, and Robert E. Leach (Boston Univ.) point out that although clinical assessment usually is better than radiography in detecting rotational deformity at fracture sites, the forearm is an exception. It appears that in the absence of comminution, a significant rotational deformity must be considered if the diameter of a long bone changes abruptly across a fracture line. The findings in a woman, aged 40, who sustained a distal radial shaft

(3–22) J. Can. Assoc. Radiol. 34:8–11, March 1983.

fracture and had local pain 5 weeks later are shown in Figures 3–8 and 3–9, and can be compared with the normal in Figure 3–10. Marked rotational deformity was confirmed at surgery and corrected; after healing, full rotation was restored. The findings in a boy, aged 12, who injured his ring finger are shown in Figures 3–11 and 3–12. Rotational deformity was clinically apparent in this case.

Severe rotational deformity can sometimes be identified radiographically from a marked disparity in diameter between the bone

Fig 3–8 (left).—Posteroanterior radiograph of forearm through plaster of Paris splint, obtained 5 weeks after injury. Measurements of diameter of shaft immediately proximal and distal to fracture of distal radius are remarkably disparate (1.5 and 2.6 cm, respectively). Note lack of radial bow and abnormal position of bicipital tuberosity.

Fig 3–9 (right).—Close-up of fracture region.

(Courtesy of Naimark, A., et al.: J. Can. Assoc. Radiol. 34:8–11, March 1983.)

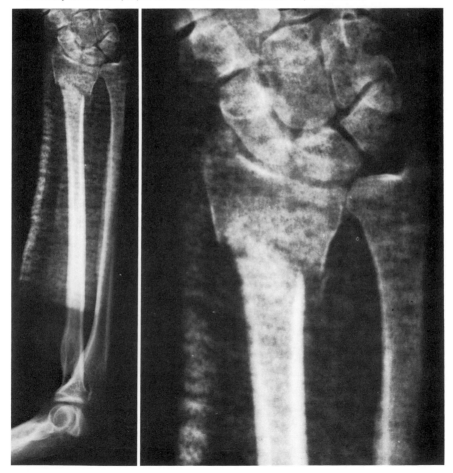

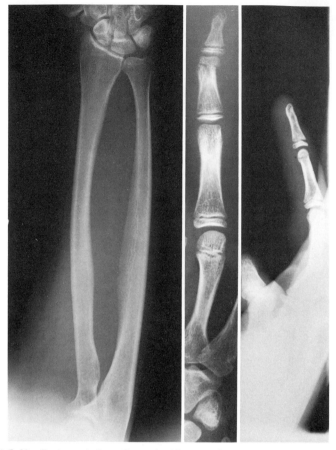

Fig 3–10 (left).—Posteroanterior radiograph of forearm of normal subject.
Fig 3–11 (center).—Posteroanterior radiograph of ring finger shows mild angulation and disparity between bone diameters immediately proximal and distal to fracture of neck of middle phalanx, indicating severe rotational deformity.
Fig 3–12 (right).—Postreduction lateral radiograph of ring finger shows that anatomical position has been restored.
(Courtesy of Naimark, A., et al.: J. Can. Assoc. Radiol. 34:8–11, March 1983.)

just proximal and that just distal to the fracture line. If the cross section of a bone at the site of fracture is ovoid and the diameter changes abruptly in the absence of comminution, significant rotational deformity is a good possibility. If displacement is severe, differential magnification has to be taken into account. Negative findings do not exclude rotational deformity. The disparate diameter sign is most important in assessing forearm trauma. The joints proximal and distal to the fracture site should be included in the study, preferably in the same film.

▶ [There is nothing new in this short article but almost every point that it makes concerning the identification of rotational deformities at fracture sites is commonly ignored, forgotten, misunderstood, or misapplied. Commiting these few facts to memory will save many patients and many clinicians much grief, particularly in the management of forearm fractures.—J.H. Dobyns] ◀

3–23 **Bony Lacerations Caused by Assault.** Compound, displaced extremity fractures inflicted by sharp heavy weapons (e.g., axes and swords) have been treated by surgeons for centuries. Assaults with such weapons as meat cleavers and machetes may be coming to be more frequent in some areas. L. A. Rymaszewski and J. M. Caullay (Glasgow) reviewed bony lacerations caused by assault in 8 patients seen between 1979 and 1983 in Glasgow. All of the wounds were cleanly incised, reflecting the sharpness and weight of the weapons used. The innocent external appearances may disguise damage to deep tissues, including fractures. In addition, a false history may be given. Radiographs are necessary if there is any doubt as to the circumstances in which a wound was sustained.

Internal fixation is used to manage these patients, and antibiotics and tetanus prophylaxis are administered. Often, only a guillotine type of injury is present. The prognosis is good when divided muscles, tendons, nerves, or vessels are repaired, and infection is unlikely. Perfect reduction of the bone fragments usually is possible; internal fixation is straightforward and is preferred as the smooth bony surfaces are inherently unstable. Also, in this series, the patients tended to be unreliable in following instructions when managed in plaster. With internal fixation, good restoration of function is usually possible. Legal implications often exist in these situations, and a thorough history and examination with careful note-taking are essential.

▶ [This article is a nice review of an injury which, although uncommon in North America, apparently is not very uncommon in some other parts of the world. It gives a reasonable approach to treatment and also an appropriate caveat regarding underestimating the amount of damage from these injuries.—J.R. Cass] ◀

3–24 **Bullworker's Fracture.** Spiral fractures of the distal humeral shaft, often with an associated medial butterfly fragment, have been described as a result of Indian arm wrestling. A. F. Lynch and P. F. O'Carroll (Dublin) report 3 cases of humeral shaft fracture occurring in healthy, athletic young men exercising with a Bullworker compression apparatus. The patients were aged 18 to 30 years. Two sustained spiral humeral shaft fractures with an associated medial butterfly fragment. One patient had a transverse distal humeral fracture. All of the fractures united uneventfully with conservative management. No patient had neurologic injury. None had had previous fractures, and routine biochemical tests gave normal results.

Increasing interest in physical fitness has led to a demand for such

(3–23) J. Bone Joint Surg. [Br.] 66-B:89–92, January 1984.
(3–24) Injury 14:351–353, January 1983.

body-building aids as the Bullworker compression apparatus. The forces generated in the lower humerus with this apparatus are similar in magnitude to those generated in arm wrestling, but the muscles of both arms are maximally contracted; hence the humerus on the nondominant side fails.

3–25 **Effects of Parathyroidectomy and Vitamin D on Fracture Healing: Fracture Biomechanics in Rats After Parathyroidectomy and Treatment With 1,25-Dihydroxycholecalciferol.** Fracture healing can be influenced by a variety of biologic factors. Both high doses of vitamin D_3 and vitamin D deficiency retard healing. Olle Andreen and Sven-Erik Larsson (Univ. of Umeå, Sweden) examined the biomechanical effects of selective parathyroidectomy and low doses of 1,25-dihydroxycholecalciferol [$1,25(OH)_2D_3$] in adult male Sprague-Dawley rats with closed tibial fractures. Results in 49 rats having parathyroidectomy and 49 given daily intraperitoneal injections of 30 ng of $1,25(OH)_2D_3$ for 5 days a week were compared with those in 51 control animals given no treatment. The fractures were left to heal for periods of 7–48 days.

Parathyroidectomy led to impaired fracture healing and several delayed unions. Tensile strength, elastic stiffness, and failure energy of the fractures were significantly lower at the start of the healing period than in control rats. Treatment with $1,25(OH)_2D_3$ was associated with increased bone formation and mineralization in early fractures, but no increase in tensile strength or failure energy compared with findings in control animals. Increased bone turnover appeared to result in early resorption of periosteal callus. Later in the healing period, fracture strength decreased compared with that in control rats. Elastic stiffness initially rose to above control values as a result of increased mineralization, but later declined to control levels.

These findings indicate that parathyroidectomy impairs fracture healing in the rat, probably through inadequate differentiation of osteoprogenitor cells and remodeling of callus. Administration of $1,25(OH)_2D_3$ appears to increase callus bone turnover with early mineralization, resulting in a temporary increase in elastic stiffness but not an increase in tensile strength.

3–26 **How Stiff Should Semirigid Fixation of the Human Tibia Be? A Clue to the Answer.** Semirigid fixation of fractures permits union to occur rapidly through the medium of external callus with little or no stress-protection osteopenia in the bone around the implant. The chief difficulty is in knowing how much movement is sufficient to promote good external callus while avoiding nonunion. Keith Tayton and John Bradley (Cardiff Royal Infirmary, Cardiff, Wales) examined the eight-hole carbon fiber-reinforced plastic (CFRP) plates used to fix 20

(3–25) Acta Orthop. Scand. 54:805–809, December 1983.
(3–26) J. Bone Joint Surg. [Br.] 65-B:312–315, May 1983.

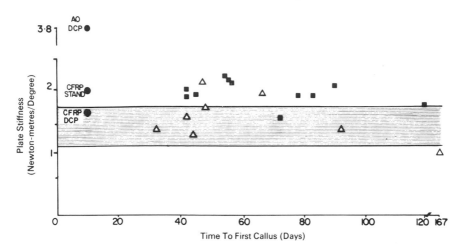

Fig 3–13.—Graph comparing stiffness of implanted CFRP plates and time for external callus to become apparent on film. There is no direct relationship between the two. Open triangles = patients who experienced significant pain; solid squares = other patients; solid circles = unused tibial plates for comparison. (Courtesy of Tayton, K., and Bradley, J.: J. Bone Joint Surg. [Br.] 65-B:312–315, May 1983.)

closed, displaced fractures of the middle third of the tibia to determine how well the material withstood clinical stresses and whether the stiffness of the plate could be related to the clinical outcome.

A 10% variation in stiffness of unused CFRP plates was not uncommon. The 8-hole standard CFRP broad plate was found to be about one-half as stiff as the steel plates tested. The stiffness of the plates could not be related to the first appearance of external callus, extent of callus, or time to sound bony union within the range of stiffness analyzed. An exception was a patient with a faulty plate that became very flexible who ultimately developed a hypertrophic nonunion. Stiffness was clearly related to aching pain at the fracture site. Most patients with significant pain had plates with stiffness values of 1.0 to 1.75 newton-meters per degree (Fig 3–13). The 2 patients with higher values had deep infection, and the 1 with a lower value was the patient with hypertrophic nonunion.

There is no single stiffness value for CFRP plates that by itself promotes rapid callus production. It appears that semirigid plates should have a stiffness above 1.75 newton-meters per degree in order to satisfactorily fix a tibial shaft fracture. Current CFRP plates, with a stiffness of about 2.0 newton-meters per degree, give satisfactory results. Nonunion is more likely when a plate with a stiffness below 1.0 newton-meter per degree is used.

▶ [The strength of this article is that it examines the human fracture, and so provides results that are directly relevant to design of semirigid plates in orthopedic surgery. The main conclusion of the study is the clinical observation that plates with less rigidity than 1.75 newton-meters per degree are associated with pain at the fracture site. In this regard it may have been helpful had the weight of the patients been provided, for this surely influences the stresses across the fracture site in ambulatory patients.

However, the strength of this paper is also its weakness. Human fracture studies cannot consistently provide comparable fractures. The variability in shape and comminution of the tibial fractures may help to explain the lack of effect plate rigidity had on the rate of fracture union. The 15% infection rate in these closed tibial fractures is noteworthy and hopefully merely reflects a statistical exaggeration in a small sample.—P.J. Kelly] ◄

4. Joint Replacement: The Hip

4–1 **ICLH Surface Replacement of Hip: Analysis of First 10 Years.**
M. A. R. Freeman (London) and Gary W. Bradley (Univ. of California
at San Diego) reviewed the results of ICLH resurfacing in 204 hips.
Patients were followed for at least 2 years after operation, the average follow-up being 3.2 years. The average age at operation was 56
years. Seven patients had bilateral surface replacements, and 14 others had a stemmed prosthesis on the other side at the time of follow-
up. Osteoarthritis was the diagnosis in 168 treated hips. Twenty hips
were operated on previously.

In 79% of hips the results were comparable to those obtained in
hips successfully replaced with stemmed prostheses. Three-fourths of
the patients were able to walk for a longer time than before operation, and range of motion was improved in a similar proportion.
Nearly 90% of these hips had a total range of motion of 140 degrees
or more. Thirty-five of the 43 failures were attributed to aseptic loosening. Infection was responsible for 3 failures, ectopic ossification and
femoral neck fracture for 2 each, and dislocation for 1. The overall
failure rate was 21%, but the rate in patients with inflammatory arthropathy was 39%. Design error was a factor in 58% of the failures,
and technical errors were implicated in 81%. The perioperative complication rate was 8%. One patient died of a cerebral infarct 9 days
postoperatively. Three patients had nonfatal pulmonary embolism.
Examination of the femoral heads from 24 hips in which the procedure failed found no avascular necrosis.

Resurfacing arthroplasty of the hip may be advantageous in some
instances, but proper patient selection is necessary and careful operative technique essential. The procedure is still under development
and at present is limited to physiologically young patients without
inflammatory arthropathy. Design modifications have resulted in an
acetabular component that now is much less than hemispheric, is
thicker walled, and is fixable without cement.

▶ [Resurfacing the hip joint is virtually dead as a surgical alternative in the armamentarium of most hip surgeons. The results shown in this and other recent reports
clearly explain why.

It has been advanced that errors in patient selection, operative technique, or size
of the prosthesis could be responsible for a large proportion of the failures. Yet no
statistical proof of this is shown. In our own experience with an admittedly smaller
number of patients (60), the failure rate, even excluding those cases in which obvious

(4–1) J. Bone Joint Surg. [Br.] 65-B:405–411, August 1983.

errors of patient selection or operative technique were committed, approached 20% in 2 years, an obviously unacceptable rate. The culprit of this procedure is, as mentioned, aseptic loosening of the components. At the present time, design constraints (a necessarily large femoral component coupled with a necessarily thin acetabular component, even if metal-backed) are responsible for increased stresses at the bone cement interface conducive to unavoidable loosening. It is possible, however, that surface replacement might "resurface" in the future as a porous ingrowth biological fixation prosthesis.—M.E. Cabanela] ◀

4–2   **Complex Total Hip Replacement for Dysplastic or Hypoplastic Hips Using Miniature or Microminiature Components.** Steven T. Woolson and William H. Harris (Boston) reviewed the results of 69 total hip replacement procedures performed in 1971 to 1979 using miniature or microminiature femur components in 48 female and 9 male patients (average age, 46 years). More than two thirds of the patients had a diagnosis of congenital dysplasia or dislocation of the hip. More than half the hips had been operated on previously. The patients were small in stature, with an average height of 5 ft 1½ in. The acetabular volume was generally small, and acetabular deficiency was present. Fifty-five hips were operated on in 47 patients and were evaluated after 2 years. Microminiature or miniature Harris CDH femoral prostheses were used for all hips, and a miniature acetabular component was used in 90% of the hips.

Intraoperative complications occurred in one fifth of the hips, and postoperative complications developed after about one third of the operations. Sixteen percent of the hips dislocated postoperatively. Eight hips have been revised. Eighty-seven percent of the hips that were not revised were painless or slightly painful when last assessed. Three hips were markedly painful. Only 3 patients had to use 2 canes or 2 crutches to ambulate. Six hips had to be revised because of component loosening and 2 because of recurrent dislocations. The overall incidence of loosening in the 110 femur and acetabular components followed up for at least 2 years was 11%.

The results of total hip replacement using miniature and microminiature components in this series were gratifying, despite many technical difficulties. For all but 1 of the 8 hips that were failures, the only feasible alternative to complex reconstruction was resection arthroplasty. Because of the complexity of reconstruction, the procedure should be performed at centers where experienced surgeons and adequate facilities are available.

▶ [This is a very important paper and should be read carefully by all orthopedic surgeons who perform total hip surgery. This study includes all of Doctor Harris' personal patients, analyzed by Doctor Woolson. It points out the many important aspects of total hip replacement in the patient with a dysplastic or hypoplastic hip. Of special concern are the number of nerve palsies following surgery, namely, 4 in their series of 69 operations. Not only is the nerve in an altered anatomical position, but the muscles normally buffering the nerve from surgical trauma are hypoplastic in these

(4–2)   J. Bone Joint Surg. [Am.] 65-A:1099–1108, October 1983.

patients. There is also a high dislocation rate as compared to the normal population (11 of 69 hips (16%) in their series). In addition to the cause of dislocation which they mention, anteversion of the neck and posterior position of the greater trochanter are usually present. Most of the neck is removed during surgery, so putting in the femoral component at a normal attitude is not difficult; but the trochanter must invariably be transposed more anteriorly so that it will not abut on the posterior portion of the acetabulum on external rotation, and lever out the hip.

One of the problems I have encountered has been loosening of the acetabular component, especially in the younger age group, even when bone grafting has been used. The authors found five loose acetabular components. In analyzing my own series, I found that this is probably due to two related factors. One, the acetabular unit is put in too much vertical tilt. The other, the lack of varus built into the miniature femoral components. This puts a direct valgus thrust against the superior aspect of the acetabular component and does not allow for an even, more central, distribution of loading forces. I understand that some of Doctor Harris' later models of femoral units have more normal anatomical neck angles, and these should be used.—Ed.] ◄

4–3 **Total Hip Replacement in Juvenile Chronic Arthritis.** Failures of total hip replacement (THR) increase over time, mainly because of mechanical loosening, and many young patients are expected to outlive their prostheses. Brynjólfur Mogensen, Håkan Brattström, Leif Ekelund, and Lars Lidgren (Univ. of Lund, Sweden) reviewed the results of 50 THR procedures performed on 33 patients with juvenile chronic arthritis, followed up for an average of 77 months after operation. The 19 female and 14 male patients had an average age of 26 years when operated on. Twenty-eight patients had a diagnosis of juvenile rheumatoid arthritis during follow-up, and 5 had a diagnosis of ankylosing spondylitis. All patients had polyarthritis during follow-up. The average duration of disease before operation was 18 years, and the duration of hip symptoms was 13 years. Pain and poor motion were the most common indications for THR. A total of 28 previous operations had been performed on 24 hips. Soft tissue-releasing procedures were necessary in 19 cases. The McKee-Farrar and Howse-Arden prostheses were used most often. Adequate prophylaxis with cloxacillin was used in 41 operations.

The hospital stay averaged 56 days. Two postoperative dislocations occurred, and 2 patients required hip mobilization with the use of general anesthesia after the operation. Late complications included one deep infection in a patient who was not given any antibiotics preoperatively; another patient was suspected of having deep infection. Clinical loosening required reoperation on 4 hips. All but 1 of the patients not requiring reoperation had satisfactory relief of pain during follow-up. Flexion was usually the same or better than before the operation. Walking improved moderately, but the patients considered the improvement to be very significant. All patients not reoperated on were satisfied with the overall results of THR during follow-up. Radiography showed loosening in 10 hips during follow-up evaluation.

(4–3) Acta Orthop. Scand. 54:422–430, June 1983.

It is likely that at least one revision arthroplasty will be necessary in patients having THR for juvenile chronic arthritis usually because of mechanical loosening. It is best to delay THR in young patients if possible. Arthroscopy should be used at an early stage to determine whether synovectomy is necessary. Synovectomy of the hip should always be considered before THR is performed if cartilage destruction is not great.

▶ [In a recent long-term follow-up review of total hip arthroplasties performed in patients 20 to 40 years old, we found very similar results to those reported here. Although rheumatoid patients do not generally subject their artificial joints to the same stresses as patients with other conditions, we have seen a number of failures, particularly acetabular loosenings, related to recurrence of rheumatoid synovitis with bony erosion underneath the cement.

Also, in a published report from our institution (Stauffer, R.N.: *J. Bone Joint Surg.* [Am.] 64-A:983, 1982), acetabular loosening was observed more frequently in patients who had had previous cup arthroplasties, and femoral loosening was observed more frequently in patients who had had previous femoral endoprostheses. This is contrary to the findings observed in this paper.

High loosening rates of total hip arthroplasty in the young, the obvious need for revision surgery, and the less satisfactory results obtained in these revision procedures, make it mandatory to intensify the search for a better alternative. At this point we don't know whether noncemented biologic fixation might be the future answer.—M.E. Cabanela] ◀

4-4 **Total Hip Arthroplasties in Patients Less Than 45 Years Old.** Lawrence D. Dorr, Glenn K. Takei, and J. Pierce Conaty (Downey, Calif.) reviewed the results of 108 total hip arthroplasties in 81 patients aged 14 to 45 years who were followed up for an average of 4½ years after the index operation. Follow-up data were available on 100 operated-on hips in 69 patients. Aufranc-Turner prostheses were used most frequently. The average age at operation was 30.5 years. The most common primary disorders were inflammatory collagen disease, osteoarthritis, and osteonecrosis. Previous surgery had been performed on 33 hips.

At last follow-up evaluation, 78% of all hips were in satisfactory condition. Of the 24 hips with unsatisfactory results, 12 had undergone revision surgery for mechanical failure, 8 were infected, and 4 caused unexplained pain. The best results were obtained in patients with inflammatory collagen disease. Only 62% of patients with a previous implant had satisfactory results. Technically satisfactory results, however, were obtained in only 42 of the 100 evaluable hips: flaws in cementing technique were identified in 16 instances, and 33 components exhibited flaws in positioning. Thus, while actual mechanical failure occurred in 12 hips, all of which underwent a revision procedure, impending failure was identified in 29% of 84 evaluable joints. This was most prominent at the acetabular site.

(4–4)   J. Bone Joint Surg. [Am.] 65-A:474–479, April 1983.

Clinically satisfactory results of total hip arthroplasty in patients aged 45 years and younger were less frequent in this series than has been reported for older patients. Although revision surgery can be performed, should the index operation fail, the subsequent outcome is not hopeful. Fusion after a failed arthroplasty or a failed revision usually is not acceptable, and resection arthroplasty then is the only alternative. The short-term benefits of hip arthroplasty in younger patients must be weighed against the considerable risk of eventual failure and the subsequent need for more difficult surgical treatment offering smaller benefit.

4–5 **Total Hip Replacement in the Previously Septic Hip.** Previous reports raise the question of whether it is ever reasonable to carry out a total hip replacement in a previously septic hip. David L. Cherney and Harlan C. Amstutz (Univ. of California, Los Angeles) performed total hip replacement in one or two stages in 33 patients with a clear history of hip sepsis within the prior 6 years and positive cultures. Sepsis had followed hemiarthroplasty in 6 hips, open reduction with internal fixation of a fracture in 8, total hip replacement in 8, and cup arthroplasty in 1. Ten other patients had total hip replacement after destruction of the hip, by hematogenous sepsis in 9 and a shrapnel wound in 1. The 17 men and 16 women had a mean age of 57 years. All were followed for at least 3 years after salvage total hip replacement. Five salvage procedures were done in a single stage in patients with positive cultures of surgical specimens. Parenteral antistaphylococcal antibiotic therapy was given perioperatively, but antibiotic usually was not incorporated in the bone cement.

Results were successful in 70% of cases. Six of the 10 deep infections were recurrences caused by the original organism. Three patients had infection with a different organism, and 1 had either a local recurrence or reseeding from a persistent pyelonephritis. The success rates were 78% where the original organism was gram positive and 58% where it was gram negative. In most patients with deep infection about a salvage prosthesis the prosthesis was removed. Six patients eventually had a Girdlestone procedure. The prosthetic failure rate was highest in patients with previous infection about a total hip replacement and those with previous infection but no previous prosthetic or internal fixation devices.

Patients with a history of gram-negative infection are now managed as if they were still infected. A full course of parenteral antibiotic therapy is given at reimplantation, and antibiotics against gram-positive organisms are used orally after operation. A resurfacing procedure is performed rather than conventional total hip replacement where possible. Antibiotics are added to the bone cement.

(4–5) J. Bone Joint Surg. [Am.] 65-A:1256–1265, December 1983.

The present success rate compares favorably with the cure rates reported for Girdlestone resection arthroplasty.

▶ [Reconstruction of the infected hip implant, either as a primary procedure or in a delayed fashion, has challenged the modern orthopedic surgeon. The authors quite correctly point out that the underlying microbiology may be the most significant prognostic factor. In the presence of gram negative bacillary infection either technique has failed in approximately one half of the patients.

When a delayed reconstruction of the previously infected hip implant is proposed, the major difficulty is to determine when it is safe to reconstruct the patient's hip. The usual laboratory parameters have proven to be less than accurate. The erythrocyte and the peripheral white blood cell count with differential and the sedimentation rate are notoriously inaccurate.

Scintigraphic examination, in particular indium-111 autogolous white blood cell scanning, may be helpful. This technique has certainly improved our ability to diagnose the low-grade infectious process about osseous structures and implanted foreign bodies. In the hands of an expert nuclear radiologist, it has an accuracy of approximately 94% to 95%.

The authors indicate that the use of antibiotic impregnated cement may be efficacious in the treatment of gram negative bacillary infections. Using this technique, Buchholz and colleagues were only able to irradicate 50% of the infections in patients with gram negative bacillary infections. Perhaps the results can be improved in this group of patients by using antibiotic impregnated cement in the delayed reconstruction of the hip.—R.H. Fitzgerald, Jr.] ◀

4–6 **Vascular Complications After Total Hip Arthroplasty** are uncommon. D. Bergqvist, Å. S. Carlsson, and B. F. Ericsson (Malmö, Sweden) report 4 cases of vascular complications associated with total hip replacement and review 25 previously reported cases. There were 22 female patients. Most complications have occurred on the left side, probably because of the more leftward lateral position of the aortic bifurcation and left iliac artery. All injuries but 1 were confined to arteries. The external iliac and common femoral arteries were involved most frequently. Acute injuries causing immediate symptoms were most often produced by excessive medial pressure from the retractor and excessive reaming in patients with acetabular protrusion. Delayed symptoms can result from a pseudoaneurysm, impaired blood flow, or distal microembolization or severe bleeding when a hip prosthesis is extracted. Either too large a volume of cement with intrapelvic spicules or intrapelvic dislocation of the socket with angulation of the artery may be involved.

Infection or reoperation cases, or both, are overrepresented among patients with vascular injury. Amputation or disarticulation has been necessary in 5 instances. Two of the previously described patients died, 1 of sepsis and 1 of pulmonary embolism. Retractors should not be used over the acetabular lip, and care is needed not to penetrate the bottom of the acetabulum when holes are drilled. Arteriosclerotic vessels in older patients are more vulnerable to injury. A socket dislocated into the pelvis should be extracted via a hypogastric incision

(4–6) Acta Orthop. Scand. 54:157–163, April 1983.

with a retroperitoneal dissection. Immediate vascular control is possible with this approach. When reconstruction is necessary in cases of pseudoaneurysm, synthetic graft material should not be used. The best method is exclusion of the pseudoaneurysm after an extra-anatomical femorofemoral crossover bypass.

▶ [Vascular complications after total hip arthroplasty can be serious and lead to large hematomas which frequently become colonized, precipitating a secondary infection of the arthroplasty. Alternatively, a compromise of the blood supply to the extremity can occur, necessitating amputation at or above the knee. Ratliff has the most extensive experience with vascular and neurologic complications following total hip arthroplasty. In his report (The Hip. *Proc. Nin. Open Sci. Meet. Hip Soc.,* 1981, pp. 276–292), the Hohmann retractor has been associated with injury to the femoral artery and vein. Reaming of the acetabulum can injure the common iliac artery, especially in patients with a thin acetabulum. Rupture of false aneurysms of the external iliac artery and the femoral artery were associated with revision surgery or resection arthroplasty for infected arthroplasties.

As the authors point out, vascular complications are more frequently associated with revision total hip arthroplasty and the surgical treatment of sepsis.—R.H. Fitzgerald, Jr.] ◀

4–7 **On Thromboembolism After Total Hip Replacement in Epidural Analgesia: Controlled Study of Dextran 70 and Low-Dose Heparin Combined With Dihydroergotamine.** Total hip replacement is associated with high rates of postoperative deep venous thrombosis (DVT) and pulmonary embolism. H. O. Fredin, B. Rosberg, M. Arborelius, Jr., and G. Nylander (Malmö, Sweden) undertook a prospective study comparing treatment with dextran 70 and a combination of low-dose heparin and dihydroergotamine (HDHE) in 116 patients having hip replacement; epidural block analgesia was used because of contraindications to general hypotensive anesthesia. Both primary and revision arthroplasties were included. The Charnley and Lubinus prostheses were used. Dextran 70 was given in a dose of 1 L on the day of surgery and 500 ml on the first and third postoperative days. Monovalent haptendextran was used to prevent anaphylaxis. The combined therapy consisted of 0.5 mg of dihydroergotaminemesylate plus 5,000 units of sodium heparin, injected subcutaneously in the abdomen every 12 hours for 10 days starting within 1 or 2 hours preoperatively. Deep vein thrombosis was diagnosed by phlebography with Urografin, and pulmonary scintigraphy was done with ^{99m}Tc-macroaggregated albumin and a dry ^{99m}Tc microaerosol.

The phlebographic findings are shown in Figure 4–1. In the lower leg, DVT was comparably frequent in the 2 treatment groups, but in the femoral segment DVT was significantly more frequent in the HDHE group. Pulmonary embolism occurred in 14 HDHE-treated patients and in 11 given dextran, for respective rates of 26% and 20%. Blood loss was comparable in the 2 groups, but 4 HDHE-treated pa-

(4–7) Br. J. Surg. 71:58–60, January 1984.

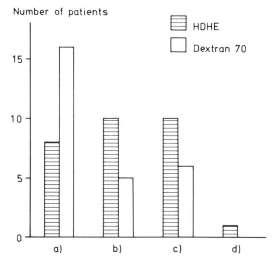

Fig 4–1.—Distribution of deep vein thrombosis in phlebograms of the treated leg: *(a)* lower leg thrombosis; *(b)* lower leg and femoral thrombosis; *(c)* isolated femoral deep vein thrombosis; *(d)* extensive deep vein thrombosis. (Courtesy of Fredin, H.O., et al.: Br. J. Surg. 71:58–60, January 1984.)

tients had bleeding complications. No anaphylactic reactions were observed. There were no deaths from pulmonary embolism in either treatment group.

Femoral DVT was less frequent in patients given dextran prophylaxis in this series, but the overall rates of DVT and pulmonary embolism were comparable in dextran-treated and HDHE-treated patients. The hemorrhagic side effects accompanying HDHE treatment are a disadvantage. Also, HDHE treatment requires subcutaneous injections twice daily for 7–10 days, whereas dextran 70 need be administered only 3 or 4 times.

▶ [There are several methods of preventing deep venous thrombosis following total hip arthroplasty. Dextran 70 (Macrodex) has been used in America with considerable success. Indeed, statistics for its use are as good as with any of the other methods. There are only two potential complications, which are, increased bleeding and hypersensitivity reaction. The other method in this study, dihydroergotamine with low-dose heparin, is seldom used in the United States, but it has been popular in Great Britain. Sodium warfarin is still used at the Mayo Clinic, with the results being perhaps superior to any others. But it does require careful monitoring for the period of time that the patient is in hospital following total hip arthroplasty.

The authors found that their only complication from using HDHE was a 7% bleeding incidence following arthroplasty. There were no complications with dextran 70. Venous thrombosis was diagnosed by phlebography done 2 weeks postoperatively on 116 patients in this study. There were no fatal pulmonary emboli. There was deep venous thrombosis in 60% of the HDHE patients and 44% of the dextran 70 patients, in contrast to some previous studies which have shown just the opposite but which were not evaluated in a similar way. Certainly these results and the results of Evarts and others in this country suggest that when dextran 70 is given carefully, with minimal dosage, it is a safe and effective method of preventing serious deep venous thrombosis, and fatal pulmonary emboli.—Ed.] ◀

4–8 **Stress Analysis of Acetabular Reconstruction in Protrusio Acetabuli.** Loosening is the most common cause of long-term failures of cemented total hip reconstructions. Roy D. Crowninshield, Richard A. Brand, and Douglas R. Pedersen (Univ. of Iowa) examined possible mechanical factors in the loosening of the acetabular component in patients with protrusio acetabuli, using an axisymmetrical finite-element model of the periacetabular bone. Polyethylene components, metal-backed components, protrusio rings, protrusio cups, and a metal medial acetabular shell were assessed in conjunction with the two surgical techniques illustrated in Figure 4–2. Stress levels and patterns of stress distribution were predicted for the component, the cement, and the bone in all instances.

Midfrontal-plane sections of the acetabular models are shown in Figure 4–3. In a protruded acetabulum, cortical bone stress on the medial part of the pelvic wall increased with medial placement of the acetabular component, while a more lateral placement reduced these

Fig 4–2.—Cross-sections of the two axisymmetrical acetabular models. Model A, protruded acetabulum is reconstructed with a normally placed component. Model B, protruded acetabulum is reconstructed with a medially placed component. For model A, five prostheses were investigated: a polyethylene cup with and without backing, a protrusio ring, a protrusio cup, and a medial metal shell. For model B, three prostheses were investigated: a polyethylene cup with and without metal backing, and a metal shell. (Courtesy of Crowninshield, R.D., et al.: J. Bone Joint Surg. [Am.] 65-A:495–499, April 1983.)

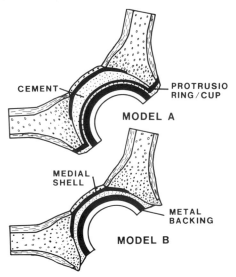

(4–8) J. Bone Joint Surg. [Am.] 65-A:495–499, April 1983.

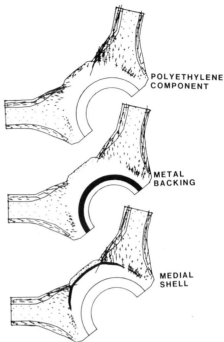

Fig 4–3.—Maximum tensile and compressive stresses on bone, calculated from the midfrontal-plane stress components for protruded acetabula reconstructed with normally placed acetabular components (see Fig 4–2, model A), are depicted by tiny crosses. The magnitude and direction of these stresses are shown by the size and orientation of the lines. The maximum cortical-bone stresses occur in the medial part of the wall. (Courtesy of Crowninshield, R.D., et al.: J. Bone Joint Surg. [Am.] 65-A:495–499, April 1983.)

POLYETHYLENE COMPONENT

METAL BACKING

MEDIAL SHELL

stresses. Metal backing of a polyethylene acetabular component caused a reduction in peak cement and trabecular-bone stress. A metal protrusio ring around the periphery of the acetabular component increased stress within the lateral part of the pelvic cortex. A complete metal protrusio cup increased stress in the same region, but substantially reduced stress in the medial part of the cortex and the trabecular bone. Prosthetic reinforcement of the medial part of the acetabular wall had little effect on stress patterns in the acetabular region.

The protruded acetabulum is especially difficult to reconstruct in a way that ensures longevity of the total hip replacement. In patients with protrusio acetabuli, the prosthetic acetabulum should be placed in a normal position. Use of a metal-backed acetabular component or a complete metal cup incorporated within the cement will reduce stress levels in the medial region of the pelvic bone, and may decrease the incidence of loosening.

4–9 **Role of Lavage in Preventing Hemodynamic and Blood Gas Changes During Cemented Arthroplasty.** If the hypotension and hypoxemia sometimes observed in conjunction with cemented hip ar-

(4–9) J. Bone Joint Surg. [Am.] 65-A:500–506, April 1983.

throplasty are due to egress of fat or release of substances produced by reaming of the medullary canal, thorough lavage of the canal might remove the offending substances. Raymond M. P. Sherman, Robert J. Byrick, J. Colin Kay, T. Robinson Sullivan, and James P. Waddell (Toronto) undertook a study in dogs to determine whether lavage of the femoral medullary canal before cement insertion would reduce the adverse hemodynamic and blood gas changes. In some dogs, 120 to 180 ml of sterile physiologic saline was injected into the reamed canal under manual pressure until the return was clear before the canal was packed with dry gauze. No venting was used in either group. Two commercially available bone cements were utilized.

The Pa_{O_2} fell significantly in control dogs, but not in the lavage group. The intrapulmonary shunt fraction increased as the Pa_{O_2} fell in the controls. No consistent changes in mean arterial pressure were found in either group of dogs. Pulmonary artery pressure increased significantly in controls throughout the operative period. Changes in the lavage group were minimal. No group differences in left atrial pressure or cardiac output were observed.

Reaming of the femoral medullary canal in dogs does not in itself cause significant changes in gas exchange of hemodynamics, but the products of reaming may produce such changes if the canal is pressurized and the contents are forced into the bloodstream. Lavage of the reamed, plugged medullary canal can eliminate hypoxemia, increased intrapulmonary shunting, and increased pulmonary artery pressure. Lavage of a plugged medullary canal should be considered as a prophylactic measure in cemented arthroplasty.

▶ [Every orthopedist who performs total hip arthroplasty should read this paper in its entirety. It is extremely important, for all of us have had the patient who experiences a sudden drop in blood pressure following insertion of the prosthesis, and fatalities have, of course, been reported. It is especially important with our newer techniques that we avoid in our patient transient hypotension and even possible cardiac arrest and sudden death. While most of us are now thoroughly lavaging the medullary cavity to remove particles of fat and blood which may interfere with the bone-cement interface, this paper points out the additional necessity for this in order to avoid the hypotensive effects from inserting methyl methacrylate under pressure.— Ed.] ◀

4–10 **Biplane Radiographic Measurements of Reversible Displacement (Including Clinical Loosening) and Migration of Total Joint Replacements.** David L. Green, Eugene Bahniuk, Ralph A. Liebelt, Erwin Fender, and Peter Mirkov (Case Western Reserve Univ.) assessed the relative motion between prosthesis and bone at the cement-bone interface in 19 total knee replacements and 33 total hip replacement cases, using simultaneous biplane radiography. Micromotion at the cement-bone interface was measured in vivo using spherical cobalt-chromium markers that were embedded in the ce-

(4–10) J. Bone Joint Surg. [Am.] 65-A:1134–1143, October 1982.

ment and the cortical bone. Reversible displacement, or relative motion during change from nonweight-bearing to weight-bearing, and migration, or relative motion over time between nonweight-bearing studies, were calculated. The resolution of the measuring system was 0.2 mm. The 52 joint prostheses, in 48 male patients, were assessed over a mean of 16 months. Eight patients were studied only once.

The range of symptomatic reversible displacement was 0.4–4.5 mm and that of asymptomatic reversible displacement was 0.3–1.9 mm. All reversible displacements less than 0.4 mm were asymptomatic. Migration up to 2.1 mm occurred without concomitant reversible displacement. All radiolucent lines were associated with measurable reversible displacement. Reversible displacement was detected 2 weeks postoperatively in half the patients. Only 13 of the 52 prostheses exhibited no motion whatever during the study. Much of the motion that was observed was asymptomatic, and some of the measured reversible displacement resolved in the course of the study.

Simultaneous biplane radiography can accurately assess motion in total joint replacements in vivo, and it may be possible to detect motion before there is clinical or radiographic evidence of loosening. The study may become an important adjunct in the postoperative management of patients with total joint replacements. Measured reversible displacement was observed in three fourths of the present cases, while only 10% of patients had clinical loosening. Resolution of reversible displacement seems to have occurred in some cases.

▶ [This article may be a very important contribution. Absolute, immobile fixation following cementing of knee and hip prostheses is obviously not possible because of the elasticity of bone trabeculae, and this explains minimal amounts of reversible displacement. If increased reversible displacement occurs, the authors postulate that it may in time lead to clinical loosening. The key then would be to stress the trabecular bone just enough to stimulate remodeling and subsequent femoral fixation, but not to overstress it to produce trabecular necrosis and loosening. Just how we accomplish this is still unanswered.

If these studies could be applied to femoral components with and without calcar collars, then the dispute between those who use calcar collar abutment (Harris et al.) and those who do not (Ling et al.) might be partially resolved. This would imply not only measuring the amount of subsidence following total hip arthroplasty, but finding just when that subsidence occurs following surgery. Does it, indeed, stop at a certain point as the noncalcar collar advocates have shown clinically? While these studies would take a good deal more time and effort on the part of the orthopedist and his patient, continuation of this interesting research seems indicated.—Ed.] ◀

4–11 **The Synovial-like Membrane at the Bone-Cement Interface in Loose Total Hip Replacements and Its Proposed Role in Bone Lysis.** A zone of radiolucency is observed at the cement-bone interface on the femoral side in more than half of total hip replacements in patients followed up for less than 10 years and on the acetabular side in one fourth of the patients followed up for 12 to 15 years. Steven R. Goldring, Alan L. Schiller, Merrilee Roelke, Carol M. Rourke, Donald A. O'Neill, and William H. Harris (Boston) examined the membrane present at the bone-cement interface in 20 patients with a loose, failed but nonseptic total hip replacement. Specimens were obtained during revision operation from sites remote from the pseudocapsule that reformed postoperatively. Both organ culture and cell culture studies were done. The membrane was assessed histologically and histochemically, and its ability to synthesize prostaglandin E_2 and collagenase was determined.

The membrane consisted of a synovial-like layer of lining cells at the cement surface, sheets of histiocytes and giant cells centrally, and a fibrous layer blending into bone. Inflammatory cells were absent. The large polygonal cells at the cement surface often had eccentric nuclei polarized away from the surface. Mitoses were not noted. Cell cultures contained stellate cells similar to those found in cultures of normal and rheumatoid synovial tissue. The membrane had the capacity to produce prostaglandin E_2 and collagenase in large amounts.

A membrane having histologic and histochemical features of synovium is present at the cement-bone interface in patients with loosening of prosthetic components after total hip replacement. The membrane can produce significant amounts of prostaglandin E_2 and collagenase, which may mediate the resorption of bone and other connective tissues. Studies of the effects of biomaterials and pharmacologic agents on the resorptive capacity of the synovial-like membrane might be of interest.

▶ [This is an important paper for those who perform total hip replacement. Similar findings have not been confirmed in total knee replacement, but they probably do apply. It is important to realize that similar membranes and similar scalloping effects have been found around the femoral endoprostheses that we have previously used without methylmethacrylate. Thus, the methylmethacrylate is not the only factor involved in producing this synovial-like tissue. Whether we will find anything similar in the porous-coated stems now being employed is questionable. Certainly, motion seemed to be the common denominator. If porous-coated prostheses are motionless, we should not expect to find the synovial interfaced between the femoral stem and bone.—Ed.] ◀

4–12 **Indium-111 Leukocyte Scanning in Evaluation of Painful Hip Arthroplasty.** The evaluation of patients with a painful hip arthroplasty can be a difficult diagnostic problem. L'Ah. Mulamba, A. Ferrant, N. Leners, P. de Nayer, J. J. Rombouts, and A. Vincent (Univ. of Louvain) performed scintigraphy with ^{111}In-labeled leukocytes in 30 patients who required reexploration after hip arthroplasty because of pain. The 15 men and 15 women had a mean age of 60 years. Twenty-one patients had had total hip replacement, usually by the Charnley procedure, 4 had had a Moore hemiarthroplasty, and 5 had had a cup arthroplasty. The mean interval without pain was 11

(4–12) Acta Orthop. Scand. 54:695–697, October 1983.

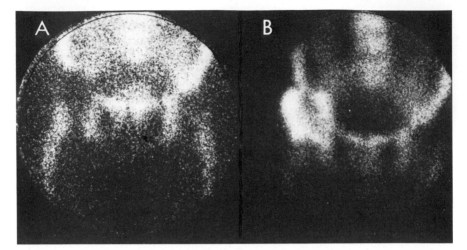

Fig 4–4.—Scintigraphy for diagnosis of infected hip arthroplasty. Patient had pain after prosthetic arthroplasty of right hip. **A,** ^{99m}Tc-sulfur colloid scan showed no uptake in right acetabulum. **B,** there was marked uptake of ^{111}In-leukocytes in regions of greater and lesser trochanters and in acetabulum of right hip. (Courtesy of Mulamba, L'Ah., et al.: Acta Orthop. Scand. 54:695–697, October 1983.)

months. The reticuloendothelial system was imaged with ^{99m}Tc-sulfur colloid at the time of leukocyte labeling.

All 12 patients with abnormal ^{111}In-leukocyte scans had organisms grown from material taken from the hip. Isolation of *Staphylococcus epidermidis* was most frequent. Preoperative hip aspiration did not yield organisms in 4 of these patients. Uptake was abnormal in the region of the false capsule and the top of the femoral shaft in 6 patients, around the greater trochanter (Fig 4–4) in 4, and in the lower shaft in 2. Only 1 of the 18 patients with normal leukocyte scans had positive bacteriologic cultures. A thick-walled abscess containing *Escherichia coli* was present in this patient.

Scintigraphy with ^{111}In-labeled leukocytes is a highly specific and sensitive means of detecting infection in patients undergoing hip arthroplasty and is recommended for patients who report pain after arthroplasty. Although normal results could be obtained in patients with impaired chemotaxis or abnormal results in patients with aseptic inflammatory disorders, no abnormal uptake not due to infection was observed in this series.

▶ [In our experience, ^{111}In autologous white blood cell scintigraphy has proven to be efficacious. It certainly should replace the old techniques of differential ^{99m}Tc-methylene diphosphonate and gallium-67 scintigraphy. In a recent prospective study comparing these two techniques, Merkel and colleagues found that sequential technetium-gallium imaging had a sensitivity of 48%, a specificity of 86%, and an accuracy of 57%. In contrast, ^{111}In-labeled leukocyte scintigraphy had a sensitivity of 83%, a specificity of 86%, and an accuracy of 88%. These differences were found to be statistically significant. When patients with a painful hip prosthesis were evaluated, the accuracy of indium scintigraphy was 94% compared to 75% with sequential technetium-gallium scanning.

I believe that the current technology necessitates an ^{111}In-leukocyte image in patients with painful prostheses.—R.H. Fitzgerald, Jr.] ◄

4-13 **Incorporation of Bone Graft Covered With Methylmethacrylate Onto Acetabular Wall: An Experimental Study.** A deficiency in the medial acetabular wall is a serious problem at replacement arthroplasty of the hip. Moshe Roffman, Michael Silbermann, and David G. Mendes (Haifa, Israel) examined the outcome of bone grafts covered with methylmethacrylate cement in deficient acetabular walls in a canine model. A Girdlestone operation was carried out through resection of the femoral head. The acetabular cartilage was removed, and a burst fracture of the medial acetabular wall was created by using a gouge. A Silastic sheet then was placed between the fragments, and grafts of corticocancellous bone chips from the resected femoral head were placed over the Silastic and adjacent bone before filling the acetabulum with polymethylmethacrylate bone cement. The cement covered the entire layer of bone grafts. The animals were killed after 6 or 10 months.

All dogs were able to bear full weight by the second week after operation, with nearly normal range of motion in most instances. Bony union between the bone grafts and acetabular wall was documented roentgenographically after 6 months. The grafts appeared viable microscopically, and highly developed strands of new bone were seen extending from the compact lamellar bone of the acetabulum toward the spongier bone of the grafts. The peripheral surfaces and marrow spaces of the grafts were lined with well-developed osteoblasts. Evidence of osteoid formation beneath the osteoblasts also was obtained. Osteoclasts were a consistent feature. The grafts had induced new bone formation as an osseous network within the connective tissue surrounding the implants. More extensive replacement of fibrous tissue by new bone was seen at 10 months.

This acetabular model would seem to be useful in assessing possible graft procedures because it promotes the acceptance of autogenous grafts and the induction of new bone. Efficient repair takes place even when a foreign material such as methylmethacrylate cement is present. Similar changes may be expected in the clinical setting.

▶ [This study substantiates the clinical experience which showed that both superior and central grafts for supplementing deficient acetabula almost invariably incorporate and act in exactly the way that they are intended. This experimental study in dogs confirms that even though the graft is covered on one surface with methylmethacrylate, it will proceed to incorporate.

I have personally never seen a graft I have placed centrally for protrusio not show every evidence of incorporation and vascularization. The same is true of grafts placed superolaterally in the dysplastic actabulum, providing there is good bone to bone

(4–13) Acta Orthop. Scand. 54:580–583, August 1983.

contact superomedially. Cement on the other surface does not seem to adversely affect the revascularization of the bone graft.

Scanning would give us additional data, but a bone scan in this area is unreliable at present. Perhaps in the future better definition can be obtained.—Ed.] ◄

4–14 **Hip Arthroplasty in Patients With Tabetic Charcot Joints.** Disabling pain can result from Charcot arthropathy of the hip secondary to tabes dorsalis, but many surgeons consider the condition to be an absolute contraindication to replacement arthroplasty. Tobin N. Gerhart and Richard D. Scott (Boston) reviewed the results of 10 hip operations in 7 patients with Charcot arthropathy secondary to tabes dorsalis. Three total hip replacements, 3 cemented Moore prostheses, 2 cup arthroplasties, 1 girdlestone procedure, and 1 fusion were carried out. The average patient age at the time of surgery was 61 years. All patients but 1 had significant pain as the chief preoperative symptom. All patients but 1 had begun treatment for syphilis at least 5 years before admission for hip surgery. Six hips were the source of acute symptoms related to subcapital fracture, while 4 were chronically symptomatic and exhibited dissolution of the femoral head. Five patients had clinically significant neuroarthropathic changes involving more than 1 joint.

Six hips were free of pain on long-term follow-up, and no patient had more pain than before the operation. Walking ability did not improve significantly, and muscle power and average motion decreased slightly. Instability was a major presenting feature, and did not improve significantly in most cases. Although orthopedists rated all the hips as poor results or failures at follow-up, all patients except those who had total hip replacement considered themselves much improved because of surgery. Two patients were entirely satisfied with the outcome. Dissatisfaction resulted from a lack of hip stability and the inability to bear weight without support.

Pain is not a favorable prognostic sign when considering arthroplasty in a tabetic Charcot hip. The main cause of poor operative results in this series was instability. All 3 total hip replacements led to chronic dislocation. The combination of debridement and resection arthroplasty is an alternative to prosthetic arthroplasty. Resection arthroplasty with complete capsulectomy and synovectomy may be the best procedure for patients with a painful Charcot hip secondary to tabes dorsalis.

▶ [The one patient with tabes dorsalis and a Charcot joint, which I personally cared for, had a similarly poor outcome.—D.J. Pritchard] ◄

4–15 **Fractures of the Distal End of the Femur Below Hip Implants in Elderly Patients: Treatment with the Zickel Supracondylar Device.** A hip implant proximal to a distal femoral fracture limits the choice of treatments, and osteoporosis in elderly patients further

(4–14) Orthopedics 6:179–183, February 1983.
(4–15) J. Bone Joint Surg. [Am.] 65-A:491–494, April 1983.

complicates the situation. Gary J. Clancey, Robert F. Smith, and Malcolm B. Madenwald (Mount Vernon, Wash.) used the Zickel supracondylar device to treat 4 elderly patients with a distal femoral fracture below an existing noncemented hip implant. They were among 416 cases of femoral fracture seen in a 4-year period. All fractures were low-energy injuries sustained in a fall. Two patients had a sliding hip screw appliance in place, 1 had an Austin Moore prosthesis, and 1 had a fixed nail plate. A closed intramedullary technique was used. The rods were inserted under fluoroscopic control without exposure of the fracture site. Large-sized intramedullary rods were used in 2 patients and medium-sized rods in the other 2. Unrestricted weight-bearing was allowed after 6 weeks.

All the fractures healed with some shortening but no rotatory or angular malalignment. There were no infectious or thromboembolic complications. None of the retained devices caused knee symptoms. The 3 patients living a year after operation had 110 to 135 degrees of knee flexion. All had resumed their prefracture activity levels. A patient who died 9 months postoperatively had resumed independent walking before her death, but she still required walking aids that had not been necessary before the fracture.

Use of the Zickel supracondylar device was uniformly successful in these cases of distal femoral fracture below a hip implant. This method is recommended if the fracture is not comminuted and the implant does not obstruct the femoral canal enough to prevent passage of intramedullary rods. Although Zickel rods are less flexible than Ender nails and require more careful maneuvering, the procedure is relatively easy and is uncomplicated.

▶ [This paper points out yet another method of treating this unusual, but often serious complication following total hip arthroplasty. The use of Rush nails and Ender's pins is a comparable method and gives excellent results. The Zickel device might be most appropriate in the very osteoporotic patient, for it gives better anchorage distally in the intercondylar region of the femur.—Ed.] ◀

4–16 **Passive Joint Position Sense After Total Hip Replacement Surgery.** Percy N. Karanjia and John H. Ferguson (Cleveland) studied 10 patients having total hip joint replacement to determine whether extracapsular mechanisms for joint position sense exist. Five patients had been operated on in the past 2–4 weeks, and the others within 2 years before the study. Most had been operated on for osteoarthritis. The procedure included total replacement of the joint surfaces, ligamentectomy, and capsulectomy. A cup-and-stem prosthesis was placed. Tests were done with a potentiometer, with the test limb encased in a pneumatic splint to prevent knee joint motion. The limb was manually flexed or extended through 0.5 degree at a rate of either 0.6 degree per second or 2 degrees per second, with the hip in

(4–16) Ann. Neurol. 13:654–657, June 1983.

10–15 degrees of flexion or extension or 45–50 degrees of flexion. The side that was not operated on was used as a control.

Barely significant errors on the side operated on were detected at 0.6 degree per second, but not at 2 degrees per second. No significant differences were associated with the various hip positions. With the limb flexed 10–15 degrees, 8 of 10 subjects were able to detect the direction of movement at 2 degrees per second 19 of 20 times on both sides. With the leg extended 10–15 degrees, all subjects detected the direction of movement at least 18 of 20 times.

The ability to detect passive hip joint position remains largely, though not completely, intact after hip joint replacement. Capsulectomy was surgically complete in all the present cases, and it is unlikely that joint receptors remained. The velocity of angular displacement seems important in the ability to perceive joint position. The joint capsule, ligaments, and joint surfaces may provide some limb motion and position information, but its absence is not clinically apparent, and these structures are not essential for kinesthesia.

▶ [Because of the very slight decline in passive joint position sense noted after total hip replacement surgery, the authors have concluded that there is support for the idea that there are extracapsular mechanisms responsible for joint kinesthesia. This may very well be true. However, they have assumed that there was a complete capsulectomy performed at the time of surgery. It should be pointed out that this is rarely the case. In most instances of total joint replacement, there is no attempt to completely remove the joint capsule. Even when a surgeon does attempt complete removal of the capsule, he is rarely successful and a good portion of the inferior capsule frequently remains.—R.N. Stauffer] ◀

4–17 **Lumbar Spinal Stenosis and Total Hip Replacement.** The association of hip pathology and spinal lesions is well known in the orthopedic field, along with spinal distress associated with excessive flexion of the hip caused by ankylosis or of tubercular origin, or congenital high posterior luxation. J. Y. de la Caffinière and J. Rocolle (Luxembourg) focus attention on the misleading clinical aspects of arthrosis of the lumbar spine, which is frequently seen in elderly patients, in whom indication for total hip replacement is common. The painful symptoms of a coxarthrosis may well be mistaken for radicular involvement—a confusion which could lead to errors in treatment.

In a series of 80 patients operated on for lumbar spinal stenosis between 1977 and 1982, there were 11 instances in which symptoms related to arthrosis of the hip and treated by total hip replacement were associated with root involvement due to lumbar spinal stenosis of degenerative origin.

Four situations were described which the orthopedic surgeon may encounter: (1) undetected arthrosis of the lumbar spine, loosened hip prosthesis; (2) arthrosis of the spine, stable prosthesis; (3) symptomatic coxarthrosis after surgical treatment of the lumbar spine; and

(4–17) Rev. Chir. Orthop. 69:323–331, 1983.

(4) an association of hip pathologic conditions and spinal lesions. Faced with a total hip replacement associated with pain of the lower extremity, and in the absence of obvious signs of loosening, lumbar arthrosis must be considered, particularly if there is no authentic limp. All these observations stress the importance of the surgeon's ability to differentiate the source of pain.

Differentiation might be easily accomplished in cases of bilateral neurogenic lameness or when the radicular discomfort originates in a topographically identifiable area. It becomes a delicate matter in the face of pain which does not exceed beyond the knee, be it anterior or posterior. Nevertheless, its descending character, and above all its nocturnal manifestation, should give rise to more elaborate exploration than simple profile films of the lumbar spine. A stenosis of the lateral portion of the lumbar spine, which often escapes detection, may be discovered.

▶ [This is a very timely reminder to the orthopedist that the association of degenerative arthrosis of the lumbar spine and spinal stenosis with degenerative disease in the hips is indeed common, and the differential diagnosis as to the source of the pain is not easy. All of us who perform hip surgery have been faced with the same problem. Certainly, if there is degenerative arthritis of the hip which is proved radiographically and clinically, it may be best in certain instances to do the total hip arthroplasty and observe the symptomatic results. A thorough neurologic examination, electromyography, probably computed tomography scanning of the spine, and occasionally myelography should precede any total hip arthroplasty, however, when symptoms suggest.—Ed.] ◀

4–18 **Reattachment of the Greater Trochanter: Use of the Trochanter Cable Grip System** is described by Desmond M. Dall and Anthony W. Miles (Cape Town, South Africa). Monofilament wiring is most often used to reattach the greater trochanter after osteotomy, but multifilament cable is more suitable. This material is versatile and easy to work with, and it has mechanical properties superior to those of monofilament wire. A "cable grip" system has been developed for using multifilament cable to reattach the greater trochanter.

The grip is an H-shaped device with two transverse bridges. Proximal hooks engage the superior crest of the trochanter, while distal teeth provide positive location of the grip. Two horizontal cables are located through drill holes in the femur close to the osteotomy surface. These cables are looped inside the femoral canal and allowed to set in the femoral cement. After being passed through the bridges and tensioning, they are fastened by crimping the bridges. Bench tests showed considerably less vertical and anteroposterior movement with the trochanter cable grip system and the Charnley staple clamp combined with the 3-wire technique than with the 2- and 3-wire techniques.

The trochanter cable grip system was used in 321 hips that have

(4–18)   J. Bone Joint Surg. [Br.] 65-B:55–59, January 1983.

been followed up 6 months or longer. Presently two horizontal cables 1.6 or 2 mm in diameter are used (the latter in technically difficult cases or heavy patients). Nearly 95% of hips treated with the current technique were united in perfect position. Many of these hips showed firm bony union at 2 months. The incidence of detachment has declined to 1.5% and that of cable breakage to 3.1%. The system was used in 22 cases of surface replacement arthroplasty, with perfect results in all cases.

Rehabilitation of patients with total hip replacement has been vigorous with most patients beginning mobilization on the second postoperative day and being allowed full weight-bearing with canes or a crutch support for balance.

Reattachment of the greater trochanter after osteotomy by using the cable grip system gives excellent results, with low rates of both detachment and cable breakage.

▶ [The authors have presented an excellent report on their method of using multifilament stainless steel wires for reattachment of the greater trochanter following osteotomy. The evolution of their technique is presented. By using heavier cables and for about 2 months following surgery limiting stress with canes or crutches, i.e., partial weight bearing, their success rate showed a 94.6% union in perfect position and a nonunion rate of only 1.5%. Cable breakage was 3.1%, and it is interesting that no cables were observed to break following bony union. This is in contrast to the monofilament wire methods where wire breakage is frequently seen late after union, presumably due to the difference in modulus of elasticity between monofilament wire and bone. Presumably multifilament wire cable has more of the elasticity of bone.

We have modified our original technique of using a looped tension wire to include the anterior-posterior forces which are strong or greater than the vertical ones, and thus, use an additional circumferential wire loop in an anterior-posterior or horizontal direction. With this technique and with protection for 1 to 2 months, depending on the state of the x-ray at that time, our nonunion rate has dropped drastically.

I have always opposed the introduction of trochanter wires into the medullary cavity, feeling that this produces one more problem with possible loosening or reconstruction if loosening does occur. Yet, in this series it hasn't seemed to pose a problem.

This has proven to be a valuable way of reattaching the trochanter. It should be considered by those who are displeased with their present methods.—Ed.] ◀

4–19   **Contrast Bone Cement.** Certain problems in both initial and revision hip arthroplasty might be solved to some extent if the cement could be distinguished visually from surrounding bone and soft tissues. William L. Bargar, Kingsbury G. Heiple, Stephen Weber, Stanley A. Brown, Richard H. Brown, and Geoff Kotzar examined the value of adding aqueous methylene blue dye to acrylic bone cement. A 1-cc volume of dye solution was added to standard 40-gm packs of Simplex-P (Radiopaque), Zimmer bone cement, and Zimmer LVC bone cement. Biocompatibility studies were done in a rabbit model in which cement was placed in the proximal tibia or used in a paraspinal muscle implant.

(4–19) J. Orthop. Res. 1:92–100, 1983.

The total amount of dye leached out was less than 1.8% for all 3 cements tested. Occasional macrophages were seen in the rabbit tissues, but there was no inflammatory response (Fig 4–5). Tension, compression, and 3-point and 4-point bending strengths were not altered significantly, apart from a slight rise in 4-point bending strength for contrast Zimer (regular) bone cement. Dough, set, and working times were reduced by 30–150 seconds. All of the contrast cements met ASTM F451 intrusion standards. Viscosity increased more rapidly for the contrast cements, but remained sufficiently low early after mixing to permit good penetration of bone. Easy removal was demonstrated in revision of cemented femoral total hip components in synthetic and cadaver femurs and in debridement of cement particles from a soft tissue background coated with blood (Fig 4–6).

Contrast bone cement appears to be effective and safe for use in initial total joint replacement surgery and in revision surgery. Working times are reduced, however, thus its use is recommended only for

Fig 4–5.—Section of tissue at cement-bone interface. **Left,** white cement is used; **right,** contrast cement is used. No qualitative differences are apparent. Hematoxylin-eosin, ×2.1. (Courtesy of Bargar, W.L., et al.: J. Orthop. Res. 1:92–100, 1983.)

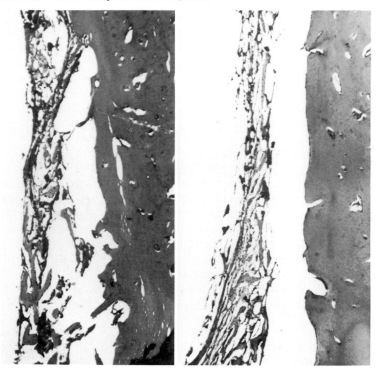

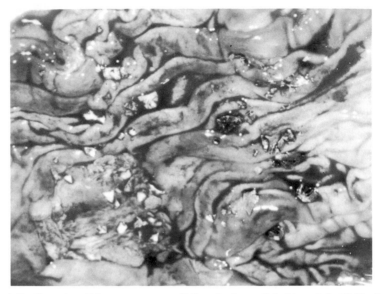

Fig 4–6.—Cement particles are seen on a soft tissue background that is coated with blood; white cement particles on left and contrast cement particles on right. Contrast cement particles are easily visualized. (Courtesy of Bargar, W.L., et al.: J. Orthop. Res. 1:92–100, 1983.)

experienced surgeons. Contrast cement containing methylene blue dye appears to be biocompatible and strong.

▶ [The addition of aqueous methylene blue dye to a standard package of acrylic bone cement is certainly helpful should removal of the polymerized acrylic bone cement be necessary. This is especially true in the presence of a deep infection where complete removal of all polymethyl methacrylate enhances the surgeon's ability to eradicate the infection and more safely reconstruct the hip at a later date.

The authors demonstrate the biocompatibility of the addition of aqueous methylene blue dye to acrylic bone cement. Furthermore, they demonstrate that the mechanical strength of the cement is not significantly altered by the addition of the dye.

In summary, this is a technique that should be adopted on a routine basis when acrylic bone cement is utilized in the operating room.—R.H. Fitzgerald, Jr.] ◀

4–20 **Dislocations in Charnley and Modified Charnley Low-Friction Arthroplasty.** S. André, P. Feuilhade de Chauvin, F. Tiberi, and M. Postel (Paris) reviewed 82 cases of dislocation (1.7%) among 4,833 total hip prostheses of the Charnley or modified Charnley type. Fifty-six cases were recurrent dislocations. Causative factors included malposition of prosthetic components, leverage from ossification or hypertrophic synovium, and nonunion after division of the greater trochanter. No cause other than muscle atrophy was apparent in 17 cases. Average patient age was 65 years. About one fourth of patients had had previous intervention. The only complications were transient

(4–20) Rev. Chir. Orthop. 69:447–453, 1983.

sciatic nerve paralysis and a postoperative hematoma. Manual reduction was carried out in most instances, always with general anesthesia and radiologic control. The prosthetic head must be directly concentric with the socket. Traction-suspension was sometimes necessary for a few days, but not for a prolonged period. All patients with malposition causing dislocation have had good architectural results. The most troublesome cases have been those with no apparent specific cause for dislocation.

Muscular deficiency may be the basic cause of prosthetic instability after hip replacement. Old age, intercurrent illness, and repeated operations on the hip may all exacerbate the deficiency. Dislocations can be minimized by insuring the correct position of prosthetic components, suppressing anterior cam effects, and providing a solid synthesis of the greater trochanter. Simple precautions can help prevent dislocations in patients recently operated on. A patient with an initial dislocation is rarely treated surgically, since many cases do not recur. Traction is not always necessary. Readaptation at a rehabilitation center is helpful in preventing recurrences. Reintervention is indicated if further dislocations occur and a mechanical cause is identified.

▶ [The experience of the authors is somewhat similar to the one reported from our own institution by Woo and Morrey (*J. Bone Joint Surg.* [Am.] 64-A:1295–1306, 1982) who found that in previous surgery about the hip, the use of the posterior approach and failure of union of the trochanteric osteotomy increased the risk of instability of the hip postoperatively. In the present study, the approach did not seem to affect adversely the incidence of dislocation, but the presence of previous surgery as well as the pseudarthrosis of the greater trochanter did. In this paper, I found the paragraphs on recurrent dislocations without apparent cause interesting. I suspect many of these dislocations are related to alterations in the myofascial tension which would be very difficult to discover. But I am certain that even with the most perfect surgical technique there is a minimum incidence of dislocation that cannot be lowered.

In this study, two thirds of the dislocations became recurrent. Woo and Morrey found only that one third of the dislocated hips developed recurrent dislocation. In both studies, the early dislocation occurring before 3 months had a greater chance of being a unique episode without recurrence than a dislocation occurring late, presumably because late dislocations are related to myofascial factors more difficult to control.

We disagree with the authors in the management of the unique dislocation. Certainly the dislocations that occur perioperatively can be handled with simple measures, particularly if one has determined that the position of the components is satisfactory. However, the dislocation occurring past 3 months should probably be followed by protection, prolonged by enough time to allow the stretched or torn neocapsule to heal satisfactorily. We have utilized hip-thigh braces (a thigh lacer connected to a pelvic band through a lateral single hinge at the hip holding the thigh in slight abduction). Indeed, we have utilized this type of brace routinely in the postoperative management of certain revision hip surgeries.—M.E. Cabanela] ◀

4–21 **Prevention of Acetabular Erosion After Hemiarthroplasty for Fractured Neck of Femur.** Many consider replacement hemiarthroplasty to be the best approach to older patients with a fractured fem-

(4–21) J. Bone Joint Surg. [Br.] 65-B:548–551, November 1983.

oral neck because it permits immediate walking on a stable, painless hip. The outcome, however, can be compromised when the metal prosthetic head erodes upward into the acetabulum. Michael Devas and Barry Hinves (Hastings, England) evaluated the Hastings hip, a new bipolar prosthesis with a dynamic, self-aligning outer head. The concentric, double-articulated prosthesis was designed to eliminate acetabular erosion. A buffered impact is obtained by an 8-mm thickness of high-density polyethylene covered by a steel shell 2 mm thick. The cup moves with weight-bearing to keep the thinnest part in the line of force through the hip.

Review was made of 161 procedures done for femoral neck fracture or resultant problems. The 146 women and 15 men had an average age of 78 years. Results were excellent in 59 of the 97 hips followed for a year or longer. These hips flexed more than 90 degrees, with no pain or limp when one cane was used. Another 11 hips had good results, 16 had fair results, and 6 had unsatisfactory outcomes. Five dislocations occurred; 2 were in patients in whom prototype prostheses were placed. No erosion occurred in any hip.

Acetabular erosion has not occurred in elderly patients who have had hemiarthroplasty with the Hastings hip for femoral neck fracture. The hips have been as comfortable as after a Thompson or Austin Moore replacement, and hip motion has, in general, been better.

▶ [We have had a very similar experience with two comparable series of patients, one treated with a Thompson prosthesis and the other with a Bateman bipolar prosthesis. The patients with the Bateman prosthesis did better overall. However, in the elderly and relatively inactive patient, the Thompson prosthesis proved to be a very satisfactory solution for the displaced femoral neck fracture. Younger patients who place more demands on their hips did better with the bipolar design. This was particularly true of the patients with avascular necrosis, where the Thompson prosthesis produced a very high rate (88%) of failures whereas the Bateman design yielded 80% of satisfactory results.—M.E. Cabanela] ◀

4–22 **Femoral Head Prosthesis With a Built-in Joint: Radiologic Study of the Movements of the Two Components.** G. H. M. Verberne (Rotterdam) evaluated 20 patients who had primary implantation of the Variokopf prosthesis for intracapsular fracture of the femoral neck. All were older than age 70 years and had displaced fractures. The ball-and-socket prosthesis was implanted via an anterior approach. The femoral component was fixed with acrylic cement. Mobilization and weight-bearing were encouraged as soon as the wound allowed, usually within 3 days of operation. The prosthesis consists of a nonfenestrating femoral component articulating through a ball head with a headpiece made of high-density polyethylene covered by a metal shell.

Mean age at operation was 83 years. The built-in joint soon lost mobility and was almost completely stiff 3 months after operation.

(4–22) J. Bone Joint Surg. [Br.] 65-B:544–547, November 1983.

Only the difference in abduction movement between the first and the third month was significant. Fifteen patients walked independently with or without cane support a month after operation, and 16 did so at 3 months. Four patients had moderate pain a month after operation, and 9 reported pain at 3 months.

Hemiarthroplasty has a definite place in the treatment of intracapsular femoral neck fractures, but there seems to be little if any advantage in use of a prosthesis with an inner bearing. Such joints cannot be expected to prevent the acetabular erosion that can follow femoral head replacement for fracture of the femoral neck. Conversion to a total hip arthroplasty may be difficult.

▶ [This is a rather controversial topic. One of the claimed advantages of the bipolar endoprosthesis, as mentioned here, is the prevention of acetabular erosion by allowing some of the stress to be dissipated into the inner joint. It should follow, therefore, that if the inner joint does not move as apparently proved in this paper, then acetabular wear should occur essentially the same as it does with conventional solid femoral head prostheses. This is fortunately not true. In our experience as well as in the experience of many others, the clinical results that one can expect with bipolar endoprostheses, particularly when done for fractures, are better than those occurring with conventional Moore or Thompson prostheses. These could be related not only to the presence of motion at the inner bearing, but to the cushioning effect of the inner bearing material itself.

The question whether motion at the inner bearing occurs or not has been addressed by several investigators. Bateman found that in the patients he has studied with his prosthesis (22 mm inner bearing), motion is always present at the inner bearing on weightbearing. Chen et al., studying the Monk prosthesis (25 mm inner bearing), had similar findings. Krein, in a study of a group of 17 hips at our institution, found inner bearing motion present but variable in all cases. Thus, we have no question that motion occurs at the inner bearing particularly with the small sized heads (22 to 26 mm). The apparent discrepancies shown by the results observed in this series might be due to the large size of the inner bearing utilized by the Variokopf prosthesis. The most important factor in promoting motion at the inner bearing in preference to the outer bearing is the lesser amount of friction in the former. This differential between outer bearing and inner bearing friction is maximized in favor of the inner bearing by the smaller size heads. Thus, the use of a 32 mm inner head would decrease the chance of inner bearing motion.—M.E. Cabanela] ◀

4–23 **Total Articular Resurfacing Arthroplasty: Analysis of Component Failure in Sixty-Seven Hips.** Initial reports on surface replacement arthroplasty of the hip were encouraging, but longer follow-up has indicated a high rate of failure. William C. Head (Dallas) reviewed the outcome of total articular resurfacing arthroplasty with the Tara device performed on 67 hips of 63 patients between 1978 and 1981. The most common diagnoses were osteoarthritis and avascular necrosis. Only patients with radiographic evidence of good bone stock had the operation, and younger patients were considered good candidates. The average age at operation was 49 years. Use of the Tara prosthesis in patients aged 60 and older was based chiefly on their activity level.

(4–23) J. Bone Joint Surg. [Am.] 66-A:28–34, January 1984.

The average follow-up was 3.3 years. Most hips were operated on by an anterolateral approach without trochanteric osteotomy. There were no postoperative wound infections. No patient had a reduced range of motion, and only 1 had heterotopic bone formation, without pain or impaired motion. Loosening of the femoral component in 1 hip was caused by a technical error. The acetabular component loosened in 7 hips, all but 1 of which were revised to conventional hip replacement without problems. The findings in 1 of these patients are shown in Figure 4–7. The rate of impending failure, with radio-

Fig 4–7.—X-ray views of hips in patient with osteoarthritis. **A,** 2 months postoperatively. **B,** 26 months postoperatively. There is loss of bone stock in the inferior part of the femoral neck owing to impingement of the stem on the medial aspect of the cortex. The acetabular component is separated at the bone-cement interface, with loss of screw fixation. Some subsidence is apparent on the femoral side. (Courtesy of Head, W.C.: J. Bone Joint Surg. [Am.] 66-A:28–34, January 1984.)

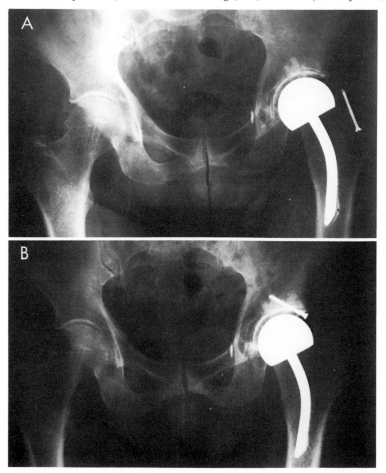

graphic evidence of component failure but not significant pain, was 22.4%. The expected total failure rate is 34.3%.

The results obtained with the Tara prosthesis seem less encouraging as the length of follow-up increases. The present results are comparable to those reported with other types of surface replacement procedures for which longer follow-ups are available. Actual and potential failure has occurred in about a third of the patients. The femoral side of the arthroplasty appears to be generally sound, but the acetabular side is highly suspect. The problems of excessive loss of acetabular bone stock from the larger component, poor distribution of cement, and micromotion at the bone-cement interface must be solved if this approach is to remain viable.

▶ [This report of the so-called Tara resurfacing arthroplasty is the first that uses a large patient number, namely, 67 hips. There was an actual failure rate of 11.9% and an impending failure rate of 22.4% for a 34.3% total failure rate. These patients were followed from 2½ to 3½ years after surgery.

The author is pessimistic about this operation. The main reason for the possible failure is the large size of the head necessitating a large acetabulum with increased frictional forces, thus predisposing to loosening of the acetabular component. This is the major complication. This is another operation designed to replace total hip arthroplasty in the younger patient. It seems to be going the way of the other resurfacing procedures.—Ed.] ◀

5. The Hip

5-1 **Osteoarthritis of the Hip Treated by Intertrochanteric Osteotomy: Long-Term Follow-Up.** Astor Reigstad and Tore Grønmark (Oslo) used the simple medial displacement technique of intertrochanteric osteotomy to treat 103 osteoarthritis hips in 101 patients between 1966 and 1973. Two thirds of the patients were women, and the mean age was 58 years. No significant rotation, extension, or flexion was produced during the osteotomy. No tenotomy or myotomy was performed. Physiotherapy was given for a variable period after surgery. The mean follow-up was 12½ years.

Complications included fatal pulmonary embolism and nonunion requiring reoperation. Overall, 70% of operations had good results a year postoperatively and another 11% had some effect. Some benefit was apparent in 51% of hips after 5 years and in 30% after 10 years. The proportion of patients having total hip replacement or arthrodesis was 24% at 5 years and 42% at 10 years. Regression of osteoarthritis after osteotomy was observed in 12 hips, whereas deterioration occurred in 67 hips during follow-up. The only combination of factors significantly associated with outcome was a preoperative femoral neck-shaft angle exceeding 120 degrees and an operative medial displacement of the femoral shaft of 20 mm or more. Hips with a large neck-shaft angle appeared to do better after osteotomy.

The clinical effects of intertrochanteric osteotomy are unpredictable and less enduring than previously thought. It would appear that the operation is indicated for younger patients because pain relief and functional results compare unfavorably with those obtained with total hip replacement in patients with osteoarthritis of the hip. The correlation noted between regression of arthritis changes and pain relief in this and other series may indicate that, in some patients, the osteotomy can repair the joint.

▶ [It is interesting that after all these years here is a report on McMurray osteotomy. This operation was used for most any patient with osteoarthritis with little or no specific indications regarding the type of osteoarthritic involvement. It was a medial displacement procedure, usually with varus, although in this report some patients had a valgus osteotomy.

This series is a potpourri, and tells us very little about specific indications for a specific osteotomy. We have progressed far beyond "one operation for all patients with osteoarthritis." Although Bombelli's writings, including his book, may be somewhat complicated to some readers, there are specific three-dimensional aspects of

(5–1)   J. Bone Joint Surg. [Am.] 66-A:1–6, January 1984.

osteotomy which must apply to each patient. All cannot be treated the same. Thus, I think the results of this study cannot be used to support or condemn the operation of intertrochanteric osteotomy. In my hands, with more specific detail regarding types of osteoarthritis, i.e., superolateral, medial, or inferomedial, degree of wedge, creation of varus or valgus and extension or flexion, the results have been far superior to the McMurray type which the authors have used (and which I used from 1954 to 1960). Nonetheless, in this series there was still a 30% benefit from the operation at 10 years. They concluded that more medial displacement of the femoral shaft improved the long-term result and that varus osteotomies fared better than valgus. But an individual breakdown of each patient was not made, which would be the only way to tell the value of these conclusions.—Ed.] ◀

5–2   **Complications of Intertrochanteric Rotational Osteotomy.** Sugioka described an intertrochanteric anterior rotational osteotomy that reportedly arrests the progress of femoral head osteonecrosis and preserves enough bone stock for later femoral head replacement should this become necessary. Ethan M. Braunstein, Barbara N. Weissman, J. Leland Sosman, and Michael Drew (Harvard Med. School) reviewed the x-ray findings in 4 men, aged 20 to 49 years, who had idiopathic femoral head osteonecrosis or, in 1, disease secondary to high-dosage corticosteroid therapy. Alcohol was a possible contributing factor in 2 cases. Follow-up ranged from 12 to 30 months. One patient with a healed osteotomy continues to have some pain. Another has had progressive femoral head collapse on continued corticosteroid therapy. The third patient had nonunion of the osteotomy, and the fourth had revision to a bipolar endoprosthesis because of continued pain a year after initial operation.

Two patients had grade II changes preoperatively and 2 had more advanced changes. In all cases the necrotic segment of femoral head was rotated anteriorly on postoperative roentgenograms and was no longer weight-bearing. Three patients had union at the osteotomy site 6 months after operation. The patient with painful nonunion had sclerosis and a widened osteotomy gap. Further femoral head collapse was evident in 1 patient a year after operation.

The usefulness of this operation remains controversial, as these results suggest. Femoral osteotomy of any type has produced mixed results in cases of osteonecrosis or Perthes disease. Roentgenography is an accurate means of assessing intertrochanteric osteotomy. Progressive collapse of the femoral head is predictive of clinical failure, but the patient may worsen clinically even without x-ray progress of disease. The absence of x-ray changes assures a successful outcome.

▶ [In a series of 21 Sugioka osteotomies followed for 2 years, I have obtained less than satisfactory results in 9 patients. As mentioned in this paper, the operation is technically difficult and progression of the disease process and continued pain have been the cause of failure. Technetium bone scanning done preoperatively and serially postoperatively showed that further interruption of the blood supply to the femoral head had occurred after the operation in many of our patients. I am convinced that technically it is almost impossible to respect the posterior column artery of Sugioka

(5–2) Skeletal Radiol. 10:258–261, November 1983.

and affect a satisfactory rotation. Proper use of a compression hip screw supplemented by cancellous screws if necessary is essential to assure stability of the osteotomy. In all of our 21 cases, union was present by 10 weeks. We have temporarily stopped performing this procedure and are awaiting longer follow-up to assess the long-term results. But at the present time, I think it is unlikely that this operation will remain in the armamentarium of the orthopedic surgeon who deals with avascular necrosis of the femoral head.—M.E. Cabanela] ◄

5–3 **Chiari's Pelvic Osteotomy in Adults: Review of 68 Procedures.** Despite the impressive success of total hip replacement, indications for conservative surgery do persist, particularly for the sequelae of congenital dislocations. J. Le Saout, B. Kerboul, J. F. Roch, and B. Courtois (Brest, France) consider the Chiari osteotomy a valid solution when it is too late for a shelf procedure or when femoral osteotomy will apparently fail.

In terms of biomechanics (Fig 5–1) Chiari's procedure has a twofold aim; to increase the joint surface and to decrease the load by shortening the medial lever arm. In the present series the authors did not adhere to the original technique, but used a slightly wider approach for control of the osteotomy site. Fixation with 1 screw rendered cast immobilization unnecessary. The use of a fracture table appears essential in the adult; it allows better control of the chisel without the impeding edge of the standard table. Translation is the important stage. To relax traction completely, the foot is removed from the shoe of the orthopedic table; simple abduction is then sufficient to mobilize the bones without the need for local maneuvers. If anterior coverage of the head seems insufficient or the osteotomy appears too high, an anterior graft may be placed between the capsule and the upper fragment.

A total of 68 osteotomies were performed between 1968 and 1982

Fig 5–1.—Diagram showing forces at hip in a lateralized hip and after pelvic osteotomy of Chiari. (Courtesy of Le Saout, J., et al.: Ann. Orthop. Ouest 15:23–34, 1983.)

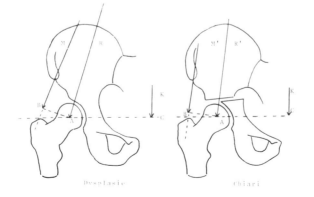

(5–3) Ann. Orthop. Ouest. 15:23–34, 1983.

(71% of patients were younger than 40 years); 59 patients were followed up for more than 5 years, all but 1 involving sequelae of congenital hip dislocation. A bone graft was added to supplement the pelvic shelf in 11 cases. A total of 61 patients with more than 1 year of follow-up were reviewed. Pain was completely absent in 32 patients; it occurred only occasionally in 21; 8 were unchanged, and 1 was aggravated. Motion was normal or quasi-normal in 43 cases; 11 had slight limitation of flexion, 6, severe limitation. Walking was normal in 34 patients; a slight limp was observed in 19, while 8 needed crutches. Most patients recovered normal muscle strength within 12 months, although a few patients were left with a slight limp for 18 to 24 months, mostly due to the shortening of the gluteus medius or upper displacement of the greater trochanter, or both. Radiographically, improvement was seen in 13.5%, the joint line was unchanged in 76%, and deterioration was observed in 10.5%.

Among factors influencing results, degenerative hip arthritis seemed most prominent. A uniformly narrow joint line promises a good result. However, severe narrowing limited to the upper part of the joint will almost always lead to failure. Technically the procedure is almost always feasible; the exception occurs in cases of extremely high dislocation, where the osteotomy would reach the sacroiliac joint, impeding all translation. A lateralized hip without degenerative signs has the best indication for success.

▶ [Alternatives to total hip replacement should always be considered in the treatment of osteoarthritis of the hip. Intertrochanteric osteotomy, and even occasionally arthrodesis, are perfectly feasible alternatives in certain patients.

This paper presents another alternative, that is, pelvic osteotomy a la Chiari, who described this procedure before his recent death. The authors carry through with their study of 68 operations (they mention 68 originally but list only 65 in the paper.) Fifty-nine patients had follow-up of more than 5 years. Confusing, however, is the fact that they have added a bone graft to supplement the pelvic shelf in 11 patients. Sixty-one patients with a follow-up of more than 1 year were analyzed as to results, with absence of pain in 32 and only slight pain in 21. There was an 85% improvement rate. Eight were unchanged and 1 was made worse. Ankylosis occurred spontaneously in 1 patient. There was no real change in motion otherwise. Radiographically, there was thought to be an improvement in 13.5% of cases with better joint line. Seventy-six percent had no change and 10% had deterioration.

This operation should be considered in patients in the younger age group, and indeed, the good results were found in those patients in their 30s. The authors concluded that the poor results correlated with the supralateral type of degenerative arthritis. When there was a more generalized type, the results were better. They also found that poor results were found more commonly when there was insufficient medial displacement.

I am personally not convinced that the Chiari osteotomy in the adult, even the young adult, is a good procedure, and I think we should wait for more evidence before it is performed in the usual osteoarthritis patient. The procedure does, of course, decrease the load on the hip by shortening the lever arm, and it does increase the total surface of the femoral head available for load. The possible indication for this procedure would most likely be in the patient with degenerative arthritis due to moderate dysplasia.—Ed.] ◀

5–4 **Anteversion of the Acetabulum and Femoral Neck in Normals and in Patients With Osteoarthritis of the Hip.** Increased anteversion of the femoral neck appears to be a factor predisposing to idiopathic osteoarthritis of the hip. Olav Reikerås, Ingjald Bjerkreim, and Alf Kolbenstvedt (Oslo) used computed tomography to measure anteversion of the acetabulum and its relation to anteversion of the femoral neck in 47 normal subjects of both sexes, aged 23 to 74 years, and 39 patients with idiopathic osteoarthritis of the hip. The 27 female and 12 male patients had a mean age of 65 years. All were disabled to the degree that operation was indicated and underwent intertrochanteric osteotomy or total hip replacement.

The anteversion angle of the femoral neck was significantly larger in patients with osteoarthritis than in normal subjects, whereas the collum femoris acetabulum angle was significantly smaller. The anteversion angles of the acetabulum did not differ significantly. The two anteversion angles were not correlated in normal subjects, and neither was correlated with age. Findings were comparable in the patients.

There normally is no correlation between the anteversion angle of the femoral neck and that of the acetabulum. An unfavorable relation between the two angles may contribute to osteoarthritis of the hip; the femoral anteversion angle is the important factor. The findings presumably reflect poor adaptation of the femoral head to the acetabulum.

▶ [We are continually being challenged as to the cause of degenerative arthritis of the hip. It does seem to be a systemic predisposition in certain individuals, for they show generalized degenerative changes in most of their joints, including the hip. In others, however, it seems rather localized to the hip and the usual attempts to define any biomechanical cause for the overload or incongruity are often unsuccessful. The opposite hip will sometimes help us in assessing the natural history, but often the two hips are involved to the same degree and thus there is no way of comparing. This work suggests that anteversion of the femoral neck may be a mechanical predisposition to degenerative arthritis in some individuals.—Ed.] ◀

5–5 **Evaluation of Primary Resection of the Head of the Femur With or Without Subtrochanteric Angulation Osteotomy.** W. Kuesswetter, G. Wolf, and T. Stuhler (Würzburg, Federal Republic of Germany) reviewed the results of primary resection of the femoral head, with or without subtrochanteric angulation, in 56 patients with osteoarthritis of the hip. Average follow-up after operation was 11½ years. The 46 women and 10 men had an average age of 64 years. Twenty-six had primary osteoarthritis, 23 had osteoarthritis secondary to dysplasia, 5 had posttraumatic changes, and 2 had arthritis after infection.

Nineteen patients underwent a resection angulation osteotomy, 2 of them bilateral. Seventeen patients had other surgery on the con-

---

(5–4) Acta Orthop. Scand. 54:18–23, February 1983.
(5–5) Int. Orthop. 7:17–23, 1983.

tralateral hip joint, most often varus osteotomy. The femoral head was resected through an anterolateral approach to the hip joint. The osteotomy presently is fixed with prebent 8-hole AO plates. Extension of the distal fragment by 10 to 15 degrees is advantageous. External rotation of the proximal fragment by 15 to 20 degrees improves the support of the femoral stump on the pelvis.

All but 4 patients were satisfied with the results of the surgery. Six patients had slight to moderate pain on occasion when resting, 7 occasionally had severe pain on weight-bearing. All but 3 patients gained considerable relief from pain after operation. Forty-three patients were able to walk 1 km or more without pain. Functional results, graded by the system of Shepherd, were good or very good in 41% of cases and satisfactory in another 39%. Average leg shortening was 3.7 cm. Mobility of the hip joint was significantly increased after operation. Radiographic examination showed reactive changes in the proximal femur in the area of loading. The larger the area of support for the proximal femur in the acetabulum, the fewer the reactive changes.

Nearly all patients in this series were satisfied with the late results of femoral head resection, although they often felt that the hip was unstable. Muscular development is important in the functional results obtained from this procedure. A wide area of support of the proximal femur is an important goal of surgery.

▶ [This paper deserves careful scrutiny. Certainly the increased frequency of the serious technical difficulties observed with revision for total hip replacement have dampened the enthusiasm for this procedure that was felt a few years ago. However, I question whether the average American patient is ready today to accept results that are less than good in 60% of the cases, which is the case here with primary resection of the femoral head.

I think that the value of this paper rests in that it shows that adding an angulation osteotomy to the procedure (which would make late conversion to total hip replacement much more difficult) does not improve the long-term result of femoral head resection. The search for a better alternative to total hip replacement in the young patient continues. But at the present time I think it can be said that, at least on the North American continent, resection of the femoral head remains largely a salvage procedure and not a primary one in the surgical treatment of hip disease.—M.E. Cabanela] ◀

5–6 **Posttraumatic Avascular Necrosis of the Femoral Head Predicted by Preoperative Technetium-99m Antimony-Colloid Scan: An Experimental and Clinical Study.** The earliest abnormalities in avascular necrosis of the femoral head found at radiographic study are seen 6 months or longer after subcapital fracture. Radioisotopic bone scanning done within a month after injury may accurately predict avascular necrosis, but conventional imaging using ^{99m}Tc-labeled phosphonate is not reliable in the first 48 hours.

J. Harvey Turner (Fremantle, Australia) used ^{99m}Tc-antimony col-

(5–6) J. Bone Joint Surg. [Am.] 65-A:786–797, July 1983.

loid to visualize the bone marrow of the femoral head within 24 hours of interruption of the blood supply by subcapital osteotomy and section of the ligamentum teres in rabbits. Imaging was carried out 1 hour after intravenous injection of 5 mCi of the radionuclide. In addition, 30 consecutive patients admitted within 24 hours of subcapital fracture of the femoral neck were scanned before internal fixation of the fracture. For scanning 10 mCi of ^{99m}Tc-antimony colloid and a gamma camera with a large field of view and a parallel-hole collimator were used.

The rabbit studies consistently showed loss of marrow activity over the affected femoral head. This focal absence of activity persisted for 3 weeks. Imaging with ^{99m}Tc-methylene diphosphonate failed to show any abnormality for as long as 48 hours after osteotomy. Histologic studies showed absent or reduced hematopoietic tissue in the femoral head. Among the patients, preoperative bone marrow scans showed a preserved blood supply to the femoral head in 16 of 30 cases. Ten of 14 patients followed up at 2 years had recovered uneventfully. Only 1 of the other 4 patients had evidence of avascular necrosis. (The findings in 1 patient with avascularity of the femoral head who was followed up for 18 months are shown in Figure 5–2.) There was 1 false positive and 1 false negative prediction of avascular necrosis. Inactive bone marrow in the femoral head prevented interpretation of scans in 2 cases.

Imaging with ^{99m}Tc-antimony colloid appears to be a reliable

Fig 5–2.—Man aged 59 years with avascularity of femoral head. Anteroposterior film shows Garden grade II subcapital fracture of right femur. Bone marrow scans with ^{99m}Tc-antimony colloid, performed within 24 hours after fracture, show focal absence of activity in head of right femur, compared with that in left femur. Such appearance is consistent with that of avascularity of right femoral head. (Courtesy of Turner, J.H.: J. Bone Joint Surg. [Am.] 65-A:786—797, July 1983.)

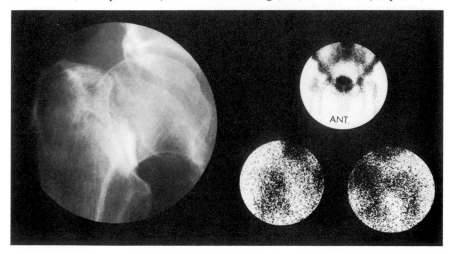

means of identifying avascular necrosis of the femoral head within 24 hours of injury. The method can be used to help decide between closed reduction with internal fixation and primary prosthetic replacement.

▶ [Predicting avascular necrosis (AVN) as the outcome of a subcapital femoral neck fracture using radiography is difficult within the first 6 months, particularly with patients with displacement (Garden classification II and III). A bone scintigram (diphosphonate) performed after 48 hours may be positive but show a low sensitivity due to the superimposed bone remodeling response. Scintigraphy of the bone marrow with the standard ^{99m}Tc-labeled sulfur colloid has been proposed in the past for early recognition of AVN (Meyers, M. H.: *Clin. Orthop.* 130:202–209, 1978). However, the results were generally disappointing due to the poor uptake in the proximal femur resulting in frequent false positive results or noninterpretable images.

The newer ^{99m}Tc-antimony sulfur colloid (^{99m}Tc-SB2 S3), now in phase III clinical studies in the United States and commercially available on a restricted basis, has a higher affinity to bone marrow due to a smaller particle size. The authors show quite convincingly that this theoretical advantage may indeed improve sensitivity and specificity for the early detection of AVN in these patients within 24 hours. Unilateral low colloid uptake by scintigraphy in 12 patients within 24 hours resulted in AVN in 11 patients 2 years later, while of 16 patients with normal scintigrams, 15 had a normal healing. All patients had closed reduction with internal fixation, and scintigrams were performed preoperatively. The author's suggestion, that preoperative evaluation for vascular supply of the femoral head by scintigraphy with ^{99m}Tc-SB2 S3 may assist in making the appropriate choice for endoprosthetic replacement or with internal fixation as a primary procedure, deserves renewed consideration by those who have been disappointed in the colloid bone marrow scintigrams used previously.—H.W. Wahner] ◀

5–7 **Effects of Surgical Procedures on the Blood Supply to the Femoral Head.** Increasing interest in resurfacing arthroplasty of the hip has raised questions regarding the vascular supply of the adult femoral head and the importance of anastomoses between the epiphysis and the metaphysis, since retinacular vessels supplying the area of the capital femoral epiphysis are often damaged in exposure and reaming of the femoral head. Leo A. Whiteside, David R. Lange, William R. Capello, and Barry Fraser (DePaul Health Center, Bridgeton, Mo.) used the hydrogen washout method to determine the rate of blood flow in the femoral head and neck in adult dogs subjected to careful reaming of the femoral head. In some cases the retinaculum was stripped circumferentially. Dogs with degenerative arthritis from hip dysplasia and traumatic arthritis produced by osteotomy of the acetabulum were also studied. The circulation of the femoral head in the adult dog normally depends on retinacular vessels. Vascular anastomosis between the epiphysis and the metaphysis generally are no larger than capillary size.

Stripping of the retinaculum, or combined reaming of the femoral head and stripping of the retinaculum, devascularized the femoral head in normal dogs. Reaming alone did not compromise the femoral head blood flow. The arthritic femoral heads had higher blood flow rates than normal. Flow rates decreased significantly after reaming

(5–7) J. Bone Joint Surg. [Am.] 65-A:1127–1133, October 1983.

and stripping, but fairly high rates persisted in all instances. Numerous vessels crossing between the epiphysis and the metaphysis were found in all specimens, in contrast with the dogs that had normal femoral heads.

There is clinical and laboratory evidence that the adult femoral head is highly dependent on retinacular vessels, and that intramedullary vascular channels become more prominent in the osteoarthritis hip. Much of the arthritic femoral head appears to be supplied by the medullary circulation. Care is needed to preserve the retinacular vessels during hip operations.

▶ [Two good techniques, postmorphological and washout, were used in determining the blood supply to the femoral head in these dogs. Certainly the clinical relevance of this paper is that the circulation to the femoral head should be retained particularly during surface replacement and osteotomy. One has a little more latitude in the arthritic femoral head because of compensatory vascular anastomoses between the epiphysis and the metaphysis.—Ed.] ◀

5–8   **Treatment of Posttraumatic Avascular Necrosis of the Femoral Head by Multiple Drilling and Muscle-Pedicle Bone Grafting: Preliminary Report.** Avascular necrosis is a complication of intracapsular fracture of the femoral neck, and it also may follow reduction of a traumatic hip dislocation. D. P. Baksi (Calcutta) treated 29 patients with posttraumatic avascular necrosis of the femoral head by multiple drilling of the bone, removal of necrotic bone, and implantation of a muscle-pedicle bone graft into the femoral head and neck. Twenty-eight had had intracapsular femoral neck fractures, 17 with nonunion. One patient had had reduction of a dislocated hip. Average age was 35 years.

Grafts were obtained from the quadratus femoris and intertrochanteric crest (Figs 5–3 and 5–4) in 21 cases, from the gluteus medius insertion and greater trochanter (Fig 5–5) in 6, and from the sartorius origin and ilium (Fig 5–6) in 2. With united fractures a posterior approach was used in all cases. A longitudinal gutter was cut over the posterior surface close to the superior border of the femoral head and neck to receive the graft, which was trimmed to fit the gutter before being placed. With ununited fractures multiple drill holes were made into the femoral head to thoroughly decompress it. Such fractures were reduced, packed with free bone grafts, and fixed with pins before inserting the muscle-pedicle graft. Patients with united fractures were allowed up 6 to 8 weeks after surgery; others were not allowed up for 12 weeks.

Follow-up averaged 38 months. Twenty patients had excellent results with no hip pain, little or no functional restriction, and favorable radiographic findings (Figs 5–7 through 5–12). Five patients had good results (Figs 5–13 and 5–14), 3 had fair results, and 1 had a poor outcome. One pin was extruded, and another penetrated into the

(5–8)   J. Bone Joint Surg. [Br.] 65-B:268–273, May 1983.

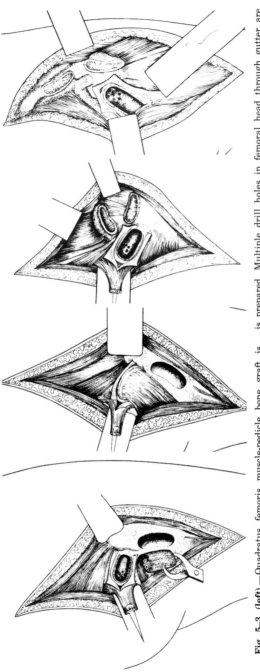

Fig 5-3 (left).—Quadratus femoris muscle-pedicle bone graft is prepared with multiple drill holes into femoral head through gutter. Gemelli and obturator internus are seen detached and retracted medially.

Fig 5-4 (center, left).—Quadratus femoris muscle-pedicle bone graft is placed in prepared gutter.

Fig 5-5 (center, right).—Gluteus medius muscle-pedicle bone graft is prepared. Multiple drill holes in femoral head through gutter are shown.

Fig 5-6 (right).—Sartorius muscle-pedicle bone graft is prepared. Multiple drill holes in femoral head through gutter are seen. Straight head of rectus femoris is seen divided near its origin.

(Courtesy of Baksi, D.P.: J. Bone Joint Surg. [Br.] 65-B:268–273, May 1983.)

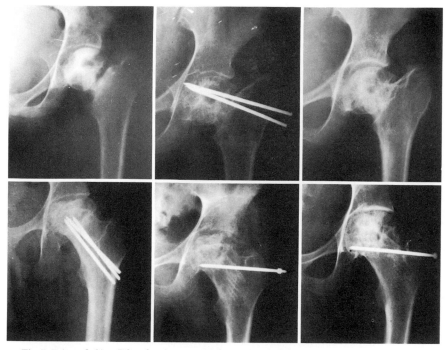

Fig 5–7 (top, left).—Film showing ununited transcervical fracture of neck of femur with partially absorbed neck and increased density of most of femoral head. Solitary "cystic" area can be seen (stage 2 necrosis).

Fig 5–8 (top, center).—Three months after operation film shows diminution of area of density of femoral head and advanced union of fracture site. Two Moore's pins are seen; a third was removed because it was being extruded.

Fig 5–9 (top, right).—Sixty-two months after operation film shows that most dense areas of femoral head have been replaced by coarse bony trabeculae and fractured neck has united satisfactorily; mild coxa vara is present.

Fig 5–10 (bottom, left).—Film showing wide area of femoral head infarcted and separated from healthy bone by radiolucent zone 2–3 mm wide 2 years after union of transcervical fracture treated by Moore's pins. Mild flattening of upper part of femoral head is seen (stage 3 necrosis).

Fig 5–11 (bottom, center).—Four months after operation film shows infarcted area has been partly replaced by coarse bony trabeculae and radiolucent zone is bridged by new bone. Portion of graft is visible over femoral neck fixed by Moore's pin.

Fig 5–12 (bottom, right).—Film 42 months after operation shows satisfactory healing of infarcted area with more normal trabecular pattern and less flattening of femoral head. Traces of residual density of femoral head are still visible perhaps due to laying down of new bone on dead trabeculae.

(Courtesy of Baksi, D.P.: J. Bone Joint Surg. [Br.] 65-B:268–273, May 1983.)

pelvis. Five patients developed 10 to 20 degrees of coxa vara after union of a previously ununited femoral neck fracture. In 9 cases restricted movement was considered a result of inadequate physiotherapy after surgery. Six patients with gluteus medius pedicle grafts had weak hip abduction.

Multiple drilling and muscle-pedicle bone grafting for avascualr necrosis of the femoral head consistently relieved pain in these cases.

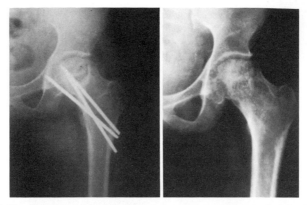

Fig 5–13 (left).—Twenty months after satisfactory union of transcervical fracture treated by Moore's pinning film shows that most of femoral head has necrosed and is separated from healthy bone by radiolucent zone 2 mm wide. Mild collapse of femoral head and step formation below upper acetabular margin are seen (stage 4 necrosis.)

Fig 5–14 (right).—Five months after operation film shows advanced healing of necrotic area and bridging of radiolucent zone by new bone. Further improvement occurred during later follow-up studies.

(Courtesy of Baksi, D.P.: J. Bone Joint Surg. [Br.] 65-B:268–273, May 1983.)

The quadratus femoris graft appeared to be the most vascular. Unlike use of the gluteus medius graft, use of the quadratus femoris graft did not significantly weaken the hip.

▶ [Osteonecrosis of the femoral head following a femoral neck fracture which heals, or following dislocation of the hip, will invariably heal. However, physicians and surgeons have failed to devise a technique to permit healing and yet maintain the anatomical integrity of the subchondral bone and geometry of the femoral head. Placing either a dead piece of bone (the Phemister technique) or a free vascularized tissue transfer into the femoral head and neck cannot maintain the structural integrity of the subchondral bone and geometry of the femoral head. Thus, the treating physician must wonder whether these techniques are superior enough to protected weight-bearing of the hip while it heals.

The clinical experience reported by Dr. Baksi states that a free tissue transfer may permit revascularization and healing of the femoral head in a more rapid fashion. If this is the case, then the period of protected weight-bearing could be reduced.

Doctor Baksi's experience with 29 patients is, indeed, commendable. With a minimum follow-up of 22 months and a maximum follow-up of 60 months, he reports on 25 of the 29 patients. In reports of the manuscript, Dr. Baksi may be a bit enthusiastic in his evaluation. The follow-up x-rays in cases 1, 3, and 20 certainly are not normal. Early degenerative arthrosis is evident in all 3 patients, and certainly all 3 will need further treatment at some future date. However, this technique may put off any type of reconstructive surgery for a considerable period of time.

Doctor Baksi is to be commended for an excellent piece of clinical work. Although the exact alteration of pathophysiology of osteonecrosis of the femoral head following free tissue transfer has not been delineated, it would appear that a free tissue transfer enhances healing and shortens the recovery time. If the patient is protected from weight-bearing during the healing period, geometric alterations of the femoral head can be prevented. In those patients who experienced these geometric alterations of the femoral head, it would appear that a free tissue transfer may prevent further collapse of the femoral head.—R.H. Fitzgerald, Jr.] ◀

5–9 **Three Brothers With Algodystrophy of the Hip.** Algodystrophy of the hip is a rare disorder that sometimes follows trauma and is characterized by sudden or progressive pain in the groin, trochanteric region, thigh, or knee. There is often a limp and functional weakness of the extremity. Films may show osteoporosis of the femoral head and acetabulum. Repair requires 4 to 7 months. Middle-aged men and pregnant women usually are affected.

J. Albert and H. Ott report the development of algodystrophy of the hip in three brothers who were born in southwestern Italy and had been living separately in Switzerland for 10 years. None had a history of trauma, fever, or systemic disease or had evidence of predisposing factors such as diabetes, hyperlipidemia, anxiety, or depression. Progression of the disorder in the youngest brother is described below.

Man, 30, rapidly developed right hip pain that radiated to the knee and he began to limp in December 1978. He improved spontaneously after 4 months of bed rest. In March 1979 films showed osteoporosis in the upper external quarter of the femoral head, which later resolved. In September 1981 there was atrophy of 1.5 cm of the right quadriceps. In April 1982 pain and limp occurred on the left side. Hip mobility was normal, but movement induced pain over the trochanter. In June 1982 a bone scan showed increased uptake in the left femoral head (Fig 5–15). Salmon calcitonin therapy gave good clinical results.

All 3 affected brothers were HLA-identical. In 2 cases the hips were affected successively. Bone resorption in the hip may be followed by involvement of the lower limbs, as in 1 of the brothers. The familial pre-

Fig 5–15.—Bone scan in June 1982 shows increased uptake in left femoral head. (Courtesy of Albert, J., and Ott, H.: Ann. Rheum. Dis. 42:421–424, August 1983.)

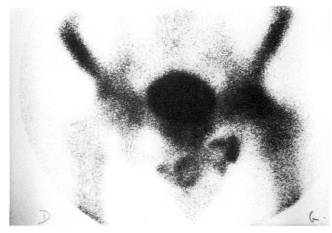

(5–9) Ann. Rheum. Dis. 42:421–424, August 1983.

sentation of algodystrophy in these subjects prompts consideration of the possible existence of a genetic factor in development of the disease.

▶ [Although the etiology and pathogenesis of this syndrome are uncertain, it is important that the orthopedist, rheumatologist, and other physicians be able to recognize this syndrome in order to avoid unnecessary treatment. The process may simulate an infection or tumor on superficial evaluation. Because the illness seems self-limited, treatment should be conservative. The cases involving the hip are strikingly similar, but osteoporosis may also occur in the knee, ankle or foot, or shoulder as well as in the hip. Incidentally, the term "transient osteoporosis" was first used in the description of a Mayo Clinic series (*Ann. Intern. Med.* 68:539–552, 1968). That article and a subsequent article (*J. Bone Joint Surg.* [*Am.*] 55-A:1188–1196, 1973) suggested that bone necrosis may develop early followed by resorption and then increased bone formation. The association of hip osteoporosis with similar changes in the ankle, foot, and knee do point toward a pathogenesis somehow related to reflex dystrophy or algodystrophy.—G.G. Hunder] ◀

5–10 **Radiologic Appearance of Appositional New Bone on Medial Part of the Neck of the Femur in Coxarthrosis.** Appositional new bone and osteophytes often are encountered in the region of the femoral head and acetabulum in the presence of coxarthrosis, but new bone has been less frequently described on the medial part of the femoral neck. D. Orlic and I. Ruszkowski (Univ. of Zagreb, Yugoslavia) examined the radiographs of 448 hips with coxarthrosis in 304 patients. Appositional new bone formation was seen on the medial part of the femoral neck in 87.5% of the anteroposterior radiographs. The extent of new bone formation usually was much greater on the posterior surface of the femoral neck than on its medial margin. Well-trabeculated cancellous bone was present between the new bone cortex and the persisting cortex of the femoral neck. The development of appositional new bone was not always associated with definite changes in the articular part of the hip, but it was observed shortly after a limp developed on the affected side. The most common pattern, seen in nearly half of the hips examined, consisted of appositional bone covering the entire length of the femoral neck from the lower edge of the femoral head to the shadow of the lesser trochanter.

This new bone formation is considered to be a response to the abnormal forces produced by limping in patients with coxarthrosis. The specific pattern of appositional new bone may depend on the type of limp, the presence of a flexion deformity, and anteversion of the femoral neck. Appositional bone usually is much more extensive on the posterior surface of the bone than on the medial margin of the femoral neck. Subluxation of the hip is not the most significant factor in the development of appositional new bone on the medial part of the femoral neck.

▶ [For many years I have observed the appearance of new bone formation on the medial part of the femoral neck in coxarthrosis. I first began looking for some evidence of lateral location of the femur in relation to the pelvis to explain this on a

(5–10) Int. Orthop. 7:11–16, 1983.

purely stress basis (subluxation) as propounded first by Weiberg (Weiberg, G.: *Acta Chir. Scand.* 83 [Suppl.]:58, 1939). But I observed that many patients had no evidence of lateral luxation of the femoral head in relation to the acetabulum and still had bone formation in this region. The authors of this article believe that this can happen because of a limp which throws the body weight more medially and thus, according to Wolff's law, builds up bone on the medial aspect of the femoral neck. But I have also observed the formation without limp.

I believe another logical explanation for the appearance of new bone formation is the accumulation of detritus from the degenerative hip. This detritus collects in the "axilla" of the hip joint near the capsular attachment where most of these ossifications occur. The fact that they have been seen without any radiographic evidence of osteoarthritis, i.e., in the very early stages and in patients without limp or lateral luxation of their hip joint, would give some credence to this theory. Thus, besides the biomechanical cause for the ossification, the biologic cause is possible. For years I have taught residents to look for this very early sign of osteoarthritis, as it sometimes is the only radiographic sign of degenerative disease in the hip.—Ed.] ◄

5–11 **Diagnostic Value of Traction During Radiography in Diseases of the Hip: Preliminary Report.** J. Vegter and J. A. C. van den Broek (Helmond, Holland) found that a diastasis can be produced between the femoral head and the acetabulum by applying manual traction on the lower extremity, and that the resultant "vacuum" phenomenon clearly outlines the shape, thickness, and extent of the cartilage. Traction is applied to the ankle of the supine patient as the hip is visualized under image intensification. A roentgenogram is made when maximal diastasis is achieved between the femoral head and the acetabulum (Fig 5–16). Further exposures can be made in

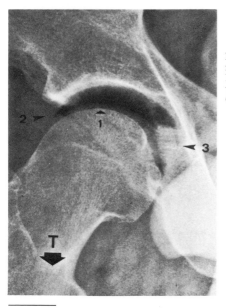

Fig 5–16.—Vacuum arthrogram of normal hip taken during traction *(T)*. *1*, cartilage of femoral head; *2*, limbus articularis; and *3*, ligamentum teres. (Courtesy of Vegter, J., and van den Broek, J.A.C.: J. Bone Joint Surg. [Br.] 65-B:428–432, August 1983.)

(5–11)   J. Bone Joint Surg. [Br.] 65-B:428–432, August 1983.

medial and lateral rotation and flexion and axial views obtained. There is no age limit to the study. The finding of diastasis without vacuum indicates the presence of free fluid in the joint.

Traction roentgenography of the hip is a simple, noninvasive means of assessing the joint cartilage and detecting hip effusion. The vacuum phenomenon is readily produced in children and adolescents, especially females. The use of a muscle relaxant may be helpful in patients with advanced osteoarthritis. In newborn infants, the shape of the unossified femoral head and acetabulum can be appreciated, replacing conventional arthrography. In cases of hip dysplasia the extent of the lateral acetabular rim is visualized, and its behavior is readily monitored. It has been impossible to produce the vacuum phenomenon in congenital hip dislocation. The authors now perform traction roentgenography wherever doubtful symptoms are present. Joint aspiration is not indicated when a vacuum phenomenon is elicited.

5–12 **Traction Radiography of the Hip and Fluid in the Hip Joint.** Clinical signs of hip disease are often related to the presence of fluid in the joint. Hans A. C. van den Broek and Joost Vegter (Helmond, The Netherlands) point out that fluid in the hip can be detected noninvasively by traction roentgenography. Traction on the joint normally creates a "vacuum" between the femoral head and the acetabulum, and this effect does not occur when fluid is present. The diastasis that normally occurs between the femoral head and the acetabulum is seen because of the physiologically lax hip joint capsule. Maximal traction is gradually applied to the lower extremity during fluoroscopy, and when the vacuum sign is seen a film is exposed. A series of roentgenograms can be obtained with the leg in various positions if the cartilage of the femoral head or acetabulum is to be evaluated.

Traction roentgenography of the hip can be useful in diagnosing fluid in the joint in such conditions as purulent or rheumatoid inflammation and Perthes' disease. Congenital hip dysplasia, femoral head necrosis, arthrosis, and osteochondritis dissecans can be evaluated in this way. Traction roentgenography has also been used to examine the wrist and metacarpophalangeal joints. A muscle relaxant may be used to obtain good diastasis on traction. An alternative approach is use of the frog leg position and fast film exposure.

▶ [Traction radiography has been discussed by other authors as a method of determining the presence of fluid in the hip, shoulder, and other joints. This author describes the traction techniques and ultrasound as a method of detecting fluid. However, findings on routine radiography as well as computed tomography and nuclear magnetic resonance may also provide noninvasive means of diagnosing joint effusions. A negative pressure phenomenon resulting in a vacuum is useful if it is present. However, in certain patients, because the degree of discomfort and therefore lack of cooperation may result in an indeterminant study, the lack of a vacuum sign may not necessarily indicate the presence of the fluid.

(5–12) Diagn. Imaging 52:76–84, Mar.–June, 1983.

The method is nonetheless helpful and useful in specific clinical situations and the author provides an excellent description of the technique and indications for its use.—T.H. Bergquist] ◄

5–13 **Villonodular Synovitis in the Hip Joint Diagnosed by Arthrography: Report of a Case.** It may be difficult to diagnose pigmented villonodular synovitis, especially if no bony abnormalities are present. T. Nybonde, W. Mortensson, and B. Robertson (Stockholm) report a case showing the value of arthrography in evaluating patients with atypical hip symptoms.

Girl, 13, had acute left lower quadrant abdominal pain. She had previously had recurrent urinary tract infections and at age 10 had been operated on for bilateral lens dislocation. Pain subsequently moved toward the left hip, and joint mobility became restricted. Roentgenography yielded normal findings, but activity was slightly increased in the hip area 3 hours after injection of ^{99m}Tc-methylene diphosphonate. The patient's condition improved spontaneously, but hip swelling, pain, and limited motion were present a few weeks later; two x-ray studies were normal. Symptoms recurred in 2 months, when computed tomography showed a small amount of fluid in the joint. Anti-inflamatory drugs and analgesics had no effect. Tomography was not helpful, but arthrography showed a pedunculated synovial tumor 2 cm in diameter (Fig 5–17), which was excised at arthrotomy and found to represent pigmented villonodular synovitis. The patient re-

Fig 5–17.—Arthrography. Arrows point to tumor attached to capsular wall in anterolateral compartment of joint. (Courtesy of Nybonde, T., et al.: Acta Radiol. [Diagn.] [Stockh.] 24:67–70, 1983.)

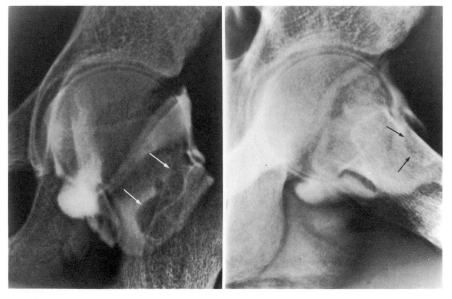

(5–13)   Acta Radiol. [Diagn.] (Stockh.) 24:67–70, 1983.

ported being free from severe hip pain 6 months after operation, but there was slight pain in several other joints.

The nature of pigmented villonodular synovitis is unclear. The most common site is the knee. Arthrography in general is useful in demonstrating focal synovial abnormalities. The study is recommended for evaluation of patients with obscure hip symptoms. Sonography probably would be useful for documenting both diffuse and localized synovial lesions. Circumscribed villonodular synovitis is treated by excision of the affected synovia; recurrences are rare.

▶ [Arthrography is very useful in evaluating subtle synovial changes. The appearance of the arthrogram in this report is somewhat atypical, but does emphasize the efficacy of this technique.

Pigmented villonodular synovitis may be difficult to differentiate from synovial chondromatosis or nonspecific proliferative synovitis. Double contrast technique may be necessary in subtle cases.—T.H. Bergquist] ◄

5–14 **Calcific Tendinitis of the Gluteus Maximus Tendon (Gluteus Maximus Tendinitis).** Only 7 cases of gluteus maximus tendinitis have been reported previously. J. F. Wepfer, J. G. Reed, G. M. Cullen, and W. P. McDevitt (St. Joseph's Hosp., Milwaukee) describe 7 patients with this condition, 6 women and 1 man aged 30 to 67 years. Four were encountered in a 25-month period. Most patients have had severe pain in the hip and upper part of the thigh posteriorly and have had tenderness over the gluteal tubercle on examination. Two of the authors' patients had sudden onset of severe pain, 3 had mild to moderate pain over weeks to months, and 2 were asymptomatic. The symptomatic patients have been followed for 2 years or longer, with no recurrence of pain. No history of trauma or unusual activity was obtained in any case.

Calcific tendinitis usually is best appreciated in the lateral projection. In the anteroposterior view, a faint, amorphous calcific deposit may be seen just below the greater trochanter, overlying the femoral cortex and part of the medullary cavity. Larger deposits project laterally into the soft tissues. A radionuclide bone scan may show intense localized uptake in the region of calcification. The differential diagnosis includes myositis ossificans, cartilaginous tumors, synovioma, and gluteofemoral bursitis.

▶ [Calcific deposits about tendons, bursae, capsule, and ligaments are a common source of pain. This particular entity is described as calcific tendinitis in the gluteus maximus tendon where it is attached to the linea aspera. There is a bursa just under this tendinous attachment, as the authors have noted. In one such patient on whom I operated, the calcium was, indeed, in this bursa and not directly in the tendon. These deposits can only be seen at times with rotational views, and the key is to suspect and then prove, as the authors have clearly shown.—Ed.] ◄

5–15 **Analysis of the Late Effects of Traumatic Posterior Dislocation of the Hip Without Fractures.** Traumatic posterior hip dislo-

---

(5–14) Skeletal Radiol. 9:198–200, February 1983.
(5–15) J. Bone Joint Surg. [Br.] 65-B:150–152, March 1983.

cation without fracture has generally been considered to be an uncomplicated state once treated successfully. S. S. Upadhyay, A. Moulton, and *F*. Srikrishnamurthy reviewed 74 cases of simple traumatic hip dislocation seen between 1936 and 1978. The 58 males and 16 females had an average age of 29 years when injured. Average follow-up was 14½ years. All patients had a dislocation without fracture, or with only a minimal chip fracture of the posterior acetabular rim, and had grade 1 cases in the Thompson-Epstein system.

Good to excellent results were obtained in 56 hips, with no appreciable pain or limp, except after a day of hard work with weight-bearing, and no more than 25% restriction of motion. Roentgenograms showed no more than minimal arthritic changes. Eight hips had a fair and 10 had a poor outcome. These hips all developed osteoarthritis, and 6 patients had avascular necrosis within 3 years of injury. Osteoarthritis was most frequent in miners, including those injured in an automobile accident, and avascular necrosis was most common in patients injured in automobile accidents. The occurrence of osteoarthritis increased over time. Arthritis was infrequent in patients younger than age 15 years and did not occur in the elderly. Two patients in whom the diagnosis was missed initially later developed avascular necrosis. There were 2 cases of sciatic palsy.

Satisfactory clinical and roentgenographic results were obtained in a large majority of cases of traumatic posterior hip dislocation without fracture in this series. The predicted long-term rate of avascular necrosis was 8%. Osteoarthritis was most prevalent in patients aged 31 to 40 years. It may be more likely to develop if heavy work is continued after the dislocation.

▶ [The authors review simple traumatic dislocations of the hip, i.e., those without fracture. The average follow-up is 14.7 years. Twenty-four percent of these patients developed osteoarthritis. This, therefore, emphasizes that what we see on the x-ray is bone. Cartilage damage at the time of the traumatic dislocation is not assessable either clinically or by x-ray. It is perfectly obvious that many of these patients will have cartilage injury at the time of their dislocation, which will develop in later years into osteoarthritis. We should all be aware of this complication of dislocation, and so advise our patients.—Ed.] ◀

6. Joint Replacement: The Knee

6–1 **Results of Total Knee Arthroplasty With a Nonconstrained Prosthesis.** J.-M. Cloutier (Montreal) reviewed experience with a nonconstrained total knee prosthesis (Fig 6–1) used since 1977. The geometry of the femoral component simulates the normal anatomy of the knee, and the flat articular surfaces of the tibial component permit unconstrained rotation, rolling, and sliding as dictated by the retained cruciate ligaments. Precise placement of the components is necessary so that the ligaments are symmetrically taut and the limb is in physiologic valgus alignment. Templates are used to perform the four osteotomies needed to correctly implant the components, as shown in Figures 6–2 to 6–4. Polyethylene plateau units of various

Fig 6–1.—Prosthesis assembled. Articular surface of femoral component duplicates normal anatomy. Carbon-reinforced polyethylene plateaus are secured to U-shaped metal retainer by a press-fit at operation. (Courtesy of Cloutier, J.-M.: J. Bone Joint Surg. [Am.] 65-A:906–919, September 1983.)

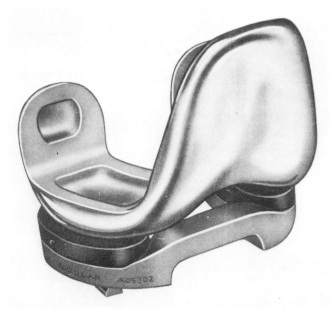

(6–1) J. Bone Joint Surg. [Am.] 65-A:906–919, September 1983.

thicknesses are tested until the proper degree of ligament tension is present, in both flexion and extension, before the components are cemented in place.

A total of 107 arthroplasties in 83 patients were followed for 24 to 54 months. Average patient age was 58 years. The diagnosis was rheumatoid arthritis in 68 knees, osteoarthritis in 35, and osteonecrosis in 4. In all but 1 case of painless ankylosis, operation was performed for painful, incapacitating arthritis. Results were excellent or good in 91% of knees by the rating system of the Hospital for Special Surgery. In 98 knees pain was adequately relieved and the limb was in physiologic valgus alignment. Only 3 knees were mediolaterally unstable in extension. The average arc of flexion was 103 degrees. Three fourths of the patients were able to climb up and down stairs normally. Gait studies in some of these patients showed a normal flexion arc of the knee. Complications included 3 deep wound infections and 1 case of aseptic loosening of the femoral component. One patient not in the series died of pulmonary embolism in the postoperative period.

A nonconstrained cruciate-preserving prosthesis can relieve pain and provide adequate axial limb alignment and stability in over 90% of knees for which total arthroplasty is indicated. Nearly nor-

Fig 6–2 (left).—Jig 1 in place for performance of anterior and posterior osteotomies. As viewed from front, with knee flexed to about 90 degrees, shorter rod is parallel to longitudinal axis of tibia and longer rod is parallel to same axis of femur. Once jig is in position, it is fixed to femur by two drills inserted through holes visible in jig.

Fig 6–3 (right).—With knee in 90 degrees of flexion and ligaments maintained symmetrically taut by distractor, three osteotomies (two femoral and one tibial) are done perpendicular to long axis of tibia and parallel to one another as viewed from front.

(Courtesy of Cloutier, J.-M.: J. Bone Joint Surg. [Am.] 65-A:906–919, September 1983.)

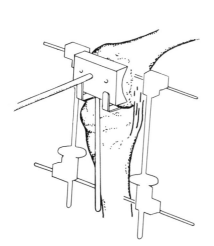
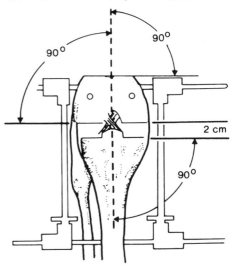

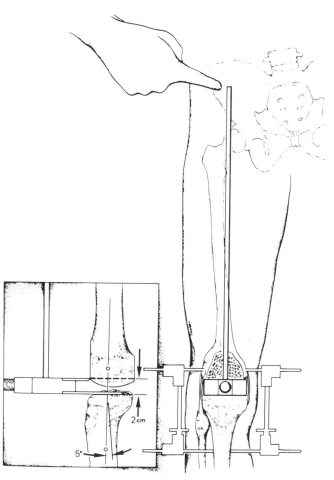

Fig 6–4.—Jig 2 has four blades, one for each condyle, and attached aligning rod. With knee in extension and ligaments maintained taut by distractor, correct alignment is achieved when rod points in direction of femoral head while long blades of jig are held against previously osteotomized surfaces of tibial plateaus. Site of distal femoral osteotomy (broken line on inset) is then marked at level of short blades. (Courtesy of Cloutier, J.-M.: J. Bone Joint Surg. [Am.] 65-A:906–919, September 1983.)

mal kinematics are preserved, and knee function is improved. The method is not used if the posterior cruciate ligament is torn or attenuated. It is rarely indicated for use in revision arthroplasty except in selected knees with a failed compartmental replacement in which bone loss is not too marked and the posterior cruciate ligament is intact.

▶ [The author presents the early results with a minimally constrained knee replacement. The results are quite good at 2 years, as they are with almost all total knee replacements. The author does make several points that bear emphasis. (1) The posterior cruciate ligament is almost always present. (2) The knee ligaments are usually adequate if properly balanced and constraint in the prosthesis is not necessary. (3) The development of precise instrumentation to make precise osteotomies has been a major contribution to improving the results of knee arthroplasty. The author does not feel that the case for patellar replacement has been conclusively made, and on this point I would not agree.

The final answer to what is the most desirable compromise between conformity of articular surfaces and, consequently, constraint and nonconformity with increased rotation translation and gliding, will be elucidated in time. In many patients, a flat tibial component produces an effective pivot shift with rapid walking, but it is not known whether this will cause increasing instability with time as it does in normal knees. On the other hand, conformity with constraint has been proven to increase the rate of loosening at bone-cement junction. I look forward to a report on the results in these same patients at 5 years and 10 years.—R.S. Bryan] ◄

6–2 **Long-Term Results of Stanmore Total Knee Replacements.** The Stanmore knee replacement, one of the first-generation constrained prostheses, is a simple hinge having no intrinsic provision for physiologic rotation. R. J. Grimer, M. R. K. Karpinski, and A. N. Edwards (Birmingham, England) reviewed the outcome of 103 sequential Stanmore knee replacements in 90 patients treated from 1973 to 1978 and followed for up to 9 years 3 months. Thirteen patients had bilateral arthroplasties. The 77 women and 13 men had an average age at operation of 68 years. The diagnosis was osteoarthritis in 41 and rheumatoid arthritis in 49. Fifty-one knees had undergone 66 previous operations. All patients had severe pain, limited joint mobility, and instability. Contraindications included previous knee infection and peripheral vascular disease. Obesity and osteoporosis were relative contraindications. The average follow-up was 68 months.

Overall, 64% of the patients were satisfied at the last follow-up. Pain returned in some patients after the initial postoperative assessment, and walking ability sometimes declined. Flexion deformity was consistently reduced after operation, and the range of flexion remained improved. Varus-valgus deformity was consistently corrected after operation. Several patients had retropatellar pain at follow-up. There were 2 femoral and 2 tibial fractures (Fig 6–5), all causing marked difficulty. Seven knees became infected. Eight prostheses were removed for aseptic loosening, and a number of others are loose but have not been revised. The cumulative success rate was 80% at 7 years, based solely on whether the prosthesis was still in place.

The Stanmore knee retains a role in knee arthroplasty, but its place in primary arthroplasty should be limited except in patients with severe incapacity. Factors predicting the success of the Stanmore knee in individual patients have not been identified. Occurrence

(6–2) J. Bone Joint Surg. [Br.] 66-B:55–62, January 1984.

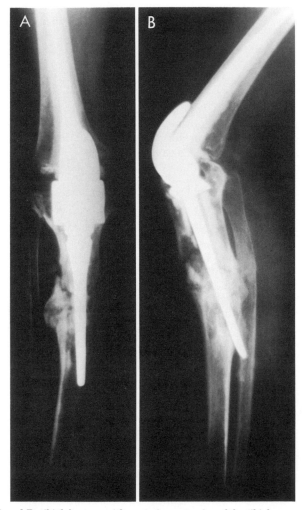

Fig 6–5.—**A** and **B,** tibial fracture with posterior protrusion of the tibial component. (Courtesy of Grimer, R.J., et al.: J. Bone Joint Surg. [Br.] 66-B:55–62, January 1984.)

of the chief complications, fracture and infection, is difficult to predict or prevent, and difficult to treat.

▶ [This is a very well-reported series of hinge replacements using a Stanmore knee prosthesis. The authors reported a cumulative success rate of 80% at 7 years, but they also reported an 18% complication rate; 7% infections, 7% gross loosening, 4% fractures. These are in keeping with the good early results and the complication rate reported with other types of hinges. I would suggest that hinges have no role at all in primary knee arthroplasty and only a very limited role in revision knee arthroplasty. It is far wiser to utilize external bracing and an unconstrained total knee arthroplasty than it is to use an internally constrained prosthesis. To realize the validity of this point one has only to look at the x-rays to recognize the extent of bone destruction when failure occurs.—R.S. Bryan] ◄

6–3 **Total Condylar Knee Prosthesis in Gonarthrosis: a 5- to 9-Year Follow-up of the First 100 Consecutive Replacements.** John N. Insall, Roger W. Hood, Laura B. Flawn, and Dennis J. Sullivan reviewed experience with the first 100 consecutive patients to have 125 knee arthroplasties with the original total condylar-I prosthesis for osteoarthritis or osteonecrosis at the Hospital for Special Surgery, New York. Average follow-up after operation was 6½ years. One hundred knees were available for evaluation in 79 patients after 5 to 9 years of follow-up. These patients had an average age of 68 years; 69 were women. A patellar replacement was not used in 10 early cases. The average preoperative range of motion was 87 degrees.

One prosthesis was removed because of sepsis. Four knees underwent revision because of pain and 2 because of subluxation. Two tibial components were loose. Sixty-four knees were rated as excellent, 27 as good, 2 as fair, and 7 as poor at follow-up. In all knees rated as poor the prosthesis had to be removed. Only minimal changes in varus or valgus alignment and in fixation of the prosthetic components occurred over time. Some lucency was associated with 41% of the tibial components, but there were only 2 complete or circumferential lucent lines, both associated with loose components. No definite evidence of wear of the polyethylene tibial component was demonstrated in any knee. Most failures were attributed to errors in surgical technique.

Over 90% of knees were rated as in good or excellent condition, and a slight improvement in the average range of motion was observed over time. Proper alignment is important. Posterior subluxation of the tibia can occur postoperatively if a tight fit in flexion is not achieved. Stair-climbing and related activities are impaired by lack of a firm fulcrum. Some proposed modifications seem to be worthwhile, but caution is indicated until further clinical data are available, since apparently minor design changes can have unexpected adverse effects. Some design deficiencies may prove to be useful over the long term by inhibiting extremely active use of the knee.

▶ [The authors report an excellent long-term follow-up of the total condylar prosthesis. A 7% reoperation rate and a 92% satisfactory result at follow-up is excellent. The 41% incidence of tibial component radiolucent lines is of concern. Although 81% of the lucent lines did not progress after the first year, the potential for loosening still exists.

Since the prosthesis utilized a nonmetal backed tibial component in this early series, the high frequency of radiolucent lines is not unanticipated. The importance of this study lies in the long-term follow-up of a prosthetic design that is still widely used today and which is mimicked by other designs. The importance of correct sur-

(6–3)   J. Bone Joint Surg. [Am.] 65-A:619–628, June 1983.

gical technique is emphasized. The authors recognized some of the deficiencies in the early prosthetic design; the sacrifice of the posterior cruciate ligament, and the potential for posterior subluxation, as well as some loss of motion due to the loss of the fulcrum provided by the posterior cruciate ligament.

It is hoped that other authors will be able to present excellent results with similar prostheses.—J.A. Rand] ◀

6–4 **Total Knee-Replacement Arthroplasty: Results With the Intramedullary Adjustable Total Knee Prosthesis.** Nas S. Eftekhar (Columbia Univ.) followed up 112 patients (130 knees) for 4 to 9 years who had undergone insertion of an intramedullary adjustable total-knee prosthesis. The prosthesis is designed to permit unconstrained rotation. It consists of a metal tray supporting a high-density–polyethylene tibial component, an intramedullary stem, and two condylar intramedullary projections on both the femoral and tibial components. The indications for arthroplasty were pain and functional disability in patients with advanced rheumatoid disease or osteoarthritis, and failure to improve after previous surgery. Infection and neurotropic changes contraindicated total knee replacement. Most patients were in their 60s or older. A minimum of bone was removed from the tibia in installing the prosthesis. Much emphasis was placed on postoperative physiotherapy and rehabilitation of the knee.

Scoring for pain, function, stability, and motion yielded 73% poor scores and 27% fair scores preoperatively. Postoperative scores were good in 77% of cases, fair in 15%, and poor in 8%. Over 90% of patients without other functional disabilities had good results at follow-up evaluation. Two deaths occurred, 1 from pulmonary embolism and 1 from sepsis following attempted arthrodesis for deep-wound infection. Reoperation was necessary in 4 of 5 patients with deep infection, and in 5 other cases for different reasons. A nonprogressive lucent line around the tibial component was noted on roentgenograms in 32% of 117 evaluable knees. Two prostheses were considered to be clinically loose; 1 because of trauma and 1 because of malpositioning of the tibial component. No revision surgery has yet been performed for component loosening.

Clinical loosening of the intramedullary adjustable total-knee prosthesis has been infrequent in this series after 4 to 9 years of follow-up. At present, the procedure should be reserved for older patients with osteoarthritis and for patients of any age with polyarthritis and severe disability whose pain is not controlled by conservative measures. Osteotomy is preferable for less-deformed, younger, and more active patients.

6–5 **Total Knee Arthroplasty in Juvenile Rheumatoid Arthritis.** Juvenile rheumatoid arthritis is a leading cause of disability in children. A. J. Sarokhan, R. D. Scott, W. H. Thomas, C. B. Sledge, F. C.

(6–4) J. Bone Joint Surg. [Am.] 65-A:293–309, March 1983.
(6–5) Ibid., pp. 1071–1080, October 1983.

TABLE 1.—Age Distribution at Operation on 29 Knees	
Age at Operation	No. of Knees
Less than 15 yrs.	4
16 to 20 yrs.	8
21 to 25 yrs.	10
26 to 30 yrs.	4
31 to 35 yrs.	2
36 to 40 yrs.	1

(Courtesy of Sarokhan, A.J., et al.: J. Bone Joint Surg. [Am.] 65-A:1071–1080, October 1983.)

Ewald, and D. W. Cloos (Brigham and Women's Hosp., Boston) reviewed the results of 29 knee replacement procedures performed on 17 patients with an American Rheumatism Association diagnosis of juvenile-onset rheumatoid arthritis between 1971 and 1981. The patients were followed for 2 years or longer after operation. The 14 females and 3 males had an average age at operation of 23 years (Table

Fig 6–6 (left).—Preoperative lateral roentgenogram showing 90-degree knee flexion contracture with distal femoral deformity secondary to healed supracondylar fracture.

Fig 6–7 (right).—Lateral roentgenogram showing gain in extension after serial manipulations and application of casts.

(Courtesy of Sarokhan, A.J., et al.: J. Bone Joint Surg. [Am.] 65-A:1071–1080, October 1983.)

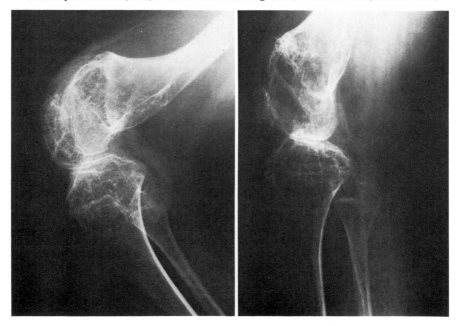

TABLE 2.—AMBULATORY STATUS OF 17 PATIENTS

Status	No. of Patients	
	Preop.	Postop.
Non-walker	4	1
Household walker	3	0
Limited community walker*	10	4
Full community walker†	0	12

*Either required assistive devices to walk outside of home or able to walk 2 blocks or less, or both.
†Able to walk unlimited distance without assistive devices.
(Courtesy of Sarokhan, A.J., et al.: J. Bone Joint Surg. [Am.] 65-A:1071–1080, October 1983.)

1). Twelve patients had bilateral procedures, 6 during a single hospital stay. Eleven patients had previously been operated on. The preoperative ambulatory status is shown in Table 2. Measures were taken to reduce flexion contractures before operation in 5 patients

Fig 6–8 (left).—Preoperative lateral roentgenogram showing posterior subluxation of tibia on femur.
Fig 6–9 (right).—Postoperative film showing use of custom-made miniature posterior stabilized prosthesis to correct subluxation.
(Courtesy of Sarokhan, A.J., et al.: J. Bone Joint Surg. [Am.] 65-A:1071–1080, October 1983.)

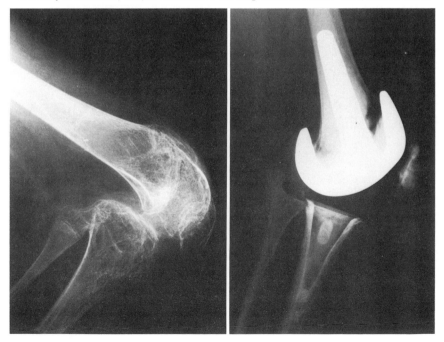

(Figs 6–6 and 6–7). Instability was managed by use of a more constrained prosthesis to correct capsular or ligamentous insufficiency. Miniature or custom-made components (Figs 6–8 and 6–9) were necessary in 12 knees.

Passive flexion of 90 degrees or more was achieved in all but 4 of the 29 knees that were operated on, and these 4 could be flexed from 60 to 80 degrees. Twenty-one knees required manipulation after operation. All knees but 1 were pain free when evaluated an average of 5 years after operation. All patients but 1 were able to negotiate stairs. The average range of active flexion was 86 degrees in the 27 knees evaluated. About one third of the knees had a radiolucency at the bone-cement interface, but no lucency more than 1 mm wide was apparent. Two patients who had required surgical revision, 1 for deep infection and 1 for pain and instability, were not satisfied with the outcome. The latter patient was the only 1 who could not walk postoperatively. Complications included 1 posterior tibial subluxation. Four patients required resurfacing of the patella because of pain. No prosthesis has had to be revised because of loosening.

Skeletal immaturity may not contraindicate knee arthroplasty in patients with progressive deformity from juvenile rheumatoid arthritis. Maximal flexion is promoted by manipulation and, where indicated, serial casting before operation. Custom-made and minisized components are necessary in some knees. Patellar resurfacing should be done at knee arthroplasty. Hip arthroplasty should be done first if there is significant involvement of the hip.

▶ [This is a well-documented series of patients with most unique problems. The author's injunction, that adequate preoperative evaluation be undertaken so that the proper type of prosthesis might be employed, is well taken. The continuous passive motion machine postoperatively may assist these patients in achieving a more rapid rehabilitation.—R.A. Klassen] ◀

6–6 **Total Knee Arthroplasty in Hemophilic Arthritis.** Chronic arthropathy caused by hemarthrosis is a disabling complication of hemophilia. M. Small, M. M. Steven, P. A. Freeman, G. D. O. Lowe, J. J. F. Belch, C. D. Forbes, and C. R. M. Prentice (Glasgow) performed total knee replacement using the Geomedic prosthesis in 5 patients, aged 22–37 years, with severe hemophilia A or, in 1 case, hemophilia B. These patients had factor levels below 1 unit/dl and had chronic arthropathy of the knee that had failed to respond to conservative treatment. Surgery was done for frequent bleeds, severe pain, and limited motion. Radiographs showed severe destructive changes in all cases. The goal was to increase the factor VIII or IX level to more than 80% before operation, maintain the level over 50% for 4 days, and, subsequently, maintain plasma levels at 30% for the rest of the hospital stay. Two patients received tranexamic acid.

(6–6) J. Bone Joint Surg. [Br.] 65-B:163–165, March 1983.

All patients had markedly less pain or total relief after knee replacement, and 3 eventually gained a greater range of motion. Two of the 3 patients who had worked full-time before the operation returned to work. Hemarthrosis in the operated joint was reduced markedly or abolished during long-term follow-up in 4 cases. No patient developed hepatitis. Perioperative blood loss required replacement of 1 to 3 units of whole blood in all cases. Subsequently, 2 patients had hemorrhage into the operated joint, controlled by infusion of plasma concentrate.

Surface replacement of the knee with the Geomedic prosthesis reduced pain substantially and improved mobility in the hemophilic patients with chronic, refractory knee arthropathy. Removal of a minimal amount of bone permits revision procedures to be done if the prosthetic joint deteriorates. Hopefully, chronic arthropathy can be prevented in future patients by more extensive home treatment, minimizing the need for orthopedic procedures.

▶ [This very small series of 5 hemophilic patients who underwent total knee arthroplasty confirms reports of other considerably larger series. There seem to be consistent reports of markedly decreased pain, improved function, and greater frequency of hemarthrosis following the total knee replacement procedure. In our experience a few patients have had bleeds subsequent to total knee replacement, however, these bleeds have been very small. In a series of 17 patients, we have had none who suffered massive bleeds into the knee.—R.N. Stauffer] ◀

6–7 **Reimplantation for Salvage of an Infected Total Knee Arthroplasty.** Some have suggested reimplantation of an infected total knee prosthesis as a delayed procedure after removal of an infected arthroplasty. Between 1970 and 1981, James A. Rand and Richard S. Bryan (Mayo Clinic and Found.) attempted salvage of an acutely infected total knee arthroplasty by implantation of a new prosthesis within 2 weeks of removal of the infected one in 14 patients. Mean patient age at reimplantation was 61 years. The diagnosis was osteoarthritis in 7 patients, rheumatoid arthritis in 4, and posttraumatic arthritis in 3. Six patients had had other operations on the knee before total arthroplasty. Four of the 11 evaluable patients refused arthrodesis, and 4 had severe involvement of the other knee or lower extremity. In 3 instances the surgeon believed that bone loss was too great for arthrodesis.

Eight patients had a functioning total knee arthroplasty at final follow-up, 5 had an arthrodesis, and 1 had an above-knee amputation. Salvage succeeded in 6 of 7 patients with low-virulence infections but in only 2 of the 7 with high-virulence infections. Two of the patients with a functioning prosthesis were left with significantly restricted motion, and 1 patient had moderate pain. The success rate excluding these patients was 35%. Four patients had complications of wound healing after reimplantation. The x-ray findings in a patient with

(6–7)   J. Bone Joint Surg. [Am.] 65-A:1081–1086, October 1983.

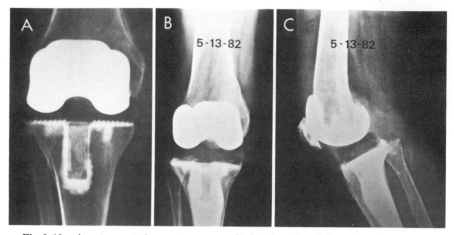

Fig 6–10.—A, anteroposterior roentgenogram of infected total condylar arthroplasty. **B** and **C,** anteroposterior and lateral films, respectively, made 4 years after reimplantation. Generalized lucent line measuring less than 1 mm is present at bone-cement interface of tibial component. (Courtesy of Rand, J.A., and Bryan, R.S.: J. Bone Joint Surg. [Am.] 65-A:1081–1086, October 1983.)

mild knee pain and normal stability 4 years after reimplantation are shown in Figure 6–10. This patient had a range of motion of 0 to 100 degrees.

The best results of reimplantation were obtained in patients in this series who were infected with an organism of low virulence. Implantation of a new total knee prosthesis within 2 weeks of removal of an infected one should not be done unless a low-virulence organism or other unusual clinical circumstance is present. A longer delay before the new prosthesis is implanted might improve the results.

6–8 **Two-Stage Reimplantation for Salvage of Infected Total Knee Arthroplasty.** John N. Insall, Francesca M. Thompson, and Barry D. Brause (Hosp. for Special Surgery, New York) reviewed the results of 11 two-stage reimplantation procedures done to salvage infected total knee arthroplasties in 10 women, 7 with osteoarthritis and 3 with rheumatoid arthritis. Mean age at the index arthroplasty was 67 years. Three infections were overtly systemic. All components of the prosthesis and all cement were removed, and reimplantation of a total condylar-type prosthesis was performed after 6 weeks of parenteral antibiotic therapy, during which serum bactericidal concentrations were maintained at a peak dilution of 1:8. Average follow-up was 34 months.

The outcome in 2 cases is shown in Figures 6–11 and 6–12. No patient had recurrence of the original infection at follow-up, but 1 had a hematogenous infection with a different organism secondary to

(6–8) J. Bone Joint Surg. [Am.] 65-A:1087–1098, October 1983.

an infected bunion. The results were considered to be excellent in 5 knees, good in 4, and fair in 2. The most common complication was weakness of the extensor mechanism with an extension lag. Only 1 knee was moderately painful. Ten knees had no ligament instability. No x-ray evidence of loosening was obtained in any joint at the last follow-up evaluation.

The results of reimplantation for infected total knee arthroplasty are not comparable with those of the primary operation. All the patients in this series were satisfied with the outcome. Antibiotic therapy alone is inadequate in these cases. The surgical procedures are technically difficult and time consuming, and there are no shortcuts. Extensor weakness has been the major problem after reimplantation. Two patients required a walking aid for this reason. Two other patients required a patellectomy for wound closure

Fig 6–11.—Case 1. Woman, 64, was seen 3½ years after Guepar arthroplasty. **A,** admission film, made when patient was in extremely toxic state due to acute infection of knee and cellulitis that was spreading proximally along lateral aspect of thigh to hip. Knee was aspirated, and culture of specimen grew *Staphylococcus aureus*. Despite intravenous antibiotic administration, patient's condition became progressively worse, and prosthesis had to be removed as emergency procedure. **B,** roentgenogram made after removal of prosthesis, when patient's condition improved remarkably. She was afebrile within a few days. However, at 6 weeks, some inflammation and induration of wound remained, though culture of aspirated material showed no growth. Antibiotic therapy was discontinued, and cylinder cast was applied. **C,** roentgenogram made after reimplantation with standard total condylar prosthesis was carried out 4 weeks later, at which time wound appeared benign. Although original prosthesis had been hinged, residual soft tissue sleeve was adequate to give good stability, though titanium mesh was required to fill defect in tibial cortex. Rehabilitation was delayed by some superficial skin necrosis, but after follow-up of 41 months, patient had range of knee flexion from 0 to 85 degrees and excellent clinical result. (Courtesy of Insall, J.N., et al.: J. Bone Joint Surg. [Am.] 65-A:1087–1098, October 1983.)

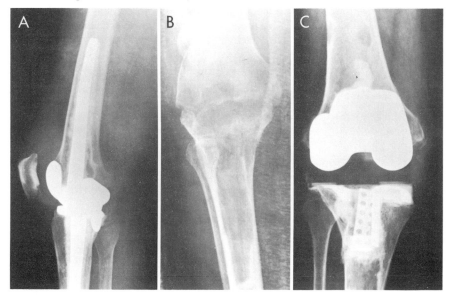

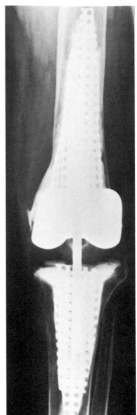

Fig 6–12.—Case 10. Roentgenogram made 72 months after reimplantation, showing use of titanium mesh to reinforce cement. Patient originally had had Guepar prosthesis, and only two hollow cones of femoral and tibial cortical bone remained after its removal. (Courtesy of Insall, J.N., et al.: J. Bone Joint Surg. [Am.] 65-A:1087–1098, October 1983.)

after reimplantation, and 1 of them had an extension lag and required a walking aid.

▶ [Management of a patient with an infected total knee arthroplasty is quite difficult. The selection of the patient for delayed reconstruction involves the evaluation of many parameters. In general, the microbiology of the infectious process is quite important. As Doctors Rand and Bryan stress, the more virulent the organism, the greater the risk of recurrent sepsis. However, Doctor Insall and his co-workers were able to eradicate the infectious process in 2 patients with the isolation of *Pseudomonas aeruginosa*. Only 1 out of 4 patients in whom *Staphylococcus aureus* was isolated developed another infection, which was of hematogenous origin.

The quality of the soft tissues, especially about the knee, is terribly important. Scarred and fibrotic soft tissues will frequently preclude close apposition of the incision following reconstruction. The selection and monitoring of antimicrobial therapy is equally as important as careful surgical technique in the management of this group of patients. Doctor Insall and his co-workers have utilized a serum bactericidal titer maintaining bactericidal levels at a peak dilution of 1:8. Such monitoring may not be available in all community hospitals. However, in most community hospitals it is possible to monitor peak and trough levels. Such monitoring is critical if aminoglycoside therapy is prescribed.

The preceding two manuscripts point out the advantages of reconstructing an infected total joint arthroplasty in a delayed fashion. It allows the body's host defense mechanism to remove residual bacteria that are always left behind following surgical debridement. It also permits the surgeon to identify those patients who may have a residual abscess or other soft tissue infection. This technique has proved to be efficacious in patients with infected total hip arthroplasties (Jones, D. R., and Fitzgerald, R. H., Jr.: *Orthop. Trans.* 7:515, 1983).

In summary, the quality of the soft tissues, the bacteriology of the infectious process, and the patient's general health are probably the most important parameters that must be carefully scrutinized prior to deciding whether to reconstruct an infected total knee arthroplasty. Most patients will be best treated with excision of the components and arthrodesis of the involved knee.—R.H. Fitzgerald, Jr.] ◄

6–9 **Failed Total Knee Prosthesis Secondary to Metal Hypersensitivity.** Prem Kumar, Christopher Bryan, James Bowler, and Robert D'Ambrosia (Louisiana State Univ.) report data on a patient with metal hypersensitivity that led to failure of a total knee prosthesis.

Man, 56, had persistent disability after initial incision and drainage for left knee injury and subsequent arthrotomy with removal of a meniscus. Total knee replacement was then done using a cobalt-chromium-nickel prosthesis. Pain persisted, and joint swelling developed 2 days after operation. The patient previously had an eczematous rash associated with wearing a necklace, ring, and metal wrist band. Hypertension was treated with hydrochlorothiazide. The prosthesis appeared to be positioned and aligned satisfactorily. Arthroscopy showed inflamed synovium but no component loosening or loose bodies. The synovial fluid was 4 + positive for protein and contained 1,100 white blood cells per cc with 60% lymphocytes. Histologic study of the synovium showed highly vascular granulation tissue replacing the connective tissue and focal lymphocytic infiltrates in some sections. Fluorescence microscopy showed no specific abnormalities. Contact patch testing produced a strongly positive reaction to nickel. The prosthesis was replaced by a titanium model free of nickel, and the patient became asymptomatic.

Metal hypersensitivity was the probable cause of prosthetic failure in this patient. Nickel in the prosthesis presumably produced a cell-mediated immune response, leading to synovitis and joint effusion. Metal hypersensitivity should be considered as a cause of prosthetic failure when other causes are not apparent. A history of rash developing after jewelery is worn should increase the suspicion of metal allergy.

6–10 **Use of Pulsing Electromagnetic Fields to Achieve Arthrodesis of the Knee Following Failed Total Knee Arthroplasty: Preliminary Report.** Pulsing electromagnetic fields have been used to help salvage resistant nonunions and congenital pseudarthroses of long bones. Louis U. Bigliani, Melvin P. Rosenwasser, Nina Caulo, Mary M. Schink, and C. Andrew L. Bassett (Columbia Presbyterian Med. Center, New York) evaluated this approach in 20 patients who underwent knee arthrodesis after a total joint arthroplasty had failed.

(6–9) Orthopedics 6:1459–1462, November 1983.
(6–10) J. Bone Joint Surg. [Am.] 65-A:480–485, April 1983.

The 13 women and 7 men had an average age of 60 years. Eighteen patients had had an infected arthroplasty; 1 each, mechanical loosening and recurrent dislocation. Arthrodesis had been attempted a total of 25 times, usually with external fixation frames. The most common indication for initial arthroplasty was osteoarthritis. Fourteen patients began coil treatment 6 months or more after arthrodesis and were considered to have nonunion, while 6 had a diagnosis of delayed union. A voltage of 1–1.5 mV per centimeter of bone width was provided for 10–14 hours a day.

The average follow-up after the completion of coil treatment was 19 months. Seventeen patients had clinical and roentgenographic evidence of union at follow-up. They included all 6 patients with delayed union. The average duration of coil treatment was 6 months. All 12 patients who had had a semiconstrained arthroplasty achieved a successful arthrodesis. The 3 patients in whom coil treatment failed had long-standing nonunions, and they had not followed the prescribed protocol. All the patients with solid union were free of pain and able to walk. They had better walking ability than before treatment, although many still required an assistive device because of their general physical condition.

Pulsing electromagnetic field therapy appears to be an effective adjunct when arthrodesis of the knee is necessary after removal of a failed total joint replacement. All patients in the present series who cooperated with the treatment did well. The treatment now is used as soon as there is evidence of delayed union.

▶ [Arthrodesis after failure of total knee arthroplasty is subject to many variables: the success of the method of treatment of infection; the quality and amount of bone remaining; the adequacy of the fixation achieved; and the cooperation of the patient. Twelve of these 20 patients had semiconstrained total knees. Since I have observed fusion occurring as long as 2 years after the attempted arthrodesis, I am impressed but not overwhelmed by the success of nonweight-bearing, plaster, and pulsating electromagnetic fields. I am more impressed with the success in 5 of 8 patients with constrained total knees and thus more severe bone loss. Any adjunctive method in these patients, and especially a noninvasive method, is valuable. The authors have stressed the importance of strict adherence to the protocol. This is not a magic wand, but if properly used it is another weapon in our armamentarium.—R.S. Bryan] ◀

6–11 **Nerve Palsy After Knee Arthroplasty in Patients With Rheumatoid Arthritis.** Peroneal nerve palsy is a seemingly rare complication of knee arthroplasty. Kaj Knutson, Ido Leden, Gunnar Sturfelt, Ingmar Rosén, and Lars Lidgren (Univ. of Lund) reviewed the occurrence of nerve dysfunction in 41 consecutive patients who had 42 knee arthroplasties in 1980. The total condylar knee was used in 20 instances, the Attenborough stabilized prosthesis in 19, and the Marmor modular knee in 3. Eight operations were revisions of arthroplasties that had failed biomechanically, and 2 were revisions of infected arthroplasties. Mean patient age was 54 years. Thirty-eight

(6–11) Scand. J. Rheumatol. 12:201–205, 1983.

patients had classic and 3 had juvenile rheumatoid arthritis. In 16 patients, neurophysiologic studies were carried out before and an average of 34 days after operation.

Four patients had clinical evidence of peroneal palsy postoperatively that was verified electrophysiologically. Two with an Attenborough prosthesis developed palsy immediately after operation; 1 of these patients had a complete palsy. Another patient developed palsy 5 months postoperatively after a hemarthrosis. One patient with a total condylar knee replacement developed a complete palsy after 24 hours. Three other knees had only electrophysiologic evidence of peroneal palsy. All palsies resolved within 6 months of operation. Correction of a flexion contracture exceeding 10 degrees appeared to predispose to peroneal palsy, particularly when combined with a varus change in alignment. The preoperative electromyographic findings did not predict the occurrence of nerve lesions after operation. The hospital stay was significantly prolonged by the development of peroneal palsy.

Clinical peroneal palsy was more frequent in this series of patients undergoing knee arthroplasty than in previous series. A reduction in flexion deformity followed by correction of valgus deformity seemed to predispose to peroneal palsy, presumably through stretching of the nerve. There is no indication that preoperative neuropathy is an important predisposing factor. In patients with fixed flexion deformity, the peroneal nerve could be released and inspected through a separate lateral incision. Bandages and plasters must be well padded. Patients who require more than 10 degrees of correction of a flexion deformity should be warned of the risk of nerve palsy.

▶ [Peroneal nerve problems have been reported in every series of knee replacements. Thirty percent of patients in whom I do knee arthroplasty have rheumatoid arthritis. In reviewing my last 145 patients, I found none with clinically diagnosed peroneal symptoms. I check carefully for this. In previous years I have noted several such cases that were associated with the onset of swelling from therapy or pressure from the bed or dressing. In my practice the usual hospital stay after knee replacement is only 14 days, however, and the development of late onset transient peroneal palsies would have been missed, as would the development of only subclinical manifestations. There are, of course, many variables involved and it is difficult to compare series. Careful studies such as this will help us to define the etiology of peroneal palsies.—R.S. Bryan] ◀

6–12 **Why Not Resurface the Patella?** Jean-Paul Levai, Hugh C. McLeod, and M. A. R. Freeman (London Hosp. Med. College) reviewed the results of knee replacement with the ICLH prosthesis in 47 patients with rheumatoid arthritis and 24 with osteoarthritis, operated on between 1977 and 1979. In 24 of the rheumatoid knees the articulating surface of the patella was replaced with a polythene prosthesis, which in 16 was fixed with cement. In the other 23 patients the patellar surface was trimmed to fit the femoral component. Fif-

(6–12) J. Bone Joint Surg. [Br.] 65-B:448–451, August 1983.

teen of the patients with osteoarthritis had the articulating surface
of the patella replaced, 9 with cement and 6 without. Nine others did
not have the patella resurfaced.

Only 2 of the 24 patients with rheumatoid disease who had the
patella resurfaced had pain, and neither required analgesia. Five of
the other 23 patients had pain in the front of the knee, and 1 required
analgesia. The posterior surfaces of 10 unreplaced patellas became
eroded (Fig 6–13), but erosion was not clearly related to pain in the

Fig 6–13.—Skyline views showing erosion of unresurfaced patella. **A,** 1 year after operation;
B, 2 years after operation; and **C,** 4 years after operation. (Courtesy of Levai, J.-P., et al.: J. Bone
Joint Surg. [Br.] 65-B:448–451, August 1983.)

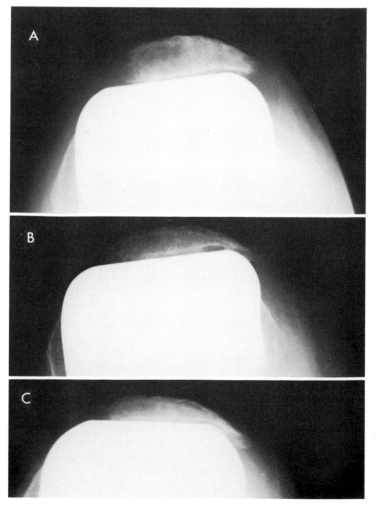

front of the knee. All patients with osteoarthritis in whom the patella was resurfaced were free from pain. Four of the 9 others had peripatellar pain, necessitating analgesia in 2. The posterior surfaces of 6 unreplaced patellas were eroded. In neither group were the resurfaced patellas roentgenographically abnormal. The operative technique did not influence the occurrence of postoperative synovitis. There were no symptomatic or x-ray differences between knees in which the patellar component was fixed with cement and the others. Three patellar fractures were discovered on roentgenography; none was displaced or symptomatic. Two patients not included in the series had patellar fractures with displacement; 1 had had the articulating surface of the patella replaced, and 1 had not.

Resurfacing of the patella at knee replacement reduces peripatellar pain and has no apparent adverse effects. It is suggested that this be a routine part of total knee replacement. The component can be fixed without cement.

▶ [I find myself in complete agreement with the authors of this paper, although many experienced orthopedic surgeons would disagree. The reader would do well to study Figure 6–13 which has a demonstration of patellar erosion. I have encountered many knees, especially in rheumatoid patients, with the patella worn thin and the anterior portion of the femoral condyles almost worn to the level of the anterior cortex of the femur. Wear against a metal flange can hardly be expected not to occur, and in many total knee revisions has become so severe that resurfacing is not possible. My experience is slightly different from the authors. I have encountered more fractures in nonreplaced patellae than in those with replacement, probably because I replace all that are not too thin and osteoporotic.

The authors have stated it well: why not resurface the patella?—R.S. Bryan] ◀

7. The Knee

7-1 **Local Anesthesia for Diagnostic and Operative Arthroscopy of the Knee.** G. O. Read (Univ. of Witwatersrand) has used local anesthesia extensively for diagnostic and operative arthroscopy of the knee since 1981. The goals are blockade of the femoral nerve, local infiltration of the patellar fat pad, and provision of adequate intra-articular anesthesia. A 20-ml volume of 0.5% bupivacaine with 1:200,000 epinephrine is injected via a lateral parapatellar approach after any hemarthrosis or effusion is aspirated, and a mixture of 5 ml of bupivacaine with epinephrine and 5 ml of 1% lidocaine is infiltrated on either side of the patellar tendon. A 23-gauge needle is used to infiltrate the prepatellar fat pad. Another 10 ml of the mixture is used to block the femoral nerve just below the inguinal ligament.

This approach was used in 100 consecutive patients, and 6 others received both local anesthesia without femoral nerve block and a general anesthetic when reconstruction of major ligament damage was necessary. Twenty-three arthroscopic operations were carried out. The average procedure time was 65 minutes. Five of the 100 patients had significant discomfort, but the procedure was completed. One procedure was abandoned. Two of the patients with significant discomfort had severe synovitis. No complications occurred.

It is unnecessary to use a tourniquet when this local anesthetic approach for arthroscopy is employed. The patient retains the ability to flex the knee, and patellar-femoral tracking can be assessed dynamically when a tourniquet is not present. If adequate facilities are available, there is no reason why arthroscopy of the knee should not be performed on outpatients with local anesthesia. Sedation is not used before or during the procedure. Considerable financial savings should result.

▶ [The author presents an interesting technique for local anesthesia which supplements the use of intra-articular anesthetic with local nerve blocks. The important sensory nerve supply to the knee is well outlined by the author, and the reported success rate is admirable. This technique, however, would not be amenable to use with a tourniquet and leg holder as is frequently utilized for arthroscopic surgery. However, for a diagnostic arthroscopy, this appears to be a viable technique which will help minimize cost to the patient and should be considered.—J.A. Rand] ◀

7-2 **Arthroscopic Meniscectomy: Short- and Medium-term Results** are reported by J. O. Ramadier, P. Beaufils, J. Y. Dupont, J.

(7–1) S. Afr. Med. J. 64:471–472, Sept. 24, 1983.
(7–2) Rev. Chir. Orthop. 69:581–590, 1983.

Benoit, and A. Frank. Two hundred sixty-five patients, most of them male and two thirds of them younger than age 40, were seen with a traumatic meniscal lesion. Fifty-eight percent of the patients participated in sports regularly. There were 283 meniscal lesions in 272 knees (11 with a lesion of two menisces). Associated lesions were very common. Of 240 arthroscopic meniscectomies performed in these cases between 1980 and 1982, 198 were reviewed with a follow-up of between 3 and 6 months and 101 were reviewed with a follow-up of between 6 months and 2 years.

Intraoperative and postoperative complications were infrequent: 3 cases of phlebitis, 1 case of hemarthrosis and 1 case of septic arthritis. The last case occurred in 1 of the 8 occasions in which arthroscopy had to be completed by an arthrotomy.

Social and functional rehabilitation was very rapid. Hospitalization time was 2 days and the patients resumed work and sports activities two to three times faster than after meniscectomy by arthrotomy. The results were excellent in 85% of the cases, slightly better than after arthrotomy. Prognosis was worse when patellar or tibiofemoral chondral lesions were present. They were not as good in cases of lateral meniscus lesions, particularly with an associated lesion of the anterior cruciate ligament. However, two thirds of patients with this disorder had noticeable improvement.

The present follow-up is not sufficient to evaluate long-term results. Hopefully, the results will be stable, as the meniscectomy was partial in three fourths of the patients. Evaluation of the incidence of recurrence and unobserved lesions will only be possible later.

▶ [The authors present a rather large series of arthroscopic meniscectomies but, unfortunately, followed them for only a short period of time. The information provided by the authors adds little to what has been presented before by other authors in the literature. The treatment program in the patients included a variety of procedures other than arthroscopy including extra-articular ligamentous reconstruction and peripheral reattachment of the meniscus probably via the arthrotomy. The authors' findings, that a tear of the anterior cruciate indicates worse results with arthroscopic meniscectomy compared to intact anterior cruciate, is worthy of note. A longer term of follow-up of this group of patients would be useful. However, the finding of improved subjective stability in the patient following partial meniscectomy in the presence of anterior cruciate deficient knee is important. The increased frequency of poor results associated with degenerative changes in the knee has been noted by several authors, as well as the authors of this paper.—J.A. Rand] ◀

7–3 **Arthroscopic, Open Partial, and Total Meniscectomy: Comparative Study.** M. D. Northmore-Ball, D. J. Dandy, and R. W. Jackson compared the outcome of different types of meniscectomy in a series of 219 knees treated at two centers. Seventy-one were managed by arthroscopic partial meniscectomy, 45 by open partial meniscectomy, and 103 by open total meniscectomy. Overall mean follow-up was 4.3 years. Sex ratios and mean ages were not markedly different

(7–3) J. Bone Joint Surg. [Br.] 65-B:400–404, August 1983.

in the 3 treatment groups. The ratio of longitudinal tears to other types was about 4:3 in both the arthroscopic and the open surgical groups. Chondromalacia was present in 28% to 38% of the different groups.

Patients who had arthroscopic treatment used a walking aid for a mean of only about 2 days, compared with 12 days for those who underwent open partial meniscectomy and 25 days for those who had total meniscectomy. Arthroscopic partial meniscectomy was associated with a shorter delay before return to sports activity than were the open procedures. The late symptomatic results were excellent or good in 90% of arthroscopic cases, 85% of open partial cases, and 68% of open total cases. Arthroscopic treatment was superior to open operation in patients with bucket-handle tears and flap tears and in patients with and those without chondromalacia. The benefit of arthroscopic operation was especially evident in cases of lateral meniscal damage.

Partial meniscectomy by a closed technique with arthroscopic control is a substantial advance in the treatment of a large majority of symptomatic meniscal tears. Widespread meniscal damage remains a rare indication for total meniscectomy. Meniscal reattachment may occasionally be indicated. Arthroscopic partial meniscectomy, however, is the preferred treatment for the common types of meniscal injury in which it is practicable.

▶ [This study attempts to place the value of an arthroscopic partial meniscectomy on more scientific and carefully controlled clinical grounds. The study investigates two variables with respect to tears of the meniscus; partial vs. complete excision, and open vs. arthroscopic surgery.

The groups are carefully selected in such a way as to study only the specific question of interest. Most of the follow-up is by questionnaire, and there are no radiographic or physical examination data. Furthermore, the follow-up periods and patient ages are not strictly comparable among the groups. The group with the complete open meniscectomy is on average approximately 8 years older than the group with partial arthroscopic meniscectomy.

Despite these minor points, this study does offer some significant data with respect to the result of the present popular modality for treating meniscal tears. A prospective study of this clinical question would be welcomed. However, it is probably not possible since relatively few surgeons are performing open complete meniscectomies at the present time.—B.F. Morrey] ◀

7–4 **Irrigating Solutions for Arthroscopy: Metabolic Study.** Normal saline is routinely used to distend the joint at arthroscopy and to irrigate the synovial cavity during and after arthroscopic operation, but little firm evidence supports its use. Brian F. Reagan, Vincent K. McInerny, Benjamin V. Treadwell, Bertram Zarins, and Henry J. Mankin (Harvard Med. School) measured rates of proteoglycan synthesis by determining the incorporation of $^{35}SO_4$ into slices of bovine articular cartilage during short-term in vitro incubation in various

(7–4)   J. Bone Joint Surg. [Am.] 65-A:629–631, June 1983.

solutions. Several standard solutions were compared with Ham F12 medium, a complex, ionically balanced salt and amino acid solution used for tissue culture. Neither normal saline nor phosphate-buffered saline supported metabolic activity as well as Ringer's lactate or acetate, both of which approximated Ham F12 solution. Incorporation of label increased modestly with phosphate-buffered saline and progressively with Ringer's lactate solution. Acetated Ringer's solution performed nearly as well as Ringer's lactate.

Ringer's lactate supports chondrocyte metabolism for 8 hours in this ex vivo organ culture system. Since its cost is the same as that of normal saline, it seems reasonable to use Ringer's solution for arthroscopic procedures.

▶ [The authors have performed an in vitro study of the effect of various irrigating solutions on articular cartilage and metabolism. It is worth noting that the use of saline does not support articular cartilage metabolism in vitro. On the basis of their in vitro studies, the authors recommend Ringer's lactate as a more physiologic solution than normal saline for arthroscopic irrigation.

All other conclusions follow from the data that they have obtained. The clinical correlation has not been proved. The ready availability of saline and its widespread use in thousands of arthroscopic cases throughout the country without adverse clinical effects would indicate that caution should be practiced before the results of these in vitro studies can be applied to the clinical setting.—J.A. Rand] ◀

7–5 **Symptomatic Anterior Cruciate-Deficient Knee.**—*Part I. Long-term functional disability in athletically active individuals.*—The best treatment of a knee with a deficient anterior cruciate ligament is uncertain. Frank R. Noyes, Pekka A. Mooar, David S. Matthews, and David L. Butler (Univ. of Cincinnati) reviewed the outcome in 103 patients seen between 1976 and 1978 with chronic instability of the anterior cruciate ligament. The 75 males and 28 females had a mean age of 26 years. Two thirds of the patients were involved in high school or college sports and the rest in recreational sports, with 4 exceptions. About half the patients were seen for gradual deterioration in joint function and increasing symptoms. About one-fourth had had a second injury. Initial injury had occurred an average of 5½ years previously. A total of 65 menisci had been removed from 51 patients.

Only 7% of patients had a diagnosis of anterior cruciate ligament injury initially. Most patients had received supportive treatment of some type, but over a third had received no specific treatment. One fifth of patients were unable to return to sports activity after the initial injury, and only about a third were participating in strenuous or competitive activities. About a third of patients had moderate to severe symptoms related to walking. Meniscectomy did not appear to have reduced the frequency of symptoms, and some patients may

(7–5)   J. Bone Joint Surg. [Am.] 65-A:154–162, February 1983.
        Ibid 65-A:163–174, February 1983.

have had more marked symptoms after the procedure. X-ray evidence of significant arthritis was present in 21% of the 91 patients evaluated. Ten patients had degenerative changes in the lateral compartment of the knee.

Patients who continue to participate in athletic activities after anterior cruciate ligament injury and are not properly treated or counseled at the outset frequently have significant functional disability, even in usual daily activities. Meniscal damage and arthritis of the knee may follow reinjury in these patients. Those who are unable to compensate for functional loss of the anterior cruciate ligament require early and continued treatment to prevent serious disability.

Part II. Results of rehabilitation, activity modification, and counseling on functional disability.—Noyes, Matthews, Mooar, and Edward S. Grood managed 84 patients with symptoms of chronic anterior cruciate laxity by rehabilitation, modification of activities to avoid recurrent symptoms, and use of a knee brace for activities. All patients had definite physical signs of chronic laxity of the anterior cruciate ligament. The 60 males and 24 females had an average age of 28 years. The average time from initial knee injury to final evaluation was 8 years. The patients were followed closely and examined periodically.

The spectrum of initial disability was wide. Over one third of patients improved with nonoperative management and were well compensated at follow-up, with no more than minimal symptoms during normal activities or recreational activities that could not be performed before treatment. Some symptoms did persist in these patients, usually in association with strenuous sports activities. One third of patients remained the same during conservative management. One third became worse, with significant symptoms on recreational activities and often on daily activities. Eighteen patients eventually had reconstructive operations, and 18 others were considering operation when last evaluated. It was often difficult initially to predict the outcome. The occurrence of reinjury was significantly related to the overall severity of the state of the knee at final evaluation. Many patients failed to comply with recommended activity modifications or substitutions. This was due in part to the importance of sports participation to these patients.

The course of patients with chronic anterior cruciate laxity during conservative management is difficult to predict, emphasizing the wisdom of postponing operation, especially in view of the uncertain long-term success rate of current reconstructive procedures. Activities that cause even sporadic reinjuries should be avoided, even if significant symptoms are absent. Arthroscopy may be useful in some cases to delineate the extent of joint deterioration and indicate the need for early operation. Reconstruction is considered only for patients with functional disability who are unwilling to modify their athletic life-styles or who have symptoms on routine daily activities.

▶ [The articles by Noyes et al., Giove et al. (see abstract 7–10), and the report by Hejgaard (see abstract 7–15) are very valuable additions to the literature. In the past, a lack of studies on the natural history of the anterior cruciate ligament injury made it difficult for the surgeon to decide appropriate treatment for the acute injury. Our experience is similar to that outlined by Noyes in that approximately one third of patients with an acute anterior cruciate ligament disruption will be well compensated and have only minimal symptoms. Another one third will do quite well but will have symptoms of cruciate instability with activities on the extended knee. However, this group will get by reasonably well with activity modification, bracing, and a good re-habilitation program. The other one third will have disabling symptoms related to their anterior cruciate ligament insufficiency with recurrent episodes of painful sub-luxation and effusion.

Based on these studies, one might reserve repair or primary reconstruction of the anterior cruciate ligament disruption for the young athletic individual who can be expected to place great demands on the knee. Reconstruction must be reserved for those individuals with significant disability related to chronic anterior cruciate insuf-ficiency with recurrent episodes of painful subluxation. Certainly, in these individuals, repeated episodes of significant subluxation will cause damage to the joint. The long-term studies of anterior cruciate insufficiency by Marshall, Jacobson, Dameron, and Noyes all indicate that the untreated cruciate ligament injury results in a slow but progressive deterioration of the articular surface and that osteoarthritis increases with time. Hopefully, the newer techniques of the vascularized patellar tendon graft in reconstruction of the anterior cruciate insufficient knee will provide predictable restoration of stability that will help prevent the repetitive insult to the articular sur-face with subsequent degenerative disease.—F.H. Sim] ◀

7–6 **Acute Anteromedial Rotatory Instability: Long-term Results of Surgical Repair.** Jack C. Hughston and Gene R. Barrett reviewed the results of surgical repair of anteromedial rotatory instability in 154 knees of 150 patients who were followed for 2 to 21 years after injury. Patients with associated anterior cruciate ligament and men-iscal injuries were included, but those with combined rotatory insta-bilities and straight instabilities were not. Eighty-six males and 3 females with an average age at injury of 19½ years were followed for an average of 8 years. All but 4 of the 93 knees in this group were injured during sports activities, most by contact. Anteromedial rota-tory instabilities of 2 + or greater were repaired. The middle third of the medial capsular ligament, tibial collateral ligament, and poste-rior oblique ligament were all torn in 85% or more of the knees that were operated on and the anterior cruciate in 59%. The medial me-niscus was torn in 58% of knees and the lateral meniscus in 10 joints. Three knees had a fracture of the lateral tibial plateau.

The objective results were satisfactory in 73% of knees and the functional ratings in 89%. Meniscectomy slightly reduced the propor-tion of satisfactory objective ratings, but anterior cruciate repair did not. Nine knees required further reconstructive operations. Over two thirds of the patients injured in organized athletics returned to an at

(7–6) J. Bone Joint Surg. [Am.] 65-A:145–153, February 1983.

least equal level of athletic activity, and over 90% either returned to such activity or thought they would be able to.

Lack of repair of a torn anterior cruciate ligament does not compromise the results of acute repair of the medial ligament. The bad reputation of the so-called anterior cruciate-deficient knee is probably related to associated injuries that are not repaired at initial operation. The medial meniscus should be repaired where possible. Repair of the posterior oblique ligament is the key to medial stability at the moment of static fixation. Recurrent injury and the need for reoperation are infrequent when a high-quality repair of the medial ligaments is carried out at initial operation.

▶ [This classic article by Drs. Hughston and Barrett contributes a great deal to our knowledge and understanding of knee ligament instabilities. It certainly supports our current thinking about the importance of the medial meniscus, particularly as an adjunct to stability. The authors have shown that an adequate repair of the secondary restraints on the medial aspect of the knee can provide a good result despite an irretrievable injury to the anterior cruciate ligament, which is the primary restraint. In our experience, had there been significant injury to the secondary capsular and ligamentous restraints on the lateral side of the knee, it would have been unlikely that anterolateral instability would have required late ligament reconstruction.—F.H. Sim] ◀

7–7 **Accuracy of Double-Contrast Arthrographic Evaluation of the Anterior Cruciate Ligament: Retrospective Review of 163 Knees With Surgical Confirmation.** Helene Pavlov, Russell F. Warren, Mark F. Sherman, and Paul D. Cayea (New York Hosp.-Cornell Univ. Med. College) evaluated double-contrast arthrography for assessing the state of the anterior cruciate ligament (ACL) in 163 patients with knee problems who were operated on between 1978 and 1981. The 129 males and 34 females had an average age of 27 years. Eighty-five patients had acute injuries and were examined within 3 weeks of the most recent injury. Arthrography was done with about 5 ml of 60% diatrizoate meglumine, epinephrine, and 50 cc of room air. After passive exercise the ACL was examined during a simulated anterior drawer maneuver by a horizontal cross-table lateral roentgenogram and fluoroscopic spot films. The menisci were then evaluated. The normal appearances of the ACL are shown in Figure 7–1 and abnormal findings in Figures 7–2 and 7–3.

Ten knees underwent arthroscopy and 153, arthrotomy. The ACL was torn in 97 knees, and a meniscal abnormality was present in 63 of these and in 41 without ACL abnormality. Arthrographic diagnoses were 95% accurate in confirming the ACL as intact or abnormal. The diagnosis was 91.4% accurate in individual diagnostic subgroups and 95% accurate in acute cases. Arthrography was 69% accurate in distinguishing a lax, intact ACL from a torn ligament with intact synovium.

(7–7) J. Bone Joint Surg. [Am.] 65-A:175–183, February 1983.

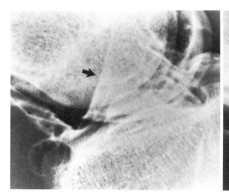

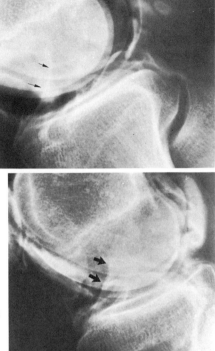

Fig 7–1 (above left).—Spot film showing normal anterior cruciate ligament. Anterior edge of anterior cruciate ligament is ruler-straight *(arrow)*.

Fig 7–2 (above).—Lax anterior cruciate ligament demonstrated by bowed, concave anterior surface of ligament *(arrows)*.

Fig 7–3 (right).—Torn anterior cruciate ligament in which investing synovium is intact. Anterior synovial edge of anterior cruciate ligament is wavy and lumpy *(arrows)*.

(Courtesy of Pavlov, H., et al.: J. Bone Joint Surg. [Am.] 65-A:175–183, February 1983.)

Double-contrast arthrography, performed and interpreted carefully, is an accurate means of evaluating the anterior cruciate ligament and menisci in a single examination. The study is 95% accurate in determining whether the ACL is intact or torn. Arthrography is helpful in identifying patients for whom arthrotomy or arthroscopic operation may be advised.

▶ [The paper is well structured and provides an excellent discussion of the technique and criteria for interpretation of cruciate ligament injuries. Other techniques have also been described in detection of the cruciate ligament injuries including xeroradiography with or without tomography, double contrast techniques with tomography, and computed tomography. These techniques are time-consuming and often result in more radiation exposure for the patient. However, because of the difficulty associated with diagnosis in these patients, these techniques may be warranted in certain cases. Since the clinical examination is usually highly accurate, arthrography is more commonly performed in patients in whom the clinical picture is not completely clear. Nuclear magnetic resonance imaging may be an additional useful technique to evaluate the cruciate ligament. We have detected the cruciate using this technique, however, experience in determining abnormalities in the ligament is limited at this time. Further experience may demonstrate that this technique will provide a noninvasive means of evaluating a ligament.

The description of the technique and results in this paper further emphasize the fact that close communication is necessary between the referring physician and the radiologist so that proper evaluation of the suspected meniscus or ligament injury can be obtained. Special views, positioning, and techniques are required depending on the clinical situation.—T.H. Berquist] ◀

7–8 **Acute Posterolateral Rotatory Instability of the Knee.** Jesse C. DeLee, Mark B. Riley, and Charles A. Rockwood, Jr. (Univ. of Texas, San Antonio) reviewed data on 12 cases of isolated acute posterolateral instability of the knee that were among 735 cases of knee ligament injury treated in 1971 through 1977. The 9 male and 3 female patients were aged 13 to 50 years. Sports activities were responsible for 5 injuries, motor vehicle-pedestrian accidents for 4, and a fall for 3. A direct blow to the anteromedial tibia was noted by 9 patients.

All repairs were done within 2 weeks of injury in patients with 2 + or more varus instability with 30 degrees of knee flexion. Examination under anesthesia was performed in 6 cases. The goal of surgery was to advance the arcuate ligament complex back to its anatomical site in a bony bed proximally or distally. Five patients had a fracture of the fibular head. The arcuate ligament complex was found at surgery to be torn in all cases. In 8 cases the biceps femoris tendon was avulsed from the fibula. The lateral meniscus was damaged in 3 cases.

Eleven patients were followed up an average of 7½ years after operation. Ten patients had 1 + or less laxity on varus stress testing at 30 degrees, and 1 patient had 2 + laxity. Result of the posterolateral drawer test was 1 + or less in 10 cases and 2 + in 1 patient. The external rotation recurvatum test was negative in 9 patients. No patient had a positive test for anterolateral rotatory instability at followup. Both peroneal nerve palsies resolved without further treatment. Eight patients had good and 3 had fair subjective results. No patient reported significant pain on routine daily activities. Objective results were good in 8 cases, fair in 2 cases, and poor in 1 patient who had a postoperative infection requiring drainage. Functionally, there were 7 good results and 3 fair results. The 1 patient with a poor result had a limp and was unable to participate in recreational sports activities.

Acute posterolateral instability results from a blow to the anteromedial tibia with the knee in extension. Surgery is indicated if there is 2 + or greater varus instability at 30 degrees of knee flexion in association with a positive external rotation recurvatum or posterolateral drawer test. Primary repair led to a stable, functional knee in 8 of 11 patients in this series without evidence of degenerative joint disease an average of 7 ½ years after operation.

▶ [The authors present an excellent review of an unusual ligamentous injury of the knee, the isolated acute posterolateral rotatory instability. There must be a great deal of suspicion of this injury for appropriate diagnosis and subsequent treatment to be decided on. The importance of the posterolateral drawer and external rotation recurvatum sign are emphasized. The reverse pivot shift should also be carefully per-

(7–8) Am. J. Sports Med. 11:199–207, July–Aug. 1983.

formed. The authors emphasize that it is important to look for small avulsion fractures either from the lateral tibial plateau margin or fibular head as an indication of significant ligamentous injury. This should be carefully sought on radiographs of individuals with acute ligamentous injuries.

Although the series is small, the findings of the authors are impressive and consistent. The pathology involving the arcuate complex with an intact anterior cruciate is somewhat different than that reported by other authors, but it is certainly compatible. The excellent results, with the long-term follow-up showing only 3 patients with degenerative changes, would support the authors' view toward early surgical repair. The need for augmentation of the acute repair with an extra-articular reconstruction was not completely addressed by the authors but should be considered if ligamentous repair is performed later or the quality of the repair is suboptimal.—J.A. Rand] ◄

7–9 **Knee Function and Muscle Strength Following Distal Iliotibial Band Transfer for Anterolateral Rotatory Instability.** Magnus Odensten, Yelverton Tegner, Jack Lysholm, and Jan Gillquist (Univ. of Linköping, Sweden) evaluated 60 consecutive patients undergoing distal iliotibial band transfer for chronic anterolateral knee instability to determine whether those with reduced activity after surgery overestimate their knee function. The 44 men and 16 women were aged 19–45 years at the time of surgery. Thirty-five patients had posteromedial capsular reefing as well, and 12 had medial collateral ligament reconstruction. Also, 25 patients had meniscal surgery. Knee function was evaluated by a scoring system, static stability testing, and a standardized function test that assessed thigh muscle strength and included 1-leg jumping and figure-of-8 running. The average follow-up was 40 months.

Eight patients underwent further surgery on the anterior cruciate ligament for persistent instability. A significant increase in mean score was noted in 43 other patients (Fig 7–4). Scores for instability and pain correlated closely with total scores. Quadriceps strength correlated significantly with the knee scores and was significantly less in the treated leg than in the untreated leg. Functional results were generally unsatisfactory. Few patients had normal findings in all

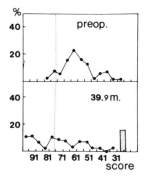

Fig 7–4.—Distribution of scores in 60 patients undergoing distal iliotibial band transfer preoperatively and at 40 months postoperatively. Dotted line indicates 77 points, representing the borderline between excellent/good and fair/poor results. (Courtesy of Odensten, M., et al.: Acta Orthop. Scand. 54:924–928, December 1983.)

(7–9) Acta Orthop. Scand. 54:924–928, December 1983.

tests, chiefly because of inadequate restoration of stability. Jump ratios between the 2 legs correlated significantly with scores. Running times were significantly related to quadriceps and hamstring muscle strength in both the treated and untreated extremities. Although significant improvement in knee function was observed 40 months after the distal iliotibial band transfer, most patients continued to experience significant symptoms during daily activities.

▶ [The results of this study are similar to the results we have found with distal iliotibial band transfer for anterolateral rotatory instability. While persistent instability seems to be the most important factor related to a poor functional result, the authors nicely correlate persistent quadriceps weakness with an adverse result. This emphasizes the importance of a systematic, carefully supervised postoperative rehabilitation program.—F.H. Sim] ◀

7–10 **Nonoperative Treatment of the Torn Anterior Cruciate Ligament.** Primary repair of a rupture of the anterior cruciate ligament can be difficult or impossible, and the results of repair and reconstruction are unpredictable. Therese P. Giove, Sayers John Miller III, Barbara E. Kent, Terry L. Sanford, and James G. Garrick reviewed the results of nonoperative management by rehabilitation emphasizing strengthening of the hamstrings in 24 patients with a diagnosed anterior cruciate ligament tear. All were men, aged 18 to 40 years, who had unilateral knee instability, with or without associated anterolateral instability or meniscal damage. The muscle rehabilitation program included isometric and isotonic exercises and isokinetic exercises performed on the Cybex II. Ten patients underwent medial meniscectomy before evaluation; in 3 of them the lateral meniscus was also removed.

Five patients exhibited positive valgus laxity and 1, positive varus laxity. Anterior instability was prevalent, but no knee had rotational instability on anterior drawer testing. Thirteen injured knees showed degenerative changes on roentgenography, compared with 7 uninvolved knees. No significant differences in range of motion were found between the 2 knees. Quadriceps and hamstring strengths were similar in the 2 extremities. Three patients returned to their preinjury level of sports participation, and 11 others averaged full activity. Two subjects participated only minimally in sports activities because of the knee injury. Sports participation was greater in subjects whose hamstrings were as strong as or stronger than their quadriceps in the injured extremity.

Adequate rehabilitation of the hamstring muscles can promote return to sports activities after a tear of the anterior cruciate ligament. An exercise program emphasizing strengthening of the hamstrings provides a possible alternative to extensive operations. Such an exercise program certainly should be considered in postoperative rehabilitation.

(7–10) J. Bone Joint Surg. [Am.] 65-A:184–192, February 1983.

7–11 **Acute Tears of the Posterior Cruciate Ligament: Clinical Study and Results of Operative Treatment in 27 Cases.** Mario Bianchi (Univ. of Milan) reviewed the results of operation for acute posterior cruciate ligament tears in 27 patients, 21 males and 6 females aged 14–58 years. Motor vehicle accidents were the cause of 14 cases and sports activities, especially skiing, of 9. Only 8 patients had an isolated tear of the posterior cruciate ligament. Eight others also had anterior cruciate tears. The most common finding was disruption of the distal third of the posterior cruciate ligament or disruption at the femoral level. Isolated tears with a tibial fragment avulsion fracture were managed by Trickey's posterior approach. An anteromedial approach was used to repair associated tears of the medial compartment. With a distal tear at the ligament level, the posterior cruciate ligament was reinserted into the tibia through holes drilled in the bone. Immobilization was for 6–8 weeks after operation. Partial weight-bearing ambulation was allowed 2–4 weeks after the cast was removed.

There were no operative complications. Twenty-five patients were followed, about half of them for 4 to 5 years. The objective results were good in 48% of patients, fair in 44%, and poor in 8%. The subjective results were good in 70% and fair in 30%. Fifty-five percent of patients had a good and 45%, a fair functional outcome. Both patients who underwent reconstruction of the posterior cruciate ligament had fair results.

Although good objective results were not obtained in a substantial majority of these patients with acute trauma to the posterior cruciate ligament, most were satisfied with the outcome because they were able to return to their work and to the sports activities they practiced before being injured.

▶ [The main value of this article is that it provides additional but not completely new data regarding cruciate ligament injuries. As with previous reports, the appropriate diagnosis is often difficult. Associated medial collateral or lateral collateral injuries with the posterior cruciate tear occur with an equal frequency of about 15%, and this is worth noting. The disparity between the objective and subjective results have been consistently reported and is the rule rather than the exception. Although not mentioned, one wonders whether or not immobilization with skeletal fixation may have improved the results. Finally, the data are not presented in such a way as to justify the recommendation that the injury should be treated within 48 hours. This recommendation does, however, concur with the recommendations of others.—B.F. Morrey] ◀

7–12 **The "Isolated" Posterior Cruciate Ligament Injury** is discussed by John R. McCarroll, Merrill A. Ritter, John Schrader, and Sandra Carlson (Methodist Hosp., Indianapolis). Apparently isolated injury of the posterior cruciate ligament, which is responsible for the basic stability of the knee, is not frequent. The mechanism of injury was

(7–11) Am. J. Sports Med. 11:308–314, Sept.–Oct., 1983.
(7–12) Physician Sportsmed. 11:146–151, February 1983.

analyzed on videotape in a soccer player who incurred this injury when receiving a violent blow to the anterior surface of the tibia during knee flexion while attempting to slide-tackle an opponent. A 1+ posterior drawer sign was present immediately after injury. X-ray films taken next day were normal. Examination with anesthesia showed a 2+ drawer sign but no other abnormality. Arthroscopy showed bleeding in the posterior cruciate ligament just above the tibial attachment. Exploration showed only a posterior cruciate tear. The patient did well after repair and extensive rehabilitation, with no residual knee instability.

Three of 4 patients with isolated tears of the posterior cruciate ligament sustained tears of the ligament off the tibia, whereas 1 case had a spiral interstitial component. None of the patients had other damage requiring repair. All injuries were caused by a violent blow to the anterior tibial surface with the knee flexed. All patients returned to full activity.

Surgical treatment of isolated tears of the posterior cruciate ligament and rehabilitation are necessary to insure consistently good results.

▶ [While the posterior cruciate ligament may be injured by a variety of mechanisms depending on the forces involved in the sport, the astute observation of this mechanism in soccer by Dr. McCarroll and his colleagues will certainly advance the diagnosis and treatment of posterior cruciate ligament injuries in soccer. Advances have been made in recent years in the diagnosis and treatment of posterior cruciate ligament instabilities. The author is one of the leaders in this area and this report has demonstrated conclusively that the patellar tendon is the best substitute for the posterior cruciate ligament. Our early experience with the vascularized patellar tendon graft as a substitute for the posterior cruciate ligament either acute or chronic as advocated by Dr. Clancy in the following abstract has been very favorable.—F.H. Sim] ◀

7–13 **Treatment of Knee Joint Instability Secondary to Rupture of the Posterior Cruciate Ligament: Report of a New Procedure.** William G. Clancy, Jr., K. Donald Shelbourne, Gary B. Zoellner, James S. Keene, Bruce Reider, and Thomas D. Rosenberg (Univ. of Wisconsin, Madison) have undertaken to correct knee instability due to rupture of the posterior cruciate ligament with a free graft of one third of the patellar tendon with both its tibial and patellar attachments. The operation was done on 48 patients, aged 16 to 39 years, who were seen between 1977 and 1981 with either an acute midsubstance tear of the ligament or, in 33, chronic ligament insufficiency. Twenty-three patients were seen after 2 years or longer. Ten (group I) had undergone repair of an acute interstitial rupture, whereas the other 13 (group II) had had symptoms of chronic disability and functional instability of the ligament. The respective average follow-ups were 41 and 31 months. Two group I patients also had posterolateral reconstruction, and 4 had reconstruction of the anterior cruciate lig-

(7–13) J. Bone Joint Surg. [Am.] 65-A:310–322, March 1983.

ament at the same time. The free graft procedure is illustrated in Figure 7–5. Successful operation depends on correct placement of the bone tunnels. A cast is used for 6 weeks after operation and a knee immobilizer for 2 weeks more.

All group I patients resumed normal activities and were able to participate in recreational or competitive sports. Stability was excellent in 8 of the 10 patients and good in the 2 others. All 7 group II

Fig 7–5.—*A* to *G,* surgical technique. Note off-center placements of tunnels with respect to normal sites of attachment of posterior cruciate ligament. Points marked "K wire" are sites of insertion of guidewires used to locate tunnels. (Courtesy of Clancy, W.G., Jr., et al.: J. Bone Joint Surg. [Am.] 65-A:310–322, March 1983.)

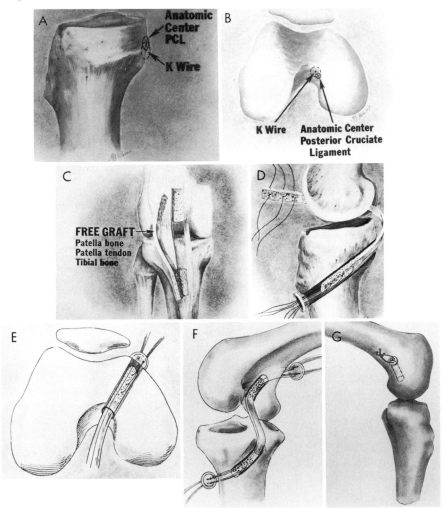

patients with isolated chronic insufficiency of the posterior cruciate ligament were satisfied with the outcome. Only 1 of them had pain on daily activities. The overall results were considered to be excellent in 2 patients and good in 4, with 1 failure. Five of the 6 patients with other ligament injury felt that their knees were improved, and 1 thought that the knee was normal. Five of these patients resumed sports activities. The overall results were considered to be excellent in 1, good in 4, and fair in 1. About 60% of all patients had articular injury of the medial compartment, but only 2 patients had marked degenerative changes on preoperative roentgenograms.

Good functional results can be obtained by using one third of the patellar tendon as a free graft in both acute and chronic cases of posterior cruciate ligament injury. The long-term effect of the procedure on degenerative joint changes remains to be determined.

7–14 **Current Concepts in Treatment of Ligamentous Instability of the Knee** are reviewed by William T. Simonet and Franklin H. Sim (Mayo Clinic and Found.). A stepwise approach is used to evaluate patients for ligament injury of the knee. Acutely injured patients should be assessed as soon as possible, using anesthesia if necessary. Arthrography is reserved for cases in which the physical findings are equivocal and the need for operation can be clarified. Arthroscopy is now used to confirm intra-articular injury and for treatment of meniscal lesions. Minor acute injuries of the collateral ligaments alone have been managed nonoperatively. Patients with isolated disruptions of the medial collateral ligament with an intact anterior cruciate ligament (ACL) can be treated nonoperatively with satisfactory results. The management of ACL injuries is controversial. Most patients with chronic instability of the knee ligaments are adequately managed nonoperatively or with minimally invasive methods such as arthroscopic or open partial meniscectomy or meniscal repair.

Ligament repair is indicated if a bony avulsion is present or most of the ligament can be brought into apposition with a raw bony insertion and the ligament substance is not disrupted. Otherwise reconstruction is done by using the middle third of the patellar tendon as a graft. Meniscal and capsular injuries are also treated. Repair with simple augmentation by the semitendinosus muscle is another option. Many reconstructive measures are available for chronic ligamentous instability. The patellar tendon is used to reconstruct acute and chronic injuries of the ACL. Acute disruptions of the posterior cruciate ligament are managed aggressively, especially in young, active patients. Chronic instability of this ligament is now reconstructed by using the middle third of the patellar tendon with a bone block.

Xenograft and prosthetic ligaments hold promise for use in the management of ligamentous instability of the knee. Long-term stud-

(7–14) Mayo Clin. Proc. 59:67–76, February 1984.

ies are needed to determine whether currect techniques provide lasting stability and prevent early osteoarthritis.

▶ [This is a particularly pertinent review of ligamentous instability of the knee. The authors now believe that a vascularized patellar tendon graft gives the best results when reconstruction of the anterior cruciate ligament is indicated. Although not mentioned in the article, there has been no subsequent postoperative patellar tendon problem either from the vascularized graft or from the older nonvascularized Jones procedure. Loss of strength was not found to be significant, although there have been some patients with patellofemoral pain syndrome probably due to immobilization following surgery. They are now moving their knees almost immediately after operation.—Ed.] ◀

7–15 **Prospective Stress Radiography in 38 Old Injuries of the Ligament of the Knee Joint.** Old, neglected ligament injuries of the knee joint pose many treatment problems. Niels Hejgaard, Henrik Sandberg, Adam Hede, and Klaus Jacobsen (Univ. of Copenhagen) used a stress radiographic technique to assess the course of chronic ligament injuries in 38 patients who were treated from 1974 to 1975. The patients had a median age of 25 years, and were followed up for a median of about 7 years. All injuries but 1 occurred during athletic performances. All but 5 patients had isolated ligament injuries, 16 involving the anterior cruciate ligament. There was only 1 posterior cruciate ligament injury. Four patients also had meniscal injuries.

The operative procedures were performed 18 days to 20 years after injury. Twelve patients had exploratory arthrotomy, 13 had primary suture or reefing of a weak ligament-capsule, and 13 had ligament reconstruction because of laxity.

Instability was relieved in all patients with medial laxity and in 1 of the 2 patients with lateral laxity. The anterior drawer sign disappeared in almost all cases. Rotatory instability was present in 6 patients preoperatively and in 14 during follow-up; it usually exceeded 6 mm. Only a few patients, however, had a troublesome sensation of instability. Ligament reconstruction reduced instability substantially. Only 16% of patients had a troublesome loss of function during follow-up.

Acute repair of knee ligament injuries is definitely indicated. Untreated injuries do better than has been thought, especially if the menisci are preserved. Simple reefing of medial structures or a McMurray tenodesis provides good results in cases of valgus instability. Marked and total instabilities are best treated by central ligament reconstruction. Gonylaxometry is very useful for accurately assessing instability preoperatively.

7–16 **Treatment of Chronic Anteromedial Instability of the Knee** is discussed by M. Lemaire and C. Miremad (Paris). In the athletic or active patient, treatment is based on the relative independence of active stability and passive stability. Effective treatment of anterome-

---

(7–15) Acta Orthop. Scand. 54:119–125, February 1983.
(7–16) Rev. Chir. Orthop. 69:591–601, 1983.

dial instability aims to restore mobility, so lengthy postoperative immobilization of the leg in a plaster cast and passive repair of the ligaments are contraindicated. The best results occur with effective operation very early after the first accident. Repetitive accidents distend the capsule and create new lesions, especially meniscal. The worst results occur when, at intervention, an important chondral lesion already exists. The error that occurs most often, and which is the most serious, is performing a meniscectomy and neglecting the ligament injury when meniscal and ligament lesions coexist.

Satisfactory techniques of treatment that allow early mobilization without the use of a plaster cast are difficult to perform and require precision. Lesions at the upper end of the medial ligament are repaired using the gracilis, and lesions of the lower end are corrected by using the semitendinosus. The principal technical points are to determine the precise position of the upper insertion of the medial ligament and the ideal tension of the released ligaments and capsule, to fix the tendons through the bone, and to avoid any plaster immobilization. A special instrument is used to make curved tunnels through the bone to use to anchor the plasty. Carbon fibers have been used for reinforcement in 452 cases, without any complications attributable to bioincompatibility.

Walking without weightbearing is allowed until the fifteenth postoperative day. Three weeks of reduction are considered necessary after that. The time off work is about 60 days. Results were satisfactory if the lesions were not too old and there were no lesions of the articular cartilage. Associated meniscus lesions were treated by partial resection or suture repair. Good results were obtained in 60% to 90% of cases following combination injuries and are maintained for the medium term. Long-term results (15–20 years) are not yet known.

▶ [We have used the semitendinosus for moderate medial collateral ligament laxity (Fenton procedure) but find that this does not control the anteromedial translation of the tibia on the femur in more marked cases. We prefer the posteromedial reconstruction described by Slocum as it provides both static and dynamic medial support.—F.H. Sim] ◀

7-17 **Ambulatory Care of Medial Collateral Ligament Tears.** Cast treatment of less-marked medial collateral ligament injuries can lead to severe muscle atrophy and prolong the rehabilitative period. Merrill A. Ritter, John McCarroll, Franklin D. Wilson, and Sandra R. Carlson (Methodist Hosp., Indianapolis) evaluated a program of controlled limb mobilization in athletes with grade 1 or grade 2 medial collateral ligament injuries. All 45 subjects had mediolateral stability with the knee in full extension and a solid end point on testing in 30 degrees of flexion with no more than 2+ laxity. Mild rotatory laxity was acceptable. The subjects were followed for an average of about 2

(7–17) Physician Sportsmed. 11:47–51, July 1983.

years. A knee immobilizer and crutches were used after diagnosis and range-of-motion exercises begun as the acute trauma subsided, followed by isotonic hamstring and quadriceps exercises. The crutches and splint were retained for 3 weeks or until 60% of normal leg strength was regained. Functional exercises involving mild resistance and slow movement were then introduced, with bicycling and swimming as tolerated. Straight running was allowed when 80% of normal strength was present.

Forty-one of the 45 athletes returned to their baseline level of sports activity in an average of 44 days. Two others with positive Lachman tests resumed sports after 8 months of rehabilitation, neither at the preinjury level of activity. One subject required a meniscectomy, and another needed removal of a pathologic synovial plica. Seventeen of the 41 patients who recovered soon after injury had both medial laxity and an anteromedial drawer sign. Knee laxity remained the same or improved by 1 degree in these patients; it worsened in only 1.

Ambulatory management has proved to be effective in athletes with medial collateral ligament tears who do not require operation. Protected mobilization of the injury promotes the most rapid recovery of ligament stability. The use of Cybex equipment is recommended, since its variable speed can specifically accommodate the given patient's reconditioning needs.

▶ [The authors present a series of athletes with isolated medial collateral ligament and medial capsule injuries who were treated by early rehabilitation with muscle strengthening and motion. They reported successful results in 85% of patients.

The results achieved by these authors appear to be encouraging and support a trend towards earlier mobilization of knees after ligamentous injury to maintain muscle tone and to improve the strength of ligament healing. The authors did not comment on the use of continuous passive motion, but this certainly has proved to be a satisfactory technique experimentally. The authors also do not comment regarding the use of arthroscopy for diagnosis. Perhaps this would improve their ability to treat these patients by defining the lesion as truly isolated rather than with associated meniscal pathology.

The authors did not comment regarding the use of a cast brace or a mobilization brace other than the immobilizer. In another recent series by Indelicato, this has proved to be a viable technique.—J.A. Rand] ◀

7–18 **Meniscal Pathology and Osteoarthritis of the Knee.** Many are concerned about leaving a tear of the posterior third of the meniscus at arthroscopy for fear that osteoarthritis may develop. N. R. M. Fahmy, E. A. Williams, and J. Noble (Manchester, England) examined the relation between meniscal lesions and degenerative joint disease in a series of 115 amputation and cadaver specimens. About 60% of the subjects were males, and 53% were younger than age 65 years. There was no evidence of significant ligamentous insufficiency in any knee. Two knees had undergone medial meniscectomy.

(7–18) J. Bone Joint Surg. [Br.] 65-B:24–28, January 1983.

Over 90% of specimens exhibited fibrillation, erosion, or both, in the medial and lateral tibiofemoral areas. Fibrillation was often present beneath the most posterior part of the undersurface of the lateral meniscus. Meniscal pathosis was present in 57% of specimens. Both menisci were abnormal in 17% of knees, the medial meniscus only in 38%, and the lateral meniscus in 28%. The pathologic change consisted almost entirely of horizontal cleavage lesions. No overall differences in the severity or distribution of tibiofemoral degeneration were evident with respect to whether the meniscus was damaged or normal. Articular changes were as often remote from the meniscus as adjacent or related to it. Gross arthritic changes in the medial tibiofemoral joint were seen in the 2 cases of medial meniscectomy, but the articular surfaces were much better preserved laterally in these cases. Fibrillation was evident in the tibiofemoral articulation in a substantial majority of cases with normal menisci. Arthritic changes were present in 10 of 14 cases with unstable meniscal tears.

There is little evidence from this study that meniscal tears cause osteoarthritis, or vice versa. Remnants of degenerated menisci may have a protective effect on the underlying articular surface. The frequent occurrence of fibrillation or erosion beneath the posterior part of the lateral meniscus warrants further study.

▶ [The authors present a pathologic study of 150 knees correlating meniscal pathology and degenerative changes on the articular surface. It is noteworthy that the knees were obtained from either necropsy or amputation specimens, and there is no history relevant to the symptomatic status of the knee.

Their findings have no direct correlation between meniscus pathology and degenerative changes, but do correlate with a previous report by Casscels. Unfortunately their series contains mostly horizontal cleavage tears. It does not contain the large flap tears in the menisci which are the lesions that are most symptomatic in patients with degenerative meniscus tear.

Their conclusion, that a horizontal degenerative meniscus tear does not correlate with osteoarthritis and does not necessarily require resection, is compatible with the conclusions of Casscels. The increasing importance of the meniscus is well recognized and commented on by the authors. Meniscectomy is not an innocuous procedure.

The question that remains unanswered by this investigation is the significance of degenerative flap tears in the meniscus, which are symptomatic and common findings in the degenerative knee. Do these lesions need to be treated by partial meniscectomy to relieve symptoms and to prevent areas of degenerative arthritis from impingement of the flap? Hopefully the authors will continue their investigations in this area.—J.A. Rand] ◀

7–19 **Meniscectomy for Tears of the Meniscus Combined With Rupture of the Anterior Cruciate Ligament.** An unstable knee with both a ruptured anterior cruciate ligament and a torn meniscus is a common clinical problem. F. W. N. Paterson and E. L. Trickey attempted to find ways of identifying patients who are likely to be relieved by meniscectomy alone and those who also require reconstruc-

(7–19) J. Bone Joint Surg. [Br.] 65-B:388–390, August 1983.

tion of the anterior cruciate ligament. Forty patients with both injuries confirmed at arthrotomy who underwent meniscectomy alone were assessed. The 32 men and 8 women had a mean age at surgery of 28 years. The mean time from injury to presentation was about 3½ years, and the mean follow-up after meniscectomy was 5 years. Three patients had a previous meniscectomy on the same knee.

Twenty-two patients had a bucket-handle meniscal tear, 16 had a posterior horn tear, and 1 each had an anterior horn tear and a transverse injury. Good results were obtained with regard to symptoms of instability in 22 cases, fair results in 8, and poor results in 10. Good results were obtained by 18 of 23 patients with bucket-handle meniscal tears and by 3 of 15 with posterior horn tears. Two patients with bucket-handle tears and 8 with posterior horn tears had a poor outcome. One of those with a bucket-handle injury had a poorly developed quadriceps despite intensive physiotherapy.

In general, a patient aged 30 or older with an unstable knee, signs of anterior cruciate insufficiency, and a bucket-handle meniscal tear can be expected to have a good result from meniscectomy only. A poor outcome can be anticipated in an athlete younger than age 25 with a posterior horn tear of the meniscus. Early reconstruction seems warranted in these cases, and it would be convenient to combine the 2 procedures with the patient under a single anesthetic. Meniscectomy did not produce increased instability in the patients in this study, with one exception.

▶ [The authors address a difficult clinical problem, namely, the anterior cruciate deficient knee with associated meniscus pathology. Since the meniscus acts as an important secondary stabilizer in the absence of a functioning anterior cruciate ligament, meniscectomy has been seen to increase ligamentous laxity in the knee and to potentially aggravate symptoms of instability.

However, the results of resectioning the damaged meniscus or of partial meniscectomy have not been widely reported on. The authors were able to salvage 75% of 40 knees with meniscectomy, without the use of anterior cruciate reconstruction. Although the surgery was done through arthrotomy, the potential for arthroscopic management of the lesion exists with considerably less morbidity than would be incurred with arthrotomy, and considerably less morbidity than with an associated ligamentous reconstruction. Since the natural history of the patient presenting with an anterior cruciate deficient knee is difficult to define initially, a management program that entails minimal morbidity should be pursued prior to reconstruction.

The authors do not address whether or not repair of the meniscus would be useful if there is a posterior peripheral tear of the medial meniscus, which is quite common with the anterior cruciate deficient knee. Since the posterior horn tear of the lateral meniscus frequently accompanies severe anterolateral instability with impingement of the posterior horn of the lateral meniscus between the tibia and femur, patients presenting with these lesions might be expected to do poorly. Conservative meniscal resection with a partial meniscectomy appears to be a reasonable step in the management of these most difficult clinical problems.—J.A. Rand] ◀

7–20 **The Microvasculature of the Meniscus and Its Response to Injury: An Experimental Study in the Dog.** Little is known about

(7–20) Am. J. Sports Med. 11:131–141, May–June 1983.

the vascular anatomy of the meniscus and its role in meniscal healing. Steven P. Arnoczky and Russell F. Warren (Hosp. for Special Surgery, New York) examined the microvasculature of the canine meniscus and its response to injury in adult mongrel dogs. Arterial perfusion studies were done using India ink. In some dogs, the medial meniscus was completely bisected, and arterial perfusion was performed at intervals up to 10 weeks after the operation. In others, the effects of a vascular access channel on healing of a longitudinal lesion in the avascular part of the medial meniscus were assessed.

The genicular arteries were seen to give rise to a perimeniscal capillary plexus within the synovial and capsular tissues of the knee joint. The vascular network supplied the peripheral border of the meniscus, with the vessels oriented mainly circumferentially and penetrating the meniscal stroma for a short distance and ending in small capillary loops. Vascular penetration extended for 15% to 25% of the width of the meniscus. The posterolateral part of the lateral meniscus was without penetrating perimeniscal vessels. The vascular response to complete transection of the medial meniscus arose from the peripheral synovial tissue. Complete healing with fibrovascular scar tissue was observed 10 weeks after the injury. Longitudinal incisions in the avascular part of the meniscus failed to heal, but when these lesions were connected to the peripheral synovial tissues at their midportion by a vascular channel, the entire lesion healed with fibrovascular scarring within 10 weeks.

The peripheral part of the canine meniscus is supplied by vessels from a perimeniscal capillary plexus that originates in the peripheral synovial and capsular tissues. The role of the peripheral synovial tissues in the reparative process suggests that these tissues should be preserved and used in the surgical repair of meniscal lesions.

▶ [The authors present an excellent experimental study on revascularization of meniscal injuries. They again confirm the importance of 25% to 30% of meniscae being vascular and capable of biologic reaction in healing. A finding that a vascular access channel may allow healing to progress into the previously avascular area of the meniscus and effect healing is most interesting. Caution, however, must be exercised when considering these findings and relating them to the human knee. Peripheral reattachment of meniscal injuries have become an accepted mode of management. However, extreme caution should be practiced before a lesion is created in the peripheral rim of the meniscus extending into a more centrally located lesion as this may disrupt the circumferential collagen fibers in the meniscus, resulting in a loss in their ability to function and maintain hoop stresses. This certainly would result in an adverse mechanical function of the meniscus. It is hoped that the authors will extend their studies to mechanical function and stress analysis of the healed meniscus following their surgical procedure. Perhaps they can extend their studies to other animals before this technique is applied to human meniscae.—J.A. Rand] ◀

7–21 **Effects of Postoperative Joint Immobilization on Articular Cartilage Degeneration Following Meniscectomy.** Removal of a

(7–21) J. Surg. Res. 35:461–473, December 1983.

meniscus from the knee imposes both further and abnormal mechanical stresses on the cartilage surfaces and can produce degenerative changes over time. There is no uniform approach to management of the meniscectomized knee. P. Ghosh, J. M. Sutherland, T. K. F. Taylor, Ghery D. Pettit, and C. R. Bellenger (Univ. of Sydney) examined the effects of postoperative joint immobilization on cartilage changes after medial meniscectomy in greyhounds. Some dogs walked immediately after operation, whereas in others the joint was immobilized by a Kirschner half-pin fixation splint for 5 weeks after meniscectomy. The dogs were killed 6 months after meniscectomy.

The articular cartilage appeared to be degenerated in all dogs, especially at the medial tibial plateau. No significant differences in the collagen content of cartilage were evident. Under nondissociative conditions only, twice as much proteoglycan was extracted from the medial femoral condyle of dogs that bore weight on their joints immediately after operation as from those of immobilized dogs. The proteoglycans of medial tibial plateau cartilage from the contralateral joints of immobilized dogs were more readily extracted and showed a significant depression of uronic acid concentration compared with both controls and tissues from other joint surfaces.

Short-term immobilization after meniscectomy may be beneficial in maintaining the integrity of articular cartilage, since excessive loading may accelerate cartilage degeneration in this setting. How long the joint should be immobilized is uncertain. The role of muscle contraction and the resultant transarticular pressure remains to be defined, but it would appear to be important with respect to chondrocyte function.

▶ [I believe the experiment in this study is poorly designed in that the authors are comparing a bilateral meniscectomy in a dog, one side of which is immobilized so that all the weight is born on the contralateral side. This, of course, is excessive weight-bearing immediately postoperatively, and they infer that weight-bearing is detrimental. In the normal clinical situation, the patient is not undergoing bilateral meniscectomy but actually experiences partial weight-bearing on the one side with early motion. The authors, therefore, are comparing excessive weight-bearing on one side to immobilization on the contralateral side, which does not have any clinical relevance. Their conclusions are contradictory to those of Salter, who has shown the beneficial effects of early motion on the nutrition of articular cartilage. The methodology of proteoglycan analysis is satisfactory, but I believe their overall experimental design is poor.—J.A. Rand] ◀

7–22 **Meniscofluoresis: Aid in Determining Prognosis of Meniscal Tears.** Meniscal tears formerly were considered incapable of healing, but experimental and clinical evidence exists that some tears can be repaired surgically, particularly those around the periphery of the meniscus. Clinically, it is difficult to assess the extent of vascularization of the meniscal rim. Gary S. Fanton and Jack T. Andrish

(7–22) Cleve. Clin. Q. 50:379–383, Winter 1983.

(Cleveland Clinic) used fluorescein dye to evaluate the vascularity of knee menisci in dogs and related the area of dye penetration to the success of meniscal healing. Adult dogs received 20 mg/kg of 10% fluorescein dye solution intravenously, and the menisci were examined 15 minutes later using a long-wave ultraviolet (UV) lamp. A transverse or longitudinal full-thickness cut then was made in the meniscus. The transverse tears were either entirely within the nonfluorescent region or extended peripherally to the area of fluorescence. The animals were sacrificed at intervals up to 12 weeks postoperatively.

Fluorescein dye penetrated the vascular part of the meniscus and fluoresced under exposure to UV light. The tears made in the fluorescent part of the meniscus healed, whereas those in the nonfluorescent portion did not (Fig 7–6). There was substantial variation in the size of the fluorescent zone in different animals.

Fluorescein injection is a useful means of assessing the intrinsic vascularity of the canine meniscus. The rim of fluorescence appears to correlate closely with findings reported in previous anatomical studies that defined the meniscal blood supply. This approach might

Fig 7–6.—Healed longitudinal tear made previously in a fluorescent zone of the meniscus (4 weeks); probe indicates end of tear. (Courtesy of Fanton, G.S., and Andrish, J.T.: Cleve. Clin. Q. 50:379–383, Winter 1983.)

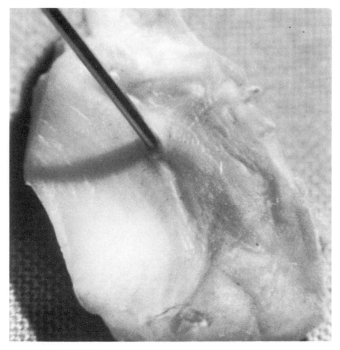

prove to be an accurate and safe means of determining which clinical meniscal tears can be repaired rather than excised.

▶ [The authors present an excellent experimental study on the potential for meniscal healing following a variety of surgically created tears in the canine model. They have clearly shown that fluorescein is an excellent method for detecting the extent of vascularity in the meniscus and correlates with healing ability. The clinical applicability of these findings is yet to be proved. Certainly their technique would appear to merit further investigation and has the potential to be quite valuable in the situation of an acute peripheral tear of a meniscus. However, since many of these menisci will heal, the further value of the procedure is questionable. In lesions that penetrate further into the substance of the meniscus, potential for healing versus meniscectomy might be better assessed using this technique that allows arthroscopic repair of the meniscus since this is the area that is difficult to reach through an arthrotomy incision. The value of this technique in the chronic tear has not been assessed and this would certainly be an area for further investigation.—J.A. Rand] ◀

7–23 **Suture of New and Old Peripheral Meniscus Tears.** Per Hamberg, Jan Gillquist, and Jack Lysholm (Univ. of Linköping, Sweden) undertook a prospective study of 50 patients undergoing vertical peripheral meniscal tear repair between 1977 and 1980. The 41 men and 9 women had a mean age of 27 years. Three fourths of the injuries were related to sports activities, usually soccer. All of the tears were demonstrated arthroscopically. Forty-three medial and 8 lateral meniscal tears were repaired. Associated ligament tears also were reconstructed in 42 cases. Fifteen patients were treated within 2 weeks of injury. The meniscal tears were repaired with 2–0 Vicryl sutures. A cylinder cast was applied for 5 weeks with the knee flexed to about 30 degrees. Isometric quadricep exercises and hamstring-strengthening exercises were begun after cast removal, and full weight-bearing was allowed when a full range of motion was restored, usually after 4 weeks.

Mean follow-up was 18 months. No symptoms of meniscal tear were present in 84% of cases. Repeated arthroscopy, carried out a mean of 12 months after injury in 27 of these cases, showed all tears to be healed. Eight patients developed symptoms of a new meniscal tear and underwent endoscopic meniscectomy. Four of the 8 had a tear at the original repair site; 2 in association with new injury. Only 1 of the 15 tears repaired within 2 weeks of injury subsequently ruptured, and not at the initial repair site.

Although many have suggested total meniscectomy for patients who have a peripheral meniscal rupture combined with ligament instability, meniscectomy leads to some degree of knee instability, especially where an anterior cruciate ligament tear is also present. Recent studies indicate better functional results of ligament reconstruction where the meniscus was intact. It seems advisable to repair a ruptured meniscus rather than to remove it in patients with concomitant ligament injury. It is important to debride an old tear so

(7–23) J. Bone Joint Surg. [Am.] 65-A:193–197, February 1983.

that revascularization will increase the chance of healing. The frequency with which repaired old tears reruptured in this series was low, considering that all ruptures were sutured if the main body of the meniscus was intact.

7-24 **Vertical Position of Patella.** Current radiographic methods of demonstrating patella alta do not give consistent results. The condition involves a high position of the patella in relation to the femoral condylar groove, which is difficult to define radiographically. O. Norman, N. Egund, L. Ekelund, and A. Rünow (Univ. of Lund) describe a new radiographic method for estimating the vertical position of the patella in extension. The patella is examined in its most proximal position during maximal extension by the supine patient, with the leg elevated and the foot rotated outward about 10–15 degrees. A lateral radiograph is obtained with the central ray directed at the ventral aspect of the joint space. The lengths of the patellar ligament, patella, and articular surface of the patella, the femoral condylar plane, and the vertical position of the patella in relation to the femoral condylar plane are recorded.

Studies were done in 57 males and 34 females with meniscal lesions; the average age was 33 years. The vertical position of the patella, or distance from the distal edge of the articular surface to the femoral condylar plane, was related to body height, as were the lengths of the ligament, patella, and articular surface of the patella. The absolute lengths of all parameters were greater in males than in females. The relative length of the patellar ligament was the same in males and females, but the relative length of the patella was less in females, and the Insall index, or ligament/patella ratio, was greater. The relative length of the articular surface of the patella was less in females. The relative length of the vertical position of the patella was the same in both sexes. The vertical position of the patella could be expressed as the vertical index, or ratio to body height, the mean being 0.21 ± 0.02.

This is a simple and reproducible means of estimating the vertical position of the patella. Previous methods have overlooked the importance of hyperextension. Both the vertical index of the patella and the Insall index are clinically relevant measures and are useful in analyzing the biomechanics of the patellar articulation. The Insall index can be normal or increased at the same vertical index, and vice versa.

▶ [The authors present an interesting study of normal patients in whom they found a correlation between body height and patella position with the knee in extension under maximal quadriceps contraction. They also identified the differences in the various parameters used to measure patellar position between the male and female. The latter findings are similar to those of other authors such as Aglietti and Insall.

The true definition of patella alta varies depending upon the technique used and,

(7–24) Acta Orthop. Scand. 54:908–913, December 1983.

indeed, any additional information that would help define this condition would be most useful. Unfortunately, the authors did not address the problem of how one is sure the patient is making a maximal contraction throughout the time required for the radiographs. They also do not address the problem of the patient with a lateral subluxation if asymmetric quadriceps pull may result in tilting the patella and whether or not this would affect this measurement. The authors' findings merit further investigation in a series of patients with patellar instability.—J.A. Rand] ◄

7–25 **Management of Meniscal Cysts.** The recognition that the meniscus has an important role in knee function has promoted a more selective approach to meniscectomy. E. A. Williams, D. R. A. Davies, and Jonathan Noble (Univ. of Manchester) reviewed experience with 16 patients who had a meniscal cyst and symptoms of varied severity. Three patients with mild local symptoms and no tear on arthroscopy were observed. Seven with moderate or severe symptoms but no more than minimal meniscal damage on arthroscopy had local excision of the cyst alone. Six patients with a significant meniscal tear, such as a large horizontal cleavage or a bucket-handle tear, underwent both meniscectomy and excision of the cyst at the same time.

Average patient age was 31 years. All but two cysts were associated with the lateral meniscus. Only 7 patients recalled injury to the knee. Average follow-up was 22 months. A patient with a small radial meniscal tear and mild symptoms has done well on observation. One with a small degenerate lesion and no symptoms of mechanical blockage has done well after excision of the cyst alone. Only 1 of the patients without a meniscal tear at arthroscopy has had a recurrence, and underwent reexcision with meniscectomy.

Meniscectomy should no longer be done routinely when a meniscal cyst is present. Not even all tears require removal of the meniscus. The authors now perform meniscectomy only when significant meniscal damage is found at arthroscopy. Only 1 patient has subsequently required meniscectomy for recurrence of a cyst.

► [This is a rather brief report with limited follow-up and relatively few details. The major value is found in the authors' recommendation of a simple excision of a meniscal cyst if there is no other meniscal pathology. The traditional teaching has suggested that the entire meniscus be removed. This relatively small group of patients with relatively short-term follow-up does suggest that cyst removal may be an alternative to complete meniscectomy.—B.F. Morrey] ◄

7–26 **Idiopathic Osteonecrosis of the Knee: Etiology, Prognosis, and Treatment.** P. Aglietti, J. N. Insall, R. Buzzi, and G. Deschamps reviewed experience with 91 patients who had idiopathic osteonecrosis of the femoral condyles affecting 105 knees. The 69 women and 22 men had an average age of 66 years. The lesion was in the weight-bearing region of the medial femoral condyle in over 90% of affected knees. Thirty of 75 evaluable patients were more than 20% overweight. Bone densitometry showed a slight reduction in bone density

(7–25) J. R. Coll. Surg. Edinb. 28:246–249, July 1983.
(7–26) J. Bone Joint Surg. [Br.] 65-B:588–597, November 1983.

in 7 of 33 cases and a significant decrease in 4. Most patients had a history of sudden, well-localized pain in the knee. An effusion was present in 59% of knees, a flexion contracture in 28%, and true locking in 9.5%. Average duration of symptoms was 15 months.

A lesion larger than 5 sq cm or more than 40% of the condyle in width had a relatively poor prognosis. Seventeen of 22 conservatively treated knees had an excellent or good outcome and 1 a poor outcome. Results were satisfactory in 55% of 11 knees managed by arthrotomy alone and in 87% of those treated by osteotomy. Arthrotomy was also performed in 21 of the latter cases; it did not significantly improve the results of high tibial osteotomy. The average amount of valgus in knees with excellent results was 10 degrees. All but 5% of 37 knees managed by total replacement has a satisfactory outcome. Average follow-up was 4½ years. Over half the patients had excellent results from total knee replacement. Results were best with the total condylar prosthesis.

Conservative management is indicated for 6 months after onset of symptoms from idiopathic osteonecrosis of the knee, and this approach can be maintained if a lesion less than 5 sq cm in size with a ratio of less than 40% is present. Operation is indicated for larger lesions when symptoms do not resolve. High tibial osteotomy or knee replacement should be selected according to the same criteria as in osteoarthritis. Advanced patient age and an expected low activity level favor replacement.

▶ [This paper brings us up to date with experiences at the Hospital for Special Surgery. Idiopathic osteonecrosis was originally described by Ahlbäck, Bauer, and Bohne in 1968. This most valuable contribution has continued to interest John Insall and his group at the Hospital for Special Surgery. He and others have emphasized that most osteonecrosis in stage I will spontaneously resolve since only scintigraphy will substantiate the involvement and routine x-rays are negative. Lotke has shown that the actual size of the necrosis is the important determinant as to whether spontaneous healing will take place, or whether there will be further progression, ultimately requiring surgery. The authors put the role of osteotomy and total knee replacement in the more severe cases in perspective.—Ed.] ◀

7–27 **Bilateral Simultaneous Spontaneous Rupture of Quadriceps Tendons: Five Case Reports and Review of the Literature.** Rupture of the quadriceps tendon is uncommon, and only 6 reports of bilateral simultaneous rupture of these tendons have appeared in the English literature. A. G. MacEachern and J. L. Plewes report 5 additional patients with this injury, all of whom were men older than age 50. The diagnosis was delayed in 3 patients. The chief clinical features are diffuse swelling about the knee, a visible or palpable suprapatellar defect, and inability to lift the straight leg despite a functioning quadriceps and normal activity in other leg muscle groups. Operative repair was done bilaterally in all 5 patients, without a pro-

(7–27) J. Bone Joint Surg. [Br.] 66-B:81–83, January 1984.

tective wire pullout suture. Immobilization in plaster for 6 weeks was followed by physiotherapy. Even late repair was associated with a return to useful function. All patients had satisfactory results and were independent with or without a walking aid; none required long-term external knee splinting.

This injury frequently affects elderly persons and confusion with other causes of inability to use the legs, (e.g., mild stroke) may delay the diagnosis. A previously reported patient had gout and another had hyperparathyroidism. The most common cause of bilateral simultaneous ruptures appears to be sudden, violent contraction of the quadriceps with the knees slightly flexed and the feet fixed. Obesity may be a feature. A weakened quadriceps tendon may result from obesity, degenerative changes, or repeated minor injury. Repair by a variety of methods was successful in all 5 patients.

▶ [The authors present an excellent review of the literature and add 5 cases of patients with bilateral ruptured quadriceps tendons. All of these were not spontaneous but related to minor trauma and injury. A diagnostic confusion that these patients may present with is worthy of note. The classic clinical features of swelling about the knee, palpable defect, and inability to raise the straight leg should raise a suspicion of this diagnosis. The ability to obtain satisfactory results with delayed operative intervention should encourage operative treatment as the majority of these patients continue to function following surgical repair.—J.A. Rand] ◀

7–28 **Static and Dynamic Loading Patterns in Knee Joints With Deformities.** Use of high tibial osteotomy for treatment of degenerative arthritis of the knee is based on the assumption that correcting

Fig 7–7.—Center of joint pressure (Z0) is located mostly in medial condyle during walking for normal individuals. (Courtesy of Harrington, I.J.: J. Bone Joint Surg. [Am.] 65-A:247–259, February 1983.)

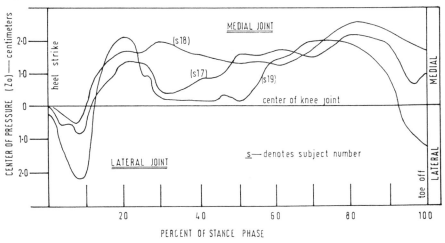

angulation will shift the center of joint loading and unload the damaged compartment. It has not been clearly shown, however, that a definite correlation exists between angular deformity of the joint and the knee joint load. Ian J. Harrington (Univ. of Toronto) used a dynamic experimental method to assess joint force transmission at the knee in 16 subjects with varus, valgus, or flexion deformity, and compared the results with those obtained by static coronal-plane analysis. Both normal-walking and one-legged-stance analyses were made with the use of a force-platform cinephotographic technique. Three normal subjects also were assessed.

Fig 7–8 (top).—Center of joint pressure (Z0) is located in medial condyle during level walking for subjects with varus deformity.
Fig 7–9 (bottom).—Center of joint pressure (Z0) shifts into medial compartment of knee for some individuals with valgus deformity during periods of maximum transmission of joint load.
(Courtesy of Harrington, I.J.: J. Bone Joint Surg. [Am.] 65-A:247–259, February 1983.)

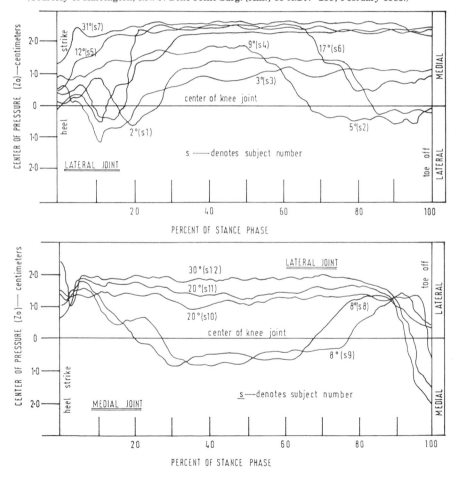

The normal subjects exhibited characteristic load peaks corresponding to hamstring, quadriceps, and gastrocnemius muscle contractions. The center of pressure was localized to the medial compartment throughout most of the stance phase, especially on maximum load transmission (Fig 7–7). The magnitude of joint force generally was less in the patients with deformity than in the normal subjects. There was a general tendency toward an increased total load with increased joint angulation in all planes, but the relationships were not clearly predictable. The center of pressure varied throughout the stance phase and was not directly related to the magnitude of angulation of the joint. The findings in varus deformity are shown in Figure 7–8; those in valgus deformity, in Figure 7–9. In patients with flexion deformity, the chief deformity was in the sagittal plane. Both static and dynamic analyses showed the center of joint loading to be in the medial compartment.

The distribution of force between the condyles of the knee joint seems to depend on the position of the center of gravity of the body and the external forces acting on it, rather than on the obliquity of the axis of the femur relative to the tibia. Factors other than structural limb deformity probably influence joint loading to a significant degree. Walking speed is an important variable. Compensatory mechanisms that reduce joint force when deformity is present probably exist, and the results indicate it is easier to compensate for a valgus than for a varus deformity. Gait analysis is necessary to dynamically analyze the biomechanical function of the knee joint before and after osteotomy or joint replacement.

▶ [Biomechanical analyses of joint force determination have vacillated between detailed theoretical approaches and simplified methods in the hope of meeting practical demands for clinical applications. This paper represents an example of an attempt to solve the joint dynamic force distribution problem in knees with deformity, both in the sagittal and frontal planes. A rather complex method was used to dispute the results obtained previously using simple static analysis, and although the results presented here appear to contradict those obtained by using static analysis, the two studies are different, both in their objectives and their prospective clinical applications. None of the static two-dimensional analyses would claim that their results could predict what the knee joint forces distribution should be under dynamic walking conditions. These simplified analyses only attempted to provide an objective means of guiding the amount of knee osteotomy correction, similar to that used for total knee component placement and orientation.

On the contrary, the results of the present three-dimensional dynamic analysis seem to compliment the static analysis since they help to illustrate that the joint alignment basic simple static analysis may be insufficient to correct the overloading condition on the medial compartment of the knee. Consequently, overcorrection is generally recommended for genu varum. On the other hand, overcorrection would appear unnecessary for valgus deformities because of the inherent medial thrust of the knee joint under walking conditions.

Any static or dynamic analysis involving human joints, regardless of its degree of complexity, cannot avoid the necessary assumptions and simplifications due to modeling difficulties, as well as experimental errors. It is difficult to predict the joint contact force center location of the knee, particularly in the frontal plane, due to its extreme sensitivity to smaller error. Therefore, it is impossible to assess whether the data obtained from one analysis is more valid than that of another unless an instrumented transducer is used, as suggested by the author.

Finally, to use a complex and tedious method to predict the knee osteotomy angle for every patient to be operated on appears to be unrealistic because of the large amount of time involved, especially when the technique to be used still faces many uncertainties. It would seem feasible and potentially beneficial to conduct the ground reaction force vector analysis in the frontal plane, as suggested by Johnson and Waugh (*J. Bone Joint Surg.* [Br.] 62-B:346–349, 1980) because of its simplicity. However, such a method also encounters the same problem, that of achieving the required data resolution because of its high sensitivity to measurement errors.—E.Y.S. Chao] ◄

7–29   **Composition of Normal and Osteoarthritic Articular Cartilage From Human Knee Joints: With Special Reference to Unicompartmental Replacement and Osteotomy of the Knee.** The management of osteoarthritic knees with grossly normal-appearing articular cartilage remains unclear. More rational decisions could be made if the functional capacity of apparently intact cartilage was known. R. Brocklehurst, M. T. Bayliss, A. Maroudas, H. L. Coysh, M. A. R. Freeman, P. A. Revell, and S. Y. Ali (London) determined the water and proteoglycan content, as well as rate of sulfate incorporation, in cartilage from 19 osteoarthritic knees undergoing total replacement and in samples from 14 normal adult knees from cadavers and amputation specimens. Only knees with little or no degenerative change were included in the control group. The incorporation of $^{35}SO_4$ was determined, and cartilage samples immediately adjacent to those used for the biochemical studies were examined histologically.

There were no significant differences between grossly intact cartilage from osteoarthritic knees and cartilage from control joints. Surface-fibrillated specimens had a higher water content in the surface layers, but no abnormality in the content or synthesis rate of glycosaminoglycan. Deeply fibrillated cartilage had an increased water content throughout its extent, as well as reductions in both the content and synthesis rate of glycosaminoglycans.

These findings suggest that degenerative changes in osteoarthritic knees are focal in origin. Some histologically and biochemically normal cartilage may persist in knees exhibiting frank osteoarthritic changes. In view of the dependence of the mechanical properties of cartilage on its chemical composition, residual intact cartilage probably is functionally normal. A mechanical rather than a metabolic origin for osteoarthritis of the knee seems likely, at least in some instances. The so-called wear-life of cartilage in an intact compartment might be normal if subjected to normal loads; corrective osteotomy or unicompartmental joint replacement would seem to be a rational approach if the intact side is not overloaded postoperatively.

▶ [This study confirms what we have seen in the clinical setting; very seldom is there

(7–29)   J. Bone Joint Surg. [Am.] 66-A:95–106, January 1984.

evidence of progressive degenerative change in the opposite compartment after upper tibial osteotomy, even though overcorrection of the varus is carried out. I have seen degenerative changes only in those knees in which there was rather marked overcorrection. We can assume from this study, as the authors state, that at least one cause for osteoarthritis is overload, and that osteoarthritis is focal. With the increased interest now among surgeons to perform arthroscopy prior to upper tibial osteotomy (or unicompartmental arthroplasty), if the opposite compartment is normal in appearance by arthroscopy or by standing x-rays, it is probably good articular cartilage and not basically osteoarthritic. We can be better assured, therefore, of a lasting result as far as that compartment is concerned after osteotomy or unicompartmental joint replacement.—Ed.] ◄

7–30 **Limb-Threatening Potential of Arteriosclerotic Popliteal Artery Aneurysms.** Walter M. Whitehouse, Jr., Thomas W. Wakefield, Linda M. Graham, Andris Kazmers, Gerald B. Zelenock, Jack L. Cronenwett, Thomas L. Dent, S. Martin Lindenauer, and James C. Stanley (Univ. of Michigan) reviewed experience with 61 patients who had 88 arteriosclerotic popliteal artery aneurysms and were treated between 1943 and 1982. The 59 men and 2 women had a mean age of 67 years. Aneurysms were bilateral in 44% of patients. Risk factors associated with arteriosclerosis were frequent in this population. One third of patients had coronary artery disease, and 5% had cerebrovascular disease. Extrapopliteal aneurysmal disease was present in 60% of patients and in 78% of those with bilateral popliteal aneurysms.

Angiography often underestimated the size of the popliteal artery aneurysms. Over half the aneurysms were symptomatic. Gangrene was present in 8 extremities. No ruptures occurred. One fourth of the popliteal aneurysms were totally occluded at the time of diagnosis, and 5 were associated with peripheral embolization. Fifty-six popliteal aneurysms in 44 patients were operated on. There were 44 primary arterial reconstructions, usually by the reversed autogenous saphenous vein bypass method. Three reconstructive operations failed early, and there were 3 late failures. Five of these 6 patients had amputations. A total of 9 patients required major amputations, 4 as primary procedures. All these patients had symptomatic aneurysmal thrombosis. Three of 17 patients who were not operated on had severe ischemic complications on an average follow-up of 25 months, and 2 of them required amputations.

The natural course of untreated popliteal artery aneurysms is unclear, but one third of patients can be expected to have serious ischemic complications within 3 to 5 years. Reconstructions generally use reversed saphenous vein with a proximal end-to-side anastomosis. Resection should be done only if significant local symptoms or venous obstruction have developed. Abdominal aortic aneurysms are usually treated first, but popliteal and femoral aneurysms can often be treated simultaneously.

► [This excellent study by Dr. Whitehouse and his colleagues is of great importance

(7–30) Surgery 93:694–699, May 1983.

to orthopedic surgeons. One must include a popliteal artery aneurysm in the differential diagnosis of posterior knee and leg pain. The authors have shown that early recognition and surgical correction of popliteal artery aneurysm will lessen the potential of this disorder to threaten the limb.—F.H. Sim] ◄

7–31 **Release Surgery in Stiffness of the Knee.** Quadricepsplasty has been recommended for chronic knee stiffness if manipulation and physiotherapy fail. Norvald Langeland and Bjørg Carlsen (Univ. of Oslo) have found that quadricepsplasty can be avoided in most instances and that good results can be obtained with a simpler surgical procedure. Four men and 3 women with a mean age of 36.5 years underwent excision of scar tissue from the superior recess, patellofemoral joint, and anterior part of the tibiofemoral joint and release of the retinacula and sliding mechanism on the medial and lateral sides of the joint (Fig 7–10). Knee stiffness had been present for an average of 26 months and for up to 66 months in these cases. Lengthening of the rectus tendon was necessary in 1 case, but it was not

Fig 7–10.—Schematic drawing demonstrating capsule and retinacula gliding backward on femoral condyles when knee is moved from extension to flexion. If these structures are adherent to bone in encircled area *(left),* flexion becomes impossible. (Courtesy of Langeland, N., and Carlsen, B.: Acta Orthop. Scand. 54:252–255, April 1983.)

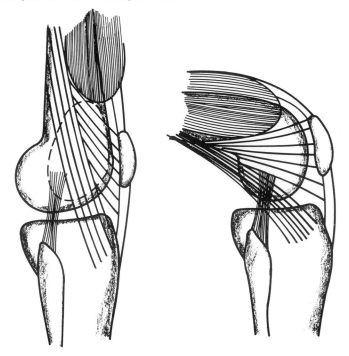

(7–31) Acta Orthop. Scand. 54:252–255, April 1983.

usually necessary to interfere with the posterior part of the capsule or joint. The knee was alternately placed in flexion and full extension after operation.

Median follow-up after surgery was 27 months. Patients gained a median of 66 degrees of flexion and 10 degrees of extension. None had less than 90 degrees of total motion after operation. Three patients regained normal knee function and have no pain. Another has only transient pain, and still another has only a slightly positive anterior drawer sign.

This release procedure produces a gain in mobility comparable with that obtained with the Thompsen quadricepsplasty in patients with chronic stiffness of the knee. It is a less extensive operation and leaves the patient with better muscle function. It is very important to alternate the position of the knee between 90 degrees of flexion and full extension after operation. Assisted active and active flexion and extension and exercises against intermittent resistance also are important. Forced massive movements should be avoided, and the patient's tolerance of pain should not be exceeded. Release surgery usually should be done only after more than a year of knee stiffness.

▶ [While the title is a misnomer since this article deals primarily with inability to flex the knee, the importance of the medial and lateral sliding mechanisms is appropriately emphasized and illustrated. Although few cases are presented in this article, this is not uncommon with such reports. The diverse etiology of the condition is likewise typical. The major disadvantage is that significant improvement of knee flexion is demonstrated to be possible by joint surgery without the more complicated quadricepsplasty, a message that the practicing orthopedic surgeon would do well to remember when confronted with such a problem.—B.F. Morrey] ◀

8. Back and Neck

8-1 **Chymopapain, Chemonucleolysis, and Nucleus Pulposus Regeneration.** Chymopapain injection of the intervertebral disk may alter sciatic pain in patients with disk herniation, but its mechanism of action is unclear. David S. Bradford, Katherine M. Cooper, and Theodore R. Oegema, Jr., (Univ. of Minnesota) examined the effects of chymopapain in dogs and in an in vitro study of human intervertebral disks obtained at operation from patients with idiopathic scoliosis who were undergoing anterior reconstructive spinal surgery. Adult mongrel dogs received injections of 1 mg of chymopapain per disk in 0.1 ml of buffer, a midrange dose. Proteoglycan synthesis was analyzed using ^{35}S-sulfate.

Disk space narrowing was observed radiographically in the injected dogs within 2 weeks. Complete loss of proteoglycan was demonstrated by safranin-O staining of the nucleus pulposus, cartilaginous endplates, and annulus fibrosus. The nucleus pulposus retained the ability to synthesize proteoglycans, but these were degraded by endogenous proteolytic action. The disk was increased in height within 3 months after chymopapain treatment when intense safranin-O staining returned to the annulus and the cartilaginous end-plates and very prominent staining was observed in the nucleus. The proteoglycan monomer was slightly larger than in control samples. Within 6 months there was a further increase in disk height, and histologic findings returned to normal. The proteoglycans isolated from the nucleus pulposus at this time were physicochemically essentially the same as those from control samples. The studies of human disk tissue confirmed low protease activity and extensive degradation of proteoglycan by added chymopapain.

Whether pain relief from enzymatic dissolution of the nucleus pulposus is the result solely of a biochemical effect on disk proteoglycans remains uncertain. Direct chemical and anti-inflammatory effects have been proposed. Restoration of disk height after chymopapain injection is owing not to replacement by fibrocartilage, but to replacement with matrix containing proteoglycan resembling that of the normal nucleus pulposus. Chymopapain injection would appear to be a more physiologic treatment than surgical excision is.

▶ [Doctor Bradford's work in the dog model reinforces our clinical impression, and Dr. Lyman Smith's earlier experience, that the intervertebral disk is capable of regen-

(8–1) J. Bone Joint Surg. [Am.] 65-A:1220–1231, December 1983.

eration after chemonucleolysis. We have found, as have others, the most notable being Leon Wiltsie, that serial x-rays done at 3, 6, and 12 months, and at 3 years, do show that the lumbar interspaces of a significant number of patients who have undergone chemonucleolysis have rewidened.—B.M. Onofrio] ◄

8–2 **Technique for Chemonucleolysis.** Henry W. Apfelbach (Lake Forest, Ill.) outlines a technique of chemonucleolysis based on accurate placement of the needle within the intervertebral disk space. General anesthesia provides better physiologic control should anaphylaxis develop, and maintenance of the patient's position is easier, especially when the procedure is prolonged. Local anesthesia should not be used until 20 or 30 patients have been treated by a given surgeon. When myelographic and CT findings are equivocal, diskography may serve a diagnostic purpose in showing whether chemonucleolysis should be done at the L5–S1 level. Routine lumbosacral spine x-ray studies should be available. The inexperienced operator should obtain proper needle placement at the L4–L5 level initially. The needle is at about 45 degrees, 8–11 cm from the midline. The L5–S1 needle generally is inserted 30 degrees caudad to the L4–L5 needle. Conray is the best contrast medium at present.

Enzyme is injected 15 minutes after diskography and can be prepared as the x-ray films are being developed. The recommended dose is 3,000 units, injected over about 3 seconds. The endotracheal tube is left in place as long as possible. Anaphylaxis, if it occurs, does so almost instantly and usually within the first 10 minutes, although it has been described as developing up to 1–2 hours after enzyme injection. The patient is usually kept in the recovery room for 90 minutes and monitored closely. The intravenous line should be kept open for at least 3 hours.

▶ [I would take issue with Dr. Apfelbach's first paragraph in which he states that "the keystone of performing chemonucleolysis is proper needle placement." I think the keystone should be proper and precise diagnosis which in turn is followed by technically proficient needle placement. Whether or not the procedure is done under general or local anesthesia is up to the discretion of the operating surgeon. It is best performed with a perfectly positioned patient. Local anesthesia allows for subtle but real movement, which may confound needle localization while using biplane fluoroscopy. Under "diskography," it is misleading regarding the potential transdural approach to difficult needle placement at the lumbosacral disk. Transdural approach is absolutely contraindicated, not in the opinion of some, but in the opinion of all who are involved with chemonucleolysis. With the present state of the art, conscious violation of the intrathecal space is absolutely contraindicated. Diskography, using as a model a three-level diskogram, is turning back the clock 20 years to a time when diskography and chemonucleolysis was done at multiple interspaces. It is the present concern of all those involved with chemonucleolysis that the needles be placed in the spaces that, preferably by myelography or myelography and computed tomography (CT) scanning or less preferably by CT scanning alone, a disk protrusion or extrusion has been identified. Performing routine diskography at three levels is unnecessary and invites the use of chemonucleolysis for degenerating disks which are

(8–2) Orthopedics 6:1613–1616, December 1983.

otherwise clinically asymptomatic and it increases the risk of intradiskal infection in spaces which need not be violated at all.—B.M. Onofrio] ◄

8–3 **Chemonucleolysis Under Local Anesthesia.** Curtis W. Spencer III (Mem. Hosp. Med. Center, Long Beach, Calif.) believes that general anesthesia is unnecessary during chemonucleolysis, since local anesthesia has proved to be effective and safe. Dual-needle diskography has been used, with biplane image intensification. Histamine antagonists are given before the procedure, and a narcotic and antiemetic are given an hour before chemonucleolysis. Diskography is performed in a fluoroscopy suite after hydrocortisone administration. More diazepam or narcotic can be given intravenously as needed, or 40% nitrous oxide in oxygen can be administered. The medial edge of the iliac crest is anesthetized with 1% lidocaine before an 18-gauge needle is placed in the L5 disk. Pure oxygen is given after needle placement, and diskography and chemonucleolysis are carried out. Narcotics can be given to relieve the pain of chemonucleolysis, but not to the point of total sedation. Diphenhydramine is given intravenously for persistent itching and burning. Hypotension need not be treated unless it persists.

General anesthesia for chemonucleolysis masks early signs of anaphylaxis. Local anesthesia is safer and allows the patient to report when a nerve root is hit by the needle. The recovery period is shorter, and the postoperative sequelae of general anesthesia are avoided. A large majority of patients are comfortable and cooperative throughout the procedure.

► [With regard to this subject I would always point out that the major disadvantage of a local procedure is the tendency to perform this procedure in a less-than-optimal setting. Subtle movements of the patient would confound optimal needle placement as well.

In the end, the technique that is most desirable for each individual patient is the technique that best serves the physician who carries out the procedure. There are no absolute criteria with regard to the best way of accomplishing optimal needle placement when carrying out chemonucleolysis.—B.M. Onofrio] ◄

8–4 **Anaphylactic Reactions Following Intradiskal Injection of Chymopapain Under Local Anesthesia.** Brad B. Hall and John A. McCulloch reviewed data on 4,282 patients with a diagnosis of herniated nucleus pulposus who received intradiskal chymopapain injection under local anesthesia between 1970 and 1981; 15 of these patients (0.35%) experienced an anaphylactic reaction. All injections were done in an operating room under sterile conditions, and the patients were monitored closely. Local anesthesia was augmented by diazepam and fentanyl administered intravenously. In some cases a small amount of thiopental was administered just before chymopapain injection.

(8–3) Orthopedics 6:1617–1618, December 1983.
(8–4) J. Bone Joint Surg. [Am.] 65-A:1215–1219, December 1983.

Ten women and 5 men, average age 43 years, sustained an anaphylactic reaction. Eight patients had known allergies to drugs, and 1 was sensitive to stinging insects. Six of these patients also reported allergies to foods or other substances. None had a significant family history of allergy or atopy. In all, 25 disk spaces were injected. Hypotension developed as the first symptom in only 3 patients. Eleven reactions occurred within 5 minutes of chymopapain injection. The systolic blood pressure fell to below 80 mm Hg in all cases, and 8 patients had no detectable blood pressure at some point. Anxiety, nausea, and paresthesias were frequent complaints. Nine patients had swelling or angioedema, chiefly in the facial region, and 5 had urticaria. An average of 3.8 L of fluid replacement was required during treatment of hypotension. Eleven patients received epinephrine intravenously. None required intubation. Twelve of the 15 patients reported an excellent outcome when followed up an average of 51 months after treatment. Only 1 patient reported a new allergy, that is, urticaria occurring after codeine use.

Intradiskal chymopapain injection should be done under local anesthesia augmented with neuroleptic drugs so that early warning signs of anaphylaxis will be recognized. Such reactions are best managed pharmacologically without general anesthesia. All reported deaths associated with chymopapain anaphylaxis occurred in procedures done under general anesthesia. Anaphylaxis did not affect the final outcome of chymopapain injection in the present series.

▶ [The conclusions of Hall and McCulloch as to the optimal nature of local anesthesia in chemonucleolysis reside within the discretion of the authors and their experience. It should not be interpreted as being the "only" or the "best" method to be used in diskolysis. I would think that excellent anesthesiologic coverage of every case is the absolute requirement in carrying out chemonucleolysis. Certainly the experience these authors have had with a significant number of cases makes any observation they make valid. Their opinions should be considered by the less experienced who are developing their own technique.—B.M. Onofrio] ◀

8–5 **Lumbar Intervertebral Diskolysis with Collagenase.** John W. Bromley (New York Univ.) and Jaime G. Gomez (Bogota, Colombia) undertook an experimental evaluation of collagenase (Nucleolysin) in 52 patients with herniated lumbar disks who were refractory to conservative treatment. The patients, aged 20–61 years, had been symptomatic for 2 months or longer and had failed to respond to at least 2 weeks of bed rest, often with pelvic or Buck's traction. None had had previous back surgery or had major neurologic deficits. None had myelographic defects at more than one level. Enzyme was injected into the nucleus after confirming the needle position. The dose ranged from 300 to 600 units. Ambulation began after 24 hours or when the patient was comfortable. All procedures were done with local anesthesia.

(8–5) Spine 8:322–324, April 1983.

Only 1 of the 4 patients given 300–350 units of Nucleolysin had a good outcome, but 78% of the 46 evaluable patients given 500–600 units had good results. Only 1 patient had a recurrence necessitating surgery for disk extrusion. Thirteen percent of patients had poor results, and 5 of the 6 were operated on. Disk sequestration was observed in 4 of these cases. Radiographic follow-up showed narrowing of the disk space after 4–6 weeks, which did not progress after 2 months. No significant laboratory abnormalities were observed, and no infectious or other complications resulted from enzyme injection.

Collagenase injection of the herniated lumbar disk is a simple, safe procedure with a high success rate. It is a useful extension of conservative management. Failures due to disk sequestration require surgical treatment. Current diagnostic procedures do not always permit a diagnosis of disk extrusion preoperatively. A double-blind study of collagenase injection is under way.

▶ [Diskolysis using collagenase is a treatment modality still under investigation. It would appear from early results that the problem of anaphylaxis which occurs in about 1% to 2% of patients undergoing diskolysis with chymopapain is not a problem when collagenase is used. However, it would appear that any inadvertent intrathecal injection of collagenase might be more of a problem than when chymopapain is used. The exact mechanism by which either collagenase or chymopapain bring about pain relief is still not known. Is the ultimate effect simply due to settling and narrowing of the disk space or is there some immunologic or chemical effect which is as yet undemonstrated? We will look forward to further reports of the efficacy of collagenase diskolysis and particularly look forward to the results of a double-blind study in the near future.—R.N. Stauffer] ◀

8–6 **Safety and Efficacy of Chymopapain (Chymodiactin) in Herniated Nucleus Pulposus With Sciatica: Results of a Randomized, Double-blind Study.** Manucher J. Javid, Eugene J. Nordby, Lee T. Ford, William J. Hejna, Walter W. Whisler, Charles Burton, D. Keith Millett, Leon L. Wiltse, Eric H. Widell, Jr., Robert J. Boyd, St. Elmo Newton, and Ronald Thisted report the results of a double-blind trial comparing intradiskal chymopapain injections with a placebo in patients at seven centers with single-disk herniations and persistent radicular pain that had failed to respond adequately to at least 6 weeks of conservative therapy. All patients were aged 18 to 60 years and had neurologic abnormalities. None had been operated on. Study patients received 6,000 units of chymopapain, injected under fluoroscopic guidance.

Failure was suggested by both the patient and investigator in 31 of 53 placebo-treated patients and in 15 of 55 drug-treated patients. Of 32 placebo patients whose conditions failed to respond and were subsequently treated with chymopapain, 29 had a successful outcome. In no patient did anaphylaxis develop. Back spasm was the most common adverse effect of both chymopapain and placebo injections.

Chymopapain appears to be clearly superior to saline in the treat-

(8–6) JAMA 249:2489–2494, May 13, 1983.

ment of patients with lumbar-disk herniation. The procedure is safe when performed by experienced surgeons. Patients in this study showed a success rate of 82% when treated with chymopapain initially, and a rate of 91% when given chymopapain treatment after failure with a placebo injection. Chemonucleolysis with chymopapain is a useful alternative to laminectomy in surgical candidates. The responses observed in placebo patients could be due to additional conservative treatment after the saline injection, to the natural course of the disease, to mechanical change at the injection site, or to a psychogenic placebo effect.

8–7 **Computed Tomographic, Myelographic, and Operative Findings in Patients With Suspected Herniated Lumbar Disks.** Nazih A. Moufarrij, Russell W. Hardy, Jr., and Meredith A. Weinstein (Cleveland Clinic) performed sector computed tomographic (CT) examination in 50 consecutive patients operated on for lumbar disk herniation. None had previously had lumbar laminectomy or had a diagnosis of lumbar canal stenosis. Lumbar myelography also was performed in 46 patients. The CT scanner was modified to obtain sections 12.7 cm in diameter. Sections 4 mm thick were obtained with the patient supine. In 8 cases, metrizamide was introduced into the subarachnoid space before CT scanning.

Twenty-five patients had CT findings of a soft herniated disk; 10, spondylitic compression in the lateral recess or foramen; 4, a combination of disk herniation and spondylitic compression; 1, a dural cyst. In 10 cases, the CT findings were negative and myelography correctly predicted the lesion in 8 of these 10. Sector CT correctly predicted the nature of the lesion in 48% of all cases, was incorrect in 28%, and gave incomplete findings in 24%. The study was most accurate when the only finding was a disk protrusion; it correctly predicted the findings in all but 1 of these 25 cases.

Sector CT is useful in assessing patients with sciatica. The study correctly predicted the operative findings in about half the present cases, and was correct in all but 1 of 25 patients with a soft herniated disk only. Myelography can be omitted when CT shows a soft disk protrusion, but it should be done if spondylosis or a mixed lesion is shown by CT scanning.

▶ [The authors take several interesting points of view. I would, however, take issue with their statement that when findings of a CT scan demonstrate a soft disk protrusion, myelography may be omitted. I believe that myelography does what CT scanning in the lumbar area cannot do at the present time, that is, evaluate the intradural contents. We have all had the experience of myelographically proved findings not leading to satisfactory postoperative results. To assure one that an intradural process has not been missed, which has been concomitant with the disk protrusion, myelography is an absolute necessity. Computed tomography scanning as the sole means of diagnosis in lumbar disk surgery has a built-in failure rate of approximately 4% because of missed intradural tumors, whether they be symptomatic or asymptomatic.

(8–7) Neurosurgery 12:184–188, February 1983.

The false negative examinations that occurred in 9 out of the 50 patients examined is a much higher false negative CT scan rate than is seen at our institution.—B.M. Onofrio] ◄

8–8 **Differential CT Diagnosis of Extruded Nucleus Pulposus.** A majority of nucleus pulposus herniations can be diagnosed by the presence of a focal computed tomographic (CT) abnormality at the disk margin, but the appearances of nuclear fragments penetrating the posterior longitudinal ligament and anulus are unclear. Alan L. Williams, Victor M. Haughton, David L. Daniels, and John P. Grogan (Med. College of Wisconsin) reviewed the preoperative CT findings in 57 patients in whom a diagnosis of extruded nuclear fragment was made at laminectomy and in 31 with similar findings in whom anomalous root sheaths or epidural tumors were subsequently diagnosed. In the last 20 cases the density of tissues within the spinal canal was measured with a computer program and a region-of-interest technique.

All CT studies of patients with surgically confirmed extruded disk fragments showed asymmetry of epidural fat and compression of displacement of a root sheath or the dural sac. An epidural soft tissue mass was seen in 52 studies; in 27 cases it was contiguous with the disk. In 14 cases the disk fragment was seen caudal to the intervertebral disk. Findings were similar in 15 patients with anomalous, conjoined nerve root sheaths. Dilated root sheaths in 6 cases caused the sheaths and the epidural fat to appear asymmetric. The findings in patients with epidural tumor resembled those in patients with extruded disk fragments superficially. Tissue density measurements distinguished between extruded disk fragments and the root sheath anomalies; the disk fragments had considerably higher Hounsfield unit values than the root sheath anomalies.

Computed tomographic study of extruded lumbar disk fragments may show a sharply marginated epidural mass, migration of the fragment, and occasionally a normal or nearly normal posterior disk margin. Nerve root sheath anomalies and neoplasms may produce similar changes, but these can usually be distinguished from extruded disk fragments. Intrathecal contrast study occasionally is useful.

► [Many neuroradiologists cannot achieve the 95% detection rate implied in this article. It is my understanding that the next revision of a similar article by this group will quote 80%. Our detection rate is even lower than 80%. In a group of young patients, one might approach the author's accuracy rate, but the inclusion of older patients lowers everyone's results. This study should not encourage reformatting which, in our hands, is useless. The article is otherwise excellent.—B.M. Onofrio] ◄

8–9 **Treatment of the Persistent Sciatic Artery** in 2 patients is described by David T. Mayschak and M. Wayne Flye (Univ. of Texas at Galveston). Only 37 patients with persistent sciatic artery have been

(8–8)   Radiology 148:141–148, July 1983.
(8–9)   Ann. Surg. 199:69–74, January 1984.

reported in the world literature. The extremity may be at jeopardy through atheromatous degeneration, leading to aneurysmal dilatation, occlusive thrombosis, or thromboembolism. A man aged 55 with hypertension had bilateral calf claudication of several months' duration. The right popliteal pulse and both pedal pulses were absent, and angiography showed occlusion of the proximal part of a persistent sciatic artery on the right. The superficial femoral artery on this side was hypoplastic. Distal runoff was poor. On the left side the persistent sciatic artery was hypoplastic and the superficial femoral artery was complete. A woman aged 60 with sudden right leg and hip pain had complete persistent sciatic arteries and aneurysms in both upper thighs; hypoplastic superficial femoral arteries ended in the distal thighs. The right and then the left persistent sciatic arteries were ligated at the level of the sciatic foramen and divided at the junction with the popliteal artery; saphenous vein bypass grafts were placed end-to-end between the common femoral and popliteal arteries.

The estimated incidence of persistent sciatic artery is about 0.05%. Nearly half of the reported patients had bilateral involvement. Aneurysm formation occurs in up to 15% of patients. The vessel is complete in most instances. Associated hemihypertrophy of the pelvis or leg has been described. A pulsatile mass in the buttock represents aneurysmal dilatation of the vessel. The superficial femoral system is atretic in the distal thigh, usually terminating at the adductor hiatus. The persistent sciatic artery passes deep to the gluteus maximus and hamstring muscles and along the posterior surface of the adductor magnus before entering the popliteal fossa. The vessel is prone to early atheromatous degeneration and aneurysm formation. A dilated aneurysm can produce neurologic symptoms through sciatic nerve compression. Doppler study is helpful in tracking the vessel. Surgery involves exclusion of the anomalous artery from the circulation and revascularization of the extremity. An aneurysm is best managed by exclusion from its point of exit from the pelvis to its junction with the popliteal artery and construction of a femoral-to-popliteal bypass.

▶ [I have never seen a clinical problem associated with a persistent sciatic artery as described in this article. I am impressed that orthopedists probably should be aware of this potential arterial problem, but it is so very rare that I cannot see how a big issue can be made of it.

The principles of management either of aneurysmal or of occlusive disease would be the same for this vessel as for any other in that area, and certainly the orthopedic surgeon must deal with any adjacent arterial problem regardless of the name of the vessel involved. The anatomy could only be shown by good arteriography, and I don't see how anyone could be suspicious of this vessel unless the patient happened to be one of the unusual members of the population to have some type of hemihypertrophy of the pelvis or leg, or a short leg as has been reported in 1 or 2 cases. The pulsating mass in the buttock would be an indication for arteriography, which generally would delineate the problem and would demonstrate the importance of that unusual vessel in supplying blood to the lower extremity.—P. Bernatz] ◀

8–10 **Flexion and Extension Radiography of the Lumbar Spine: A Comparison With Lumbar Diskography.** Richard C. Quinnell and Harold R. Stockdale (Nottingham, England) reviewed four methods of quantifying relative intervertebral body movement from static flexion-extension films of the lumbar spine, and compared the value of each technique in indicating sites of disk degeneration with that of lumbar diskography. Lateral lumbar spine films were taken in the extremes of flexion and extension in 30 seated patients with mechanical low back disorders.

The analytic methods included the angular displacement technique of Begg and Falconer, the Tanz modification of this method, the method of Pennal et al. in which a point of zero instant velocity is deduced, and the linear anteroposterior displacement method. A total of 111 disk spaces was evaluated. The most accurate means of identifying disk degeneration was that of measuring the linear displacement of one vertebra in the anteroposterior plane. None of the methods, however, was free of artifacts.

A single set of flexion-extension films cannot be expected to be of much value in the management of patients with low back pain. Serial studies may be useful in such areas as assessment of the stability of spinal fusions. The best means of quantifying relative intervertebral body movement may be to measure linear anteroposterior displacement. The radiation dose is an important consideration; the dose is unacceptable unless improved patient management can reasonably be expected.

▶ [This is a most interesting study. The questionable clinical value of diskography has again been demonstrated. There are, however, a number of problems with this study. In a recent study of the three-dimensional motion of the lumbar spine in normal young volunteer subjects, we found that the amount of motion present at each vertebral segment was extremely variable. Therefore, the "normal" amount of motion for a given segment is not known and cannot be used as a basis for comparing individual subjects studied by the authors' proposed technique. Furthermore, it appears that the subject of segmental instability is a good deal more complex than simply the amount of translation of one vertebral segment on another in the coronal plane. It appears that subtle evidences of segmental instability occur which are a matter of the derangement of rotary motion which occurs during flexion-extension. A patient under study could have an apparently normal amount of translation or angulation of one vertebral segment on another as viewed by the bending x-rays but yet have marked instability because of the aberration of accompanying rotational motion which occurs at that same level.—R.N. Stauffer] ◀

8–11 **Use of Epidural Morphine To Decrease Postoperative Pain in Patients Undergoing Lumbar Laminectomy.** The presence of opiate receptors in the spinal cord helps explain the prolonged segmental analgesia produced by epidural narcotic administration. Glenn R. Rechtine, Charles M. Reinert, and Henry H. Bohlman undertook a double-blind study of the efficacy of small doses of preser-

(8–10) Clin. Radiol. 34:405–411, July 1983.
(8–11) J. Bone Joint Surg. [Am.] 65-A:113–116, January 1984.

vative-free epidural morphine in reducing discomfort after lumbar laminectomy in 50 consecutive patients. An epidural catheter was passed through the laminotomy defect at the end of surgery, and 3 mg of preservative-free morphine, morphine in a 1:200,000 epinephrine solution, or normal saline was injected. Surgery was done under nitrous-narcotic anesthesia, with inhalational agents used to control blood pressure administered as needed. Most patients had diskectomy.

The patients given epidural morphine were comfortable for about 16 hours after operation, and those given saline were comfortable for 7 hours. Significantly less systemic analgesia was needed in the first 24 hours after surgery by the morphine-treated patients. Total pain scores in the first 24 hours after operation were significantly lower in the morphine-treated patients, but comparable numbers of narcotic doses were used in all 3 groups of patients. No appreciable advantage accrued to the use of epinephrine with morphine. No patient had respiratory depression. One had pruritus of the lower extremities.

Epidural morphine administration is an effective and safe means of analgesia in patients having lumbar laminectomy. The chance of subarachnoid injection is minimized by placement of the catheter under direct vision. Several patients did not require any supplemental postoperative analgesia. The smallest effective dose of morphine should be used, and patients must be monitored for respiratory depression. Preservative-free morphine should be used to prevent the development of paraplegia from the caustic preservatives contained in standard preparations.

▶ [I think the best argument against the placement of an epidural catheter and the injection of epidural narcotics to control postoperative pain in the lumbar disk patient is found in the third sentence of the conclusion where it states: "The catheter is placed under direct vision and therefore the chance of inadvertent subarachnoid injection is minimized." With lumbar disk surgery, one of the more ominous surgical complications is the creation of a dural rent or leak and if there is any chance of increasing that possibility I think that the epidural narcotic catheter placement should be avoided. The hallmarks of the onset of neurologic complications in the immediate postoperative period include motor or sensory abnormalities and/or sphincter disorders which might alert us to the early occurrence of an epidural clot. Masking or modifying any of these early warning signs would not be in the patient's best interest.—B.M. Onofrio] ◀

8–12 **Epidural Morphine for Control of Pain After Spinal Surgery: Preliminary Report.** Epidural opiate treatment has been used successfully to control pain that follows obstetric, abdominal, and orthopedic procedures. Henry H. Schmidek and Scott G. Cutler (Univ. of Vermont) evaluated epidural analgesia with morphine in 5 patients undergoing spinal operations. Three had lumbar disk protrusions, 1 had a gibbus deformity involving T12–L2, and 1 was undergoing decompressive lumbar laminectomy for spinal stenosis. A small

(8–12) Neurosurgery 13:37–39, July 1983.

Portex epidural catheter was used until pain was absent for 24 hours without the need for analgesic. Administration of preservative-free morphine solution began when the patient requested medication for pain, and the dose was titrated according to the degree of discomfort, ranging from 2 to 6 mg. Pain relief was impressive in all instances, and the patients had essentially pain-free postoperative courses. No patient had evidence of respiratory depression or urine retention. Patients were observed in an intensive care setting for the first postoperative day.

Use of an epidural catheter for morphine administration for up to 5 days after spinal operations is an effective means of relieving postoperative pain. No complications requiring treatment have occurred. Respiratory depression is the most serious possible complication, and appropriate monitoring is necessary. Naloxone should be available. Tachyphylaxis and tolerance to morphine have not been observed during 2 to 5 days of intermittent opiate use. Epidural morphine administration has also been used in 6 patients with percutaneously placed catheters who had pain from benign or malignant disorders. No infection has resulted from epidural catheterization on follow-up for an average of 4½ months. The catheter is managed like a parenteral hyperalimentation line.

8–13 **Indwelling Epidural Morphine for Control of Postlumbar Spinal Surgery Pain.** Epidural morphine administration is an effective means of controlling pain and in relatively brief applications is safe. Charles D. Ray and Russel Bagley (Abbott-Northwestern Hosp., Minneapolis) used relatively small doses of morphine in a small volume to relieve pain in the most painful phase of postoperative recovery in 25 patients. The results were compared with those obtained in 25 other patients undergoing lumbar spine operations who received standard parenteral and oral doses of narcotics. The groups were clinically comparable before operation. Portex epidural catheters were used. Patients received 1–3 mg of morphine per injection in a volume of 1–3 ml.

The results were distinctly better than those of standard narcotic treatment in terms of pain control, side effects, and overall facilitation of recovery after operation. The 9 patients who had had previous lumbar spine operations with standard analgesia were pleased with the results of epidural treatment. Less than one tenth of the parenteral amount of narcotic was necessary in epidural patients. The patients were more alert and cooperative than those treated conventionally, and they ambulated earlier. The hospital time was shortened by 1 to 2 days. The overall clinical results 6 weeks and 6 months after discharge were similar in the two groups. No complications were attributable to the epidural morphine approach.

(8–13) Neurosurgery 13:388–393, October 1983.

Since these 25, about 150 more patients have received postoperative epidural morphine analgesia with excellent results and no major side effects. Several patients have had increased difficulty voiding or neurogenic itching, which has generally resolved within 8–12 hours.

▶ [Although no one would be surprised by the success of epidural morphine in limiting low back and leg pain secondary to the operative procedure in the postoperative laminectomy patient, I believe one has to look at the potential side effects of this treatment, namely, respiratory depression and an increased rate of operative wound contamination by indwelling catheters at the wound site and epidural space. I think the method is totally unwarranted because of the potential risk of these two complications. Although it is a tempting philosophy, I believe its use would increase the already significant types of postoperative complications a laminectomy patient is subject to and I would condemn it. It is a far different circumstance in patients with thoracotomies because of complications due to poor inspiration. In this instance it enhances their postoperative results allowing early ambulation.

I would have to apply the same comments to this paper as well. The placement of epidural catheters is unfortunately not always epidural and may have the unpleasant side effect of being intradural which adds to the risk of cerebrospinal fluid leak in addition to the respiratory suppression and added risk of operative wound infection. I would condemn the procedure.—B.M. Onofrio] ◀

8–14 **Indications for Metrizamide Myelography: Relationship With Complications After Myelography.** Metrizamide has replaced Pantopaque as the contrast medium of choice for lumbar myelography. Harry N. Herkowitz, Richard L. Romeyn, and Richard H. Rothman examined the relation between complications of myelography and the absence of objective clinical and myelographic evidence of lumbar disk herniation in a retrospective review of data on 248 patients and on a prospective series of 110 patients in whom lumbar disk herniation was suspected. There were 170 males with a mean age of 44 years and 188 females with a mean age of 41.5 years. Studies were done by injecting 12 ml of metrizamide with a 22-gauge needle at the L3-L4 interspace after 5 ml of cerebrospinal fluid was withdrawn. Patients were not allowed to lie flat for 12 hours after the procedure.

Complications occurred in 53% of all patients; headache and nausea-vomiting were most frequent. The incidences of complications were 30% in 112 patients who had abnormal clinical and myelographic findings and 70% in the 180 with only subjective symptoms and normal myelographic findings. The proportion of patients of the latter type was much higher among those receiving compensation than among patients not receiving compensation. In the prospective series, 10 of 31 patients with abnormal clinical and myelographic findings and 38 of the 60 with only subjective symptoms had headache. Headache was severe in 3 of the former and in 26 of the latter. The average hospital stay of patients with complications was 3.4 days longer than that of patients without complications after myelography.

Complications of metrizamide myelography were nearly 2½ times

(8–14)   J. Bone Joint Surg. [Am.] 65-A:1144–1149, October 1983.

more frequent in patients in this study in whom suspected lumbar disk disease was not confirmed than in those with abnormal myelographic findings. Both headache and nausea-vomiting were increased in the former group. Compensation patients more often had normal findings and complications of myelography. Myelography should, in general, be restricted to patients with objective physical findings who are being considered for surgical treatment of lumbar disk herniation.

▶ [The authors are to be commended for looking at myelography and the symptomatic response to it, and then correlating these findings with the presence or absence of clinical signs that confirm lumbar nerve root irritation prior to myelography. I believe those who have had significant experience in the treatment of low back disorders are well aware that any procedure done for the Group B patient has a higher rate of morbidity. In defense of myelography in those patients in whom conservative management has failed, there always resides an honest attempt to rule out organic disease prior to placing a label of "functional disorder" on patients suffering from back and leg pain. Although it is not surprising that headache, nausea, and vomiting is more common in those patients, I believe in many instances the short-term morbidity is justified if it lends support to a nonaggressive form of surgical management. When pain is the substrate of most low back disorders that may potentially be surgical, I believe myelography has its place in an effort to finalize the sorting process into absolute conservative or absolute operative patient categories. Despite our safeguards with regard to attempting to avoid the group B patients as far as surgery is concerned, there are innumerable gray zone patients who have clinical and x-ray findings which point toward a diagnosis of disk fragments and in whom an experienced surgeon will know that the likelihood of obtaining a good result is minimal. Unfortunately, we have no fail-safe mechanism to guarantee either conservative or aggressive therapy. Myelography, even though it has its drawbacks, certainly even in the patient who is not suspected of having a surgical disease, has its place.—B.M. Onofrio] ◀

8–15 **Atrophy of Sacrospinal Muscle Groups in Patients With Chronic, Diffusely Radiating Lumbar Back Pain.** Muscle atrophy developing after surgery for lumbar back pain syndromes is reflected by radiolucency in the sacrospinal muscle group on the operated side on computed tomography (CT) examination. In its most severe form it is a result of replacement of muscle tissue by adipose tissue. E. M. Laasonen (Helsinki) sought these changes in patients with chronic or subacute radiating lumbar back pain who underwent lumbar CT. Patients whose symptoms were attributable to a single lumbosacral nerve root were excluded. A total of 156 patients underwent scanning without contrast medium. At least 2 interspaces were examined, usually including L5-S1.

Sacrospinal muscle atrophy was seen in 31 patients (20%), bilaterally in 11, and in 29 (31%) of 94 patients operated on for radiating lumbar back pain. Only 2 patients with bilateral atrophy were not operated on; 1 had tuberculous spondylitis, and the other, ankylosing spondylitis. Usually, a homogeneous or nearly homogeneous lucency of the muscle area was observed. The entire transverse area of the

(8–15) Neuroradiology 26:9–13, January 1984.

sacrospinal muscle group appeared atrophied in most instances. Atrophy usually began 6–24 mm below the level of surgery. Strong correlations were not found between the radiologic and clinical findings. Severe denervation potentials were observed on electroneuromyography in 7 of the 9 patients studied, 2 had no active potentials.

The muscle atrophy in these patients is thought to represent neural damage caused during surgery. It was seen regardless of the type of surgery performed or the number of operations carried out. The appearance of these changes may well contraindicate further surgery, or may call for physiotherapy.

▶ [The authors are to be commended for their most interesting observations. The cause of the spinal muscle atrophy, however, remains obscure. Is this due to direct muscle injury at the time of surgery? Is it due to denervation from damage to the posterior primary division of the spinal nerves? Or might this finding even be present preoperatively and, in fact, be a contributing cause to the segmental instability which underlies the patient's symptoms of back pain?

Since virtually all of the patients in the study were postoperative, these questions cannot be answered. We would look forward with great interest to a prospective study which would allow the assessment of preoperative to postoperative change. It might also answer questions about whether or not this muscle atrophy is irreversible or whether it could be affected by vigorous exercise regimens.—R.N. Stauffer] ◀

8–16 **Evaluation of an Exercise Program for Back Pain.** Low back pain is one of the most common causes of disability, and an inexpensive, widely available treatment program could significantly reduce health costs. Hans Kraus, Willibald Nagler, and Alexander Melleby (New York) evaluated a 6-week exercise program established at YMCAs throughout the United States for persons with low back pain. Classes meet twice a week with trained instructors, and participants also exercise at home. The program includes relaxation exercises and a gradually increased sequence of limbering, strengthening, and stretching exercises, all limited to three repetitions at a time. Subjects are evaluated by the six-item Kraus-Weber test battery for muscular fitness.

Results in 11,809 persons completing the exercise program at 800 YMCAs in all 50 states between 1977 and 1981 were assessed. Less pain was reported by 80.7% of participants at the end of the program. Demographic variables did not influence the results to any degree, and the duration of low back pain was not a significant factor, nor was previous treatment relevant. The results in 580 patients who had had spinal operations were comparable with those in the other subjects. Nearly 90% of subjects evaluated whose trunk muscle strength had improved substantially, perceived less back pain.

This simple exercise program has reduced low back pain significantly in about 80% of a large group of subjects. It is effective even in patients who have had spinal operations. Back exercise programs are presently in operation at 936 YMCAs throughout the country.

(8–16) Am. Fam. Physician 28:153–158, September 1983.

The effort represents the largest organized low-cost approach to dealing with low back pain in persons who do not require or who have failed to respond satisfactorily to operation.

▶ [The benefit people with low back pain reportedly received from the efforts described in this article is important for several reasons. First of all, it is a program that utilizes medical and nonmedical team members. Secondly, since the YMCA provided the organization and facilities, it was a cost-effective way to care for individuals with low back pain. Further follow-up studies and refinement of methods could provide even more specific help.—M.C. McPhee] ◀

8–17 **Risk Factors in Low Back Pain: An Epidemiologic Survey.** J. W. Frymoyer, M. H. Pope, Janice H. Clements, David G. Wilder, Brian MacPherson, and Takamaru Ashikaga (Univ. of Vermont) undertook a survey of 1,221 men, aged 18–55 years, who were seen in a family-practice facility between 1975 and 1978; the survey was undertaken to assess the socioeconomic and medical impact of low back pain in this population. The facility is the only local medical site for about 8,000 rural and suburban persons. The response rate was 67%.

While 30% of subjects had never had low back pain, 46% had had moderate pain, and 24% had had severe symptoms. Those with severe back pain had significantly more lower extremity symptoms, had sought more medical care for back pain, and had lost more time from work than those with moderate back pain. Risk factors for severe pain included jobs that required repeated heavy lifting, the use of jackhammers or machine tools, and the operation of motor vehicles. Patients with severe back pain were more likely to smoke cigarettes and to have greater tobacco consumption. Patients with moderate back pain were more often joggers and cross-country skiers than were subjects without back symptoms or those with severe low back pain.

Smoking was significantly associated with medically reported episodes of low back pain in this male population. Emotional, recreational, and occupational differences do not seem to explain this association, and it may be that cigarette smoke or a constituent has a direct adverse physiologic effect on the spine. Nicotine has been shown to reduce vertebral-body blood flow in dogs. Complex occupational risk factors for low-back pain exist. Recreational activities are, in general, not closely associated with the symptom. These findings may not be representative of those to be discovered in a highly urban population or in different climates. Ongoing studies of the various risk factors that may be causally related to low back pain are needed.

8–18 **Study Revealing a Tall Pelvis in Subjects With Low Back Pain.** Better knowledge of factors predisposing to low back pain would be helpful in advising potential recruits into occupations involving heavy manual work. W. F. Merriam, R. G. Burwell, R. C. Mulholland, J. C. G. Pearson, and J. K. Webb (Nottingham, England)

(8–17)   J. Bone Joint Surg. [Am.] 65-A:213–218, February 1983.
(8–18)   Ibid., [Br.] 65-B:153–156, March 1983.

used anthropometric methods to evaluate 300 men, aged 20 to 65 years, 174 of whom were prone to low back pain and had been seen at back pain clinics. Subjects with acute low back pain were not included. The subjects prone to back pain had a mean age of 42 years, compared with 38 for control subjects. The former had a greater standing height than those not prone to back pain. Analysis of both pelvic height and suprapelvic height, besides subischial height, indicated that the relatively large standing height of the pain-prone subjects was due to the pelvic component only. The finding persisted when data on subjects matched for age and occupation were analyzed. A significantly greater bi-iliac or pelvic width was also found in the subjects prone to back pain, but this effect was less marked. Back pain could not be significantly correlated with body weight.

Subjects prone to low back pain in this survey tended to have a greater standing height due to a greater pelvic height. A tall pelvis might describe a larger arc during gait, leading to greater stress in the lower lumbar region. The pelvis has become shorter and wider during evolution to provide large bony areas for the origin of muscles that maintain the upright position. Persons with a tall pelvis and longer pelvic lever arms might represent an evolutionary group predisposed to low back pain. The identification of other factors might permit advice to be given on a prophylactic rather than a therapeutic basis.

▶ [All clinicians are aware that taller people have more low back problems (including disk protrusion), than short people. These authors have attempted to show that the difference in pelvic height is significant in back pain.

They don't explain, to my satisfaction at least, exactly what "pelvic height" is. They use both true and apparent increases in their assessment, but they have concluded that a relatively larger true skeletal pelvic height was present in those patients who had low back problems.

We should continue to look at this problem anthropometrically and substantiate, if possible, this very interesting finding.—Ed.] ◀

8–19 **Mechanical Function of the Lumbar Apophyseal Joints.** M. A. Adams and W. C. Hutton (London) carried out studies on cadaver lumbar spines to assess the mechanical function of the apophyseal joints. When an intervertebral joint is loaded in shear, the apophyseal joint surfaces resist about one third of the shear force, resulting in a high interfacet force. High stress is present in cartilage in the upper joint margins in full flexion, when the shear force is highest. Joint rotation can occur if the articular facets of the apophyseal joints are asymmetrically oriented. The apophyseal joints resist some intervertebral compressive force in lordotic postures. The posterior anulus is protected in torsion by the facet surfaces and in flexion by the capsular ligaments. Once the posterior spinal ligaments have been sprained in hyperflexion, the wedged disk can prolapse into the neural canal if subjected to a high compressive force.

(8–19) Spine 8:327–330, April 1983.

The lumbar apophyseal joints allow limited movement between the vertebrae and protect the disk from shear forces, excessive flexion, and axial rotation. The joints are not well suited to resisting intervertebral compressive forces and usually are relieved from this by the disks. The ligaments of the apophyseal joints are most likely to be injured in bending forward and to the side. The joint capsule could be a source of pain in sustained lordotic postures.

▶ [This is a concise summary of the mechanical function of the lumbar apophyseal joints based on studies carried out by the authors and also by other investigators—chiefly, the Toronto group of Farfan and co-workers. There appears to be little question that the mechanics of the posterior apophyseal joints and the anterior intervertebral disk are intimately related. Degenerative disease of the lumbar spine is a process involving the entire motion segment. The mechanics of the lumbar intervertebral disk has been exhaustively studied. An understanding of the mechanics of the apophyseal joints represents a void in our knowledge, however, studies such as discussed in this article are rapidly filling this void.—R.N. Stauffer] ◀

8–20 **Anomalies of the Lumbosacral Nerve Roots: Review of 16 Cases and Classification.** Arvo Neidre and Ian MacNab reviewed 16 cases of lumbar nerve root anomaly found at operation. All but 2 of the patients were operated on for symptoms of an associated disk herniation. Half the cases were discovered at repeat exploration. Only 6 patients initially were seen with established neurologic deficits. One patient without disk herniation had spinal stenosis and the other had spondylolysis. There was no consistent association with bony vertebral anomalies.

Seven patients had type 1 anomalies, which include those of conjoined roots arising from a common dural sheath. Three of them had the type 1B variant, in which the roots are almost conjoined, producing a nerve root that exits at right angles to the dural sheath like a cervical nerve root. Five patients had a type 2 anomaly, with two nerve roots exiting through one foramen. One of them had the type 2B variant, in which nerve roots are present in all foramina, but one foramen contains two separate roots. Three patients had a type 3 anomaly, with adjacent nerve roots connected by a root in the form of an anastomosis. One patient had a combination of type 2 and type 3 anomalies.

Recognition of type 1 lumbosacral nerve root anomalies is important so as to avoid root or dural damage when a root is displaced at diskectomy. If two nerve roots are present in one canal, foraminotomy should be included in the initial operation. If a type 2 anomaly is present, decompression should be done with the diskectomy. If anomalous areas are not adequately decompressed, symptoms persist in a high proportion of cases. In none of the patients in this series was the anomaly the only pathologic change that was present.

▶ [I think that Dr. MacNab again shows a leader in lumbar spine surgery by re-em-

(8–20) Spine 8:294–299, April 1983.

phasizing that lumbar nerve root abnormalities may complicate an otherwise apparently straightforward operative approach to the lumbar disk. This point needs to be re-emphasized periodically to jar the complacent attitude that commonly surrounds lumbar disk surgery. I think he is to be applauded for restating a frequently overlooked situation.—B.M. Onofrio] ◀

8–21 **The Long-term Results of Fusion In Situ for Severe Spondylolisthesis.** J. R. Johnson and E. O'G. Kirwan (London) reviewed the long-term results of fusion in situ in 12 female and 5 male patients with severe lumbosacral spondylolisthesis who were followed up for 7 to 20 years, and for an average of 14 years after the operation. At the time of operation the 12 female and 5 male patients had an average age of 16 years. All had low back pain of gradual onset, usually accompanied by stiffness, and 6 also had neurologic symptoms and signs of weakness or paresthesia. Low back motion was restricted in most patients. The average slip was 78%, and the average sacral inclination was 38 degrees. Posterior or posterolateral intertransverse fusion was performed. The most recent patients had 3 weeks of bed rest, followed by 18 to 20 weeks in a Gauvain brace.

The average time taken for patients to return to work or school after the operation was 3½ months. No major complications occurred. At follow-up, 7 patients had occasional backache, and the same number had occasional stiffness. Two patients had continued to have sensory changes in their legs. All patients but 1 were able to touch their ankles with their fingertips. The average straight leg raising was 80 degrees. Four patients had minimal neurologic signs; 2 had the signs preoperatively. Only 4 patients believed that their deformity was worse than before the procedure. No significant increase in forward slip or inclination of the sacrum occurred in any patient since the last evaluation, 5 years after operation. There was no obvious pseudarthrosis, although 2 patients had minimal degenerative changes above the level of fusion. Six of the 8 women who conceived had normal deliveries. Only 1 patient had to change from heavy manual to sedentary work after the operation, and none had lost time off work in the previous year. Very few patients treated by fusion in situ for severe lumbosacral spondylolisthesis complain about their appearance at long-term follow-up.

This would appear to be a safe, reliable method of treating spondylolisthesis. No late complications or significant degenerative changes in the lumbar spine above the level of fusion have occurred. It is not necessary to decompress the nerve roots at the time of operation.

▶ [This long-term follow-up of a small number (17) of patients who had fusion in situ for severe lumbar spondylolisthesis indicates surprisingly good results, without any attempt at reduction of the deformity before fusion. The patients were almost universally satisfied with the results of the operation and the majority did not find any de-

(8–21) J. Bone Joint Surg. [Br.] 65-B:43–46, January 1983.

formity to be objectionable. There is no detail given as to the degree of spondylolisthesis in the patients, but one would assume from the description that all patients had either grade 3 or 4. This paper indicates that perhaps the recent interest and description of reduction of the spondylolisthesis—with its frequent neurologic complications—is perhaps unwarranted.—R.N. Stauffer] ◄

8–22 **Spinal Instability Due To Malignant Disease: Treatment by Segmental Spinal Stabilization.** Management of patients with spinal instability from neoplastic vertebral destruction involves both prevention of cord injury and control of pain owing to mechanical instability. Thomas J. Flatley, Marc H. Anderson, and George T. Anast (Med. College of Wisconsin, Milwaukee) used the segmental spinal instrumentation of Luque, designed to treat neuromuscular scoliosis, in 7 patients with malignant tumors. One patient had a complete vertebrectomy and the others had varying neural deficits or pain. All 5 patients with pain experienced marked relief after surgery, and 3 of the 5 with a neural deficit improved. One patient remained unchanged, and 1 with paraparesis later became paraplegic.

Boy, 16 years, had spinal metastasis from an osteogenic sarcoma in the distal right femur. A pulmonary metastasis was resected 4 months after high amputation through the thigh and institution of high-dose methotrexate therapy. Chemotherapy was continued for 6 months. Collapse of the body of L1 was present without neural deficit. A complete anterior and posterior vertebrectomy was done at the L1 level via a bilateral lateral extracavitary approach. Stabilization was provided by double Luque-rod fixation from T10 to L4. Anterior fusion was delayed until a tumor-free margin was verified in all histologic sections. The patient walked with a Jewett brace postoperatively. Controlled collapse of T12 on L2 soon was evident, and an anterior interbody fusion was done using iliac bone. Biopsy of paraspinal tissue in the area of the excised body of T12 showed tumor tissue. The patient remained ambulatory with a brace until his death 6 months postoperatively from aortic and pulmonary metastases. Alignment of the spine was stable after interbody grafting.

All 7 patients benefited from stabilization. The only complication directly related to rod instrumentation was partial loss of reduction caused by cutting the wires through the lamina in the youngest patient. The use of 4.8-mm rods proved adequate. Most patients underwent laminectomy for either biopsy or decompression of the cord or nerve roots. Spinal fusion should be done in addition to rod fixation when the patient is expected to live for more than a year. An orthosis is useful in a young, active patient. The use of methylmethacrylate appears warranted only when there is extensive destruction of bone. Five patients died, at an average of 1 year postoperatively; 4 of the 5 were able to walk at last follow-up.

▶ [Safe and successful treatment of spinal cord tumors, both primary and metastatic, can be achieved with current methods of surgical management and stabilization. Multiple level total vertebrectomy followed by strut grafting and using either a fibular rib or a vascularized rib graft can provide adequate anterior spinal stability, which is

(8–22) J. Bone Joint Surg. [Am.] 66-A:47–52, January 1984.

then augmented with posterior instrumentation to provide total spine stability. These authors have demonstrated the effectiveness of using the Luque-type fixation. One theoretical and structural problem that can occur when a total vertebrectomy is performed is collapse. The type of fixation these authors have recommended will not prevent this collapse, and the authors have recognized this fact in the paper. In these instances, a combination of a distracting and a compression system of fixation, with the addition of a segmental wiring may provide a more stable structural unit. It has been our experience in a much larger series that bone healing does occur satisfactorily and that preoperative radiation and chemotherapy do not appear to have a deleterious effect on bone healing. Postoperatively, we use a two-piece modeled polypropylene jacket for added support, or a halo cast, depending on the level of the lesion.—R.A. Klassen] ◄

8–23 **Lumbar Grafts, Pressure Atrophy, and Spinal Stenosis** are discussed by Raphael Cilento and Otto C. Kestler. An increasing number of cases of spinal stenosis that have followed primary laminectomy and secondary lumbar fusion have been reported in recent years. Apart from various congenital causes, spinal stenosis may be acquired from trauma, operation, degeneration, disk protrusion, inflammatory or degenerative arthritis, gouty arthritis, and hyperostosis. Stenosis seen after spinal operations may be due to arachnoid scarring or may represent actual bony overgrowth. Posterior fusion is the most common surgical antecedent of spinal stenosis. Fusion-induced overgrowth can be explained as a reaction to meningo-osteovertebral injury. More marked stenosis may occur if disk removal precedes arthrodesis. Spinal stenosis that follows microlaminectomy may be a result of uncontrolled bleeding and the introduction of organisms. The chief symptom of spinal stenosis is continuous, severe pain in the back, buttocks, thigh, and leg; it is usually worse on one side. Limb paresis and loss of bowel and bladder control may also occur, as well as impotence. Computed tomography can help rule out vascular damage from operation. Spinal cord tumor must always be a consideration.

Spinal stenosis should be managed as conservatively as possible, even if a complete cauda equina block is present. Antibiotic therapy may be indicated, and nonsteroid anti-inflammatory agents are useful. Decompression is indicated only for the "bone block" type of spinal stenosis. Arachnoid scarring should not be treated surgically if at all possible. If decompression is done, as minimal a procedure as possible should be performed. If the spine becomes extremely unstable after any laminectomy, a two-stage spinal procedure should be considered.

► [This paper does well to remind orthopedists, especially the younger generation, that posterior spinal fusion was not an uncommon operation in the past and that the iatrogenic syndrome of spinal stenosis could result from it. Today lumbosacral fusion is less common, and when it is done it is usually done laterally which should not predispose to spinal stenosis unless there is an accompanying arachnoiditis or another inflammatory element.—Ed.] ◄

(8–23) J. Neurol. Orthop. Surg. 4:119–123, July 1983.

8–24 **Idiopathic Coccygodynia: Analysis of 51 Operative Cases and a Radiographic Study of the Normal Coccyx.** Idiopathic coccygodynia has been attributed to a variety of pathologic states, most often those involving trauma, but little attention has been given to subluxations of the coccygeal vertebrae or to the x-ray features of the coccyx in general. Franco Postacchini and Marco Massobrio (Univ. of Rome) obtained anteroposterior and lateral roentgenograms of the sacrum and coccyx from 120 subjects with no history of coccygodynia. The 60 males and 60 females were aged 14 to 71 years. Lateral x-ray films showed four types of configuration: type I, with the coccyx curved slightly forward and its apex pointing down and caudally; type II, with a more marked curve and an apex pointing straight forward; type III, a sharply forward-angulated coccyx; and type IV, with the coccyx subluxated anteriorly at the level of the sacrococcygeal joint or the first or second intercoccygeal joint. Over two thirds of subjects had a type I configuration, whereas 17% had a type II pattern. Types III and IV were seen in 6% and 9%, respectively.

Fifty-one patients with idiopathic coccygodynia underwent coccygectomy between 1960 and 1980. Mean age was 34 years. Mean duration of symptoms before operation was 2½ years. Onset was associated with a fall or a blow to the coccygeal region in 25 patients. Moderate to severe pain on pressure over the coccyx was present in all cases. A type III coccyx was found in 23% of patients and a type IV pattern in 22%. Twelve patients had a total and 31, a partial coccygectomy. The results were considered to be excellent in 33% of the 36 evaluable patients, good in 55%, fair in 5%, and poor in 5%. The results could not be definitely related to the coccygeal x-ray pattern or to the extent of operation.

Most patients with idiopathic coccygodynia respond well to conservative measures, which should be tried for at least 3 months. Coccyges with a type II, III, or IV configuration seem more likely to become symptomatic than those with a type I configuration. Coccygectomy, where indicated, is usually effective in relieving symptoms.

▶ [This very good and appropriate study classifies the anatomical variations in the configuration of the coccyx. I feel the most important aspect of the study is the evaluation of the normal configuration. The authors have thoroughly evaluated the surgical results and find no definite relationship between the result and preoperative radiographic evaluation of the coccyx. I would agree that those individuals in whom mechanical discomfort is predominant over the tip of the coccyx or at the angle usually do well following surgical excision of the coccyx.—L.F.A. Peterson] ◀

8–25 **Fatiguing Weakness: Initial Symptom in Cervical Compressive Radiculopathy.** Exercise-induced weakness in the lower extremities has been described in patients with lumbar spinal canal ste-

(8–24) J. Bone Joint Surg. [Am.] 65-A:1116–1124, October 1983.
(8–25) Surg. Neurol. 19:354–357, April 1983.

nosis. James S. Lieberman, Guy Corkill, and Robert G. Taylor (Univ. of California at Davis) report findings in 3 patients with cervical compressive radiculopathy in whom upper limb muscle weakness occurred only during sustained or repetitive exercise.

Man, 33, noted cervical and interscapular pain of about 1 week duration 6 months previously when lifting a heavy load. Acute neck and interscapular pain and radicular pain in the left arm occurred 2 weeks before evaluation when the patient ducked quickly into a car. Tingling was present in the C6 distribution. Sensory symptoms resolved in a few days, but the pain persisted and weak elbow flexion was noted during sustained maximal effort. Examination showed decreased neck motion on left rotation and left tilt, spasm in the left cervical muscles, and tenderness over the spinous process of C6. Left elbow flexion became weak after 20 seconds of maximal effort. The sensory and reflex findings were normal. Electromyography showed a decreased interference pattern in the left C6 arm muscles. Computed tomography and metrizamide myelography findings showed a large bone spur projecting 5–6 mm into the spinal canal on the left at the C5-C6 level. Foraminotomy and facetectomy were done at this level. The left C6 root was displaced posteriorly and angulated. A posterior surgical approach was used. Fatiguing weakness resolved soon after surgery, and the patient was well 2 years later and active in his work as a police officer.

Exercise-induced weakness can occur in patients with cervical compressive radiculopathy. Physicians may not be sufficiently aware that fatiguing weakness can be an important feature of neuromuscular disease. Standard manual muscle testing does not identify fatiguing weakness when it is the sole manifestation of a motor disorder. The fatiguing weakness is considered to represent early or mild neurologic involvement that is unmasked by exercise, rather than a manifestation of compression or ischemia.

▶ [Doctor Lieberman's paper on fatiguing weakness reinforces my impression that clinically latent neurologic weakness is often emphasized by muscle fatigue. As the authors state, it is a different mechanism from lumbar stenosis. I think it is an interesting concept. The limited number of patients in this study is, obviously, of anecdotal experience only, but it reinforces our clinical impression.—B.M. Onofrio] ◀

8–26 **Anterior Cervical Diskectomy With and Without Fusion: Prospective Study.** The anterior approach to the cervical spine has been used increasingly in preference to the posterior approach because it is less traumatic. Jarl Rosenørn, Elisabeth Bech Hansen, and Mary-Ann Rosenørn (Hvidovre, Denmark) undertook a prospective study between 1978 and 1981 comparing diskectomy alone (DE) and with interbody fusion (DEF) in a series of 63 patients operated on for herniated cervical disk. The mean age of the 40 men was 53 years, and that of the 23 women, 50 years. Patients with fracture, dislocation, or significant osteochondrosis with intervertebral foraminal or spinal canal narrowing were excluded. Twenty-four patients had acute symptoms, and trauma was a factor in 8. In 30 patients more than 1

(8–26) J. Neurosurg. 59:252–255, August 1983.

root was affected, and 6 had bilateral symptoms. The average duration of symptoms was 1 year.

Diskectomy was done in 32 patients and DEF in 31. The 2 treatment groups were clinically comparable at the outset. At 3 months there were significantly more excellent results in the DE group, and the same was true at 12 months. In the DEF group at 12 months, men had better results than women had. Hospitalization times were similar, but postoperative sick-leave periods were shorter after DE than after DEF. One patient required reoperation because of a subfascial hematoma. No wound infections, osteitis, or diskitis occurred.

Soft herniated cervical disks are best managed by DE, particularly in women. The procedure is easier to perform than DEF is, and the time of postoperative sick leave is shorter. In addition, the clinical outcome was better after DE than after DEF in the present series. The difference was chiefly owing to the poor results of DEF in women. The supporting structures in women probably are less resistant than those of men to the extension provided by the bone graft.

▶ [Several reports in the literature concerning cervical disk excision without anterior fusion have claimed equal or better results than with fusion. However, in my estimation, it will take 5 to 10 years of follow-up to see whether the suboptimal reversal of the cervical lordosis will lead to earlier degeneration at other spaces.

I would commend the authors' observations, however, in this short-term study.— B.M. Onofrio] ◀

8–27 **Methylmethacrylate Stabilization of the Cervical Spine.** Charles R. Clark (Univ. of Iowa), Kristaps J. Keggi, and Manobar M. Panjabi (Yale Univ.) have used methylmethacrylate as an adjunct to stabilization of the cervical spine in selected cases since 1970. A study group of 52 patients, with a mean age of 57, was followed up for an average of 3 years after treatment. The indications were malignant disease in 18 cases, fracture in 17, rheumatoid arthritis in 12, and osteoarthritis in 5. All patients had significant neck pain preoperatively, and many had neural symptoms. Twenty-four patients had objective neural deficits. The most common procedures were anterior vertebral-body resection with posterior fusion and interbody fusion, and posterior cervical fusion alone. Where a laminectomy had been done, the vertebrae were stabilized with wires that were incorporated in steel methylmethacrylate, and the dura was protected with steel mesh.

The spine was stable immediately after operation in all cases; no rigid external orthosis was necessary. No complications resulted from the methylmethacrylate itself. No pseudarthroses developed. One patient had an asymptomatic fracture of the cement mass but no gross instability. A solid surgical construct was consistently obtained in tumor patients and those with rheumatoid disease, as well as in the fracture cases. Most of the patients with cervical spondylosis due to osteoarthritis did well postoperatively.

(8–27) J. Bone Joint Surg. [Am.] 66-A:40–46, January 1984.

Cement is a useful adjunct to surgical stabilization of the cervical spine in patients with cord injury who have bowel or bladder dysfunction and anesthesia, who tolerate a halo vest or cast poorly. It also is used in elderly and debilitated patients who may not tolerate prolonged bed rest or the use of a halo vest. Alcoholic patients who are at risk of delirium tremens or who may be noncompliant with standard treatment can benefit from the internal stability provided by methylmethacrylate cement.

▶ [I think that this technique is a useful addition to the surgical armamentarium particularly when the orthopedist deals with patients who have significant bony destruction resulting in instability and neurologic involvement and in whom the life expectancy is markedly reduced. As the authors point out, tumor patients benefit greatly from this type of cervical stabilization, particularly in the quality of their remaining life. This technique might also be justified in certain patients with advanced rheumatoid destruction of the cervical spine, although in a significant experience of over 10 years, encompassing more than 100 rheumatoid cervical spines, we have encountered only 2 cases in which this technique might be advisable over conventional techniques. In our experience, rheumatoid patients tolerate halo thoracic immobilization far better than the literature seems to indicate. The use of methylmethacrylate stabilization for traumatic lesions of the cervical spine or of spines afflicted with cervical spondylosis is, in our opinion, not justified since conventional methods of fixation are usually more than adequate.—M.E. Cabanela] ◀

8–28 **Odontoid Hypoplasia.** T. McManners obtained measurements of the normal adult odontoid peg in the vertical and sagittal planes from 500 lateral radiographs of the upper cervical spine, for use in diagnosing odontoid hypoplasia. Measurements were made in 217 men and 283 women older than 25 years. The mean height of the odontoid was 18.0 mm in men and 16.9 mm in women. Correlation between age and peg height was not significant, but peg height was positively correlated with both height of the body of C2 and the C2 canal diameter in both men and women. An odontoid peg height of less than 11.9 mm in either men or women can be used as a criterion for diagnosing odontoid hypoplasia.

Odontoid hypoplasia is part of a spectrum of ossification and fusion abnormalities involving the upper cervical spine. It has occasionally been associated with other pathologic states. The disorder usually is readily diagnosed on standard radiographs including flexion and extension lateral views, but signs and symptoms may take some years to develop. The attachments for the alar and apical ligaments are absent, and the hypoplastic odontoid process does not act as a restraining structure within the ring of the atlas. Excessive rotation of the atlas can result, and the rudimentary peg can slide beneath the transverse ligament and cause atlantoaxial dislocation and cord compression. Campbell recommended atlantoaxial fusion in patients who have pain on motion or transitory neurologic signs.

▶ [This work provides the scientific basis for radiologic diagnosis of odontoid hypo-

(8–28)   Br. J. Radiol. 56:907–910, December 1983.

plasia. It is not known, however, how often these cases are symptomatic and require treatment.—M.E. Cabanela] ◄

8-29   **Operative Treatment of 183 Cases of Tuberculosis of the Cervical Spine.** Jing-quan Li (Tuberculosis Hosp. of Heilongjiang Province, Hulang, Heilongjiang, People's Republic of China) has presented data on 183 patients with tuberculosis of the cervical spine, who were operated on from 1960 to 1980. These patients comprised 3.2% of the 5,714 who were hospitalized with tuberculosis of the spine in that period. Ages of the 183 ranged from 5 to 45 years; most patients were aged 10–20. The ratio of male to female patients was 1.0:1.7. Duration of the condition before hospitalization was 2–15 months. Ninety-three cases had been diagnosed as sprain or rheumatism, causing delay in specific treatment. Tuberculosis of other parts of the body was seen in 109 cases.

Locations of cervical lesions were C1-C2, 18 cases; C2-C3, 21 cases; C3-C4, 31 cases; C4-C5, 43 cases, C5-C6, 48 cases; and C6-C7, 22 cases. Retropharyngeal or anterovertebral abscesses were found in all cases in this series with accompanying respiratory or deglutitory symptoms. Incomplete paraplegia was found in 15 cases.

Eradication of the tuberculous focus was performed in all cases in this series after preoperative antituberculous and general therapy for 2–3 weeks. A transoral or transhyothyroid approach was used in 23 cases under endotracheal anesthesia through interior tracheotomy. The operative procedure with these approaches was relatively simple and safe, and operative trauma was less than with other approaches. These approaches provided direct wide access to the diseased area, making it possible to remove all the tuberculous foci on both sides of the vertebrae simultaneously, and the vertebral artery and spinal and cervical sympathetic nerves were easily protected. Complications of infection or apnea were not found after operation. Nasal feeding through a stomach tube was used after operation, and the tracheal cannula was removed 5–7 days after surgery. The transoral approach was suitable for C1-C2 lesions, and the transhyothyroid approach was more convenient for C3-C4 lesions and also could be used for lesions of C2 or C5.

Anterior or posterior sternomastoid approaches were used in the remaining 160 cases (172 operations). A total of 125 operations were performed under intravenous balanced anesthesia; acupuncture anesthesia was used for the other 47. The anatomical relationships of these incisions were complicated. The vertebral artery or the spinal and sympathetic nerves might be injured or stimulated during operation. Sympathetic symptoms have been found in 12 cases after operation; all recovered completely within 1–3 months. Eradication of the tuberculous focus on the other side of the vertebrae through ster-

(8–29)   Chin. J. Orthop. 3:231–233, 1983.

nomastoid incision was relatively difficult. Secondary operations through the opposite sternomastoid approach were done in 12 cases.

Posterior fusion with bone grafting was performed 3–4 weeks after eradication in 93 cases of this series. Antituberculous therapy was used continuously for 2–3 months. The results of treatment were satisfactory. With the exception of 1 patient with cord compression who died of respiratory failure after operation, the bone lesions in these 183 patients all healed well, and the accompanying neural deficit completely disappeared in all the 14 cases. During follow-up of 1.5–7 years, no recurrences have been found.

▶ [A recent visit I made to mainland China has convinced me that they have many areas of medical expertise that would be of interest to YEAR BOOK readers. This particular paper on tuberculosis of the cervical spine in the *Chinese Journal of Orthopedics* (translated by one of our Chinese Fellows in Biomechanics, Dr. K. R. Dai) is a case in point. None of us in the western world will ever be able to accumulate this many patients and have this much experience with this particuar disease.

The approach to tuberculosis in the cervical spine is not radically different from that in the thoracic spine, which has been so aptly covered by many, especially Professor Arthur Hudson in Hong Kong. Of interest is that the neurologic deficits in these patients were markedly improved with decompression and eradication of the focus.—Ed.] ◀

9. Hand, Wrist, and Forearm

9–1 **External Fixation of Complex Hand and Wrist Fractures.** Jaquet developed a method of external fixation with a mini-exoskeletal fixateur for soft tissue and skeletal support in cases of severe hand injury. A modified technique subsequently has been used in cases of unstable Colles and Smith fractures and in wrist arthrodesis, bone lengthening procedures, and unstable forearm bone fractures with gross soft tissue injury. Stanley A. Riggs, Jr., and William P. Cooney III (Mayo Clinic and Found.) used external fixation with the Jaquet mini-fixateur in 38 patients with upper limb injuries. The forearm was injured in 5 cases, the distal radius in 23, and the hand in 10. The average patient age was 47 years. In 14 cases, another type of fixation had failed to maintain reduction. The pins were inserted with the patient under axillary block, intravenous, or general anesthesia.

All 10 hand fractures united in an average of 6 weeks, and no secondary procedures were necessary. The distal radial fractures united

Fig 9–1.—Mini-Hoffmann external fixateur applied after bone grafting. (Courtesy of Riggs, S.A., Jr., and Cooney, W.P. III: J. Trauma 23:332–336, April 1983.)

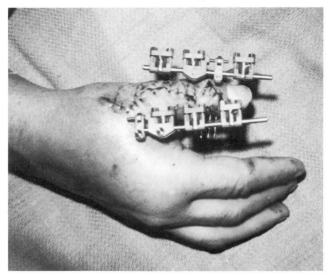

(9–1) J. Trauma 23:332–336, April 1983.

in an average of about 7 weeks. Complications occurred in 22% of cases. There were two pin-site infections but no cases of osteomyelitis at pin sites. One patient with a phalangeal fracture required inlay bone grafting for union. Application of the external fixateur in 1 case is shown in Figure 9–1.

The adaptability of the mini-fixateur frame allows the placement of pins in a wide variety of positions and angles so that they will not interfere with soft tissue care or overall hand function. Exoskeletal fixation continues to be used in cases of compound, segmental, or very comminuted fractures of the hand; unstable distal radial fractures; and septic nonunions. It has proved very useful for salvage where more traditional methods have failed. External fixation is not recommended for most phalangeal and metacarpal fractures, fracture-dislocations, or joint arthrodeses of the hand or wrist.

▶ [The authors point out the usefulness of the mini-fixateur for certain conditions of the hand and wrist such as with contaminated soft tissue defects. The grouping of phalangeal, metacarpal, and Colles' fractures, however, is not altogether satisfactory.—R.L. Linscheid] ◀

9–2 **Colles' Fracture: End Results in Relation to Radiologic Parameters.** Colles claimed that in cases of the fracture that bears his name, the injured extremity would in time be functional and free of pain despite misdiagnosis and mistreatment, but this assertion has been controversial. R. M. Rubinovich and W. R. Rennie (McGill

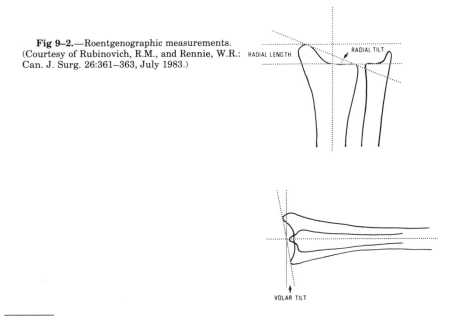

Fig 9–2.—Roentgenographic measurements. (Courtesy of Rubinovich, R.M., and Rennie, W.R.: Can. J. Surg. 26:361–363, July 1983.)

(9–2) Can. J. Surg. 26:361–363, July 1983.

Univ.) reviewed the findings in 37 patients with unilateral Colles' fracture, all but 2 of them a year or longer after injury. Range of motion, grip strength, and pinch strength were assessed clinically, and radiographic measurements were made as shown in Figure 9–2. Excellent functional results were obtained in 38% of cases; good results, in 38%; and fair results, in 24%. Strength scores but not pain, activity level, or range of motion distinguished patients in the different functional categories. In comparing the groups with respect to radial tilt, volar tilt, and radial length, the only significant difference between the groups with excellent and fair functional results was in volar tilt. All but 2 patients were satisfied with the outcome. No patient had to change work, but some noted mildly restricted activity.

All patients followed up for more than a year were satisfied with the result. Regardless of the radiologic appearances, all had similar levels of activity, pain, and range of motion. The only radiologic finding that correlated with the functional outcome was volar tilt. Grip and pinch strength declined along with volar tilt. Colles was essentially correct in stating that patients with a misdiagnosed or mistreated fracture will, in general, eventually have a complete range of motion with no pain.

▶ [The authors' conclusion would appear to contradict a number of previous studies which suggest that persistent pain, limitation of motion, and continued difficulty persist past 1 year, and that there is a definite correlation between the anatomical result and the functional end result. The loss of volar tilt does, indeed, correlate with weakness but also with chondromalacia and subluxation of the distal radioulnar joint, increased radial deviation, and mid-carpal instability patterns. The authors don't go on to state the reason for weakness following marked loss of volar tilt, but radial shortening, which moves the point of action to the left on the BLIX curve, is certainly one of the major factors.—R.L. Linscheid] ◀

9–3 **Intra-articular Metacarpal Head Fractures.** Edward C. McElfresh and James H. Dobyns reviewed experience with 100 patients who had 103 intra-articular metacarpal head fractures. If VA hospital patients are excluded, the male-female ratio was 3:1. The peak incidence of injuries was in the second and third decades. The second metacarpal was most often injured, and the thumb least often. Athletic injuries were most frequent, followed by striking objects and fights. Twenty-two injuries were open. Thirty patients, including all 22 with open injuries, had surgical treatment.

There were 4 relatively undisplaced Salter-Harris type III epiphyseal fractures, treated closed with splinting and early motion. Seventeen patients had ligament avulsion fractures. All were closed injuries. Four were operated on early, and 3 late. Of the 8 osteochondral fractures, the 5 closed injuries did well, but 1 of the 3 open injuries became infected. Obliquely, or sagittally, directed fractures occurred 22 times. Seven oblique fractures necessitated open reduction and in-

(9–3) J. Hand Surg. 8:383–393, July 1983.

ternal fixation. Four patients had vertical, or coronal, injuries. Four had horizontal, or transverse, fractures of the metacarpal heads. Comminuted metacarpal head fractures occurred 31 times in 28 patients. Five had open reduction and internal fixation with Kirschner wires. Three patients had boxer's fractures involving the joint. Six patients had injuries involving loss of bone substance; all were open, machine-caused injuries. There were 3 cases of avascular necrosis of the metacarpal head with no obvious fracture, and another case was associated with a fracture.

Metacarpal head fractures involving large intra-articular defects generally should be reconstructed to obtain a congruent metacarpal head. The digit should be mobilized as early as is technically feasible. A balance must be sought between maintenance of articular congruence and smoothness, maintenance of a stable but flexible periarticular envelope, and a rapid return to maximum normal motion.

▶ [This report reflects our experience with and the relative occurrence of metacarpal head fractures. While primarily a report on the incidence of this injury, experience with treatment is discussed, particularly with regard to the importance of open reduction and precise internal fixation of these intra-articular fractures.—W.P. Cooney, III] ◀

9–4 **Fracture of the Hook of the Hamate: Report of 6 Cases and the Suitability of Computed Tomography.** Fracture of the hook of the hamate is an uncommon injury for which routine carpal bone x-ray films are not helpful. Computed tomography (CT) can be done with the patient's palms together in a praying position to clearly demonstrate the injury. Masaaki Egawa and Toru Asai (Japan) report 6 cases of fracture of the hook of the hamate seen in the past 3 years. Three subjects were injured by swinging a bat that clipped the edge of a baseball, fracturing the bone on the nondominant hand. All patients had persistent pain on motion and localized tenderness over the injury. The symptoms were aggravated by grasping objects. Four patients had hypoesthesia in the ring and small fingers. Carpal tunnel radiographs showed all the fractures, but CT demonstrated them much more clearly in the 3 patients examined. Only 1 patient had satisfactory bone union after plaster immobilization. The other 5 patients required excision of the fragment; upper-arm block anesthesia was used. All patients were able to return to their previous work and participate in sports activities without symptoms.

This injury is a result of direct force against the hook of the hamate. Pain on wrist motion and localized tenderness aggravated by grasping an object suggest the correct diagnosis. Computed tomography of the wrist is useful in assessing fresh injuries. Immobilization is indicated as primary treatment; a short arm cast should be used for 6 weeks. Surgery is considered when conservative management is

(9–4) J. Hand Surg. 8:393–398, July 1983.

ineffective and when an ulnar nerve deficit is demonstrated. All symptoms resolve after removal of the fractured hamate hook, and patients are able to return to their usual work and sports activities.

▶ [The authors emphasize that the diagnosis should be made on the basis of patient history and physical findings with confirmation by x-ray techniques. Technetium bone scan and tomography, particularly the trispiral and hypocycloidal types in the sagittal plane, have also been helpful in making this diagnosis.—R.L. Linscheid] ◀

9–5   **Traumatic Radioulnar Synostosis Treated by Excision and a Free Fat Transplant: Report of Two Cases.** Ken Yong-Hing and Stanley P. K. Tchang (Univ. of Saskatchewan) treated traumatic radioulnar synostosis in two patients by excising the crossunion and interposing a free fat transplant. Functional results were excellent.

CASE 1.—Man, 19, developed a radioulnar synostosis in 30 degrees of pronation after fixation of an ulnar fracture with a plate and screws. The synostosis was excised, and a free nonvascularized fat transplant was placed between the bones. The bones were stripped of as little soft tissue as possible. The 7.5 × 3 × 1-cm fat graft was taken from the anterior abdominal wall. It covered all raw bone surfaces and completely filled the dead space. Full pronation returned, but there was 15 degrees less supination than on the uninjured side at last follow-up.

CASE 2.—Man, 19, had a radioulnar synostosis in neutral rotation after plate and screw fixation of radius and ulna fractures. The same procedure was done, except for circumferential stripping of soft tissues off the ulna. The range of motion was nearly normal at last follow-up.

Functional results were impressive 3 and 2 years, respectively, after excision of a traumatic radioulnar synostosis and free fat transplantation in these patients, compared with those reported from other treatments. Fat has been used as a transplant either free or with a pedicle. This approach warrants further trial in traumatic radioulnar synostosis.

▶ [The treatment of heterotopic ossification following trauma is fraught with a number of difficulties, particularily the recurrence of the heterotopic bone following excision. This is despite the use of silastic membrane and low dose radiation. The authors present the use of a free fat transfer in 2 cases in which they block the recurrence of heterotopic ossification. The mechanism is left unexplained but the results do stand as a potential technique in treating this difficult problem. The improved motion that they obtained following the original procedure is remarkable since, in most circumstances, maximal motion is that obtained at the time of the original surgery and some loss of motion can be anticipated. The authors reported the opposite, that is, further improvement in motion with time. Further studies using this technique are necessary.—W.P. Cooney, III] ◀

9–6   **Isolated Fracture of the Ulnar Shaft: Treatment Without Immobilization.** The so-called nightstick fracture occurs when the forearm is raised to shield the head from a blow. Even the most innocent-appearing crack fracture of the ulna can end in nonunion. Frederic H. Pollock, Arsen M. Pankovich, Jorge J. Prieto, and Mark Lorenz

---

(9–5)   J. Bone Joint Surg. [Br.] 65-B:433–435, August 1983.
(9–6)   Ibid., [Am.] 65-A:339–342, March 1983.

(Cook County Hosp.) encountered several patients with a healing ulnar-shaft fracture who had received no treatment, and then reviewed the records of 71 isolated ulnar shaft fractures seen between 1979 and 1981, exclusive of gunshot injuries. Fifty-four patients were followed up for at least 6 months or until healing occurred. Twelve of these patients were treated with an axilla-to-palm plaster, and 42 either with a forearm splint or a cast for up to 2 weeks or with no immobilization at all. In the latter 42 cases, an elastic wrap was applied to control swelling and provide a feeling of security.

One of the patients treated with a plaster cast showed delayed union, but normal elbow motion was regained in all cases. All of the patients treated with a forearm splint or cast or without immobilization experienced prompt healing of their fractures. The average time to union was 6½ weeks. Full joint motion was usually present at the time of union. The overall average loss of forearm rotation was 5 degrees. Two patients showed greatly limited forearm rotation when last seen. No fracture was more displaced or angulated than at the outset. None of the 4 open fractures became infected.

The nightstick fracture of the ulna usually is a low-energy injury and displacement is not likely to be extreme. Early use of the forearm therefore is tolerated, and early mobilization of the joints without external immobilization or internal fixation can be implemented. The motion that occurs at the fracture site may enhance healing. Other methods are needed in cases of completely displaced and comminuted fractures of the ulna. Overuse of the forearm can lead to excessive callus formation and impaired forearm rotation.

9–7 **Closed Treatment of Isolated Radial Head Fractures.** The management of isolated radial-head fractures remains controversial. Martin S. Weseley, Philip A. Barenfeld, and Arthur L. Eisenstein (SUNY, Brooklyn) reviewed 387 cases of isolated radial head fracture that were treated nonoperatively. Pediatric cases and cases with concomitant injuries in the same elbow were excluded. The indications for radial-head excision were a loose bone fragment restricting elbow joint motion and extensive comminution expected to result in significant loss of motion. Most injuries were classified as Mason type I. Patients' injuries were managed in a posterior splint for 1 to 2 weeks, followed by active range-of-motion exercises. A sling was used until the patient felt comfortable without it. The elbow joint was aspirated when hemarthrosis caused significant discomfort.

Mason type I fractures were followed up for an average of 5 months, and Mason type II and type III fractures for 8 months. Thirty-three of 50 patients with Mason type II fractures had excellent results, 16

(9–7) J. Trauma 23:36–39, January 1983.

had good results, and 1 had a fair outcome. Six of 8 patients with Mason type III fractures had excellent or good results, and 2, fair results. Patients with Mason type I fractures generally had excellent results, but 6 had only a fair outcome. No patient had a poor result. No patient reported pain at follow-up evaluation, but some had discomfort with unusual activity. Seventeen other patients seen during the review period had had radial head excision; 14 had excellent or good results, and 3, fair results. Cooperation with early exercises was an important factor in the outcome. Patients who moved their elbows early rarely lost more than 5 degrees of motion, regardless of the se-

Fig 9–3.—*A* and *B,* AP and lateral roentgenograms of injured left elbow in a 43-year-old male patient. *C* and *D,* AP and lateral roentgenograms of left elbow 7 weeks postinjury after closed treatment. (Courtesy of Weseley, M.S., et al.: J. Trauma 23:36–39, January 1983.)

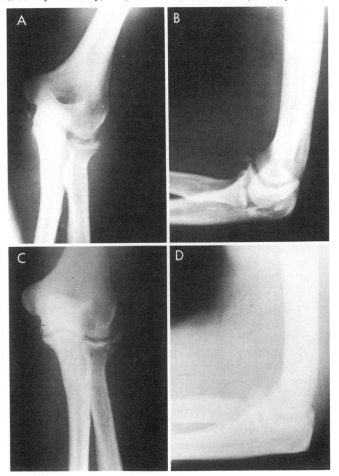

verity of the injury. The roentgenographic findings in 1 case are shown in Figure 9–3.

Patient motivation and a willingness to endure early discomfort are important to the outcome of isolated radial-head fractures that are managed conservatively. Excellent results can be obtained by a short period of immobilization followed by active range-of-motion exercises, provided the fragments are in reasonable position and a displaced fragment does not obstruct elbow motion. Many patients with Mason type II and type III fractures are older and have associated medical problems, and surgery and anesthesia can be avoided by nonoperative management.

9–8 **Sepsis in Hand Injuries.** The management of hand infections has been much improved by the availability of antibiotics. C. L. Cheng and S. P. Chow (Univ. of Hong Kong) reviewed the results obtained in 206 cases of hand infection. Males constituted over two thirds of the series. A similar proportion of patients were manual laborers. The age peak was 20–30 years. A closed puncture wound was present in 30% of patients, a crushed wound in 19%, and a laceration in 22%. About one fifth of patients had no wound. The fingertips were the most common site of injury. The thumb, index finger, and middle finger were most often affected. About 30% of patients had a paronychia. The usual presenting symptom was pain; most patients had swelling and pus formation. The most common organism isolated was *Staphylococcus aureus*. All patients received ampicillin and cloxacillin. Severe infections were treated intravenously. Definite localized infections were incised and drained. Complications were infrequent; 9 patients required secondary wound closure or skin grafting, 15 required tendon surgery or bone joint surgery, and 3 required amputation of fingers. Half the patients were discharged the day after admission.

No marked change in patterns of injury and infection of the hand has occurred. Closed puncture wounds are the most common precursor of infection, and *S. aureus* is the most common causative organism. Prevention of injuries is the chief means of preventing hand infections. Adequate training of workers, sufficient lighting at the workplace, and testing of equipment all are helpful measures. Even slight wounds should be cleaned immediately. Pyogenic tenosynovitis is treated by incision and drainage and irrigation of the tendon sheath with antibiotic solution, as well as intravenously administered antibiotics.

▶ [This is an interesting report on hand infections in the Far East. The authors point to the importance of incision and drainage (87% of patients) and antibiotic coverage by ampicillin and cloxacillin. Surprisingly, the patterns of infection are quite similar to Western studies, although 22% of the patients denied any wound or trauma and many had local remedies applied by themselves or general practioners. The authors confirm the importance of open drainage of hand infections and local wound care.

(9–8) J. West. Pacific Orthop. Assoc. 20:17–19, June 1983.

That only 40% of their patients had a staphylococcus infection confirms the necessity of cultures prior to starting antibiotics.—W.P. Cooney, III] ◄

9-9 **Hand Difficulties Among Musicians.** Little is known of occupational disabilities in concert musicians, whose work necessitates strong, rapid, repetitive hand movements and constant adjustments of the muscles and tendons of the hand, wrist, and forearm. Fred H. Hochberg, Robert D. Leffert, Matthew D. Heller, and Lisle Merriman (Massachusetts) reviewed the difficulties seen in 100 musicians during a 1½-year period. The 53 men and 47 women had a median age of 37.5 years. Three fourths were pianists, and most of the rest played stringed instruments. Most subjects had begun playing at an early age and practiced an average of 5 to 6 hours each day. Forty-nine of the musicians were examined by the authors.

The initial hand complaints often included pain, weakness, tightening, cramping, and loss of control. The pianists had noted a loss of control and speed and a loss of facility in rapid passages. The right upper arm was affected twice as often as the left. Weakness or decreased bulk or tone in the muscles was noted in half of the patients examined, and abnormal positioning was noted in about 40% of cases. Tendon contracture and pain on movement were less frequent findings. About 40% of patients had inflammatory disorders of the tendons or synovium, and a similar proportion had nerve disorders, including entrapment. The most common associated medical disorders were allergic diathesis, alcoholism, manic-depressive disorder, hypertension, and ulcer disease. Many patients had tried nonsteroidal anti-inflammatory drugs, and physiotherapy also had commonly been tried. Several subjects had undergone tenotomy and exploration of possibly entrapped nerves. Most patients' conditions were managed with a combination of nonsteroidal anti-inflammatory agents and physiotherapy. Most evaluable patients with inflammatory tendon symptoms have experienced improvement. Electrode-assisted biofeedback is being tried in patients with difficulties in motor control.

Tendonitis is a common disorder in musicians with hand complaints. It may result from rapid and forte movements where the thumb is fixed and the fourth finger is stretched. Neurologic disorders also are prevalent in this population. Most subjects have a good prognosis with conservative management.

► [This article is an important contribution to helping the physician recognize and understand overuse syndromes of the upper extremities. Musicians certainly are subject to occupational disease of the musculoskeletal system, which becomes more readily apparent with the more skilled musician. Unfortunately the diagnosis and treatment is often relegated to a series of chance encounters and colleagues with well-meaning advice. What is needed, as the authors suggest, is a study of the complex physiologic factors involved so that a rational mode of treatment can be developed.—R.L. Linscheid] ◄

(9–9) JAMA 249:1869–1872, Apr. 8, 1983.

9–10 **Nail Bed Repair and Reconstruction by Reverse Dermal Grafts.** The nail bed is often involved in fingertip injuries, and poor nail adhesion and nail deformity may result when the nail bed is allowed to granulate after nail matrix tissue is lost. Robert H. Clayburgh, Michael B. Wood, and William P. Cooney III (Mayo Clinic and Found.) used reverse dermis grafts in 9 patients with acute traumatic nail bed avulsion and in 10 having secondary reconstruction of a scarred nail bed with nail deformity. Total or partial removal of the nail plate usually is necessary. The area of scarred nail bed is sharply excised down to periosteum. A dermatome is used to raise a thick split-thickness skin flap, and a section of free dermis is excised and defatted before replacing the split-thickness skin flap. The graft usually is taken from the palmar surface of the proximal part of the forearm; the thigh also can be used. The dermal graft is tailored to fit the nail bed defect, inset in a reversed position, and secured with fine chromic sutures.

Half or less of the sterile nail bed matrix was involved in most of the patients. The final follow-up examination occurred an average of 15 months after operation. Seven of the 9 patients having primary surgery had excellent results and 1 had a fair result. A patient with an initially unrecognized germinal matrix injury and a coexisting malunited distal phalangeal fracture had a poor result. The patient with a fair result had previous trauma to the acutely injured nail bed. Only 1 of the secondarily treated patients had an excellent result, and the delay between injury and time of treatment was only 4 weeks in this case. The overall delay until treatment in this group averaged 17 months. Two patients had fair and 7 had poor results.

Free reverse dermal grafting of the avulsed or damaged fingernail matrix yields predictably excellent results in acutely treated patients. The more aggressive use of this approach to treat acute nail bed injuries may prevent the development of unacceptable nail deformities.

▶ [This article outlines a method of repair of acute nail bed injuries using reversed dermal grafts. The authors had very good results in acute repairs but poor results in the delayed reconstructions. The technical details of the procedure itself were clearly presented in the text.—J.R. Cass] ◀

9–11 **Mucous Cysts of the Digits.** Richard J. Nasca and John S. Gould (Univ. of Alabama) reviewed experience with 13 patients having surgical treatment of mucous cysts of the digits in 1975–1981. Twelve were women, and most were in their late 40s and early 50s. The distal interphalangeal joint was involved in 8 cases, the proximal interphalangeal joint in 3, and the interphalangeal joint of the thumb in 2. Right hand involvement predominated. Three patients had inflammatory arthritis. The cysts usually occurred to the radial or ulnar side of the extensor tendon and had caused marked thinning of the

(9–10) J. Hand Surg. 8:594–599, September 1983.
(9–11) South. Med. J. 76:1142–1144, September 1983.

skin. Some osteophytosis was present in all joints with an associated mucous cyst. Surgery consistently showed the cyst to communicate with the interphalangeal joint via a stalk. The bulbous part of the cyst usually was lateral to the conjoined extensor mechanism and medial and dorsal to the collateral ligament of the interphalangeal joint. The cysts contained viscous mucoid synovial fluid.

Surgery was done under digital nerve block or regional block analgesia. Loupe magnification aided in dissecting the cysts and surrounding tissues. Skin was grafted in 2 cases. Exposure did not require release of the extensor tendon insertion. No recurrences have been observed on follow-up for 6 years. No significant loss of motion resulted from surgery. The skin healed rapidly, and nail deformities resolved within 3–6 months. Aching in the joint also usually resolved completely after 3–6 months. One patient having a distal interphalangeal joint arthrodesis had rapid, stable fusion and a good functional result.

Mucous cysts of the digits should be meticulously excised within the joint in order to avoid recurrences. Osteophyte excision may not be mandatory, although it was done in most of the present cases. Improved range of joint motion should not be expected. This surgery can be safely done in an outpatient surgical setting, with the use of local anesthesia and a tourniquet.

▶ [Osteophytes may lead to the development of a one way valve mechanism through the dorsal capsule of the joint which allows synovial fluid to be pumped into the cyst with joint motion. If so, excision of the cyst itself may be of little importance if the stalk and valvular mechanism are interrupted.—R.L. Linscheid] ◄

9–12 **Reconstruction of Hand With Three Toes.** Yu Zhong-jia, et al. (Shanghai) describe the transplantation of 3 toes for reconstruction of the hand, a procedure based on successful experience in reconstruction of 2-digited hands. The second toe of the ipsilateral foot is transplanted to replace the lost thumb, and the second and third toes of the other foot are used to reconstruct the index and middle fingers (Fig 9–4). Artificial metacarpals are placed between the forearm stump and the grafted toes to serve as the bony framework of the palm. The resulting hand resembles a normal hand much more than a 2-digited hand does; also, grasping and other functional movements are more dexterous and steady. Four patients have undergone this procedure.

Bilateral toe donation is necessary to reconstruct a 3-digited hand, thus only 1 such hand can be made. The ideal solution for patients with losses of both hands would be the donation of toes from 1 foot to reconstruct a lost hand on either side.

▶ [From the Sixth People's Hospital, an inventive procedure of toe-to-hand transfer for complete loss of the hand is presented. We have performed a number of toe transfers for loss of all digits or loss of the thumb but not for complete loss of all

(9–12) Chin. J. Orthop. 3:323–326, 1983.

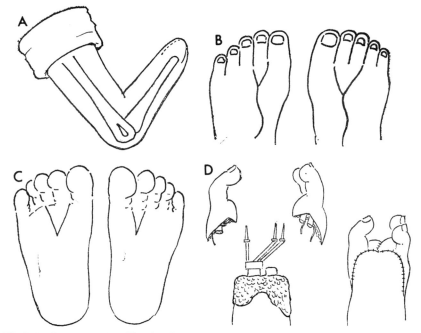

Fig 9–4.—Reconstruction of hand with 3 toes. *A,* preoperative appearance. *B* and *C,* second toe of ipsilateral foot and second and third toes of the opposite foot removed for use in reconstruction of the index and middle fingers. *D,* implantation of toes on forearm stump. (Courtesy of Zhong-jia, Y., et al.: Chin. J. Orthop. 3:323–326, 1983.)

structures. With part of the carpus remaining, this type of reconstruction has been performed by others. Transplantation to the forearm, however, has not been described. Inadequate internal fixation is a problem. Motor function to the toes must be restored. Sensibility must be sufficient. Time, cost, and results should be superior to prosthetic replacement. We must await better follow-up to determine if this would be the case.—W.P. Cooney, III] ◀

9–13 **Open Treatment of Fingertip Amputations.** R. P. Lamon, J. J. Cicero, R. J. Frascone, and W. F. Hass (St. Paul) reviewed the results of open treatment in 25 patients with fingertip amputations at or distal to the distal interphalangeal joint. The finger was cleaned after administration of digital block anesthesia. Hemostasis was secured, and the wound was covered with bacitracin ointment and a tubular gauze bandage. A 4-prong plastic splint was placed over the bandage for immobilization and protection. Five patients received antibiotics. Seven patients required debridement of nail, bone, or devitalized tissue. The wound was soaked in soap solution and the finger exercised actively 3 times a day.

The mean patient age was 28.5 years; 3 patients were children.

(9–13) Ann. Emerg. Med. 12:358–360, June 1983.

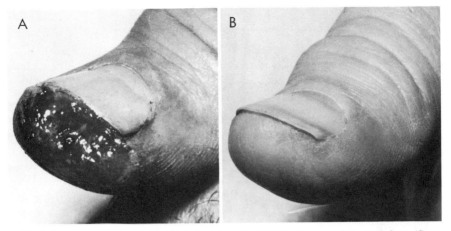

Fig 9–5.—**A,** amputation of tip of left thumb and nail. **B,** healing complete at 32 days. (Courtesy of Lamon, R.P., et al.: Ann. Emerg. Med. 12:358–360, June 1983.)

Crush injuries were most frequent. Six patients had bone involvement. No wound infections developed. The average time for complete reepithelialization was 29 days. The course of healing is illustrated in Figure 9–5. Patients were able to work within 24 hours of injury if they did not have to lift heavy objects or get their hands wet. Sensation was normal in 88% of cases at the time reepithelialization was complete. One patient had minimal loss of flexion at the distal interphalangeal joint.

Open treatment of distal fingertip amputations results in complete healing without infection, preservation of joint mobility, and the return of normal sensation. Healing occurs with normal fingerpad contours. Routine administration of systemic antibiotics is not necessary.

▶ [Treatment of fingertip injuries by open wound technique has once again been successfully demonstrated. When the injury is at or distal to the mid-nail level even with bone exposed, granulation formation and reepithelialization will occur. The authors of this paper have correctly emphasized the need for debridement of devitalized soft tissue including fingernail or bone, daily wound care and protective splinting. We have used a similar method over the past 5 years and have included the exposed distal phalanx, which will most remarkably heal by granulation tissue and reepithelialization and produce a quite satisfactory fingertip pulp which is needed to prevent a hypersensitive fingertip. While the amount of exposed bone that can be expected to granulate is less clear, we have preferred to go to soft tissue flap coverages when there is an excess of 5 mm of bone exposed and fingertip shortening is not preferable for the specific patient. However, in an industrial worker or farmer who needs to return to his job, shortening of the bone following secondary granulation and reepithelialization produces no real handicap.—W.P. Cooney, III] ◀

9–14 **Adduction Contracture of the Thumb in Cerebral Palsy: A Preoperative Electromyographic Study.** Traditionally adduction

(9–14) J. Bone Joint Surg. [Am.] 65-A:755–759, July 1983.

contracture of the thumb in patients with cerebral palsy is managed by Z-plasty of the web and total release of the adductor origin, combined with capsulodesis of the metacarpophalangeal joint when necessary. Preoperative electromyography in 2 of 21 patients in a previous study showed voluntary adductor brevis activity on grasp but no activity when grasp was released, and these patients lost some ability to pinch after release of the muscle.

M. Mark Hoffer, Jacquelin Perry, Manual Garcia, and Daniel Bullock (Rancho Los Amigos Hosp., Downey, Calif.) now perform electromyography on all prospective surgical candidates. Twenty-three children and adults with functional spastic hemiplegia and a contracted thenar-adductor space were examined by needle electromyography. The patients had some ability to grasp, but this was limited by the width of the thenar web. Cognition was no more than slightly retarded in any case.

Two patients had complete selective control of the extrinsic muscles; 10 had patterned control only on release; 2 had patterned control only during grasp; and 9 had patterned control of the muscles on both grasp and release. All showed at least some clinical evidence of selective control of the hand. Eight patients with intermittent activity in the adductor at electromyographic study had partial release of that muscle. Four others had total release of the insertion of the adductor; 2 were the patients who led to the study, and the other 2 had nearly continuous activity of the adductor at electromyographic study.

A splint was worn for at least 6 weeks after operation. All 12 patients treated surgically had simultaneous procedures, most commonly transfer of the flexor carpi ulnaris to the extensor digitorum communis. All patients had an increased width of grasp on follow-up 2 years or more after surgery. They were able to hold thicker objects and to perform new two-handed activities. The patients who had partial myotomy lost no ability to pinch, but 2 of those who had total release lost some ability to side-pinch.

Preoperative electromyographic study is helpful in selecting patients for partial or total release of the adductor muscle for spastic hemiplegia. When indicated, a combination of thumb release and tendon transfer can yield quite satisfactory and predictable results.

▶ [In this clear, concise article the authors have continued their attempt (begun with their contribution in 1979) to turn the art of upper limb cerebral palsy surgery into a science. They are sufficiently successful, so that anyone planning such surgery should read the article in its entirety as they will probably profit from their methods.—J.H. Dobyns] ◀

9–15 **Treatment of Finger Joints With Local Steroids: Double-Blind Study.** The long-acting steroid suspensions triamcinolone hexacetonide (TH) and methylprednisolone acetate (MP) are widely used in in-

(9–15) Scand. J. Rheumatol. 12:12–14, 1983.

tra-articular treatment. S. Jalava and R. Saario (Preitilä, Finland) compared the effects of these agents in 24 patients with rheumatoid arthritis and finger joint swelling, 12 men and 12 women with a mean age of 48.6 years. In a double-blind manner, the inflamed interphalangeal and proximal interphalangeal joints of one hand were treated with TH or MP; those of the other hand, with the alternate preparation. A total of 120 affected finger joints were treated. Each joint was treated intra-articularly with 0.2–0.3 ml of steroid suspension without splinting.

There were no significant initial differences between the 59 joints treated with TH and the 61 treated with MP. Joint circumference decreased significantly with both treatments, but the effect of TH persisted more than that of MP after 6 months. Benefit was evident in 75% of TH-treated joints and in 58% of MP-treated joints at this time; 3.5% and 10%, respectively, were worse than at the outset. Four patients treated with TH and 1 given MP had signs of skin and soft tissue atrophy.

Both TH and MP had significant beneficial effects on finger joint swelling in patients with rheumatoid disease in this study. After 6 months, the treatment effect persisted more in the TH-treated joints, but more adverse effects occurred with TH treatment. Only finger joints with signs of hydrops should be treated with steroid suspension. Deposition of steroid outside the joint should be avoided. The treated joints should be splinted for a couple of days.

▶ [This is a relatively well-controlled study involving 24 patients with 120 joints in whom triamcinolone was compared with methylprednisolone. A definite advantage of using intra-articular steroids particularly in rheumatoid disease have been once again established by this study. We feel this is a particularly effective method of treatment early in the course of rheumatoid arthritis when the goal is the control of individual joint inflammatory process in the hopes of avoiding surgical synovectomies. We always combine this with splinting, which the authors do not mention, and we will repeat the injection up to the 3 times at intervals of 6 months. The limitations of this study include no control group of digits, too short a follow-up to assess long-term results, and no mention of the potential hazards on joint cartilage of repetitive steroid injections.— W.P. Cooney, III] ◀

10. Elbow and Shoulder

10-1 **Cementless Total Shoulder Arthroplasty: Preliminary Experience With 13 Cases.** English and McNab developed an unconstrained total shoulder prosthesis consisting of a cobalt-chrome alloy humeral component with a sintered stem and a metal-backed, high-density polyethylene glenoid component with a sintered back. The humeral component is fixed by a press-fit within the medullary canal, and the glenoid component is fixed by placing cancellous screws into the scapula. D. Dennis Faludi and Andrew J. Weiland (Johns Hopkins Univ.) evaluated this prosthesis in 12 patients who had 13 total shoulder arthroplasties in 1978–1981. All but 2 of the humeral components were implanted without cement. The average patient age at the time of surgery was 62 years. The most common diagnoses were rheumatoid arthritis and posttraumatic arthritis. The average follow-up was 44 months.

Pain was effectively relieved by the procedure, and function was improved. The most benefit was in patients with rheumatoid disease, primary osteoarthritis, and avascular necrosis. Active range of motion improved to a modest degree, but there was no significant increase in muscle power. The roentgenographic appearance is shown in Figure 10–1. No humeral component showed lucency along the stem-bone interface, but resorption of the proximal humerus just beneath the prosthetic head was seen in 2 cases. No glenoid component showed bone resorption at the metal-bone interface. Two patients had humeral fractures during insertion of the humeral component. One patient had perforation of the humeral shaft and postoperative dislocation. One patient had a late *Staphylococcus aureus* infection, necessitating removal of the prosthesis; no primary source of infection was identified.

Criteria for shoulder replacement include intractable pain, dependency on narcotics, disabling limitation of range of motion, and radiographic evidence of destruction of the glenohumeral joint. In this series, function was improved and pain was relieved with placement of the cementless total shoulder prosthesis, but significant complications occurred. Loosening of the components was not observed. Although bony ingrowth was not documented, biologic fixation is believed to have occurred.

▶ [One should note that this is a very heterogeneous group of patients, which includes those with rheumatoid arthritis, osteoarthritis, posttraumatic arthritis, avascu-

(10–1) Orthopedics 6:431–437, April 1983.

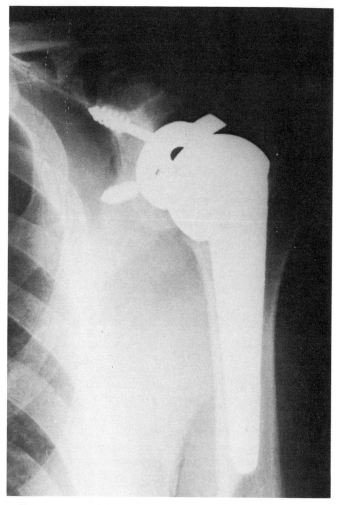

Fig 10–1.—Roentgenogram of shoulder in AP projection 31 months postoperatively. (Courtesy of Faludi, D.D., and Weiland, A.J.: Orthopedics 6:431–437, April 1983.)

lar necrosis, and failed hemiarthroplasty. Motion gained after surgery was not great and much less than is anticipated following an unconstrained total shoulder arthroplasty. The number of complications were also somewhat excessive in this small group of patients. The most dramatic finding was the absence of any detectable loosening of the glenoid component-bone interface. This is a promising prospect for bone ingrowth prosthetic systems in the shoulder.—R.H. Cofield] ◄

10–2 **Prosthetic Arthroplasty of Shoulder.** W. N. Bodey and P. M.

(10–2) Acta Orthop. Scand. 54:900–903, December 1983.

Yeoman (Bath, England) reviewed experience with shoulder arthroplasty in 26 patients operated on between 1973 and 1980 and followed for an average of 3 years. Eighteen patients had rheumatoid arthritis, 2 had long-standing posttraumatic osteoarthrosis, 1 had primary osteoarthrosis, and 5 had fresh fracture dislocations. The average patient age was 59 years. One rheumatoid patient had bilateral arthroplasties. The Stanmore and Kessel prostheses and the Neer hemiarthroplasty were used. Active assisted exercises were performed postoperatively, usually for 2–3 months.

All 21 patients having 22 elective arthroplasties had relief of pain. Motion improved most with use of the Kessel prosthesis. Most patients continued to experience improved abduction for 6 months after operation. Those with fresh fractures improved for a year. All patients believed that their daily function was improved and that the procedure was worthwhile. Complications included postoperative subluxation of a Neer prosthesis, late subluxation of a Neer prosthesis, and dislocation of a Kessel prosthesis. No infections occurred. A lucent zone was seen around the glenoid component of two Stanmore prostheses, but without measurable displacement or movement.

A painless shoulder with good internal rotation is advantageous, even if more than 60 degrees of combined abduction is not obtained. Fracture patients have obtained combined abduction of more than 90 degrees with the Neer hemiarthroplasty. Arthroplasty of the shoulder still is reserved for patients with severe, disabling pain. Prostheses with restricted rotation should be placed so as to allow free internal rotation from neutral. A linked prosthesis should be placed to maintain a depressed humeral head relative to the acromion and provide a mechanical advantage for the deltoid. This also avoids acromial impingement.

▶ [This is a heterogeneous patient group as assessed by diagnosis. It is interesting that there was no attempt at rotator cuff repair in many of the patients who received prostheses. This correlates with what is really quite poor active abduction in the patients in this series compared with other patient series. It does serve to re-emphasize what should be well known, that prostheses can achieve pain relief and return of active movement, and that strength can be achieved with musculotendinous repair. But without such repair, excellent active movement and strength will not be regained.—R.H. Cofield] ◀

10–3 **Operative Treatment of Chronic Ruptures of the Rotator Cuff of the Shoulder.** Patients with persistent, disabling symptoms from rotator cuff tears may require operation. N. P. Packer, P. T. Calvert, J. I. L. Bayley, and Lipmann Kessel (London) reviewed the results of 63 late operative repairs of chronic rotator cuff tears in 61 patients followed for a mean of 33 months. The 43 men and 18 women had an average age of 58 years. The dominant side was involved in 70% of cases. Symptoms began in conjunction with a particular incident in the same proportion of cases, but only 6 patients had significant

(10–3) J. Bone Joint Surg. [Br.] 65-B:171–175, March 1983.

trauma. Five patients had had previous operations. The average duration of symptoms before rotator cuff repair was 41 months. A transacromial approach was used in most instances. Where possible, the tear was closed by direct side-to-side suture. The distal insertion of the cuff was reattached to bone where necessary. A gap was bridged with the long head of the biceps, porcine fascia, or carbon fiber in 11 instances. In 31 shoulders, measures were taken to prevent subacromial impingement.

Pain was adequately relieved in 71% of the 56 shoulders operated on for this reason. Decompression of the subacromial space promoted pain relief. Fewer patients with pain for 2 years or longer were relieved. Thirty-nine shoulders had adequate function for most activities after operation, and another 5 were improved. Three shoulders were functionally worse after operation. Fifteen of 25 heavy manual workers returned to the same job after operation. Three patients required manipulation with anesthesia before a good result was achieved. One wound infection occurred. Eleven patients had a second attempt at operative repair. Two of the 6 who had not had decompression initially had a good result.

Repair of the torn rotator cuff is worthwhile if persistent symptoms are present and fail to respond to conservative management. Adequate subacromial decompression is an important part of the operation. The results have been especially good in patients treated for persistent pain.

▶ [The average follow-up was 32.7 months. The range is quite broad, extending down 6 months. One wonders if this follow-up is long enough for patients with reconstructive surgery on the rotator cuff. The authors even state that the average time taken to achieve a stable state averaged 9.3 months. When evaluating soft tissue surgical procedures one must know the pathology, the method of treatment, and the results. For these patients who all had rotator cuff repairs, it might be important to know the exact pathology encountered. For example, what were the size and shapes of the tendon tears. The methods of repair have been given. Direct tendon suture alone was accomplished in 20 shoulders or approximately one third of the patient group. This implies that the tendons were not torn from bone in these patients and also that the tendon tearing was rather small. It does make it difficult to understand results when these patients are grouped with others, for instance those who required carbon fiber prostheses to bridge the tendon gap.

In terms of results, it should be noted that those in whom staples were used had subsequent operations to remove the staples and those who had dislocations associated with their rotator cuff tears did more poorly than other patients. Pain relief is quite straightforwardly presented though it is a bit difficult to understand the numbers. Range of movement is described in categories rather than physical examination parameters, and it is difficult to be certain what the final results concerning the movement were.

This article is a useful addition to the literature, but some more information could have been obtained from this material that would be useful to the reader.—R.H. Cofield] ◀

10–4   **Cuff Tear Arthropathy.** Charles S. Neer, II, Edward V. Craig, and

(10–4)   J. Bone Joint Surg. [Am.] 65-A:1232–1244, December 1983.

Hiroaki Fukuda (New York Orthopaedic Hosp.-Columbia-Presbyterian Med. Ctr.) reviewed the findings in 26 patients with rotator cuff tear arthropathy whose injuries were explored between 1975 and 1983 and who underwent total shoulder replacement arthroplasty. The 20 women and 6 men had an average age of 69 years. The dominant shoulder was operated on in all but 6 patients. All had long-standing, progressive pain exacerbated by use and activity. The average duration of pain was nearly 10 years. Inability to elevate or rotate the shoulder externally also was reported. Twenty patients had no history of injury, and none had been involved in heavy labor. Steroid injection was not an apparent causative factor. Conservative measures had failed in all 26 patients. Four had become addicted to narcotics.

Examination disclosed typical signs of massive rotator cuff tear and incongruity of the glenohumeral joint in these patients. The changes caused by subacromial impingement usually were conspicuous and well advanced. All of the patients had a large, complete rotator cuff tear. The teres minor and subscapularis tendons usually were involved. Atrophied cartilage near areas of articular surface collapse had a pebblestone-like appearance. Failure of fusion of the anterior acromial epiphysis was seen in 3 shoulders. The atrophic articular cartilage usually was covered by a disorderly fibrous membrane containing connective tissue cells. At some sites the changes resembled those of osteoarthritis. Fragments of articular cartilage were present in the subsynovial layers, but were much less extensive than in a neuropathic joint.

A massive rotator cuff tear exposes a large part of the articular cartilage of the humeral head, impairs normal glenohumeral joint movement, and renders the humeral head unstable. Both nutritional and mechanical factors presumably contribute to cuff tear arthropathy. The cuff tear often requires special repair techniques, and even then muscle strength may not be dependable. Most patients are not good candidates for shoulder arthrodesis. The use of oversized glenoid components remains under investigation. Anterior acromioplasty has been done as indicated to relieve impingement. If more exposure of the supraspinatus tendon is needed, the entire acromioclavicular joint is excised; otherwise, the superficial surface of the joint is left intact.

▶ [This pathologic entity has been only well recognized in the last 4 to 6 years, and its cause at this point is uncertain. The "Milwaukee shoulder," described by McCarty and his coworkers, presents a similar clinical picture and has been attributed to changes in chemical composition of the synovial fluid. As presented in this paper, massive rotator cuff tears, cartilage loss, and deformity of subchondral bone secondary to nutritional and mechanical factors is the logical end stage of the impingement syndrome progressing from inflammation to fibrosis to partial thickness tearing to full-thickness tearing to massive tendon tearing with arthritis. This clinical presentation can be confused with what is usually termed osteoarthritis of the shoulder; but it should not be, as osteoarthritis is seldom associated with massive rotator cuff disease. Treatment for this problem is at this time not completely satisfactory as is also true, of course, for massive rotator cuff tears without arthritis.—R.H. Cofield] ◀

10–5 **Rotator Cuff Tear Measurement by Arthropneumotomography.** Conventional arthrography frequently fails to show the exact size of a rotator cuff tear or the thickness of the remaining cuff. R. F. Kilcoyne and Frederick A. Matsen III (Univ. of Washington) developed a modification of the double-contrast technique with the addition of complex-motion tomography with the patient in the upright position. The records of 33 patients with a surgically confirmed rotator cuff tear were reviewed.

After the injection of 4 ml of a 60% meglumine diatrizoate solution and 10 to 15 ml of room air under fluoroscopic guidance, the shoulder is mildly exercised, and axillary views and a bicipital-groove view are obtained. The patient then is placed upright with a 2-kg weight in the hand, and AP views in the plane of the glenohumeral joint are obtained in internal and external rotation with the x-ray tube angled 15 degrees caudally. A transscapular lateral view then is obtained. If a tear is suspected or demonstrated, tomography is carried out with the patient upright and holding the weight. Anteroposterior tomograms are obtained at 0.3-cm or 0.5-cm intervals.

Tomograms showed the rotator cuff tear better than plain arthrograms in 23 cases. The exact width of the cuff tear and the thickness of remaining cuff could be measured on tomograms. The estimated size of the cuff tear correlated well with the operative findings. In 4 cases, a suspected tear was not confirmed by tomography, and surgery was not carried out. In 8 cases, the tomograms did not add information because of technical errors.

The information obtained by double-contrast arthrography and upright tomography is helpful in planning the repair procedure. Tomography is the best way of determining whether a tear is large enough to have extended into other parts of the cuff, as well as the supraspinatus. The functional results of cuff repair are likely to be better with a smaller tear. If the remaining cuff is thick, repeated tearing or pulling out of the repair is less likely to occur.

10–6 **Symptomatic Shoulder Instability Due to Lesions of the Glenoid Labrum.** Lesions of the glenoid labrum can lead to shoulder symptoms and instability by permitting the joint to dislocate recurrently, subluxate, or click, catch, and lock when partially attached fragments are interposed between the articular surfaces. Arthur M. Pappas, Thomas P. Goss, and Paul K. Kleinman (Univ. of Massachusetts, Worcester) report 6 cases illustrating that the damaged glenoid labrum can produce symptoms by causing functional, as opposed to anatomical, glenohumeral instability. Glenohumeral axillary arthrotomography is an advantageous means of detecting labral pathologic change. The earliest is slight blunting

(10–5) AJR 140:315–318, February 1983.
(10–6) Am. J. Sports Med. 11:279–288, Sept.–Oct., 1983.

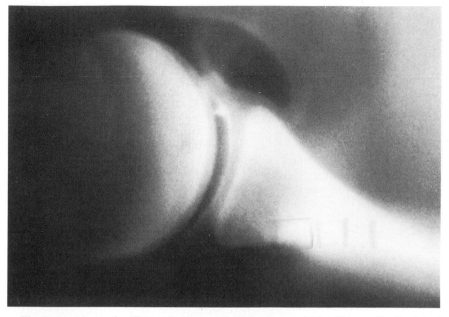

Fig 10–2.—Abnormal axillary arthrotomogram of glenohumeral joint. Note small collection of contrast medium at one point on inner aspect of anterior labrum consistent with minimally displaced tear. (Courtesy of Pappas, A.M., et al.: Am. J. Sports Med. 11:279–288, Sept.–Oct., 1983.)

and irregularity from nonspecific degenerative disease. Nondisplaced linear tears of the labrum can be detected. With a complete tear and separation of the labrum from the glenoid rim, only an irregular labral remnant may be visualized. The appearance of a minimally displaced tear of the anterior glenoid labrum is shown in Figure 10–2.

Lesions of the glenoid labrum can cause functional glenohumeral instability, due to an interposed, partially attached labral fragment, as well as anatomical instability. These lesions are sensitively detected by glenohumeral axillary arthrotomography in patients whose symptoms are unresponsive to nonoperative measures. Symptomatic labral changes can be present both anteriorly and posteriorly in the same shoulder. Arthroscopy is a minimally invasive means of both diagnosing labral lesions and treating those that produce functional instability, through removal of interposed labral fragments. Anatomical glenohumeral instability, in contrast, calls for repair of the labral lesion and capsulorrhaphy. If glenohumeral instability is both functional and anatomical, excision of labral fragments accompanies repair of the defect and capsulorrhaphy.

▶ [This article has two purposes. First, it shows the value of arthrotomography in the axillary projection to identify glenoid labrum tearing. Second, it states, as other recent articles have, that glenoid labral tearing without demonstrable shoulder instability can exist and can be symptomatic.

Other supplementary statements made in the article are, I believe, becoming more accepted. First, that the most definitive noninvasive test for determining whether one is dealing with a subluxing or a dislocating shoulder is examination under anesthesia. Second, that lesions can exist both anteriorly and posteriorly in the same shoulder. Third, that at repair of a dislocating or subluxing shoulder, a glenohumeral arthrotomy should be done to inspect the joint with particular reference to the glenoid labrum.—R.H. Cofield] ◄

10–7 **Double-Contrast Computed Tomography of the Glenoid Labrum.** The glenoid labrum is often injured during acute or recurrent shoulder dislocation, and damage to the labrum itself has been implicated in shoulder instability leading to recurrent dislocation. William P. Shuman, Raphael F. Kilcoyne, Frederick A. Matsen, James V. Rogers, and Laurence A. Mack (Univ. of Washington) performed double-contrast computed tomography (CT) of the glenoid labrum in 11 patients suspected of having labral damage or, in 1 patient, a grade I chondrosarcoma of the glenoid. The CT study was done after plain roentgenography and double-contrast arthrography. A 3-ml dose of Renografin 60 and 10 ml of air were used. The glenoid region was scanned to obtain five to nine slices 5 mm thick. Software reconstruction of the images was used to magnify the area of interest.

Only 4 patients had abnormal plain x-ray films. Double-contrast

Fig 10–3 (left).—Normal right shoulder CT arthrogram showing anterior glenoid labrum *(open arrows)* and posterior glenoid labrum *(solid arrows)*. Note how lip of labrum is continuous with glenoid articular cartilage. Also note size of normal anterior shoulder joint capsule *(arrowheads)* and attachment of capsule to anterior glenoid. *HH*, humeral head; *GL*, glenoid; and *ANT*, anterior.

Fig 10–4 (right).—Stretching of anterior joint capsule *(open arrows)*. Note discontinuity of anterior labrum *(solid arrow)* and anteriorly displaced labrum fragments *(arrowheads)*.

(Courtesy of Shuman, W.P., et al.: AJR 141:581–584, September 1983.)

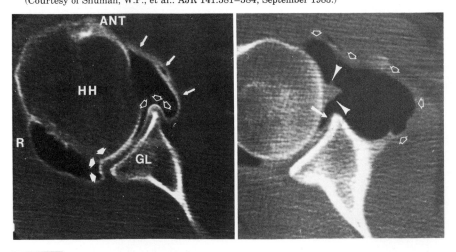

arthrography showed a normal rotator cuff in all patients. The labrum was not identified in 5 patients, and in 5 others it was inadequately visualized. The CT study showed labral abnormalities in 6 patients, 4 of whom showed discontinuity with displacement of a labral fragment. In 5 of these patients the labral abnormalities were confirmed at operation. Computed tomographic abnormalities of the anterior shoulder joint capsule were seen in 4 patients. The findings in 1 of these patients are compared with the normal appearances in Figures 10–3 and 10–4.

Computed tomography after double-contrast shoulder arthrography provides high-quality images of both the glenoid labrum and the anterior shoulder joint capsule. This may be the best means of imaging the glenoid labrum. Computed tomography is easier to perform than polytomography and is more comfortable for the patient, and the radiation dose is lower.

▶ [Computed tomography in conjunction with either air alone or double contrast arthrography, is useful in evaluating the glenoid and acetabular labrums. It allows more complete evaluation of the anterior and posterior portions of the labrum than does double contrast multi-projection or tomographic techniques. Radiation dose is probably less than it is with arthrotomography.

The procedure should be reserved for selected cases. Patients with recurrent dislocation or subtle articular changes should be evaluated using CT.—T.H. Berquist] ◀

10–8 **Arthroscopy of the Shoulder.** Robert H. Cofield (Mayo Clinic) performed 74 arthroscopic studies of the shoulder on 71 patients in December 1979 to June 1982. The most common indications for this procedure were evaluation of glenohumeral instability and assessment of the joint and tendons before acromioplasty for chronic supraspinatus tendinitis. Less frequently arthroscopy was done to diagnose or stage arthritic disease, assess long-standing periarthritis, define rotator cuff tears, visualize intra-articular fractures, or treat infections. Interscalene block or general anesthesia is preferred for arthroscopy. The joint is methodically evaluated. A second incision is made when an irrigation system is to be used or palpation of intra-articular structures is necessary.

Examination of the shoulder under anesthesia was more useful than arthroscopy itself in cases of shoulder instability. In cases of chronic tendinitis, identification of undersurface rotator cuff tears at arthroscopy permitted specific treatment. The examination was of value in staging intra-articular arthritic disorders and in evaluating articular fractures. It was, however, of minimal value in assessing rotator cuff tears and periarthritis and in treating chronic infections. Acute infections were usefully treated in conjunction with arthroscopy. The examination also was useful in a case of pigmented villonodular synovitis.

Arthroscopy of the shoulder is a useful procedure in certain set-

(10–8) Mayo Clin. Proc. 58:501–508, August 1983.

tings. It has a supportive role in cases of complicated glenohumeral instability. Arthroscopy is not necessary in evaluating or treating supraspinatus tendinitis, but it does exclude intra-articular pathologic conditions. Arthroscopy is helpful in determining proper treatment for acute septic arthritis. It probably is not appropriate for patients with chronic articular infections. Arthrography is preferred for evaluating rotator cuff tears and periarthritic conditions.

▶ [The development of arthroscopy as a technique for direct visualization of intra-articular structures has indeed been a major development in the diagnosis and treatment of joint diseases. However, as is the case with many new techniques, there tends to be some "novelty value." Arthroscopy at the present time is extremely popular and for the past several years has perhaps been performed unnecessarily in a good many situations. This article is extremely helpful in defining the proper role of arthroscopy of the shoulder joint. The extensive experience of the author very well outlines those situations for which arthroscopy is, and those for which it is not likely to be of value.—R.N. Stauffer] ◀

10–9 **Shoulder Joint Arthroscopy.** James R. Andrews (Hughston Orthopaedic Clinic, Columbus, Ga.) and William G. Carson (Tulane Univ.) reviewed the findings at shoulder arthroscopy in 118 patients (120 shoulders) examined in November 1980 to January 1983. The most common symptoms were pain, popping, and shoulder instability. Symptoms had been present for an average of 1 year before surgery.

General endotracheal anesthesia is used in these procedures. A posterior approach is preferred. A needle is inserted about 3 cm inferior to the posterolateral edge of the acromion and directed anteriorly toward the coracoid process. Saline is injected to distend the joint before inserting the arthroscope sleeve and trocar through a small skin incision. An anterior portal may also be required. If necessary, a second anterior portal can be established directly adjacent to the first. Bupivacaine solution is injected into the joint when the examination is completed. Two patients had ulnar nerve neuropraxias, and 1 had a musculocutaneous complication. Abnormalities were found in 88% of the shoulders examined.

Shoulder arthroscopy is a reproducible diagnostic procedure when carried out systematically, giving adequate attention to variations in normal shoulder anatomy. Proper orientation is essential, with consistent positioning and suspension of the arm of the patient. Examination time should be minimized. Arthroscopy of the shoulder joint can be very useful in evaluating a wide range of chronic shoulder complaints.

▶ [This manuscript describes technique and to a lesser extent arthroscopic anatomy. It is important to recognize that indications for the procedure are not outlined, nor are the diagnostic or treatment benefits. Three patients had a neuropraxia which would make one wonder about the use of upper extremity traction of 15 to 20 pounds in the anesthetized patient. The discussions of the middle glenohumeral ligament and the subscapularis tendon are a bit confusing and one wonders if in actual practice it is sometimes difficult to be certain which structure is which.—R.H. Cofield] ◀

(10–9) Orthopedics 6:1157–1162, September 1983.

10–10   **Adhesive Capsulitis of the Shoulder: Arthrographic Diagnosis and Treatment.** Adhesive capsulitis of the shoulder is a distinct entity that must be diagnosed accurately for appropriate treatment to be given. James A. Loyd and Herbert M. Loyd (Houston) reviewed the findings in 31 patients seen in 1978–1981 with clinically suspected adhesive capsulitis of the shoulder. Two had bilateral involvement. The 22 women and 9 men had an average age of 54 years. Twelve patients reported some injury, and 2 others had cervical disk disease. All patients had constant pain that interfered with daily activities, and 12 claimed to have incapacitating pain. Motion was limited in each case. The duration of symptoms averaged 6 months. Twenty-five patients had been treated previously.

Arthrography with manipulation showed a very small joint capacity in 23 cases and a moderately small capacity in 10. The biceps tendon sheath filled poorly in 10 cases, and did not fill in 3. Five rotator cuff tears, 2 of them large, were identified. Capsular rupture was seen in 21 cases, usually through the subscapularis bursa. The appearance in 1 case is shown in Figure 10–5. On follow-up after an average of 8 months, 20 patients reported no pain, and 13 had continued to have occasional minor pain. No patient had had any form of manipulation or surgery since the arthrogram. Minor limitation of motion persisted in 10 cases. Improvement generally was maximal within 3 months. Four of the 9 patients with restricted function had rotator cuff tears. The 2 patients who did not benefit from gentle manipulation of the joint at arthrography, under intra-articular lidocaine anesthesia, had manipulation under general anesthesia, and 1 of them did well.

This procedure insures an accurate diagnosis of adhesive capsulitis of the shoulder. Methylprednisolone is injected along with the contrast medium and lidocaine. Morbidity is much less than with surgery with the patient under general anesthesia. No complications occurred in the present series. The therapeutic results have been much better than with analgesics and physical therapy. This approach can markedly shorten the period of symptoms with minimal risk to the patient.

▶ [The cause of adhesive capsulitis of the shoulder is rarely known with certainty and its pathology is not well understood. This is because the natural tendency of this disorder is resolution and operative treatment is, almost without exception, ill-advised.

In such a setting, adhesive capsulitis of the shoulder is essentially a painful and stiff shoulder for which other causes of this problem, such as rheumatoid arthritis or rotator cuff tearing, have been excluded. The authors' point, that arthrography helps diagnose this problem, is a very important one and should be considered for patients with this diagnostic complex. How important distension of the shoulder capsule is in the treatment of this problem is another question. It certainly is possible to distend the capsule with fluid, but often before much in the way of distension occurs there is

(10–10) South. Med. J. 76:879–883, July 1983.

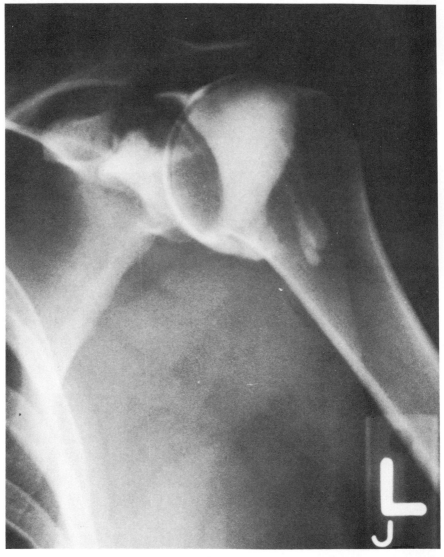

Fig 10–5.—Appearance of adhesive capsulitis in shoulder with absent axillary recess, small subscapularis bursa, and no rupture. (Courtesy of Loyd, J.A., and Loyd, H.M.: South. Med. J. 76:879–883, July 1983. Reprinted by permission of the Southern Medical Journal.)

a rupture through the subscapularis bursa or out the biceps tendon sheath. Manipulation can certainly shorten the course of adhesive capsulitis. How much in the way of manipulation was done for these patients is difficult to quantitate. If the shoulder was taken through a range of motion by the radiologist and this range was not possible before arthrography, then substantial manipulation was done. This may represent in some patients an effective way of diagnosing adhesive capsulitis and a means of supplying relative anesthesia so that manipulation can be done. It will be helpful to have more experience in this procedure. It does hold some promise. Unfortunately, in the 12 patients with adhesive capsulitis for whom I have done this without the injection of steroids, the effect in relieving their pain and stiffness has been moderate or less than moderate, and treatment for these patients has been redirected along more traditional lines.—R.H. Cofield] ◄

10-11   **Ultrastructure of the Subacromial Bursa in Painful Shoulder Syndromes.** Inflammation of the subacromial bursa often is implicated as a cause of shoulder pain, and "bursitis" frequently is diagnosed even when primary disease of a contiguous structure is apparent. Kiriti Sarkar and Hans K. Uhthoff (Univ. of Ottawa, Ont.) undertook an ultrastructure study of the subacromial bursa in 8 operative cases of shoulder pain to determine whether "bursitis" was present. Samples were taken from 3 patients with calcifying tendinitis, 2 with a tight coracoacromial ligament, 2 with a rotator cuff tear, and 1 with acromioclavicular osteoarthritis. The bursa was not considered the primary source of pain in these cases, but its secondary involvement was not ruled out.

Study of the cases of calcifying tendinitis, tight coracoacromial ligament, and rotator cuff tear showed primarily an increase in cells through the bursa wall and proliferation of endothelial cells in the vessels. The cells contained densely packed intermediate-type filaments, but showed no substantial decrease of metabolic organelles. Lipid droplets were abundant in the extracellular connective tissue of the bursae in cases of rotator cuff tear. The bursa in the case of acromioclavicular osteoarthritis showed widespread fibrin deposition and cell necrosis. No case had the bursa tissue infiltrated by inflammatory leukocytes.

These findings suggest that the subacromial bursa tends to undergo proliferative or degenerative changes in rotator cuff tendinopathies, but bursa inflammation with polymorphonuclear cell infiltration is not common. Painful shoulder syndromes that mainly affect structures such as rotator cuff tendons, acromioclavicular joint, or coracoacromial ligament, would alter the ultrastructure of the subacromial bursa, probably because of anatomical proximity. The concept of "bursitis" must be more precisely defined to be of diagnostic value.

► [It has long been my contention that the term "bursitis" should be virtually eliminated from our shoulder terminology except for very, very occasional cases of septic inflammation. Several years ago we ran a study of bursae deposits in the cuff, usually in the supraspinatus tendon. These never showed any inflammation. As the authors point out, there are degenerative changes in the bursa; but evidence of inflammation with morphonuclear cell infilatrate is absent. Let's finally stop calling this common shoulder pain due to tendon degeneration "bursitis."—Ed.] ◄

(10–11) Virchows Arch. [Pathol. Anat.] 400:107–117, June 1983.

10–12 **Polymyalgia Rheumatica: An Arthroscopic Study of the Shoulder Joint.** The nature of polymyalgia rheumatica remains unclear, but the nonspecific synovial changes have generally been considered unimportant. W. A. C. Douglas, B. A. Martin, and J. H. Morris (Brisbane, Australia) studied 19 patients with classic changes of polymyalgia rheumatica who had arthroscopic study to determine whether an underlying arthritic process could be detected. The 13 women and 6 men, aged 50 to 79 years, were followed up for a mean of 15 months. All had developed severe pain and stiffness within a period of weeks or months that was limited to the shoulders, neck, and hips. The sedimentation rate exceeded 30 mm/hour. No patient had evidence of inflammatory peripheral joint involvement. Five patients had bone and joint scans with ^{99m}Tc-methylene diphosphonate (MDP). In 4 cases the synovium was examined for immunofluorescence.

All but 2 patients had evidence of synovitis at arthroscopic study (Fig 10–6). Four patients had joint effusions. The histologic findings were generally unimpressive when compared with the picture seen with the arthroscope (Fig 10–7). Vascular dilatation, engorgement, and perivascular edema were constant findings, and round cell infiltration was usual. There was variable proliferation of the surface epithelium without irregular nuclei. Vasculitis was suggested in only 1 case. Only 2 of 5 patients showed a positive uptake on bone-joint scanning. Three of 4 samples of synovial membrane showed fibrin

Fig 10–6.—Hypertrophic edematous synovial membrane in shoulder joint. (Courtesy of Douglas, W.A.C., et al.: Ann. Rheum. Dis. 42:311–316, June 1983.)

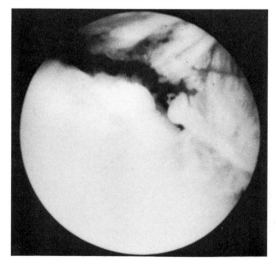

(10–12)   Ann. Rheum. Dis. 42:311–316, June 1983.

Fig 10–7.—Synovial biopsy specimen from shoulder showing vascular engorgement and synovial cell hyperplasia. Hematoxylin-eosin; ×65. (Courtesy of Douglas, W.A.C., et al.: Ann. Rheum. Dis. 42:311–316, June 1983.)

deposition on endothelial cells on immunofluorescence study. Focal IgM and C3 deposition were each seen in 2 cases. All patients responded dramatically to injections of corticosteroid into the shoulder joint, and all but 1 responded rapidly to 10 mg of oral prednisone daily. A patient who refused steroid therapy responded quite well to naproxen therapy.

Polymyalgia rheumatica appears to be a specific entity. Vascular complications are quite infrequent. Joint scanning has not proved useful in diagnosing this disorder. Immunofluorescence studies should be pursued.

▶ [Nineteen patients with polymyalgia rheumatica had shoulder arthroscopy with the Stortz 3.8 telescope. Seventeen of the 19 were found to have synovitis (Fig 10–6). By comparison, no evidence of synovitis was found in 10 control shoulders arthroscoped for "nonspecific shoulder pain." A hypertrophic edematous synovial membrane was seen at arthroscopy. Histologically, this showed lymphocytic infiltration (Fig 10–7). Random synovial samples from 12 cadaver shoulders used as controls showed normal synovium.

There are now multiple lines of evidence suggesting that polymyalgia rheumatica is in fact a misnomer and that it is instead a chronic arthritis. These are (1) consistently normal muscles biopsies, (2) positive joint scans using technetium pertechnetate, (3) positive biopsies for synovitis in such joints as shoulders, sternoclaviculars, and knees, and (4) chronic erosive radiologic changes in the sternoclavicular, manubriosternal, sacroiliac, pubic symphyseal, and even hip joints of some patients.— J.D. O'Duffy] ◀

10–13 **Magnuson-Stack Procedure (Modified) for Recurrent Shoulder Dislocation (A Long-term Follow-up).** Most previous reports of the Magnuson-Stack operation for recurrent anterior shoulder dislocation have involved too few patients or too short a follow-up interval. Michael Carroll (State Univ. of New York at Stony Brook) reviewed the outcome in 71 patients having a modified Magnuson-Stack repair for recurrent shoulder dislocation from 1963 to 1978. Ten different surgeons were involved in the study. The 60 males and 11 females had an average age of 24 years. Surgery was performed after at least 3 recurrences of shoulder dislocation. Average follow-up was 5.2 years.

A deltopectoral approach was utilized. After exploring and irrigating the joint, an area of the greater tuberosity just lateral to the biceps groove was roughened subperiosteally, and the tendon and capsule were stapled to the site to limit external rotation from 0 to 30 degrees. Nonabsorbable sutures were used to secure the new insertion to the surrounding periosteum. The shoulder was immobilized in a Velpeau sling for 3 to 6 weeks, and sports activity was limited for 3 to 6 months.

The rate of recurrence was 12.7%. Four recurrences resulted from severe trauma, while 3 occurred during throwing. Five of the 9 failures were in patients aged 17 and younger, and only 1 in a patient more than 21 years old. External rotation was subjectively limited in one third of patients. About one fourth felt limited in playing sports. One fifth of the patients described mild shoulder pain, usually associated activity. Very few surgical complications occurred. One patient developed a vascular thoracic outlet syndrome 6 months postoperatively and refused treatment. Another had occasional cyanosis of the arm. Eighty-three percent of patients were satisfied with the outcome.

The Magnuson-Stack operation is a relatively easy procedure that gives excellent results in patients older than 21 years of age. Younger patients have a much higher failure, and might best have a more extensive procedure such as the Bankart repair, or perhaps a combined operation.

▶ [This is a very insightful review of the results of operations on recurrent instability, and a particularly detailed review of the Magnuson-Stack procedure. The relationship of age to the results of the operation is particularly intriguing, and undoubtedly henceforth authors reporting on this subject will have to consider that in their reports. Recurrence is concentrated in the younger age groups, not only for the nonoperative patients, but for the operative ones as well.—R.H. Cofield] ◀

10–14 **Recurrences After Initial Dislocation of the Shoulder: Results of a Prospective Study of Treatment.** L. Hovelius, K. Eriksson, H. Fredin, G. Hagberg, Å. Hussenius, B. Lind, J. Thorling, and J. Weck-

---

(10–13) J. West. Pacific Orthop. Assoc. 20:43–48, December 1983.
(10–14) J. Bone Joint Surg. [Am.] 65-A:343–349, March 1983.

ström (Sweden) undertook a prospective study of 257 patients younger than age 40 years who were treated at 27 hospitals in Sweden between 1978 and 1979 for primary anterior dislocation of the shoulder. Either the affected shoulder was immobilized in a Velpeau dressing or sling and swathe or the arm was tied against the body for 3 to 4 weeks, or patients wore a sling as long as they benefited from it (up to 2 weeks) and were told to avoid painful abduction and external rotation of the shoulder for about 3 weeks. Follow-up evaluations were carried out 2 years later in 112 patients who used an immobilization device and in 104 who began using the shoulder as early and freely as possible. Sports accounted for most injuries in younger patients, while falls prevailed in those aged 30 to 40 years.

None of 32 patients with a fracture of the greater tuberosity reported further dislocations in the 2 years after treatment, but one third of the other patients had redislocations. Fractures were prevalent in patients aged 12 to 13 years and in those aged 34 to 40 years. Chip fractures of the glenoid rim occurred in 8% of patients, most of them older. Over half of the patients had impression fractures in the posterior part of the humeral head; these were not associated with a significantly increased rate of redislocation. Recurrences were comparably frequent in patients who used an immobilization device and in those who used the shoulder early. Nearly half of the patients aged 22 years and younger had recurrences regardless of treatment, as compared with one fourth or less of older patients.

Patients in this study were followed up for the standard 2 years, the interval in which over two thirds of recurrent dislocations are known to occur. The incidence of redislocation was not influenced by the use of an immobilization device, nor by the early and free use of the shoulder after injury.

10–15 **Acromioclavicular Separations Treated Conservatively: 5-Year Follow-up Study.** Although partial separations of the acromioclavicular joint are nearly always managed nonoperatively, controversy about the treatment of complete dislocations continues, and more than 30 different operations have been described. Håkan Bjerneld, Lennart Hovelius, and Jan Thorling assessed the long-term results of conservative treatment of complete joint separations in 77 patients seen with acromioclavicular separations in 1961–1979. In only 5 cases was an attempt made to reduce the dislocation. Five other patients were operated on. A complete separation was present in 33 of the 70 evaluable patients, excluding those treated surgically and the 2 who died during follow-up. The mean follow-up was 6 years. The mean age at injury was 35 years.

All patients with partial separations had satisfactory results, and most had an excellent outcome (table). Sixteen of the 37 patients did

(10–15) Acta Orthop. Scand. 54:743–745, October 1983.

RESULTS ON FOLLOW-UP EXAMINATION*

	Satisfactory		Unsatisfactory	
	Excellent	Good	Fair	Poor
Partial separation	24/37	13/37	–	–
Complete separation	7/33	23/33	1/33	2/33

*(Courtesy of Bjerneld, H., et al.: Acta Orthop. Scand. 54:743–745, October 1983.)

heavy physical work. Thirty of 33 patients with complete separations had satisfactory results, and 7 had excellent results. Fifteen patients with a satisfactory outcome did heavy physical work. Few cosmetic complications occurred in either group. Patients generally returned to work 4–6 weeks after injury. About half the patients with complete separations had significant remodeling of the lateral end of the clavicle, so that vertical displacement was less than the total height of the joint. In most cases, stress did not influence the displacement at the time of radiographic follow-up. Moderate to extensive calcification was noted in the area of the coracoclavicular ligaments in 21 patients with complete separations.

There appears to be no need for reduction and long-lasting immobilization in cases of partial acromioclavicular joint separation. Total separations can be adequately managed without reduction and with a short immobilization time. The joint seems to have considerable ability to adapt to the new position of the clavicle. A more horizontal joint space is formed, and in most cases, the new joint is stable and not influenced by traction on the arm.

▶ [As the authors point out, treatment of acromioclavicular separations is controversial, yet these authors are suggesting a nonoperative approach.

I think most surgeons make their mind up after a period of time. The older the surgeon, the less the urge to resort to surgery!—P.J. Kelly] ◀

10–16 **Resection of Lateral End of Clavicle: 3 to 30-Year Follow-Up.** Claes J. Petersson (Univ. of Lund) followed up 50 patients having resection of the clavicle after an average of 9 years. From 1 to 2 cm of the clavicle was removed lateral to the coracoclavicular ligament. In all, 51 procedures were done. Seventeen patients were followed up for 10 or more years. Thirty-four patients were operated on for traumatic damage to the acromioclavicular joint and 16 for nontraumatic disorders.

Thirty-seven patients having 38 operations were pleased with the

(10–16) Acta Orthop. Scand. 54:904–907, December 1983.

results at follow-up evaluation, but 11 had some residual symptoms and their outcome was considered only fair. The duration of follow-up did not influence outcome. Comparable results were obtained in traumatic and nontraumatic conditions. Overall, 27 patients had good results, 11 had fair results, and 13 had poor results. None of the treated shoulders was unstable. Five patients with a poor outcome were operated on because of persistent pain in the acromioclavicular region after clavicular fracture; 3 of these had been operated on previously. Six patients with poor results and 8 with fair or good outcomes had alcoholic or psychiatric problems. Most poor results were apparent at the end of the convalescent period. The clinical results could not be related to the presence of new bone spurs or radiopaque deposits. New bone formation was similar in the traumatic and nontraumatic cases.

About 75% of patients having resection of the lateral end of the clavicle are satisfied with the results, which appear to be maintained over time. Proper patient selection may improve the outcome. The presence of new bone at the resected end of the clavicle or radiopaque material in the resection gap is compatible with a good clinical outcome.

▶ [This is an interesting series which demonstrates that this operation can be consistently successful if one is careful in patient selection. As a sidelight, it also reinforces the concept that one should be wary of operating on patients with psychiatric disease or alcoholism if the primary indication for surgery is control of pain.—R.H. Cofield] ◀

10–17 **Ununited Fractures of the Clavicle.** Nonunion is found in only 1% to 2% of patients with fractures of the clavicle. Ross M. Wilkins and Renner M. Johnston (Denver Gen. Hosp.) reviewed the findings in 33 patients treated between 1960 and 1981 with ununited clavicular fractures. The 15 males were most often injured in the second decade of life and the 18 females in the third through fifth decades. The right clavicle was affected in two thirds of cases. Average follow-up was about 8 years. Nonunion had been present for an average of 5½ years in surgically treated patients. Fourteen patients who were not operated on had nonunion for an average of 10 years. Most patients had pain on shoulder motion, and some reported grating. Only 4 had significant weakness. Six patients were asymptomatic. Nineteen patients had a total of 25 operations. Two patients had thoracic outlet syndrome as a result of the nonunion.

The initial duration of immobilization could not be related to the development of nonunion. There were no open fractures, but two thirds of patients had completely displaced fractures, and 6 of them also had gross comminution. Seven patients showed nonunion in the area of a previously united fracture. Hypertrophic nonunion was present in 22 patients; the other 11 had atrophic nonunion. Operations

(10–17) J. Bone Joint Surg. [Am.] 65-A:773–778, July 1983.

for nonunion included resection of the pseudarthrotic middle third of the clavicle, internal fixation with a small plate and bone graft, insertion of an intramedullary pin, screw fixation with bone grafting, and local ostectomy and bone grafting without internal fixation. One patient had avulsion of the transverse cervical vein, which was ligated without sequelae. The most successful procedure appeared to be internal fixation and bone grafting. Twelve patients who were operated on achieved union, but some continued to have mild to moderate symptoms.

A significant proportion of these patients had refracture of a previously healed clavicular injury. Bone grafting with internal fixation seemed to give the best overall surgical results. Patients with atrophic nonunion may improve over time, and a patient with a nonunion should not be operated on without specific indications.

▶ [When one critically reviews the clavicle fractures they have seen over the years, the incidence of nonunion seems even higher than the usual "1% to 2%." Granted that while some of these seem relatively symptom-free, most require bone grafting.

This paper gives the results in 19 patients who had various procedures for nonunion, and emphasizes that the most successful procedure is internal fixation and bone grafting. This is not surprising, as this is the most successful operation in most ununited fractures.—Ed.] ◀

10–18 **Degeneration of the Glenohumeral Joint: An Anatomical Study.** Claes J. Petersson (Univ. of Lund, Malmö Sweden) performed 151 shoulder dissections on 41 male and 35 female cadavers to determine the prevalence of glenohumeral joint degeneration at different ages and the relation between cartilaginous degeneration of the joint and degeneration of the rotator cuff. Average age at death was 68 years; age range was 18 to 92. The most common causes of death were malignancy and cardiovascular disease. Nineteen humeral heads without gross degenerative changes, from normal-appearing joints in 11 cadavers, also were examined. Mean age also was 68 years.

Gross degeneration of the rotator cuff was seen in 25 shoulders and full-thickness cuff ruptures were seen in 23. These changes were bilateral in 87% of cases. In 12 of the shoulders with cuff degeneration the changes were localized to the inner surface of the supraspinatus tendon close to its insertion. Most full-thickness ruptures were in the supraspinatus tendon. Severe cartilage degeneration was present in 24 shoulders; in 12 of them full-thickness degeneration was present with denudation of the subchondral bone. Degenerative changes often were more marked in the glenoid cavity. Osteophytes were seen most often in the area of the tubercles and the sulcus. In 6 shoulders the long biceps tendon had ruptured. Degenerative cuff disease was much more prevalent in shoulders with cartilage degeneration.

Degeneration and ruptures of the rotator cuff, cartilage degeneration, and changes in the long biceps tendon all become more frequent

(10–18) Acta Orthop. Scand. 54:277–283, April 1983.

with advancing age. A highly significant relation between cuff and cartilage degeneration was found in the present study of cadavers. Glenohumeral degeneration was bilateral in most cases and is more frequent in women than men. There is little evidence that occupation is of major importance in the development of shoulder joint degeneration.

10–19 **Synovectomy of Elbow in Rheumatoid Arthritis.** The elbow is affected in at least half of the patients with rheumatoid athritis, but surgery is not commonly done as a means of treatment. L. A. Linclau, W. P. C. A. Winia, and J. K. v.d. Korst (Amsterdam) reviewed the results of 43 synovectomies of the elbow done between 1976 and 1980 in 33 patients with rheumatoid disease. The radial head was resected in nearly all instances. A silastic radial head prosthesis was inserted in 7 joints, and in 6 elbows the ulnar nerve was transposed. Thirty-one patients, mean age 62 years at operation, were followed up. The mean duration of disease was 17 years, and all but 3 patients had elbow symptoms for more than 1 year.

Complications included transient irritation of the ulnar nerve in 1 patient, and temporary paralysis of the posterior interosseous nerve in 2. Symptoms of synovitis were absent in 31 of 39 elbows at follow-up. Pain decreased or disappeared in 27 joints, and function improved in 21. Stability was virtually unchanged. The radiographic appearances deteriorated after synovectomy in 9 instances, but this was unrelated to clinical outcome. Twenty-seven patients were satisfied with the outcome. The overall results were considered satisfactory in 27 of the 39 elbows.

The success of synovectomy of the elbow in patients with rheumatoid disease appears related to the operative approach used rather than to the radiographic grade of destruction or duration of follow-up. The radiographic findings are of little help in deciding whether synovectomy or a prosthesis is indicated. The outcome in the present series did not appear to depend on whether a radial head prosthesis was inserted at the time of synovectomy.

▶ [This study confirms the value of synovectomy for rheumatoid arthritis and emphasizes that good results may be obtained even though the process is quite advanced. The radial head was excised in 86% of elbows indicating the high number (56%) of radiologic grades 3 and 4. Note that only 28% of elbows were followed 3 years or longer and, therefore, the series is really quite short-term. No absolute preoperative and postoperative pain, range of motion, or stability assessments were given.—L.F.A. Peterson] ◀

10–20 **Long-Term Effects of Excision of the Radial Head in Rheumatoid Arthritis.** Most have recommended excising the radial head in conjunction with synovectomy of the elbow joint, but there is biomechanical evidence that this may have such adverse effects as prox-

(10–19)   Acta Orthop. Scand. 54:935–937, December 1983.
(10–20)   J. Bone Joint Surg. [Br.] 66-B:109–113, January 1984.

imal migration of the radius or valgus deformity with traction damage to the medial soft tissues. L. A. Rymaszewski, I. Mackay, A. A. Amis, and J. H. Miller (Glasgow) examined the long-term effects of radial head excision in 40 elbows of 37 patients with rheumatoid disease, operated on in 1972–1980. The 32 women and 5 men in the series had an average age of 56 years. All patients but 2 had classical features of rheumatoid arthritis, and 32 were seropositive. The average duration of disease was 19 years, and of elbow involvement, 12 years. Silastic sheeting was interposed in 15 elbows. In 2 cases, the ulnar nerve was transposed.

Eighteen elbows were reported to be free of pain at follow-up, while in 12 there was either no relief or a worsening of pain. In 10 instances, initially good pain relief was followed by later deterioration. Elbow instability was associated with unsatisfactory results. Several patients felt that range of elbow motion was improved after operation. The use of Silastic did not appear to significantly influence the results of surgery. The radiologic findings correlated poorly with the clinical outcome. Further degenerative changes at follow-up were the rule.

Mechanical factors appeared to be a major cause of failure in this series. The axial load on the radius when an object is lifted is transferred to the ulna after radial head excision, producing considerable tension on the medial ligament to prevent valgus deformity. This adds further to the humero-ulnar force. Insertion of a radial head prosthesis may be very difficult if painful instability develops after radial head excision. Replacement should be done at the time of resection if possible.

▶ [The authors have pointed out that significant disability following radial head resection and synovectomy in rheumatoid arthritis can occur from increasing valgus deformity and stress due to absence of the radial head. They conclude, however, that these forces can be balanced by the insertion of a radial head silastic prosthesis. While this is certainly theoretically true, it is my experience that, particularly in these unstable type patients, the prostheses do not hold up. While the studies and interests of the authors are correct, I would not agree with the conclusion that the radial head prosthesis should be utilized in rheumatoid arthritis. Certainly there may be some patients in whom it would be beneficial, but in those patients with significant instability the potentials for pressures associated with the valgus stress could certainly lead to increased problems with the use of the prosthesis.—R.D. Beckenbaugh] ◀

10–21 **Entrapment Neuropathies of the Median Nerve At and Above the Elbow** are discussed by Lucido Gessini, Bruno Jandolo, and Alberto Pietrangeli (Rome). The anatomical relationships of the median nerve at and above the elbow are shown in Figures 10–8 and 10–9. Only 3 of 238 cases of median nerve entrapment occurred at and above the elbow. One patient had Struthers' ligament syndrome, and 2 had the lacertus fibrosus bicipitis syndrome. Although many cases of entrapment by Struthers' ligament have been reported, compres-

(10–21) Surg. Neurol. 19:112–116, February 1983.

sion neuropathies caused by the lacertus fibrosus bicipitis are rare.

Features of these neuropathies include disability of all muscles innervated by the median nerve without significant muscle atrophy and disordered sensitivity involving the three radial fingers and the adjacent section of the palm. Secretory and vascular symptoms are less frequent and less prominent.

Electromyographic study shows signs of denervation in all muscles dependent on the median nerve, reduction in their volitional activity, and decreased motor and sensory conduction velocities in the nerve crossing the elbow. Conduction velocities may not be reduced in the early stages of compression. The pronator teres muscle has been involved in all the authors' cases. Supracondylar entrapment by the ligament of Struthers may lead to a palpable or roentgenographically apparent bony spur in the lower third of the humerus. Soft, swollen tissue along the medial border of the arm suggests a hypertrophic brachialis or an anomalous muscle.

Median nerve entrapment at and above the elbow can be caused by

Fig 10–8.—**A,** relationship of brachial artery, median nerve, supracondylar process, and Struthers' ligament. **B,** anatomical picture of brachial artery as it splits above spur. (Courtesy of Gessini, L., et al.: Surg. Neurol. 19:112–116, February 1983. Reprinted by permission of the publisher, copyright 1983, Elsevier Science Publishing Co., Inc.)

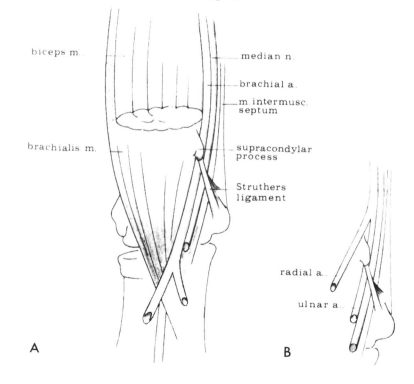

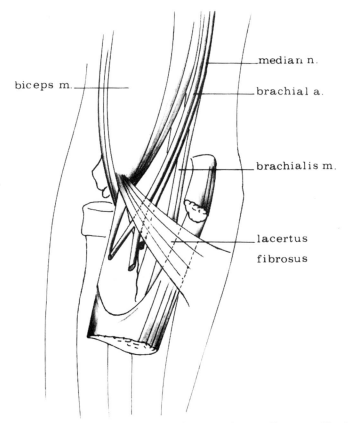

Fig 10–9.—Relationship of brachial artery, median nerve, lacertus fibrosus, and brachialis muscle. (Courtesy of Gessini, L., et al.: Surg. Neurol. 19:112–116, February 1983. Reprinted by permission of the publisher, copyright 1983, Elsevier Science Publishing Co., Inc.)

compression of the nerve beneath the Struthers ligament or compression beneath the lacertus fibrosus bicipitis due to either a hematoma or a hypertrophic brachial muscle.

▶ [With increasing awareness of carpal tunnel syndrome as the major cause of median neuropathy in the upper extremity, familiarity with more proximal neuropathies is important. The authors suggest two levels of possible entrapment which are well known. Additionally, entrapment of the median nerve further distally within the pronator is also a distinct possibility and should be sought out.—M.B. Wood] ◀

11. Foot and Ankle

11–1 **Acute Injuries of the Lateral Ligaments of the Ankle: Comparison of Stress Radiography and Arthrography.** The lateral ligaments of the ankle often are injured by inversion stress, especially in young athletes. Inversion and anterior stress radiographs have customarily been used to evaluate the ligaments, but some have recommended arthrography. Donald D. Sauser, Rendon C. Nelson, Melvin H. Lavine and Christine W. Wu (Loma Linda Univ., Calif.) compared stress radiography using the Telos apparatus with arthrography in 55 patients with acute inversion injuries of the ankle. The 35 men and 20 women had an average age of 25 years. Plain radiographs showed varying degrees of soft tissue swelling laterally but no fractures. No patient had evidence of previous ankle trauma or incongruity of the articular surfaces. Inversion and anterior stress radiography of both ankles was followed immediately by arthrography of the injured ankle. The stress views employed 15 kPa of pressure. The inversion views were obtained with the foot in about 18 degrees of internal rotation.

The range of anterior displacement of the talus in relation to the tibia on anterior stress averaged 5.1 mm in normal ankles, 6.3 mm in those with a torn anterior talofibular ligament, and 7.2 mm in those with a tear of the calcaneofibular ligament as well. On inversion stress, the angle of talar tilt averaged 2.6 degrees in normal ankles, 8 degrees in those with a torn anterior talofibular ligament, and 8.8 degrees in those with tears of both ligaments. Arthrography showed a torn anterior talofibular ligament in 33 ankles, and tears of both ligaments in 12 cases. Anterior stress views were not correlated with the arthrographic findings, and inversion stress views did not distinguish between a torn anterior talofibular ligament alone and tears of both ligaments. Inversion stress testing was very accurate in detecting ligament injury when the ankle of inversion was 10 degrees or greater, but this degree of accuracy was achieved in only 38% of cases.

Stress radiographic evaluation of the ankle ligaments has a high false negative rate. This probably could be reduced by anesthesia, but it is as easy to perform arthrography, which also has a high false negative rate when performed too long after injury. The appropriate modality depends in part on the proposed treatment.

▶ [For years, the tilting talus view has been used to demonstrate posttraumatic ligament pathology or absence of same. Yet this test can be compromised by pain, mus-

---

(11–1) Radiology 148:653–657, September 1983.

cle splinting, false negatives, and technique. Although the statistics used in this article are confusing, the conclusion should be of help to all who see and treat ankle sprains. The authors confidently state that arthrography done within 72 hours of injury has far greater reliability than stress testing of the sprained ankle. Our experience confirms this.—E.W. Johnson, Jr.] ◄

11–2 **Limiting Use of Routine Radiography for Acute Ankle Injuries.** Ankle injuries may account for more than 10% of emergency room visits. Many patients have radiographic examination of the ankle or foot, but the results of a high proportion of these studies are negative. W. Peter Cockshott, Jeffrey K. Jenkin, and Margaret Pui (McMaster Univ., Hamilton, Ontario) sent about 200 questionnaires to radiologists in 36 countries regarding the radiographic projections used to diagnose acute ankle trauma; responses were received from 170 of them. Also, a prospective study was carried out in 242 consecutive patients seen in an emergency room with 24 hours of ankle injury and having a 4-view radiographic study.

In answer to the questionnaire, the average number of routine films reported obtained for patients with ankle trauma was 2.5 worldwide, 2.9 in the United States (both hospitals and offices), 2.3 in hospitals operating as salaried health services in Europe, and 2.0 in developing countries. The overall average number of views obtained by hospital radiologists was 2.6, and in private offices, 2.4. In the prospective series, 29% of the patients had fractures. All of these had definite malleolar soft tissue swelling, as did 4% of the ankles without fractures. Older patients had fractures considerably more often than did those in the second and third decades, in whom ligamentous injuries were more frequent. All fractures were detectable in the anteroposterior or lateral view.

Radiographic examination of the injured ankle is often unnecessary. Two routine views are adequate for initial diagnosis, although additional views may be necessary for clinical management. Routine requests for radiographs of the foot, as well as of the ankle, are not warranted. Considerable cost savings could be realized by obtaining ankle x-ray studies only on high-yield criteria. Several other reports confirmed a lack of need for performing ankle x-ray examinations in patients without ankle swelling.

▶ [Limiting x-rays to patients with ankle swelling does have some merit. There is no question that radiographs are not always required, but a good clinical exam should always be performed before the radiograph is ordered. In an emergency room setting this is often not the case, and radiographs are frequently ordered prior to adequate clinical examinations. Anteroposterior and lateral views are not sufficient. One must not forget ligament injury which can be accurately assessed in 90% or more of patients, and mortise views as well as both obliques are needed.—T.H. Berquist.] ◄

11–3 **Radiographic Instability of the Ankle Joint After Evans' Repair.** The postoperative results of the Evans' repair of lateral insta-

(11–2) Can. Med. Assoc. J. 129:129–131, July 15, 1983.
(11–3) Acta Orthop. Scand. 54:734–738, October 1983.

bility of the talocrural joint are generally good, but the subjective results do not always correlate with the objective findings. S. Orava, H. Jaroma, H. Weitz, T. Loikkanen, and M. Suvela reviewed the results obtained in 42 unstable ankle joints treated by the Evans' operation in 41 patients in 1979–1981. The mean patient age at the time of surgery was 29 years. Surgery was done for clinical instability in a previously injured ankle joint. Most patients had "giving way" instability, and a majority had pain as a chief complaint. Most patients had had several ankle sprains. The talar tilt examination was positive in 29 cases; the anterior drawer sign, in 25. Follow-up was for 6 months to 2½ years after surgery.

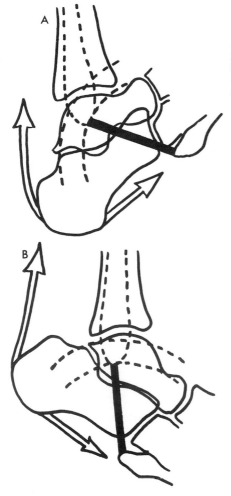

Fig 11–1.—A, in dorsiflexed ankle joint after Evans' repair, anterior subluxation is not possible. **B,** in plantarflexed ankle joint, tangential subluxation of talus may occur. (Courtesy of Orava, S., et al.: Acta Orthop. Scand. 54:734–738, October 1983.)

Patients rated 27 ankles as excellent or good at follow-up. Four ankles were unstable on clinical examination. The radiologic stress examination was positive in 19 cases. Five ankles exhibited degenerative or reactive changes that did not correlate with the operative results. Positive findings on stress radiography correlated with moderate or poor results on objective functional assessment. The subjective results correlated poorly with radiologic instability at follow-up. Even patients with adequate subjective results tended to be symptomatic during athletic activities, and many of them still used an elastic bandage during sports activity. Only 1 patient, however, was unable to continue his previous athletic activity because of ankle symptoms.

The subjective and objective results of the Evans' operation for lateral ankle instability were similar to those previously reported. Persistent radiologic instability can be explained by the lack of an intact anterior fibulotalar ligament or by the transformation of the anterior capsule and fibulotalar ligament to loose connective tissue and scar by recurrent injuries (Fig 11-1). The degree of instability present after tenodesis is difficult to assess clinically. The operation is easily performed, has minimal complications, and requires immobilization for a relatively short time. In addition to the tenodesis, the torn ligaments should be sutured or duplicated and fixed to the short peroneal tendon, especially in physically active patients.

▶ [We would certainly agree with the authors' conclusions. In a clinical and biomechanical study comparing the various types of lateral ankle ligament reconstructive techniques, Cass and Morrey found that all of the various procedures were effective and there was no significant difference between the various techniques. We, therefore, perform the simplest procedures; the Evans' procedure or the Snook-Chrisman modification of the Elmslie Procedure.—J.H. Sim] ◀

11-4 **Compression Arthrodesis of the Ankle: Evaluation of Cosmetic Modification.** Marcus J. Stewart, T. Craig Beeler, and John C. McConnell (Univ. of Tennessee) have used Charnley compression clamps in a modification of the compression method of ankle joint fusion as originally conceived by Key, and have obtained a high proportion of successful arthodesis and good functional and cosmetic results. Seventeen of 28 patients who had arthrodeses in 1955–1979 were reassessed in person by one of the authors. The average age of patients at surgery was 48 years, and the average follow-up was 4½ years. The most common indication for arthrodesis was pain from traumatic arthritis. The most common initial injury was bimalleolar fracture.

TECHNIQUE.—A longitudinal wedge of bone is removed from the medial malleolus, medial tibia, and medial talus. Through a lateral incision, a similar wedge of bone is removed from the distal tibial metaphysis, lateral talus, and medial fibula. The bone surfaces then are denuded of cartilage and sub-

(11-4) J. Bone Joint Surg. [Am] 65-A:219–225, February 1983.

chondral bone and scored, and Steinmann pins and Charnley clamps are then put in place. Compression is applied until the pins are moderately bowed. The malleoli are fastened to the tibia with a screw and serve as a bone graft.

Solid arthrodesis was present at follow-up in 93% of ankles. Five patients had tarsal motion comparable to that in the other foot. Nine others had an average reduction of 10.6 degrees, while 3 had an average increase of 13.3 degrees of motion. Most patients showed no change in midtarsal arthritis. Five patients had moderate pain when performing daily activities, and 1 had severe pain. One of the 2 patients with a failed arthrodesis has been reoperated on with a satisfactory result. One patient had persistent numbness over the dorsum of the foot after surgery. One required further surgery for painful nonunion of the distal fibular malleolus despite solid ankle fusion.

Fusion was obtained in more than 90% of cases in this series. In contrast to most ankle fusions, the resultant ankle is not too wide, and the shoe counter does not abrade the soft tissues adjacent to the malleoli. The procedure produces a functional, durable, and cosmetically superior ankle.

▶ [The authors' description of a novel technique for achieving ankle fusion is quite interesting. It appears as though the fusion does provide a pleasing cosmetic appearance for the ankle. It would appear, however, that technically the procedure would be extremely difficult. The 93% fusion rate reported is about the same as that reported for most other techniques utilizing compression across the ankle.—R.N. Stauffer] ◀

11–5   **Tarsal Tunnel Syndrome and Peripheral Neuropathy in Rheumatoid Disease.** The principal neuropathies of rheumatoid disease include nerve compression, a mild distal sensory impairment, and a severe sensorimotor disorder. Entrapment at the tarsal tunnel has been implicated in foot pain in rheumatoid patients. Louis McGuigan, David Burke, and Anthony Fleming (Sydney) studied 30 patients with classic or definite rheumatoid arthritis who had both pain and erosions in the feet. All were aged 65 or younger. None had any previous foot operations. None was diabetic. The mean patient age was 51 years, and the mean duration of rheumatoid disease was 10 years. Twelve patients had active disease at the time of the study. All patients were taking nonsteroid anti-inflammatory drugs. Six were taking prednisone and 24, a slow-acting suppressive agent.

Only 3 patients reported having a history of numbness or paresthesia, and 1 of them had no clinical abnormalities. Four patients had evidence of tarsal tunnel syndrome and no demonstrable medial plantar sensory potential. The condition was not related to disease activity. The electric abnormalities were not gross; no patient had compound muscle action potential amplitude more than 2 SD below the normal mean. Two patients had evidence of peripheral sensory polyneuropathy with absent or abnormal distal sural sensory potentials

(11–5)   Ann. Rheum. Dis. 42:128–131, April 1983.

and absent and medial plantar sensory potentials. A normal distal sural sensory potential was recorded in 77% of the patients.

Electrodiagnostic evidence of the tarsal tunnel syndrome is not rare in patients with rheumatoid disease in the feet. However, the electric abnormalities are mild, and no clinical syndrome has been observed. Distal sensory neuropathy is not common in these patients.

▶ [Diagnosis of the tarsal tunnel syndrome unfortunately is often based on the criterion used by these authors, that is, "distal motor latencies to abductor hallucis (medial plantar nerve) or to abductor digiti quniti (lateral plantar nerve) or both prolonged beyond 2 standard deviations from the normal mean for temperature and conduction distance."

Such a sole diagnostic criterion is not adequate and will lead to overdiagnosis of the so-called tarsal tunnel syndrome. To make this diagnosis, the conduction velocities of other lower extremity motor nerves would have to be normal with normal distal latencies and with the only abnormal findings being in the tibial nerve. Unfortunately, these were not recorded in this study.—K.A. Johnson] ◀

11–6   **A Dorsal Wedge V Osteotomy for Painful Plantar Callosities.** Painful plantar callus formation due to prominence of the metatarsal head is a common orthopedic problem. Excision of the metatarsal heads increases the load on the remaining heads, and oblique metatarsal osteotomies leave the final position of the distal fragments to chance, with displacement frequently resulting. Edward L. Sclamberg and Mark A. Lorenz (Cook County Hosp., Chicago) have used a dorsal closing wedge V osteotomy for treatment of painful plantar callosities due to prominence of any of the five metatarsal heads.

An inverted V is marked with its apex toward the metatarsal base at an angle of about 60 degrees, and the bone is cut with an oscillating saw as shown in Figure 11–2. The periosteal sleeve on the plantar surface is preserved. A second inverted V osteotomy is made about 3 to 4 mm distal to the first, with the two converging at the same point on the inferior cortex. Patients now are ambulated in a bunion shoe as soon as weight-bearing is comfortable.

Forty-one osteotomies have been done on 25 patients with plantar callosities in the past 3 years. The 20 female and 5 male subjects had an average age of 34 years. Eleven of them had associated bunion deformities and or hammertoes, or both. Conservative treatment had failed in all instances. Bunion deformities were osteotomized and hammertoes were corrected at the same time the dorsal wedge V osteotomy was performed. The second metatarsal was osteotomized in 18 cases and the third and fourth were osteotomized in 10 cases each.

All patients were able to bear full weight within 3 days after operation. Bony union of the osteotomy site was evident at 4 to 7 weeks with the average time being 5½ weeks. No patient had complaints related to the osteotomy site or the plantar callus at follow-up. The callosities had resolved by 6 months in all cases but 1, and

(11–6)   Foot Ankle 4:30–32, July–Aug. 1983.

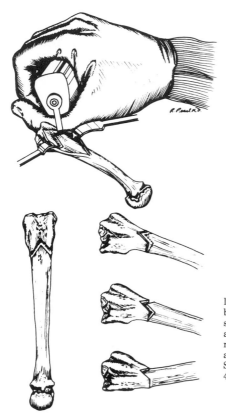

Fig 11—2.—Periosteum is split longitudinally and then retracted. Narrow-bladed oscillating saw is used to cut dorsal V-shaped wedge. Wedge is removed and pressure is applied from plantar to dorsal aspect of metatarsal head. Osteotomy closes dorsally, allowing metatarsal head to elevate. (Courtesy of Sclamberg, E.L., and Lorenz, M.A.: Foot Ankle 4:30–32, July–Aug. 1983.)

they did not recur. All patients wore normal footwear without pads.

The proximal V osteotomy of the metatarsal is a simple, predictable means of correcting plantar callosities. No significant complications have occurred. The procedure can be carried out in conjunction with other operations for related foot deformities.

▶ [The authors describe a procedure to alleviate painful plantar callosities. They state that "in all patients so treated relief of symptoms was achieved, plantar callosities were resolved, and no significant complications occurred." It is hard to imagine that any surgical procedure will invariably give such good results. Although the idea is alright, I feel that with closer scrutiny transfer metatarsalgia, incomplete correction, delayed union, wound inflammation, hypertrophic callus, and other difficulties would become evident.—K.A. Johnson] ◀

11–7 **Conservation of Metatarsal Heads in Surgery of Rheumatoid Arthritis of the Forefoot.** The forefoot is involved in at least 90% of cases of rheumatoid arthritis. Previously used operations on the

(11–7)   Acta Orthop. Scand. 54:417–421, June 1983.

forefoot relieve pain, but they shorten the foot and may make existing unsteadiness worse. Raymond J. Newman and John M. Fitton (Leeds, England) describe a procedure that avoids these problems and that can be done on early cases when the disease is localized to 2 or 3 rays. The metatarsal heads are preserved as the first metatarsophalangeal joint is fused, and the bases of the proximal phalanges of the involved rays only are excised along with cysts and synovium. Traction is used after operation to maintain the length of the operated lateral toes. A walking cast is used for 5 weeks, and a second cast is used for another month if the arthrodesis is not sound.

Seventy-nine patients with proved rheumatoid disease who had this operation in 1975 to 1978 were followed up, and data were obtained on 71 patients who had 130 forefoot operations. In 97 procedures all the toes were treated; in 33 only 3 or 4 toes were operated on. Fifty-nine patients had bilateral surgery. Average age of the 57 women and 14 men at operation was 53 years. Average follow-up was 3½ years.

All but 12% of patients reported significant improvement after operation. Twenty-five percent of patients had no pain at follow-up and another 25% had only aching. Only 5% of patients had significant pain. Nearly 60% of patients who were initially unsteady could walk normally at follow-up, but 20% of those who were initially steady became worse. Five patients required second operations, 4 for prominence of the second or third metatarsal head in the sole and 1 for a recurrent cyst. Bony fusion of the arthrodesis of the first metatarsophalangeal joint was noted in 86% of cases. There was a painless fibrous ankylosis in the remaining cases. Three superficial infections occurred, but there were no healing problems.

This conservative operation relieves pain and generally improves stability in the rheumatoid forefoot. Walking distance improved significantly in the present patients.

▶ [To adequately evaluate this surgical procedure, the extent of rheumatoid arthritis involvement of the forefoot prior to operative treatment needs to be known. With minimal involvement, preserving the metatarsal head regions seems reasonable.

There is little significant metatarsal head erosion in this example case. For the more common severe rheumatoid forefoot disease, the metatarsal head resections should probably still be a part of the surgical treatment.—K.A. Johnson] ◀

11–8   **Osteotomy in the Treatment of Osteoarthritis of the First Carpometacarpal Joint.** Degenerative changes in the first carpometacarpal joint can cause pain, weakness, and adduction deformity, and in resistant cases an abduction wedge osteotomy of the base of the first metacarpal can relieve symptoms with fewer complications than are produced by other operations.

J. N. Wilson (Royal Natl. Orthopaedic Hosp., London) and C. J. Bossley (Hutt Hosp., Lower Hutt, New Zealand) reviewed the results

(11–8)   J. Bone Joint Surg. [Br.] 65-B:179–181, March 1983.

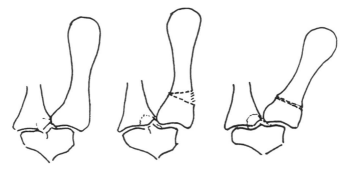

Fig 11–3.—Illustration of principle of basal wedge osteotomy in treatment of osteoarthritis of first carpometacarpal joint. To avoid instability it is important that apex of wedge coincide accurately with ulnar cortex of metacarpal. Width of base varies with amount of adduction deformity to be corrected. (Courtesy of Wilson, J.N., and Bossley, C.J.: J. Bone Joint Surg. [Br.] 65-B:179–181, March 1983.)

of 23 osteotomies performed in 20 women and 1 man who were followed up for 2 to 17 years after operation. Average age at operation was 48 years. All patients had a diagnosis of osteoarthritis. Pain was the chief presenting symptom. Examination showed crepitus and local tenderness over the carpometacarpal joint in all cases, as well as thenar wasting and decreased pinch grip.

At surgery a closing wedge osteotomy is performed at the proximal end of the first metacarpal with the base of the wedge directed radially (Fig 11–3). A wire suture is not needed if soft tissue dissection is minimal and a periosteal hinge is maintained on the ulnar side. A forearm plaster is used for 6 weeks after surgery.

All but 3 patients were completely relieved of pain. Three others had a slow response to surgery, but even they and the 3 patients with slight pain are satisfied with the outcome. Two patients have had the same operation on the other side. No relapses have occurred, and no secondary operations have been necessary. Powerful grasp and spread of the hand were restored, permitting large objects to be gripped without difficulty. In 3 cases the adduction deformity was not corrected, but grasp nevertheless was possible. At radiologic study there was no evidence of improvement in the joint, although no further deterioration was observed. All the osteotomies were united by bone healing within 3 months of surgery. The only complication was minor loss of sensation at the thumb tip in 1 patient.

Basal osteotomy of the first metacarpal has provided substantial, lasting relief of pain in patients with degenerative changes in the first carpometacarpal joint and has permitted full function of the thumb. Average follow-up now is 12 years.

▶ [The authors present a unique treatment of osteoarthritis of the first carpometacarpal joint by osteotomy. This brings the thumb out from an adducted to an abducted position and in effect changes the stress relationship across the trapeziometacarpal joint. We have had no experience with this treatment modality although it is based on the same principle used for subtrochanteric osteotomy for degenerative arthritis of the hip. Certainly, correction of radial subluxation and realignment of the thumb by abduction osteotomy would have a beneficial effect on the functional use of the thumb and secondarily may correct debilitating pain. In the authors' series, however, they mention that 3 of 21 patients had persistent pain and they don't grade other patients as to the presence of minor pain. Furthermore, they have no data with respect to pinch or grip strength which we expect would improve if pain relief was satisfactory. A classification of the degree of degenerative arthritis is also not provided and the authors don't state whether they would recommend this procedure for grade IV degenerative arthritis of the trapeziometacarpal joint. It would seem this type of procedure would be more restricted to the grade II or possibly grade III type of degenerative arthritis.—W.P. Cooney] ◄

11–9 **Mitchell Osteotomy for Hallux Valgus: Long-Term Follow-up and Gait Analysis.** Kurt D. Merkel, Yoshihisa Katoh, Einer W. Johnson, Jr., and Edmund Y. S. Chao (Mayo Clinic and Found.) reviewed data on 144 Mitchell osteotomies performed on 96 patients in 1967 to 1980. Follow-up data were available for 69 patients who had a total of 96 operations. Mean age at time of surgery was 44 years; nearly all patients were female. Mean follow-up was more than 7 years. Only 2% of patients had surgery for cosmetic reasons alone.

A double incomplete osteotomy was performed three quarters of an inch proximal to the articular surface before completing the proximal osteotomy. The distal fragment then was shifted laterally and slightly plantar-flexed. The osteotomy was secured with chromic sutures or Kirschner wire. Most patients had nonweight-bearing cast immobilization for an average of 6 weeks. Gait analysis was carried out at follow-up in 26 cases.

More than 80% of patients began wearing shoes within 3 months of surgery, and 64% had no shoe restriction at follow-up. Sixty-seven percent had no pain after operation, and only 2% had incapacitating pain. Only 3% of patients were dissatisfied with the outcome. Fifty-four percent of patients were considered to have had an excellent result, and 35% were considered to have had a good result. Postoperative plantar flexion averaged 1 degree. Three of 5 feet (60%) with 5 or more degrees of dorsiflexion had less than satisfactory results. Of the 7 feet with more than 10 mm of first metatarsal shortening, 29% had unsatisfactory results.

The postoperative hallux valgus angle averaged 14 degrees, and there was no correlation with the final result of surgery. Gait analysis showed abnormal foot mechanics, with decreased cadence, velocity, and step length, compared with control subjects. Complications included delayed union or nonunion in 3% of cases, superficial infection in 3%, and deep infection in 1%. No patient had avascular necrosis or hallux varus.

(11–9) Foot Ankle 3:189–196, Jan.–Feb. 1983.

Mitchell osteotomy gave satisfactory results in most patients in this series. Satisfactory clinical results do not, however, necessarily lead to normal foot mechanics. Gait analysis may be helpful in identifying patients who are at increased risk of postoperative metatarsalgia.

▶ [This nice paper presents important information to the surgeon who may utilize Mitchell osteotomies for treatment of hallux valgus in his practice. Of special importance is the emphasis placed on gait analysis which provides some important objective parameters for comparison of the various surgical procedures. It is clear that Mitchell osteotomy is a technically demanding procedure, and the authors correctly emphasize the critical interrelationship between shortening of the first metatarsal and plantar flexion of the distal fragment at the time of osteotomy. With patients properly selected and a procedure properly performed, patients so treated are likely to be pleased with the results.—D.C. Campbell, II] ◀

11–10 **First Phalanx Osteotomy in the Treatment of Hallux Valgus.** P. Lavigne (Alençon, France) presents a revised version of the technique for osteotomy intially published in 1974, certain defects of which might have caused a number of bad results. The revised technique has currently been used for approximately 5 years. It differs from the initial technique in the following respects. The osteotomy is more distal (8 to 10 mm from the cartilage) in order to arrive at a larger and better vascularized epiphyseal fragment, which in turn requires preservation of as much of the joint capsule as possible. The small oscillating saw is used as little as possible, serving merely to

Fig 11–4.—Illustration showing initial technique *(left)*, and current technique *(right)*. (Courtesy of Lavigne, P.: Ann. Orthop. Ouest 15:217–223, 1983.)

OSTEOTOMIE de P1

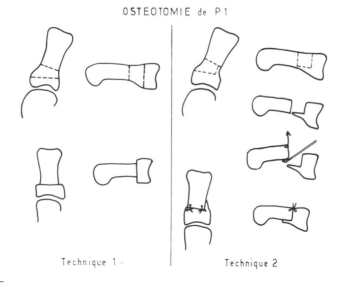

Technique 1 ·   Technique 2

(11–10) Ann. Orthop. Ouest 15:217–223, 1983.

trace the bone resection on the back of the phalange and to perform the distal resection. The lower cortex is preserved together with the proximal fragment, which not only avoids incongruency of the 2 surfaces, but protects tendon and sheath and permits faster fusion. The lateral cortex is also preserved as far as possible. Thus, the distal end of the first phalanx, after slight roughening of its inferior surface, will fit into the proximal fragment (Fig 11–4). The amount of bone to be excised must be precisely determined so as to obtain a big toe as long as or slightly shorter than the second toe. The postoperative course is simple; walking is resumed on the fourth day with an elastoplast bandage to support the metatarsals, including a felt-lined plaster sole.

In this report 210 cases were reviewed, and 55 feet were examined clinically and radiologically. For stage I hallux valgus, results were good in almost all cases, from both morphological and functional viewpoints. The patients were nearly all young women between 18 and 45 who previously had pain and difficulty in finding shoes. All had about the same type of foot, with a long big toe. For stage II hallux valgus, results were less even, concerning mostly older people with deformities often involving toes other than the big toe and with signs of incipient arthrosis of the metatarsophalangeal joint. For stage III, long-term results were nearly always poor or bad, frequently with return of the deformity (the latter connected with a loosening of the medial suture). This conservative technique is considered valid for moderate foot deformities in young women with long big toes.

▶ [This author espouses an osteotomy of the proximal portion of the proximal phalanx for the treatment of the hallux valgus deformity. He concludes that it is most useful in patients who have a moderate deformity and long great toes. It is my feeling that this procedure is most useful when the proximal phalanx has a valgus deviation when comparing the distal and proximal articular surfaces, that is, a hallux valgus interphalangeus. For deformities that include a dislocation of the first metatarsophalangeal joint, the rate of recurrence of deformity after performing the phalangeal osteotomy as described by the author has been unacceptably high.—K.A. Johnson] ◀

11–11 **Surgical Wedge Excision Versus Phenol Wedge Cauterization for Ingrowing Toenail: Controlled Study.** J. S. Varma, A. W. G, Kinninmonth, and D. W. Hamer-Hodges (Edinburgh) reviewed the results obtained in a prospective study of 67 patients with ingrowing toenail who were randomized to have either standard surgical wedge excision or phenol wedge cauterization. Twenty-three patients with onychogryphosis underwent avulsion of the nail and total phenol cauterization of the nail bed. Phenol wedge cauterization was performed with 2% lidocaine ring block anesthesia and a tourniquet applied to the base of the great toe. A 3-minute application of 89% phenol was made to the affected edge of the nail bed after the ingrowing edge was avulsed.

(11–11) J. R. Coll. Surg. Edinb. 28:331–332, September 1983.

The average healing time was 2 weeks after both treatments for ingrowing toenail. Nail spikes recurred in about one fourth of both treatment groups. Three patients treated with phenol and 7 who had conventional therapy required further treatment for symptoms. The patients treated with phenol for onychogryphosis also had an average healing time of 2 weeks. Four had a recurrence, but none required further treatment for symptoms.

Phenol wedge cauterization avoids incisions and suturing and can be carried out in the presence of infection. Postoperative pain has been less than after surgical wedge excision of ingrowing toenail. Excellent results are obtained from total phenol ablation, but the method is fairly drastic and should be reserved for symptomatic recurrences that follow phenol wedge cauterization.

▶ [The type of alcohol-phenol procedure we use deviates slightly in that we use three 30-second applications of phenol to the nail bed rather than one application of phenol for 3 minutes as mentioned in the article. In an unpublished comparison of our surgical versus phenol procedures, K. A. Johnson reports 97% satisfied patient response in 110 cases and 90% satisfied patient response in 62 patients having the chemical partial matrixectomies.—J.L. Graham] ◀

11–12 **Interdigital Neuroma: Critical Clinical Analysis.** Roger A. Mann and J. Christopher Reynolds (Oakland, Calif.) reviewed the results of excision of 76 interdigital neuromas from 56 patients, 53 females and 3 males with an average age of 55 years. Average follow-up was 22 months. Eleven lesions had previously been operated on. The chief symptom was pain localized to the metatarsal head region of the foot, aggravated on ambulation and relieved by rest. Six patients noticed progressive enlargement on the plantar aspect of the foot. In all cases pain was localized to the interspace between the metatarsal heads. Three patients had hypesthesia. Most patients had some relief from conservative management, but localized plantar pain on examination rarely responded. Anti-inflammatory agents were ineffective, and local anesthetic injections had varied results but did not give lasting relief.

Comparable numbers of neuromas were removed from the second and third interspaces. All the recurrent lesions exhibited changes of traumatic neuroma. The 6 associated synovial cysts exhibited degenerating fat and thin-walled, fibrous-appearing tissue. Eighty percent of patients who were not previously operated on were substantially improved, and another 6% were somewhat improved but had some persistent symptoms. The causes of failure were not evident. Nine of the 11 patients with recurrent neuroma were significantly improved after operation. Most patients remained limited in their selection of shoe styles, especially high heels.

Most patients with interdigital neuroma are satisfied with the results of operation, but many have residual tenderness over the cut

(11–12) Foot Ankle 3:238–243, Jan.–Feb., 1983.

end of the common digital nerve, and the procedure is not always successful. No patient has developed causalgia or sympathetic dystrophy. Those who failed to respond to operation have been managed with a broad-toed shoe and metatarsal support, anti-inflammatory medication, and occasional injections of local anesthetic, corticosteroids, or both. Ultrasound or transcutaneous nerve stimulation has been useful in a few instances.

▶ [This interesting article is a retrospective study of 56 patients upon whom 76 interdigital neuromas were excised. This exhaustive review of these 56 patients really illustrates two important points which have not been noted in the literature prior to this article. The first of these is that an equal number of interdigital neuromas from the second, as well as from the third, interspace were noted. This is entirely opposite to the literature in the past. The second difference is the presence of 6 cases with a synovial cyst in which the cyst exerted pressure against the nerve and produced symptoms in the sole of the foot. Also, these 6 patients had divergence of the toe and a progressive enlargement on the plantar aspect of the foot prior to the onset of symptoms in the interdigital neuroma. A "squishy" lump was felt on the plantar aspect of the foot. This further reinforced the suspicion of a cyst and the diagnosis was made at surgery. Only 1 of these 6 patients had rheumatoid arthritis.

The authors make the point that anyone doing surgery on interdigital neuromas should be careful to caution their patients that, at least in this series, only 80% of patients were completely satisfied with the surgery results. This approaches our experience and should be discussed with the patient preoperatively.—E.W. Johnson, Jr.] ◀

11–13 **Foot Reconstruction by Free Flap Transfer.** Major soft tissue defects of the foot, especially those involving weight-bearing areas, can be difficult treatment problems. The use of rotational and island flaps may be limited by the size and site of the defect and associated injuries, and distant pedicle flaps may be associated with considerable morbidity requiring prolonged hospitalization. Michael B. Wood, George B. Irons, and William P. Cooney, III (The Mayo Clinic and Found.) reviewed the results of free skin flap transfer done for foot salvage and reconstruction in 10 patients who were followed up for a year or longer mean, 17 months) after surgery. Surgery on the ankle was not included.

The procedures and results are summarized in the table. The recipient site was the heel in half of the patients. Overall, 7 flaps were applied to weight-bearing sites with underlying exposed bone. Three of these flaps were innervated by cutaneous neurorrhaphy at the time of transfer. The mean initial hospital stay was 10 days. All patients but 1 had a successful outcome. Four patients with successful results required secondary procedures. The single failure was caused by arterial thrombosis and flap loss in a child with a septic wound who subsequently underwent a cross-leg flap procedure. The appearances in a patient with an excellent outcome are shown in Figure 11–5.

Free flap reconstruction of foot defects has been considered only when distant pedicle flap transfer or amputation was the alternative.

(11–13) Foot Ankle 4:2–7, July–Aug., 1983.

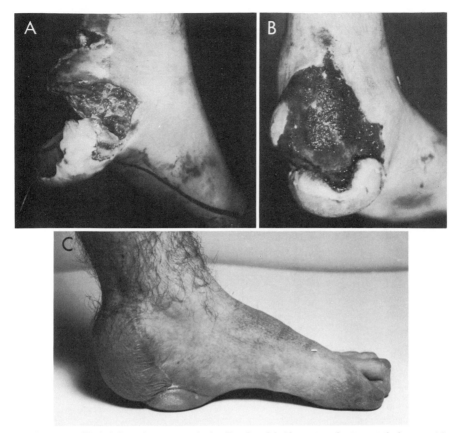

Fig 11–5.—Heel defect. **A,** preoperatively; **B,** after debridement and attempted closure with split-thickness skin graft 4 weeks after injury; **C,** free groin flap transfer 33 months postoperatively, at which time patient was ambulatory. (Courtesy of Wood, M.B., et al.: Foot Ankle 4:2–7, July–Aug. 1983.)

In adults the procedure seems as reliable as distant pedicle flap transfer is. Use of an innervated flap in a weight-bearing area of the foot may be of particular value in selected patients, such as those with poor potential for neoneurotization from the periphery because of adjacent soft tissue injury or associated peripheral nerve injury.

▶ [Treatment of major soft tissue defects of the foot, especially in the weight-bearing area, has presented a tremendous therapeutic challenge. Free flap transfer techniques have improved greatly, as shown by the authors of this paper. They have demonstrated that in a patient who has been carefully selected, free flap transfer can be highly successful in the hands of a surgeon trained in its use. Not only does it have a great potential for improving the ultimate function of a patient who has sustained a very serious injury, but may offer a very viable alternative to amputation.—D.C. Campbell, II] ◀

PATIENTS WITH FREE SKIN FLAP TRANSFERS TO THE FOOT

Case	Donor site	Innervation	Initial hospitalization (days)	No. of secondary flap procedures	Result
			Heel defects		
1	Groin	Yes	8	0	Good
2	Groin	No	8	1	Excellent
3	Groin	No	6	0	Fair
4	Groin	No	6	0	Excellent
5	Tensor fascia lata	Yes	11	1	Good
			Plantar-forefoot defects		
6	Dorsalis pedis	Yes	15	0	Good
7	Tensor fascia lata	No	8	0	Excellent
			Dorsum-midfoot defects		
8	Latissimus dorsi	No	17	2	Good
9	Groin	No			Failed
			Medial-midfoot defects		
10	Latissimus dorsi	No	Not evaluated[a]	1	Excellent

[a]Hospital stay unrelated to flap transfer.
(Courtesy of Wood, M.B., et al.: Foot Ankle 4:2–7, July–Aug. 1983.)

11–14   **Osteochondritis of the Hallux Sesamoid Bones** is characterized by localized pain and tenderness under the first metatarsal head, and fragmentation and disorganization of the sesamoid seen on roentgenography. Michael E. Kliman, Allan E. Gross, Kenneth P. H. Pritzker, and N. David Greyson (Toronto) report 6 cases of osteochondritis of the hallux sesamoid bones, 4 of them treated surgically. All patients were young women who wore fashionable high-heeled shoes. Two were dancers, 1 was a marathon runner, and 1 patient had Marfan's syndrome with marked pes cavus. In 2 cases, the medial sesamoid was involved, and in 4, the lateral sesamoid was affected. Recently scanning has proved very helpful in distinguishing between congenitally divided and pathologically altered sesamoid bones. The pathologic findings reported here consisted of osteonecrosis with some evidence of recent fracture and callus. The condition appears to represent a stress fracture with secondary osteonecrosis.

Conservative treatment failed in 4 of the 6 cases. Subsequent excision was curative in all of these cases, although 1 patient required surgical release of a postoperative rigidus. A dorsomedial approach to the lateral sesamoid was used in 3 cases. A dorsolateral transarticular approach was used in the patient with rigidus. A plantar approach to the lateral sesamoid has been proposed, but the nerve may be cut. A dorsomedial approach provides ready access to the medial sesamoid and avoids a plantar scar.

(11–14)   Foot Ankle 3:220–223, Jan.–Feb. 1983.

12. Tumors

Osteogenic Sarcoma in the American Black. The incidence of cancer in black Americans has been increasing more rapidly than in whites, and survival rates are consistently lower in blacks with the most frequent types of cancer. Andrew G. Huvos, Avital Butler, and Sara S. Bretsky (Mem.-Sloan Kettering Cancer Center, New York) reviewed the outcome in 100 American blacks in whom osteogenic sarcoma was diagnosed between 1921 and 1979. A progressive increase in admissions was evident over the period, particularly in the

Fig 12–1.—Overall survival of all osteogenic sarcoma patients, comparing blacks and whites. There is no significant difference in survival (P = .77). (Courtesy of Huvos, A.G., et al.: Cancer 52:1959–1965, Nov. 15, 1983.)

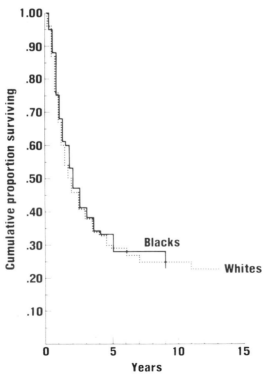

(12–1)   Cancer 52:1959–1965, Nov. 15, 1983.

1970s. Mean patient age was 19 years. Blacks were generally younger than whites at diagnosis; this was especially true of females. Sites of disease were generally similar to those in whites, except for more frequent involvement of the tibia and fibula and less frequent involvement of the humerus in blacks. The clinical stage at presentation, duration of symptoms, and histologic subclassification of tumors were similar in the two racial groups, and there were no significant differences in survival either for the entire duration of the study or for the period after 1974 (Fig 12–1). The overall 2- and 5-year disease-free survival rates for black patients were 42% and 32%, respectively. The 2-year disease-free survival of 36 patients treated after 1974 was 57%.

The generally poorer prognosis of cancer in black subjects does not seem to hold for osteogenic sarcoma. This may be attributed to an even distribution of prognostic factors or variables and to the fact that all patients have been treated comparably. The relatively less favorable survival of blacks with various types of cancer may be due in part to diagnosis at a relatively late stage of disease. Low socioeconomic status, poor overall health care, inadequate health education, and increased exposures to environmental or occupational pollutants, or both, appear to be more significant than any biologic differences.

▶ [Osteosarcoma is being studied extensively today, but epidemiologic studies analyzing racial differences have been lacking.—F.H. Sim] ◀

12–2 **Radiologic Imaging of Osteosarcoma: Role in Planning Surgical Treatment.** Precise anatomical localization of malignant bone tumors is necessary for proper selection of patients for limb salvage procedures. T. M. Hudson, M. Schiebler, D. S. Springfield, I. F. Hawkins, Jr., W. F. Enneking, and S. S. Spanier (Univ. of Florida) reviewed the radiologic findings in 50 cases of classic central osteosarcoma seen between 1976 and 1982. Fifteen patients had conventional tomography; the other 35 had computed tomographic (CT) scanning, often with contrast infusion. Forty bone scintigrams were also available, as were 42 arteriographic studies. Most of the tumors arose in tubular bones, most frequently the femur. Thirty-five had a mixed lytic-blastic appearance on plain x-ray films.

Major neurovascular involvement by tumor could be inferred from plain x-ray films in 30 cases. Few conventional tomograms added useful information, but several CT studies accurately defined soft tissue surgical margins of the tumor that were not evident on plain films. Most CT studies showed the tumor mass well enough for evaluation of its relation to major blood vessels. Many scintigrams showed an "extended" or "augmented" pattern of increased uptake beyond the true tumor margins. Nearly all angiograms showed typical malignant neovascularity and clearly indicated the relation of the tumor to

(12–2)   Skeletal Radiol. 10:137–146, 1984.

nearby major vessels. The critical surgical plane was defined in this way in a majority of cases.

The overall accuracy of radiologic evaluation in this series was high. Plain roentgenography frequently yielded most needed information on the extent of disease. Computed tomography usually showed accurately the intraosseous and extraosseous extent of disease and the reactive rims of the tumor. Scintigraphy was helpful in detecting metastases. Angiography was invaluable in demonstrating the relation of the tumor to major vessels where this was not clear from the CT findings.

▶ [Our experience generally parallels that of the authors'. Plain radiography still provides the most useful information in diagnosing osseous tumors. The computed tomography scan is extremely helpful in accurately assessing both the intraosseous and extraosseous extent of the lesion. When combined with infusion of contrast material, it usually provides the necessary information for making appropriate treatment decisions. Arteriography, in our experience, is rarely necessary in the preoperative assessment of malignant osseous lesions.—T.C. Shives] ◀

12–3 **Clear Cell Sarcoma: A Clinicopathologic Study of 27 Cases** seen at the Mayo Clinic from 1925 to 1980 is reported by Jeffrey J. Eckardt, Douglas J. Pritchard, and Edward H. Soule (Mayo Clinic and Found.). There were 18 females, average age 26 years, and 9 males, average age 33. All but 1 had a mass or swelling, and 9 had pain. The average duration of symptoms was 2½ years. Lesions tended to occur in the distal extremities, especially in the foot. Five patients had regional metastases and 1 had widespread disease at presentation. Five others had at least 1 prior local recurrence. Definitive surgery was done in all patients except for the 1 with widespread disease, in whom palliative radiotherapy was used. There were 2 incisional resections, 5 marginal resections, 18 wide resections including 12 amputations, and 1 radical amputation. Adjuvant therapy was not standardized, but generally was used in patients with regional or disseminated disease.

Twenty local recurrences developed in 10 patients during an average follow-up of 7 years. Six of these patients died of disseminated sarcoma, and only 2 were alive and well at last follow-up. Eight of the 9 patients with regional node metastasis died of widespread disease. Twelve patients in all had dissemination beyond the regional nodes; all those who died of sarcoma had pulmonary metastases, and 5 had metastatic lesions in bone. Both patients with widespread disease who survived had terminal disease at last follow-up. Eleven of the 14 survivors have been without evident disease for an average of 7½ years.

Patients with clear cell sarcoma have a poor outlook. Wide excision or "wide" amputation remains the best surgical approach, although radical extracompartmental resection might be considered. Immedi-

(12–3) Cancer 52:1482–1488, Oct. 15, 1983.

ate adjunctive radiotherapy may have a role in the management of these patients. The long interval between onset of disease and final dissemination emphasizes the need for prolonged regular evaluation.

▶ [The authors review 27 cases of clear cell sarcoma seen over 55 years at the Mayo Clinic. They emphasize that this is a primarily soft tissue tumor associated with the tendons and aponeuroses, occurring more commonly in the distal aspects of the extremities. It has a poor prognosis, as only 11 of the 27 patients remained free of disease. They emphasize that wide excision or possibly amputation would be the treatment of choice, although they were not able to specifically prove one method superior to another.—J.R. Cass] ◀

12–4 **Malignant Fibrous Histiocytoma Arising in Previous Surgical Sites: Report of Two Cases.** Malignant fibrous histiocytoma has been described as developing after radiotherapy and arising in association with bone infarcts and fractures. Tsuyoshi Inoshita and George A. Youngberg (Johnson City, Tenn.) describe malignant fibrous histiocytoma in 2 patients that developed in sites of previous surgery, 1 in an amputation stump and 1 in a hernioplasty scar. In the first patient, a man aged 92, a mass developed about 6 years postoperatively in the stump of an above-knee amputation done for arteriosclerotic gangrene. The chiefly subcutaneous tumor was a myxoid variant of malignant fibrous histiocytoma. The patient was well 22 months after tumor removal. The other patient, a man aged 35, had a tumor containing very large atypical cells that occurred in a hernioplasty scar. The diagnosis was malignant fibrous histiocytoma with a predominantly pleomorphic histiocytic pattern. The patient, who was given radiotherapy, was well 10 months after tumor resection. He also was found to have two small dermatofibromas.

Malignant fibrous histiocytoma is a sarcoma of uncertain histogenesis. Both fibroblast-like cells and histiocyte-like cells are present in varying proportions, classically in a storiform pattern and often accompanied by pleomorphic tumor giant cells and inflammatory cells. Myxoid, inflammatory, and angiomatoid variants have been recognized. At least 16 tumors have been reported to develop after radiotherapy for various types of malignancy. Bone infarcts and fractures also may precede the development of these neoplasms. Findings in the present patients represent the development of malignant fibrous histiocytoma in association with other chronic reparative reactions. Some persons may be at increased risk for the development of a fibrohistiocytic reaction.

▶ [In all such cases the possibility of coincidence must be considered.—D.J. Pritchard] ◀

12–5 **Sarcoma Complicating Paget's Disease of Bone: Clinicopathologic Study of 62 Cases.** Sarcoma is the most serious complication of Paget's disease of bone. Fritz Schajowicz, Eduardo Santini Araujo,

(12–4)   Cancer 53:176–183, Jan. 1, 1984.
(12–5)   J. Bone Joint Surg. [Br.] 65-B:299–307, May 1983.

and Mario Berenstein (WHO, Buenos Aires) reviewed 62 cases of sarcoma complicating Paget's disease, representing 6% of all cases registered in 1 center in 1940–1981. Two other cases were associated with giant cell tumor of bone without evidence of malignancy. There was only a slight male predominance. The peak incidence was at ages 50–70 years. The most frequent sites were the femur (37%), the pelvis (16%), the humerus (14.5%), and the tibia (14.5%). Most cases of sarcoma occurred in patients with polyostotic disease. Frequently, multipole foci of sarcoma developed nearly simultaneously in different areas of the same bone or in different bones. The most prevalent symptoms were swelling and increased pain. Local injury was noted in only 1 case. The alkaline phosphatase concentration usually rose abruptly, but levels were quite variable. The radiographic findings depend largely on the histologic type of tumor.

Osteosarcoma was present in nearly two thirds of cases; fibrosarcoma, in about a fourth of cases. The histologic findings were similar to those seen in sarcomas arising in normal bone, but often there was more anaplasia. One lesion involved the clavicle, a rare site of Paget's sarcoma. Only a few reported patients have lived more than 5 years after amputation or disarticulation. Only 1 of the present patients lived more than 5 years, after midthigh amputation for an upper tibial fibrosarcoma.

There appears to be a close histopathogenetic relationship between Paget's disease of bone and associated sarcoma. Sarcomas have consistently developed in bones already affected by Paget's disease. Although these sarcomas are relatively rare, their absolute number is significant because of the prevalence of Paget's disease. Not all tumors associated with Paget's disease of bone are highly malignant.

▶ [This report of a large series offers considerable information about this relatively unusual problem. Our experience is similar.—D.J. Pritchard.] ◀

12–6 **Bone Sarcomas in Paget's Disease.** Harry G. Greditzer III, Richard A. McLeod, Krishnan K. Unni, and John W. Beabout (Mayo Clinic) reviewed the records of 41 patients with Paget's disease and bone sarcoma, representing 0.9% of all patients with Paget's disease who were seen during the review period. Only 1 patient remains alive. All patients but 3 were aged 50 years and older at the time of diagnosis; the mean age was 64 years. The most common sites of involvement by Paget's sarcoma were the pelvis, femur, humerus, skull, tibia, and scapula. Most long-bone tumors were found in a metaphyseal location. Most patients were initially seen with either acute pain or increased chronic pain, and over two thirds had a palpable mass. The average duration of symptoms before diagnosis was 6 months. Thirty-five patients had osteosarcoma, and 6, fibrosarcoma. All but 2 lesions had grade 3 or grade 4 features. Twelve pa-

(12–6) Radiology 146:327–333, February 1983.

tients had distant disease at first visit, usually in the lung. Lytic features were most frequent (Fig 12–2), and all fibrosarcomas were of the lytic type. Some cases exhibited both lytic and blastic features. Tumors with a predominantly blastic pattern were rare. Both cortical destruction and contiguous soft-tissue involvement were present in most evaluable patients. Only 1 patient had multiple blastic lesions.

Eighteen patients underwent radical ablative surgery, and 6 of these had subsequent chemotherapy and radiotherapy. Nineteen patients with tumors not amenable to surgery had primary radiotherapy. Three patients were treated palliatively for pain, and 1 tumor was found at autopsy. The 5-year survival was 8%, and only 3 patients lived more than 10 years. Thirty-three deaths were directly related to primary or metastatic tumor. One patient was alive 9 months after diagnosis.

Paget's sarcoma is an uncommon complication of Paget's disease,

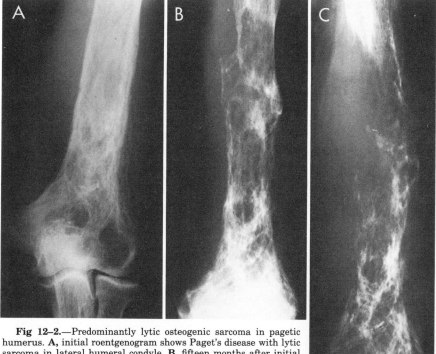

Fig 12–2.—Predominantly lytic osteogenic sarcoma in pagetic humerus. **A,** initial roentgenogram shows Paget's disease with lytic sarcoma in lateral humeral condyle. **B,** fifteen months after initial roentgenogram, tumor has progressed to involve about one third of the distal humerus. Note healing pathologic fracture. **C,** twenty months after initial roentgenogram, tumor now involves more than half of the humerus. Note extensive destruction of humerus and soft-tissue mass. (Courtesy of Greditzer, H.G., III et al.: Radiology 146:327–333, February 1983.)

but it accounts for one-fifth of osteogenic sarcomas in persons aged 50 years and older. Most lesions involve the axial skeleton, and most are lytic on roentgenography. A few patients have lived without disease for more than 10 years. Most long-term survivors have had lesions in the extremities and underwent amputation as primary treatment.

12–7 **Pelvic Ewing's Sarcoma: Advances in Treatment.** William K. Li, Joseph M. Lane, Gerald Rosen, Ralph C. Marcove, Brenda Caparros, Andrew Huvos, and Susan Groshen (Meml. Sloan-Kettering Cancer Center, New York) reviewed the results of a multidisciplinary approach to primary Ewing's sarcoma of the pelvis in 18 previously untreated patients, 14 of whom had no evidence of metastasis initially. Eight patients were managed without surgery but with chemotherapy and irradiation. Ten had prolonged preoperative chemotherapy, wide resection of the tumor, low-dose radiotherapy to the tumor site, and further chemotherapy. The 4 patients who presented with pulmonary metastases received whole-lung irradiation after treatment of the primary tumor. In later cases, continuous combination chemotherapy was used for 6 months. The most recent protocol includes cyclophosphamide, Adriamycin, methotrexate, bleomycin, dactinomycin, and vincristine. The median follow-up from the start of treatment was 3 years.

Ten (56%) patients were free of disease after a median of 57 months. All patients had objective evidence of tumor regression after combination chemotherapy. Five of the 8 patients not operated on had a relapse, as did 3 of the 10 patients who had had surgery. The patients who had had wide resection had a 3-year survival rate of 80% and a disease-free survival rate of 70%. No significant complications resulted from perioperative chemotherapy. The presence of pulmonary metastases at presentation did not preclude disease-free survival.

The use of computed tomographic scanning (Figs 12–3, 12–4, and 12–5) in conjunction with angiography and bone scanning has greatly improved surgical planning in these cases. Aggressive chemotherapy substantially reduces the soft tissue tumor burden, making surgery more effective. Wide resection now is considered if the femoral nerve and vessels are free of tumor; tumor is limited to the hemipelvis and/ or a resectable part of the sacrum; the pelvic organs are uninvolved; the proximal third of the femur is free of tumor; and widespread metastases are not present. Seven of 10 patients in the present series lived without disease for more than 3 years after surgery, chemotherapy, and radiotherapy.

▶ [The prognosis for pelvic Ewing's sarcoma is worse than for the same tumor aris-

(12–7)   J. Bone Joint Surg. [Am.] 65-A:737–747, July 1983.

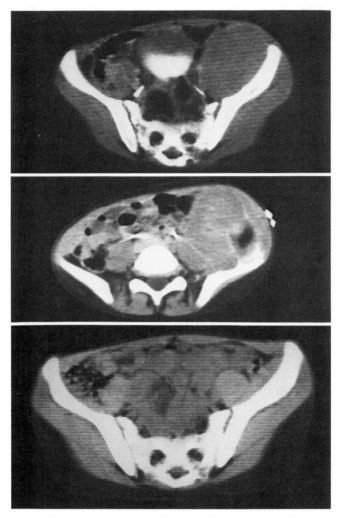

Fig 12–3 (top).—Computed tomographic (CT) scan of 9-year-old boy with Ewing's sarcoma of left ilium before chemotherapy.

Fig 12–4 (center).—Another CT scan before chemotherapy also shows significant soft tissue mass.

Fig 12–5 (bottom).—Scan after chemotherapy shows 90% reduction in size of tumor.

(Courtesy of Li, W.K., et al.: J. Bone Joint Surg. [Am.] 65-A:737–747, July 1983.)

ing in other sites. The results obtained in this report are encouraging. We still need to refine our treatment procedures, utilizing all known effective modalities in various combinations.—D.J. Pritchard] ◄

12–8 **Periosteal Chondroma: Review of 20 Cases.** Periosteal chon-

(12–8) J. Bone Joint Surg. [Am] 65-A:205–212, February 1983.

droma is a benign chondroid tumor arising under or in the periosteum on the surface of cortical bone. About 60 cases have been reported since 1952. S. Boriani, P. Bacchini, F. Bertoni, and M. Campanacci (Bologna, Italy) reviewed data on 20 patients with periosteal chondroma who were followed up for an average of 7 years. Fourteen patients were males; adolescents and young adults predominated. All lesions but 1 arose in a tubular bone, and most were at or near the end of the diaphysis. Six patients had lesions in the proximal humerus, and 5 had tumors involving hand bones. Swelling followed by moderate pain was the most common presenting pattern. The average duration of symptoms was 21 months.

Periosteal chondroma typically produces scalloping of the bone cortex, with a well-defined tumor-bone margin. The tumor bed shows a variable degree of sclerosis. In 7 cases, protruding or overhanging edges

Fig 12–6 (left).—Metacarpal periosteal chondroma with evident scalloping showing continuous border encircling the tumor.

Fig 12–7 (right).—Periosteal chondroma arising in proximal part of diaphysis of humerus with cortical bone showing evident scalloping, with mild sclerosis and without calcified matrix.

(Courtesy of Boriani, S., et al.: J. Bone Joint Surg. [Am.] 65-A:205–212, February 1983.)

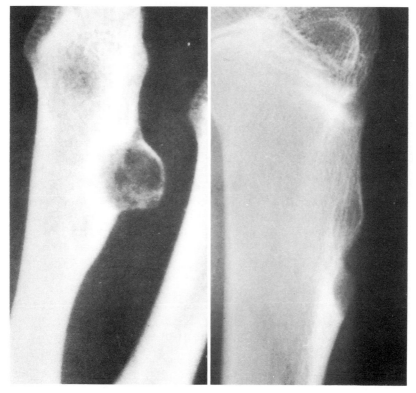

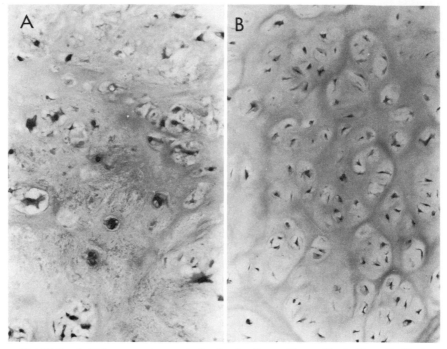

Fig 12–8.—**A,** high-power micrograph showing hyaline cartilage with starlike cells, **B,** chondroma in which enlarged hyperchromic, binucleated cells are seen. Hematoxylin & eosin; ×400. (Courtesy of Boriani, S., et al.: J. Bone Joint Surg. [Am.] 65-A:205–212, February 1983.)

completely encircled the lesion (Fig 12–6). Only 4 tumors lacked calcification or ossification of the cartilaginous matrix (Fig 12–7). These changes were striking in 7 instances. The tumors were as large as 7 × 4 cm. Immature cartilage was the predominant tissue type. Star-like cells and binucleated cells are shown in Figure 12–8. Three lesions were soft and myxoid. Mitotic figures were not seen but, where binucleated cells were frequent, nuclear pleomorphism was evident. A fibrous capsule was invariably present, and the soft tissues never were invaded.

Periosteal chondromas tend to occur at the proximal ends of long bones, especially the humerus, and in the bones of the hand. The lesion usually is graded 2 or 3 on a scale of 1 to 4 with respect to anaplasia. Marginal excision usually is effective treatment. It is important to avoid misdiagnosing this benign lesion as a more threatening tumor.

▶ [Our experience is similar.—D.J. Pritchard.] ◀

12–9 **Resection Alloplasty in Treatment of Certain Malignant Bone Tumors.** Custom-made endoprosthetic devices offer the possibility of

(12–9) Cancer 52:2180–2184, Dec. 1, 1983.

radical surgery for tumor with preservation of the affected extremity. Hakon Kofoed and Søren Solgaard (Univ. of Copenhagen) managed 13 patients seen from 1976 to 1981 with malignant bone tumors of the extremities by alloplastic replacement of the involved bone. The 7 men and 6 women had an average of 54 years. Seven patients had grade 2A or 2B primary bone tumors, and 3 others had solitary involvement by tumor that might involve other organs. All patients initially had open biopsy of the tumor. A custom-made device was used when a suitable resection device was not available. All devices were fixed using methyl methacrylate.

There were no infections and no clinical evidence of thromboembolism. One patient had temporary peroneal palsy. Early hip dislocation in 2 patients was managed by closed reduction. The 10 surviving patients were followed for an average of 4½ years. They remained in good clinical condition considering the extent of surgery that was necessary. No radiologic loosening was observed. Only 1 of 9 survivors with a device in the lower extremity required constant support in walking. Most patients were able to continue working.

Resection alloplasty is worthwhile in patients with various malignant bone tumors in the extremities. Secondary malignant tumors can be treated with good functional results in such patients, but the procedure does not seem to influence length of survival. An alloplastic procedure can be done primarily in older patients. Young patients with a long survival expectancy can have allografting primarily, with resection alloplasty reserved for use as a secondary procedure.

▶ [We agree with the authors that resection arthroplasty has a definite role in the management of primary malignant tumors of bone in carefully selected patients. While prosthetic replacement has definite advantages over other techniques and the early results have been very encouraging, the major concern is for late loosening of the prosthesis. Recent improvements in the design of these tumor prostheses should improve their durability.—F.H. Sim] ◀

12–10 **Modular System for Total Femur Replacement: Endo-Modell.**® **Development, Model Description, Operative Procedure** are discussed by E. Nieder, E. Engelbrecht, K. Steinbrink, and A. Keller (Hamburg, Federal Republic of Germany). Total femur replacement may offer a useful solution in cases of severe trauma or neoplasia; in revision arthroplasty when total joint replacement has failed, when a gross loss of bone has resulted in an unstable femur, and when no other method of treatment would provide a stable leg. Until recently, total femur components were custom-made, but now a comprehensive modular femur implant is available that reduces problems of preoperative preparation and simplifies the manufacture of custom-made designs.

In 1965 the first total femur replacement was anatomically shaped and made from cobalt chromium. Nine years later the material used

(12–10) Chirurg 54:391–399, June 1983.

was polyethylene. Then the femur was further modified by reinforcing the middle part with a metal netting to obtain greater stability. Between 1973 and 1980 the construction of the implant model changed. The first polyethylene femur proved to be subject to breakage, and titanium was used for later models. The new device can be shaped and adapted to the condition encountered at the time of preparation. One author proposed the push-through prosthesis which makes the maintenance of bone possible, although not for functional support but as muscle and tension attachment, as a physiologic implant cover, and in providing natural patellary function. This type of prosthesis can be mounted step by step and converted into a total femur replacement with either a conventional head or a saddle at the proximal end and a total axial rotating knee prosthesis at the distal end. Elongation of the entire system is feasible. Natural structures should be maintained as much as possible. Removed parts of the bone can be replaced with polyethylene segments. In septic patients, however, antibiotic cement is used.

Alternatives to total femur replacement that permit maintenance of the limb but do not involve implant methods are built-up plastics with autologous or homologous bones, resection arthroplasties and arthrodoses. Build-up plastics are especially recommended for younger patients, avoiding failure of alloplastic methods. This method is not used for older patients in whom the healing process is slow or for patients who do not have enough bone available for transplant. The resection arthroplasty is satisfactory in treating the hip but is less satisfactory for the knee. Serious defects limit the use of resection arthroplasty, since severe shortening leads to ineffectiveness of muscles, instability, and the telescope phenomenon. Arthrodosis should only be considered if only the joint is involved. Total femur replacement may be indicated in osteomyelitis when all other treatments have failed.

▶ [The authors are accumulating a great deal of worthwhile experiences in the design and application of a total femur prosthesis to reconstruct the limb following resection either of bone tumors or of their non-neoplastic conditions. However, our experience in over 100 patients with extensive neoplastic or non-neoplastic involvement of the proximal femur indicates that successful results can be achieved by proximal femoral replacement arthroplasty. We do not feel that skip metastasis are a clinical problem. A cross bone resection with a safe margin is adequate to prevent local recurrence.—F.H. Sim] ◀

12–11 **Etiology and Treatment of Simple Bone Cysts.** The cause of simple bone cysts is unclear, and since direct evidence of venous obstruction is lacking, the proper treatment is controversial. Masaki Chigira, Susumu Maehara, Satoru Arita, and Eiichi Udagawa (Gumma Univ.) managed 7 patients who had simple bone cysts by drilling multiple holes with Kirschner wires. Internal cyst pressure

(12–11) J. Bone Joint Surg. [Br] 65-B:633–637, November 1983.

was measured in 4 cases, and partial gas pressures were estimated in 3. The cysts were drilled percutaneously with wires 2 mm in diameter; the diaphyseal side of the cyst wall was perforated in several places. Two or three wires were left in place for drainage.

Internal cyst pressures were slightly higher than pressures in normal marrow in the contralateral limb, and the intracystic pressures declined during drilling. The P_{O_2} of cyst fluid was lower than that of venous blood in the same patients, but the P_{CO_2} values were similar to those in arterial and venous blood, and no differences in base excess, pH, or bicarbonate were found. Reconstruction of the cortical bone of the cyst wall was generally seen 2 to 3 months after drilling, when the cyst cavity had become radiopaque. New bone formation was evident 3 to 5 months after treatment, and healing generally was observed within 6 to 8 months (Figs 12–9 and 12–10). In 2 cases a small cyst reappeared in the same area 4 to 5 months after removal of the Kirschner wire. One patient failed to respond within 8 months and underwent curettage and bone grafting.

Obstruction of venous drainage appears to be the primary cause of

Fig 12–9 (left).—Anteroposterior roentgenogram made before operation.
Fig 12–10 (right).—Result 8 months after operation. Wires were removed at 17 months.
(Courtesy of Chigira, M., et al.: J. Bone Joint Surg. [Br.] 65-B:633–637, November 1983.)

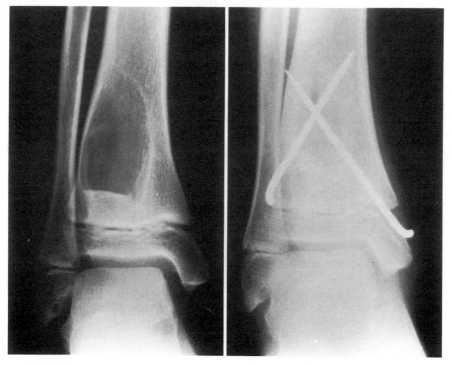

simple bone cysts. Multiple drilling may act by producing an immunologic response that in some way helps prevent recurrences. It is more likely that the wires keep the holes in the cyst wall open, permitting fluid to escape. Drilling appears to be the best treatment for simple bone cysts in young persons. Whether it is necessary to leave the wires in place remains to be determined.

▶ [I am not certain that the authors have "clearly demonstrated that obstruction of venous drainage is the primary cause of simple bone cysts," nor am I convinced that "the multiple drill-hole method is the best treatment of simple bone cysts in youth." Nevertheless, the paper is interesting. It may well be that clinical improvement after aspiration and injection with methylprednisolone, as noted by many observers, is due more to the drill-holes that are necessary to introduce the steroid preperation than to the steroid itself.—D.J. Pritchard] ◀

12–12   **Localization of Osteoid Osteomas: Use of Radionuclide Scanning and Autoimaging in Identifying the Nidus.** Osteoid osteoma is a small, painful intraosseous abnormality that consists of a nidus of irregular osteoid and calcified matrix lined by osteoblasts and osteoclasts, often surrounded by reactive, radiodense bone. Surgical excision is curative, but it may be difficult to localize the lesion both surgically and pathologically because of its small size and its location within cortical bone.

Vincent J. Vigorita and Bernard Ghelman (Hosp. for Special Surgery, New York) used preoperative radionuclide scanning to localize osteoid osteoma during surgery in 3 cases and for autoradiographic identification of the nidus pathologically. Patients received 10 mCi of ^{99m}Tc-methylene diphosphonate (^{99m}Tc-MDP) 4 hours before operation and were examined during operation by using a sterilized NaI scintillation probe and a scale rate meter. Autoimaging on undeveloped film was positive in all 3 cases. The most intensely imaged fragment corresponded to the nidus. The nidus was identified by fine-grain specimen films in only 1 of these cases.

Radionuclide scanning with ^{99m}Tc-MDP can effectively localize osteoid osteomas at operation. Autoimaging is useful for pathologic identification of the nidus of the lesion. This approach should reduce the incidence of false negative reports, which presumably are due to sampling errors.

▶ [We have seldom used intraoperative probing following preoperative ^{99m}Tc-methylene diphosphonate injection. However, this technique has, on occasion, been useful in localizing an osteoid osteoma in an anatomically difficult area.—T.C. Shives] ◀

12–13   **Spinal Enostoses (Bone Islands).** Enostoses are bone islands or focal sclerotic lesions of medullary bone that may occur at any skeletal site but are most frequent in the axial skeleton, particularly the ilia and ribs. Spinal enostoses are considered rare. Donald Resnick, Albert A. Nemcek, Jr., and Parvis Haghighi (Univ. of California, San

(12–12) Am. J. Clin. Pathol. 79:223–225, February 1983.
(12–13) Radiology 147:373–376, May 1983.

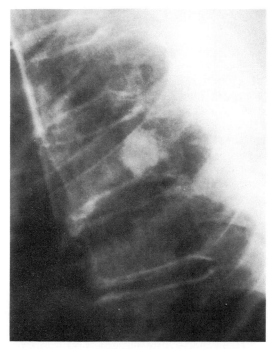

Fig 12–11.—Large spinal enostoses. Radiodense lesion, measuring 12 × 11 mm, involves posterior half of T-5 vertebral body and has brush-like radiations. Lesion did not change in size on serial radiographs over 2-week period. (Courtesy of Resnick, D., et al.: Radiology 147:373–376, May 1983.)

Diego) undertook a prospective study of the anterior aspect of the thoracolumbar spine in 100 consecutive cadavers, 99 men and 1 woman, aged 46–93 years. Radiographs were made in the frontal and lateral projections before the specimens were sectioned. Enostoses

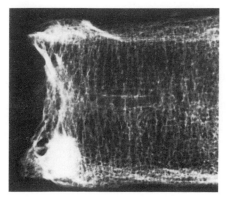

Fig 12–12.—Enostosis of T-10 vertebral body. Radiodense lesion in anteroinferior aspect measures 5 × 5 mm and has radiating spicules at margin. Lesion has intimate relationship with anterior surface of vertebral body and diskovertebral margin. (Courtesy of Resnick, D., et al.: Radiology 147:373–376, May 1983.)

were found in 14% of the cadavers. The roentgenographic appearances are shown in Figures 12–11 and 12–12. One cadaver had 2 lesions. Eight of the 15 enostoses were in thoracic vertebrae; and 7, in the lumbar spine. They ranged in size from 2 × 2 to 6 × 10 cm. The enostoses generally were circular or oblong, and they usually had irregular or spiculated borders. Histologic study of 5 lesions showed lamellar compact bone with normal haversian systems and no cartilaginous or fibrous elements. In 2 cases, part of the lesion contained cells resembling chondrocytes and locally calcified interstitial substance.

Enostoses are not infrequent in the thoracic and lumbar vertebrae, but their small size accounts for their being found infrequently by radiologists. The lesions can become large, however, and serial radiographs may show growth. Histologic study generally shows a well-defined focus of lamellar bone with radiating trabeculae that merge with the surrounding bone. Enostoses usually can be distinguished readily from osteomyelitis, or osteonecrosis, skeletal metastases, and other benign bone neoplasms. It is possible that abnormalities in development of the junction of the disk and vertebra result in cartilaginous nests or nodules within the vertebral body, which may then serve as a substrate for the development of spinal enostoses.

▶ [This paper provides an excellent review of benign enostosis of the spine. The incidence and awareness of this entity has increased in recent years and is reported by the current authors to be 14%.

It is important to differentiate these benign lesions from blastic metastases. This can be accomplished radiographically by using the criteria set forth by the authors, which include the fact that the benign lesions tend to be single, are frequently along the vertebral margin, and possess a spiculated margin.—T.H. Berquist] ◀

12–14 **Osteofibrous Dysplasia (Ossifying Fibroma of Long Bones): Study of 12 Cases.** Yasuaki Nakashima, Takao Yamamuro, Yuzo Fujiwara, Yoshihiko Kotoura, Eigo Mori, and Yoshihiro Hamashima reviewed the findings in 12 cases of osteofibrous dysplasia. The 9 girls and 3 boys had an average age of 5 years at diagnosis. Seven patients presented with tibial swelling; 4 with local pain. The average duration of symptoms was 1 month. The tibia was involved in all cases, bilaterally in 1 patient, and 1 patient also had involvement of the ipsilateral fibula. Roentgenograms showed solitary or multiple lytic lesions with thinning and expansion of the cortex (Figs 12–13, 12–14, and 12–15). The periosteum was unaltered. The lesions were generally eccentrically located and surrounded by bone sclerosis. Many patients had a bowing deformity.

Ten patients were managed primarily by curettage, with or without bone grafting, and all had recurrences. Two recent patients treated by biopsy only had no evidence of progression of disease on follow-up of 13 and 23 months, respectively. No spontaneous regression was evident in any case. The typical histologic findings were variably cellular

(12–14) Cancer 52:909–914, Sept. 1, 1983.

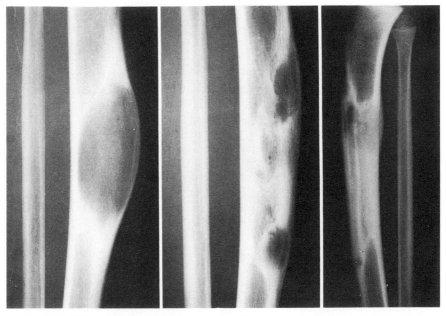

Fig 12–13 (left).—Osteofibrous dysplasia with unilocular area of rarefaction in tibia of 3-year-old girl. Treatment consisted of curettage and bone graft.

Fig 12–14 (center).—First recurrence at age of 4 years, 10 months after primary treatment.

Fig 12–15 (right).—Second recurrence at age of 5 years. Complete resection of lesion was performed.

(Courtesy of Nakashima, Y., et al.: Cancer 52:909–914, Sept. 1, 1983.)

fibroblastic proliferation in a storiform pattern with osteoid or bony trabeculae. Hemorrhage and necrosis were not evident in uncomplicated lesions. Mitotic figures were rare. Both the amount of trabeculae and the degree of calcification of trabeculae were variable. Cartilaginous foci were seen in 2 cases. Giant cells often were seen close to trabeculae. No changes of malignancy were apparent in any case.

The cause of osteofibrous dysplasia is unknown. It is not clear whether it represents a primary neoplasm of bone or a congenital anomaly. The lesion has a marked tendency to recur, but malignant changes have not been reported. Surgery may result in cure in patients over age 10 years, but ablative surgery is contraindicated in younger patients. Bracing may help prevent fractures. Conservative surgery may be necessary in patients with pseudarthrosis. There is no place for radiotherapy in the treatment of osteofibrous dysplasia.

▶ [Our experience is comparable.—D.J. Pritchard] ◀

12–15 **Closed Vertebral Biopsy.** Some but not all workers have found

(12–15) J. Bone Joint Surg. [Br.] 65-B:140–143, March 1983.

needle aspiration biopsy of vertebrae to be diagnostically useful. I. S. Fyfe, A. P. J. Henry, and R. C. Mulholland sought to clarify the factors that influence the results of vertebral biopsy in 100 consecutive cases in which spinal biopsy was carried out. A wide range of pathologic states was represented. Over a third of patients had multifocal disease. The peak number of lesions were in patients aged 50 to 70 years. All but 6 biopsies were made in the thoracic and lumbar regions. Standard image intensification or fluoroscopic control was used. The Harlow Wood vertebral biopsy needle was employed in 52 cases in an attempt to obtain a large specimen with minimal damage to surrounding soft tissue. Usually two specimens were obtained for histologic and bacteriologic studies.

Forty-four patients had marked tenderness over the spine at the level of the lesion, and 34 had some neurologic involvement at the outset. Biopsy of 52 large specimens yielded a diagnosis in 90% of cases, compared with 50% for 48 small samples. Small samples were adequate for diagnosis of tuberculosis, osteomyelitis, and myeloma, but not metastases. Complications occurred in 11 large-needle biopsies and 15 small-needle examinations. Pulmonary complications occurred only in the small-needle series. All nerve root lesions occurred with large-needle biopsies. There were no injuries to major vessels.

Needle or trephine biopsy of bone has many advantages. It is simple and does not interfere with subsequent radiotherapy, and it can be done with general or local anesthesia. Small trephines can damage specimens and tend to yield a cytologic smear rather than a histologic block of tissue. Trephines yielding specimens 2 mm or more in diameter can be expected to have a high degree of diagnostic accuracy. Patients with painful thoracic metastases and evidence of progressive cord compression should have early decompression after open biopsy rather than needle biopsy.

▶ [The authors present a series of needle biopsies of thoracic and lumbar spinal lesions in 100 patients. The number of pathologic conditions is quite variable. The authors note a significant number of complications totaling one quarter of their entire series. This complication rate alone is enough to raise concern with this technique.

The utility of the small biopsies is questioned with only a 50% yield using a needle that is less than 2 mm. The ability of the pathologist to read the biopsy depends on the pathology and the pathologist's familiarity with reviewing small samples. The problem of sampling arises when using a small core biopsy which may not be representative of the tissue of the entire tumor. This is especially true in primary bone tumors, but may be less of a problem with a metastatic lesion. The authors appropriately stress extreme caution in using this technique for thoracic metastasis or progressive cord compression because of potential further neurologic compromise.

This technique should be reserved for the individual with an obvious metastatic lesion without neurologic compromise, and should be performed by an experienced surgeon. It is wise to consult a pathologist prior to performing a needle biopsy to see if this would be an adequate sample for his evaluation.—J.A. Rand] ◀

12–16 **Sonographic Correlation in Extremity Soft Tissue Masses.** Jerry S. Apples, Salutario Martinez, Pamela A. Nelson, Eric R. Rosenberg, John M. Harrelson, and James D. Bowie (Duke Univ.) reviewed the ultrasonographic findings in 24 patients with clinical soft tissue masses of the extremities, excluding popliteal cysts. Surgical confirmation was available for 22 cases. A static or real-time gray-scale unit was used. Thirteen patients also underwent computed tomography (CT), 10 had xeroradiography, and 21 had plain roentgenography.

There were 11 fluids collections, 11 neoplasms, and 2 vascular lesions. The thigh and arm were the most common sites of the masses. All neoplasms except a metastatic lung cancer were solid. The fluid collections included 4 hematomas and 3 epidermal inclusion cysts. Ultrasound study correctly predicted 11 lesions of solid echogenicity, 8 of mixed echogenicity, and 2 with purely cystic components. Two solid masses were misdiagnosed as predominantly cystic; both were sarcomas. A benign fibroma initially was thought to be a mixed lesion. Computed tomography was more useful than ultrasound in 9 of 13 cases in determining the tissue composition of a lesion or the relation of the mass to adjacent bone. Ultrasound was more useful in 4 cases by showing internal echoes in lesions that on CT were near water density or by defining vascular channels in small hemangiomas. Ultrasound was more useful than xeroradiography in defining internal structure in 9 of 10 cases, but xeroradiography was better for identifying involvement of adjacent bone.

Computed tomography appears to be generally better than ultrasonography for evaluating extremity soft tissue masses, but ultrasound is helpful by detecting internal echoes in masses that appear to be near water density on CT. Plain roentgenography or xeroradiography should be performed initially and CT considered next to evaluate the density of the lesion. A sharp back wall and increased sound transmission are necessary for diagnosis of a cystic mass by ultrasonography.

12–17 **Pigmented Villonodular Synovitis (Giant Cell Tumor of Tendon Sheath and Synovial Membrane): Review of Eighty-One Cases.** A. Srinivasa Rao and Vincent J. Vigorita (New York Hosp.-Cornell Univ.) reviewed the findings in 81 patients with pigmented villonodular synovitis or giant cell tumor of the tendon sheath seen between 1970 and 1981. More than half of the lesions were in the finger or thumb, and more than a quarter in the knee. The average patient age was 41.5 years; patients with finger or thumb lesions were older than those with knee lesions. Females predominated. Seventy lesions were histologically nodular, and 11 were classified as vil-

(12–16) Med. Imaging 1:75–81, January 1984.
(12–17) J. Bone Joint Surg. [Am.] 66-A:76–94, January 1984.

lonodular. Most were at least partly encapsulated. Bone and cartilage were not noted except in 1 knee lesion. Fibrosis was moderate in 37 lesions and marked in 5. Mitoses were present in 43 lesions. Inflammation was evident in 20 instances.

Of 35 patients followed up for 3–144 months, 7 had recurrent lesions after surgery for pigmented villonodular synovitis performed elsewhere. Four of the other 28 patients, followed up for an average of 43 months, had recurrences. Three of 4 toe lesions recurred. There was no evidence of a relationship between the number of mitoses present initially and recurrence in the 5 evaluable lesions. All 5 recurrent lesions contained mitoses, however, whereas only 1 had mitoses initially.

Pigmented villonodular synovitis and giant cell tumors of the tendon sheath are neoplasm-like proliferations of collagen-producing polyhedral cells, often associated with multinucleated giant cells; the lesions appear to originate in the subsynovial fibroblasts or fibrohistiocytes. Excision of all nodules appears to be necessary to prevent recurrence. The cause of the lesion remains obscure.

12–18 **Neurilemomas and Neurofibromas of Upper Limb.** Neurilemoma and neurofibroma are the most common solitary neoplasms of the peripheral nerves of the upper extremity. Elio Rinaldi (Parma, Italy) reviewed data concerning 9 solitary neoplasms in the upper limb, 5 neurilemomas and 4 neurofibromas. The neurilemomas were derived from proliferation of the Schwann cells of a single nerve funiculus. They were slow-growing, completely encapsulated neoplasms with a pedicle. Few symptoms are present in affected patients. Careful intraneural dissection under optimal magnification is used to re-

Fig 12–16.—Mobilization of the ulnar nerve and enucleation of a rounded pedunculated intraneural mass in patient with neurilemoma. (Courtesy of Rinaldi, E.: J. Hand Surg. 8:590–593, September 1983.)

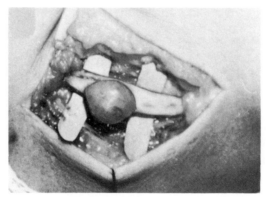

(12–18) J. Hand Surg. 8:590–593, September 1983.

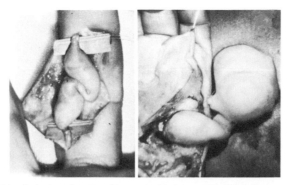

Fig 12–17 (left).—Isolation of a neurofibroma arising from the digital nerve.
Fig 12–18 (right).—Slow-growing tumor of 2 years' duration affected the hypothenar eminence. A large, multilobular, firm mass arising from a palmar sensory branch of the ulnar nerve was isolated.
(Courtesy of Rinaldi, E.: J. Hand Surg. 8:590–593, September 1983.)

move these tumors, but their enucleation is always possible, leaving the remaining funicular groups intact and functioning (Fig 12–16). Nerve resection is never indicated. Two patients had median and 3 had ulnar nerve lesions. All did well for 3 years or more after surgical enucleation.

The neurofibroma (Figs 12–17 and 12–18) can invade and destroy the funicular structure of the involved nerve because of its origin from the connective tissue of the endoneurium and perineurium surrounding the axons and Schwann cells. Intraneural dissection is not possible. Complete resection of the involved part of the nerve is necessary for tumor removal. Direct suture is possible if the gap does not exceed 1 cm. Otherwise, nerve grafting can be done, or nerve discontinuity can be left unrestored if significant functional damage is not present. Three of the present patients had simple resection leading to purely sensory loss that was considered acceptable. One patient had nerve grafting of a defect of the ulnar digital nerve of the long finger.

▶ [This article gives a nice and concise differentiation between neurilemomas and neurofibromas and reiterates well-known information which might be overlooked by the occasional surgeon.—B.M. Onofrio] ◀

12–19 **Post-Traumatic Osteolysis of Pubic Bone Simulating a Malignant Lesion.** Goergen et al., in 1978, described an unusual lytic healing pattern that simulated malignant disease after pubic bone fracture in 3 patients with a remote or absent history of trauma. Ferris M. Hall, Ronald P. Goldberg, Earl J. Kasdon, and Hyman Glick (Harvard Med. School) encountered 4 patients with similar radiographic findings after trauma. Two underwent an extensive workup and open biopsy for suspected malignant disease.

(12–19) J. Bone Joint Surg. [Am] 66-A:121–126, January 1984.

Woman, 65, complained of pelvic and chest pain a week after a fall. Results of a pelvic radiograph made at the time of injury were normal, but the pain worsened when the patient resumed walking. A pelvic radiograph made 7 weeks after injury showed a displaced fracture of the right pubic bone with bone destruction. Scintigraphy showed focally increased activity in the right pubic bone and ribs. Results of a thorough search for a primary tumor, including a breast biopsy, were negative. Radiography at 11 weeks showed a slight increase in osteolysis and an associated pubic bone fracture. Healing rib fractures corresponding to the areas of increased nuclide activity also were noted. Open biopsy of the pubic bone showed an organizing healing fracture and no evidence of tumor or infection. Symptoms were improved 6 months later when radiographs showed further callus formation, although prominent focal osteolysis persisted.

A history of trauma may be difficult to obtain in these patients or may not be obtained at all. Two of the present patients had normal findings on radiographs at the time of initial injury. Proper interpretation of biopsy material obtained from the site of a healing fracture may be difficult. The cause of posttraumatic osteolysis of the pubic bone is unknown, but the lack of impaction or motion in a single ramus fracture may be a factor. Focal osteolysis could represent an untypical form of reflex sympathetic dystrophy syndrome. The disorder may be similar to posttraumatic osteolysis of the distal clavicle. Delayed fracture healing may occur, especially when the pubic symphysis is involved.

▶ [The authors' presumption that osteolysis may occur because of the motion of the fracture fragment seems unlikely in itself, since virtually all fracture fragments move regardless of what type of immobilization is applied unless it is an opened reduction with firm fixation. Certainly, such fractures as the clavicle, the ribs and the humerus, as well as many others not treated with rigid immobilization, all do not show this pattern. More likely it is the authors' suggestion that this represents a focal form of reflex sympathetic dystrophy. Why isn't a parallel drawn with the acute form of osteitis pubis? Certainly the radiographs are most suggestive. In that classic acute form there is bone absorption, later followed by reformation and sclerosis, and no specific cause has yet been found.

The authors should pursue a long-term follow-up of these patients to see if they often develop a complete bony regenerative pattern along with the sclerotic nature seen in osteitis pubis. We should all certainly be aware of this phenomenon and not overdiagnose and overtreat our patients who present with this now fairly characteristic picture.—Ed.] ◄

13. Infections

13–1 **Bacteriologically Occlusive Clothing System for Use in the Operating Room.** Airborne bacteria are an important cause of joint sepsis after orthopedic implant procedures. Clothing occlusive to bacteria must be worn to achieve the lowest counts of airborne bacteria in a laminar-flow operating room. The total body exhaust gown can restrict movement and communication. W. Whyte, P. V. Bailey, D. L. Hamblen, W. D. Fisher, and I. G. Kelly (Glasgow) compared the total body exhaust gown with a disposable clothing system made of Fabric 450, which is much more comfortable and convenient. Dispersal

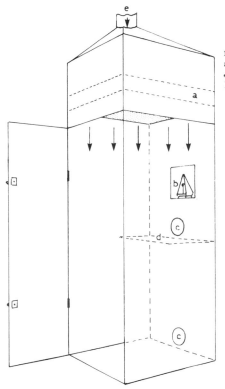

Fig 13–1.—Dispersal chamber: *a,* HEPA filter; *b,* metronome; *c,* sampling ports; *d,* shelf; and *e,* air supply. (Courtesy of Whyte, W., et al.: J. Bone Joint Surg. [Br.] 65-B:502–506, August 1983.)

(13–1)   J. Bone Joint Surg. [Br.] 65-B:502–506, August 1983.

chamber (Fig 13–1) tests were carried out in 4 subjects who exercised while wearing the different types of gown. Operating room tests were carried out with both downflow and crossflow ventilation.

The dispersal chamber tests indicated the relative ineffectiveness of wearing a surgical gown, compared with the complete system. The average airborne bacterial counts during total hip replacement were identical with the different clothing systems when downflow ventilation was used, and no significant difference was found when crossflow ventilation was utilized. With both types of clothing, counts were significantly higher with crossflow ventilation. All participants reported that the Fabric 450 system was much more comfortable and convenient than the total body exhaust system and similar to cotton clothing.

This disposable clothing system performs about as well as the total body exhaust system and is much more comfortable and convenient during hip replacement procedures. A downflow ventilation system appears to be most efficient in minimizing airborne bacteria, but a crossflow system can be used with occlusive clothing as an alternative.

▶ [Personalized isolator systems (total body exhaust gowns) are cumbersome and make communication difficult unless considerable money is invested in a communications system. The authors present an alternative technique that uses a special fabric with a hood and large mask which appears to create a comparable environment.

In 1982 Lidwell and colleagues stressed the advantages of a personal isolator system in maintaining a low incidence of postoperative wound infection following total joint arthroplasty. We now await the results of a randomized clinical trial by this group of investigators to show that their environmental studies are related to a reduction in the incidence of deep sepsis similar to that observed with total body exhaust systems.—R.H. Fitzgerald, Jr.] ◀

13–2 **Multifocal Chronic Osteomyelitis of Unknown Etiology: Report of Five Cases.** Multifocal bone lesions are rare in childhood and are of diverse etiologies. K. Kozlowski, J. Masel, S. Harbison, and J. Yu describe findings in 5 children with chronic, inflammatory, multifocal bone lesions of unknown etiology. Bone biopsy confirmed osteomyelitis in each child, but in none was a pathogen discovered.

Boy, 7 years, had inflammatory lumps over bones for 4 years that started as tender erythematous swellings and lasted for 1–2 months. The masses, which were 1–3 cm in diameter, sometimes discharged a caseous material onto the skin. New lesions appeared every few months on the elbows, hands, knees, ankles, and dorsa of the feet. Regional adenopathy was noted, but there were no signs of chronic infection or systemic disorder. Biopsies of chronic and active lesions showed chronic inflammatory epithelioid granulomas with caseation and occasional giant cells of Langhans' type. Bone biopsy disclosed necrotic bone trabeculae surrounded by coagulative necrosis. Lesions recurred throughout the next 7 years. Steroid therapy provided symptomatic relief. Antibiotics did not influence the clinical course. Radiography

(13–2) Pediatr. Radiol. 13:130–136, May 1983.

showed multiple destructive lesions that appeared to improve during follow-up. No complications resulted from the bone lesions, and the boy remains clinically well.

The other children had clinical and radiographic changes resembling those of chronic symmetric osteomyelitis. Systemic symptoms were not significant. Multifocal chronic osteomyelitis may go unrecognized for months or even years, or be treated as joint growth pains, trauma, strain, or arthritis. More severe forms may cause serious disability or even death. There is little doubt about the infectious cause of this disease, but antibiotics appear to have small effect on it. Multiple culture studies are necessary, and bone biopsy is required in each patient.

▶ [This article is a concise, yet complete, review of this perplexing condition. There is usually little or no growth disturbance of involved bones despite frequent epiphyseal and metaphyseal location of disease. Neither the clinical course nor the radiographic lesions resemble bacterial osteomyelitis, and no bacteria have been cultured despite repeated attempts by multiple authors. Some other etiologic factor is involved. It is possible that our laboratory capabilities are inadequate.—H.A. Peterson] ◀

13–3 **Predicting the Cure of Osteomyelitis Under Treatment: Concise Communication.** Osteomyelitis continues to present difficult diagnostic and therapeutic problems. It has been difficult to determine the proper duration of antibiotic therapy. Gordon D. Graham, Mi-

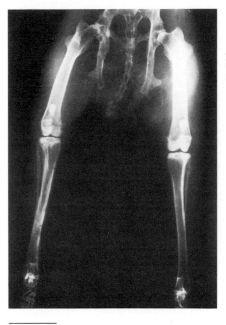

Fig 13–2.—Film of hindlegs showing periosteal elevations, early sign of osteomyelitis. (Courtesy of Graham, G.D., et al.: J. Nucl. Med. 24:110–113, February 1983.)

(13–3) J. Nucl. Med. 24:110–113, February 1983.

chael M. Lundy, Robert J. Frederick, David E. Berger, Arthur W. O'Brien, and Tommy J. Brown (William Beaumont Army Med. Center, El Paso, Tex.) evaluated the use of sequential scintigraphy with ^{67}Ga to follow the course of osteomyelitis in an animal model. Osteomyelitis was produced in adult rabbits by injecting the tibia with a suspension of *Staphylococcus aureus*, from a patient with osteomyelitis, and sodium morrhuate. Scintigraphy was performed 24 and 72 hours after injection of 2 to 3 mCi of ^{67}Ga-citrate. A small-field-of-view camera with a parallel-hole medium-energy collimator was used. Antibiotic therapy with oral rifampin and intramuscular oxacillin was begun after 4 weeks when osteomyelitis was established. Gentamicin was added after 5 weeks if no improvement was observed.

Control animals injected with sodium morrhuate alone had negative findings on scintigrams. Ten of 66 rabbits (15%) died of infection within 4 weeks of its induction. Seven (11%) had negative findings on scintigrams and negative tibial cultures. Forty-nine animals (72%) met the criteria for osteomyelitis and were started on antibiotic therapy. Twenty-five showed resolution of activity at scintigraphic study over 10 weeks and had no apparent residual infection. Eleven of 18 animals with persistently positive scintigraphic findings had positive tibial cultures when killed at 10 weeks. Animals with positive scintigraphic findings but negative cultures exhibited an impressive bony reaction. The radiographic and scintigraphic findings in infected animals are shown in Figures 13–2 through 13–4, and the scan findings are summarized in Figure 13–5.

Resolution of osteomyelitis in this animal model is associated with

Fig 13–3 (left).—Typical ^{67}Ga scan for subject with negative culture. Scan at beginning of treatment shows resolution of activity during antibiotic therapy.

Fig 13–4 (right).—A ^{67}Ga scan of same subject at end of treatment 8 weeks later.

(Courtesy of Graham, G.D., et al.: J. Nucl. Med. 24:110–113, February 1983.)

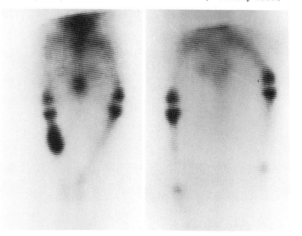

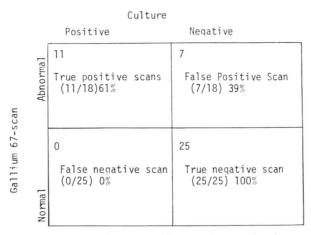

Culture

Fig 13–5.—Summary of results showing no false negative scans but frequent false positive scans. (Courtesy of Graham, G.D., et al.: J. Nucl. Med. 24:110–113, February 1983.)

a reduction in gallium accumulation. Negative findings on ^{67}Ga scintigrams appear to be strong evidence for sterilization of bone. Combined studies with gallium and ^{99m}Tc-methylene diphosphonate may be helpful when gallium accumulates in association with reparative osseous activity.

▶ [Physicians who treat patients with osteomyelitis have been hopeful that ^{67}Ga scintigraphy might prove helpful both in the diagnosis of the disease and in the establishment of an endpoint of therapy. Unfortunately, ^{67}Ga scintigraphy is taken up by reactive new bone as well as infected granulation tissue. In fact, experiments in our laboratory have demonstrated the affinity of ^{67}Ga for reactive new bone to be equal to that of infected granulation tissue.

Thus, it is not surprising that the incidence of false positive scans in this study was 39%. This of course is a very worrisome feature of the data generated in this study. When dealing with ^{67}Ga scintigraphy in the diagnosis of sepsis about musculoskeletal implants, ^{67}Ga scintigraphy has failed to diagnose 20% to 30% of the clinical infections.

At this time, ^{67}Ga scintigraphy can only be recommended as a research tool for the diagnosis and treatment of patients with musculoskeletal sepsis. It is an expensive technique. It offers little over current clinical roentgenographic findings, which are less expensive and more readily available to the practicing physician.—R.H. Fitzgerald, Jr.] ◀

13–4   **Technetium Phosphate Bone Scan in the Diagnosis of Osteomyelitis in Childhood.** D. W. Howie, J. P. Savage, T. G. Wilson, and Dennis Paterson (North Adelaide, Australia) reviewed the technetium phosphate scan findings in 280 pediatric patients seen in 1976–1981 with a clinical diagnosis of osteomyelitis. Fifty-eight patients had proved primary osteomyelitis, and 5 others had proved recurrent disease. In 45 cases, the diagnosis was based on clinical criteria only.

(13–4)   J. Bone Joint Surg. [Am] 65-A:431–437, April 1983.

Ninety-three patients had a final diagnosis of nonosseous sepsis, and 79 others had no sepsis. Studies were done with ^{99m}Tc-pyrophosphate in the first years of the study period and subsequently with ^{99m}Tc-methylene diphosphonate. A dose of about 215 μCi/sq m of body surface was used. Postinjection blood-pool scanning was followed by delayed scanning 2 hours later. Positive scans showed diffusely increased uptake initially and focal bone uptake on delayed scanning (Fig 13–6). A cold area on the delayed scan sometimes led to a diagnosis of osteomyelitis.

Scanning correctly identified osteomyelitis at all but 7 of 62 sites of disease, and was correctly negative in 74 of 79 patients without osteomyelitis. Scanning correctly distinguished all cases of cellulitis and soft tissue abscess from osteomyelitis, but osteomyelitis was diagnosed in 8 of 39 patients who had septic arthritis. Scanning was comparably accurate regardless of the duration of symptoms. It performed about equally well in all age groups and at all skeletal sites.

When 2-phase bone scanning is carried out and strict criteria are used to diagnose osteomyelitis in children, phosphate bone scanning is a highly sensitive and specific study for diagnosing osteomyelitis. Scanning usually will distinguish focal bone disease from sepsis at other sites or from nonseptic disorders. Bone scanning was sensitive in all age groups and at all skeletal sites and was independent of the

Fig 13–6.—Scan appearance of osteomyelitis in distal end of femur. (Courtesy of Howie, D.W., et al.: J. Bone Joint Surg. [Am.] 65-A:431–437, April 1983.)

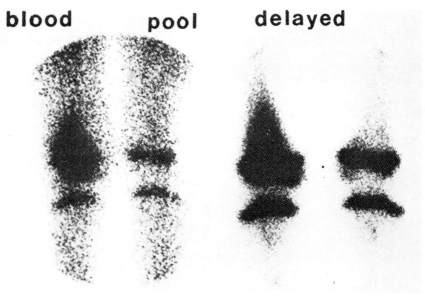

blood   **pool**   **delayed**

duration of symptoms in the present study. Other studies have found that scanning is less useful in neonates and very early in the course of disease.

▶ [This paper supports the establishment of strict criteria for the diagnosis of osteomyelitis. Technetium bone scans can enhance early diagnosis, thereby allowing better treatment and improvement in the overall results.—H.A. Peterson] ◀

13–5 **Concentrations of Some Antibiotics in Synovial Fluid After Oral Administration, With Special Reference to Antistaphylococcal Activity.** Septic arthritis is an important complication of such joint disorders as rheumatoid arthritis, and *Staphylococcus aureus* is by far the most common causative organism. It often is resistant to penicillin. M. A. Sattar, S. P. Barrett, and M. I. D. Cawley (Southampton, England) sampled synovial fluid and blood synchronously through indwelling cannulas in 20 hospitalized patients with synovial effusion of a knee joint that required aspiration and determined the relative concentrations of four antibiotics given in conventional oral doses for 1 day. Samples of synovial fluid and blood were obtained just before the first dose of antibiotic and then at 30, 45, 60, and 90 minutes and at 2, 3, 4, 6, 8, 12, 24, and 36 hours. Mean age of the 12 women and 8 men was 45 years.

Fig 13–7.—Mean serum and synovial fluid together with individual synovial fluid concentrations of amoxicillin after oral administration (7 patients) in a dosage of 250 mg 8 hourly. (Courtesy of Sattar, M.A., et al.: Ann. Rheum. Dis. 42:67–74, February 1983.)

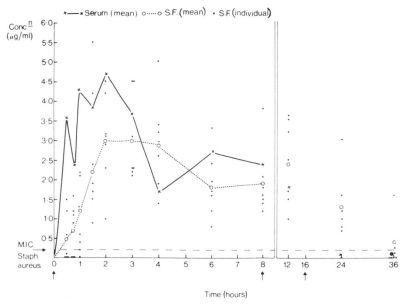

(13–5) Ann. Rheum. Dis. 42:67–74, February 1983.

Twelve had effusions due to rheumatoid arthritis or other inflammatory arthropathies.

Seven patients received 250 mg of amoxicillin every 8 hours; 6 received 500 mg of cephradine every 6 hours; 6 received 250 mg of flucloxacillin every 6 hours; and 6 received 500 mg of sodium fusidate every 8 hours. (Some patients were given doses of two of these drugs.) No morbidity resulted from the sampling procedures.

Levels of amoxicillin, cephradine, and flucloxacillin in serum and synovial fluid are shown in Figures 13–7, 13–8, 13–9. Satisfactory antistaphylococcal concentrations of both amoxicillin and sodium fusidate were obtained in synovial fluid, but cephradine levels often failed to reach the minimum inhibitory concentration for *S. aureus,* and penetration of flucloxacillin was unpredictable. The wide interpatient variations that were observed in concentrations of antibiotics in both serum and synovial fluid seemed to be independent of the underlying pathology and severity of inflammation. Concentration in synovial fluid could not be related to either clinical or laboratory indices of inflammation.

Oral sodium fusidate would seem to be appropriate as the initial treatment of nonresistant staphylococcal joint infections. Resistance may develop during treatment, and a second antistaphylococcal drug commonly is used. When the levels of drugs in the synovial fluid cannot be estimated, it probably is wise to give antibiotics parenterally

Fig 13–8.—Mean serum and synovial fluid together with individual synovial fluid concentrations of cephradine after oral administration (6 patients). (Courtesy of Sattar, M.A., et al.: Ann. Rheum. Dis. 42:67–74, February 1983.)

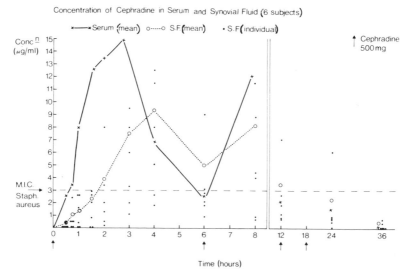

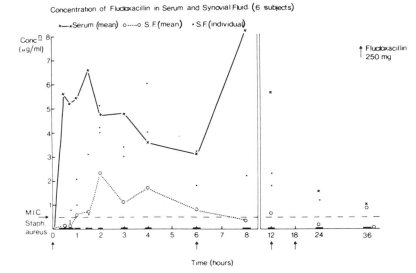

Concentration of Flucloxacillin in Serum and Synovial Fluid (6 subjects)

Fig 13–9.—Mean serum and synovial fluid together with individual synovial fluid concentrations of flucloxacillin after oral administration (6 patients). (Courtesy of Sattar, M.A., et al.: Ann. Rheum. Dis. 42:67–74, February 1983.)

in the early stages, or orally in doses greater than those usually recommended.

▶ [All physicians are concerned with the concentration of antibiotics in synovial fluid during therapy for septic arthritis. The authors' experience would suggest that amoxicillin and sodium fusidate achieve satisfactory concentrations in the synovial fluid.

The authors chose to study cephradine. Unfortunately, cephradine is not the ideal oral cephalosporin since the MIC's against staphylococci range from 1.5 to 6 μg/ml. Oral cephalothin might have been a better choice where the MIC's against *S. aureus* are usually 1.0 μg/ml. I believe cephalothin might have been as satisfactory as amoxicillin or sodium fusidate.—R.H. Fitzgerald, Jr.] ◄

13–6 Comparison Between Arthrotomy and Irrigation and Multiple Aspirations in Treatment of Pyogenic Arthritis: Histologic Study in a Rabbit Model. The goal of treatment of pyogenic arthritis is eradication of infection with preservation of joint function, but the best method of draining a joint of purulent effusion is unclear. Wayne M. Goldstein, Thomas F. Gleason, and Riad Barmada compared a regimen of antibiotics and multiple aspirations with one of antibiotics, arthrotomy, and lavage in rabbits with pyogenic arthritis induced by inoculating *Staphylococcus aureus* into the knee. Some animals had arthrotomy and lavage with normal saline after 24 hours, when swelling and a limp were present; the knees of others were aspirated daily. All rabbits received procaine and benza-

(13–6) Orthopedics 6:1309–1314, October 1983.

thine penicillin intramuscularly for 5 days starting before operation.

Comparison of uninfected rabbits (Fig 13–10) with those undergoing early arthrotomy and irrigation (Fig 13–11) showed only minor histologic abnormalities in the latter. Rare focal areas of degeneration and minimal erosive and fibrillar changes were observed. The chondrocytes appeared to be normal. Greater cartilage changes were apparent in the rabbits managed by aspiration (Fig 13–12). Diffuse

Fig 13–10.—A, coronal section of lateral femoral condyle; articular cartilage is normal. Hematoxylin-eosin; original magnification ×30. **B,** original magnification ×100. (Courtesy of Goldstein, W.M., et al.: Orthopedics 6:1309–1314, October 1983.)

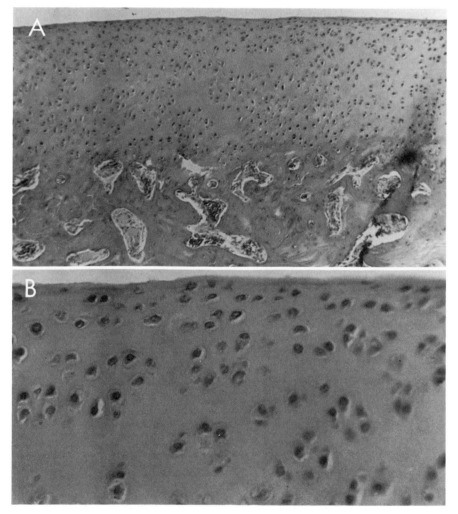

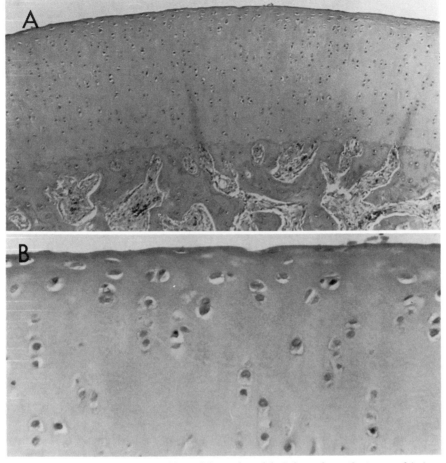

Fig 13–11.—**A,** coronal section of lateral femoral condyle 5 days after arthrotomy and irrigation. There is minimal reduction of chondrocytes in most superficial layer of articular cartilage; otherwise, cartilage appears normal. Hematoxylin-eosin; original magnification ×30. **B,** original magnification ×100. (Courtesy of Goldstein, W.M., et al.: Orthopedics 6:1309–1314, October 1983.)

erosion and widespread degeneration were seen in these. Fibrillar changes were marked and extensive.

Arthrotomy and irrigation significantly reduced articular cartilage damage in this rabbit model of gram-positive septic arthritis, compared with daily aspiration. Both groups of animals received the same antibiotic regimen. A long-term study is needed to determine if these observations are applicable to the clinical setting.

▶ [The advantages of an arthrotomy which allows the surgeon to remove infected synovium are substantiated by this research. With the Improvement of arthroscopic surgery, it might be possible to perform this procedure with a closed

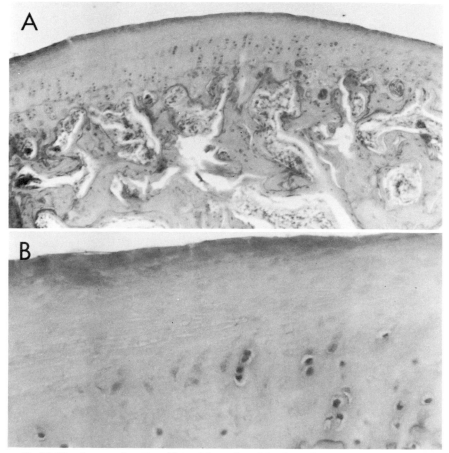

Fig 13–12.—**A,** coronal section of lateral femoral condyle after 5 days of aspiration. Superficial areas of articular cartilage are necrotic, with areas of acellularity and cloning of chondrocytes. There is diffuse fibrillar degeneration. Hematoxylin-eosin; original magnification ×30. **B,** original magnification ×100. (Courtesy of Goldstein, W.M., et al.: Orthopedics 6:1309–1314, October 1983.)

arthrotomy rather than an open procedure. Excision of infected synovium may alter catabolin production which appears to play a central role in the destruction of the glycosaminoglycans of articular cartilage in the septic process.—R.H. Fitzgerald, Jr.] ◄

13–7 **Infection After Total Hip Replacement: With Special Reference to a Discharge From Wound.** The relation between the discharging wound and late deep infection after total hip replacement is controversial. V. V. Surin, K. Sundholm, and L. Bäckman (Bȯras, Sweden) reviewed the factors associated with 34 deep infections

(13–7) J. Bone Joint Surg. [Br] 65-B:412–418, August 1983.

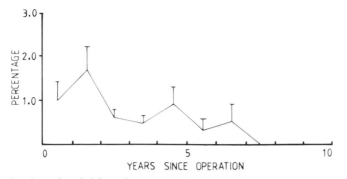

Fig 13–13.—Annual probability of reoperation for deep infection as percentage versus time since operation. Bars represent standard error (positive element only being shown). (Courtesy of Surin, V.V., et al.: J. Bone Joint Surg. [Br.] 65-B:412–418, August 1983.)

among 803 consecutive total hip replacements in patients followed for 3 to 10 years. Routine antibiotic prophylaxis was used in the last 690 operations. Deep periprosthetic infection was diagnosed within 3 months of operation in 10 patients and subsequently in 24 (Fig 13–13). *Staphylococcus aureus* was the most common isolate.

Deep infection could not be related to age, corticosteroid therapy, diabetes, perioperative complications, extreme obesity, or indication for operation. A superficial discharge, however, carried a threefold increased risk of late deep infection. Periprosthetic sepsis led to reop-

Fig 13–14.—Overall rate of reoperations for deep infection related to healing of operative wound, as percentage versus time since operation. (Courtesy of Surin, V.V., et al.: J. Bone Joint Surg. [Br.] 65-B:412–418, August 1983.)

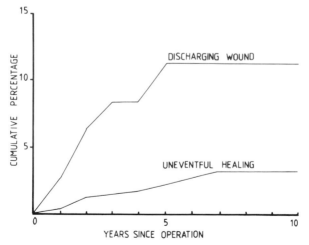

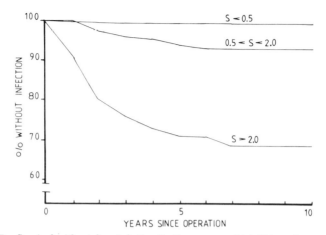

Fig 13–15.—Survival without deep infection for three groups of total hip replacement according to their prognostic scores *(S)*, as percentage versus time since operation. (Courtesy of Surin, V.V., et al.: J. Bone Joint Surg. [Br.] 65-B:412–418, August 1983.)

eration earlier in patients with postoperative wound discharge than in those with uneventful healing (Fig 13–14). The risk of deep infection was sevenfold higher when antibiotic prophylaxis was not given. Infection was also associated with postoperative complications requiring reoperation, previous hip operations, and remote infection. Multiple regression analysis indicated that the various risk factors acting together had a compound effect on the development of deep wound infection (Fig 13–15).

Deep wound infection after hip replacement is frequently associated with early wound discharge, despite complete healing when the patient leaves the hospital. Many other factors appear to contribute to deep infections in this setting, and protective measures should be directed toward all conceivable factors and routes of infection. Other factors identified in this study included serious postoperative complications, remote infection, and lack of antibiotic prophylaxis at the time of hip replacement.

▶ [The authors carefully document that the failure to administer prophylactic antibiotics requiring reoperation in the immediate postoperative period, the presence of purulent discharge from the wound, previous surgical intervention about the hip, or the presence of remote infection are associated with an increased risk of developing postoperative sepsis following total hip arthroplasty. The authors suggest that postoperative drainage from which microorganisms are isolated occurs more frequently in patients who have had previous hip surgery. Unfortunately, they do not provide the reader with the actual numbers. Thus, it is difficult to be certain if this is a statistically significant observation or a trend. Furthermore, the authors imply that such wounds may have limited ability to heal secondary to dense scar tissue. Previous hip surgery certainly has been shown in several studies to increase the risk of postoperative wound sepsis. I suspect that it relates to many factors other than just dense scar tissue in the area of the previous surgical procedure. Certainly, the vascularity of the tissues has been disturbed. This alteration of vascularity may create an area of local decreased resistance. The presence of low-grade sepsis about previously placed prosthetic devices has been shown to be a common phenomenon. Such patients must be carefully evaluated preoperatively for the presence of low-grade sepsis with aspiration, careful histologic examination of tissues obtained at the time of surgery, and aerobic and anaerobic tissue cultures prior to the administration of antimicrobial therapy. The authors fail to define this last parameter in their particular study.

Without question, the presence of postoperative wound drainage from which microorganisms are isolated must be of concern to the treating surgeon. It is frequently difficult, if not impossible, to determine whether such drainage is superficial in nature or eminates from tissues deep to the fascia. It behooves the surgeon to continue antimicrobial therapy for longer than the usual 24–48 hours in such patients. When a hematoma is forming, it is advisable to return to the operating room for decompression of the hematoma in a sterile environment. In my experience, 85%–90% of such wounds can be successfully treated without the development of deep wound infection.—R.H. Fitzgerald, Jr.] ◄

13–8 **Rectus Abdominis Muscle Flaps for Closure of Osteomyelitis Hip Defects.** Chronic osteomyelitis is expected to become increasingly prevalent with the wider use of total hip replacements. George B. Irons (Mayo Clinic) found the rectus abdominis muscle flap to be reliable for filling dead space and providing soft tissue coverage in 3 patients managed by radical debridement and long-term systemic antibiotic therapy.

Man, 48, had chronic osteomyelitis of the left hip and a history of hematogenous osteomyelitis at age 8 years. Hip fusion was done for pain at age 16. The left hip was fractured in an automobile accident at age 44. Three debridement procedures failed to provide healing. The draining sinus tract was excised and the wound debrided. Systemic antibiotic therapy was given during 4 weeks of pack changes, as the patient became afebrile and the wound granulated (Fig 13–16). The left rectus abdominis was turned down and passed extraperitoneally to the iliac fossa and through an enlarged opening in the acetabular region into the hip. The exposed part of the muscle was covered with a meshed skin graft 4 days later. The wound was still healed 6 months later, when the patient walked well with one crutch. The only symptom was numbness in the region of the hip.

The course of 1 of the other patients is illustrated in Figure 13–17. No complications occurred, and all three wounds have remained closed on follow-up for 2 to 12 months. The same principles involved in treatment of osteomyelitis of the long bones are applicable to disease of the hip, including thorough soft tissue and bony debridement, frequent wound pack changes, and appropriate antibiotic therapy. Well-vascularized muscle is used for soft tissue coverage after the infection is controlled. In 1 patient a skin island was left attached to the muscle to provide skin continuity for the wound.

► [The occasional patient with infection about the hip who has developed a second infection following a resection arthroplasty with routine wound closure and a third infection after debridement and local muscle flap, is the ideal candidate for the rectus abdominis muscle flap. This technique requires considerable resection of bone either

(13–8) Ann. Plast. Surg. 11:469–473, December 1983.

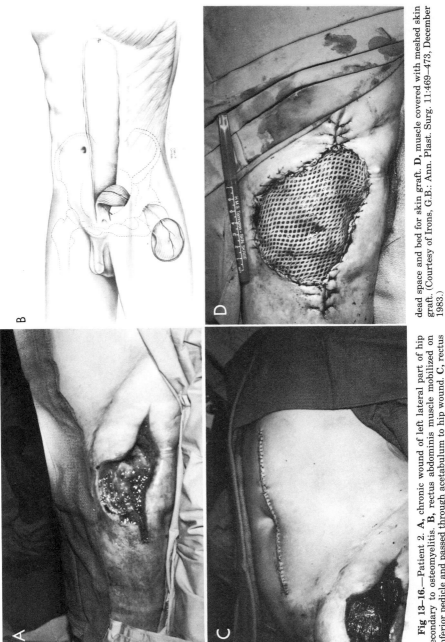

Fig 13–16.—Patient 2. **A,** chronic wound of left lateral part of hip secondary to osteomyelitis. **B,** rectus abdominis muscle mobilized on inferior pedicle and passed through acetabulum to hip wound. **C,** rectus abdominis in place in hip wound after transposition providing filler for dead space and bed for skin graft. **D,** muscle covered with meshed skin graft. (Courtesy of Irons, G.B.: Ann. Plast. Surg. 11:469–473, December 1983.)

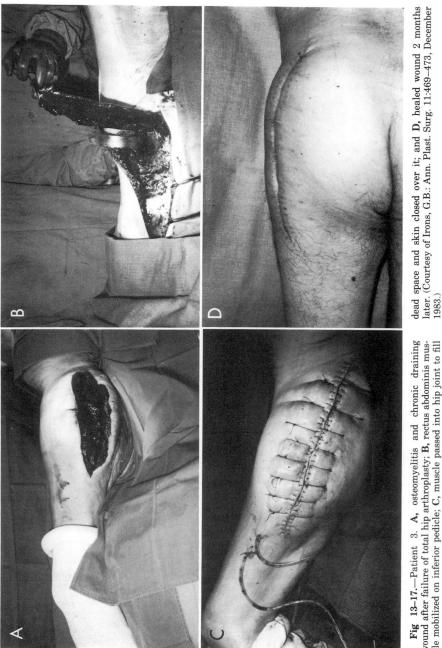

Fig 13-17.—Patient 3. **A,** osteomyelitis and chronic draining wound after failure of total hip arthroplasty; **B,** rectus abdominis muscle mobilized on inferior pedicle; **C,** muscle passed into hip joint to fill dead space and skin closed over it; and **D,** healed wound 2 months later. (Courtesy of Irons, G.B.: Ann. Plast. Surg. 11:469–473, December 1983.)

of the acetabulum or of the iliac wing. Thus, it is a purely salvage procedure requiring abandonment of all thought of future reconstruction of the hip joint.—R.H. Fitzgerald, Jr.] ◄

13–9   **Closure of Osteomyelitic and Traumatic Defects of the Leg by Muscle and Musculocutaneous Flaps.** Muscle and musculocutaneous flaps have been successfully used to provide vascularized soft tissue cover to patients with defects resulting from trauma and osteomyelitis. E. T. R. James and J. S. Gruss (Univ. of Toronto) reviewed the results of 17 such operations performed for traumatic and osteomyelitic defects in the leg. Ten patients underwent flap coverage of traumatic defects; 8 of these had compound tibial fractures. Bone grafting was carried out in 6 of the 10 cases. Many of these patients were multiple trauma victims. Two displayed a "floating-knee syndrome." Seven other patients underwent flap coverage of osteomyelitic defects. Four of them had chronic osteomyelitis complicating fracture fixation. One had a Marjolin ulcer in a long-standing pretibial ulcer. The flaps healed satisfactorily in all patients in both the traumatic-injury and infected groups. No recrudescence of infection occurred on follow-up examinations carried out for periods of 6 months to 3½ years. In one patient in the traumatic-injury group, a small sinus developed above the area of the flap after several months. The patient with the Marjolin ulcer did well.

Muscle and musculocutaneous flap transposition offers a safe means of providing soft tissue coverage for defects of the leg resulting from either trauma or chronic osteomyelitis, with predictable results. Muscle-flap transposition has the advantage of providing increased vascularity from local muscle that obliterates bone cavities and fills soft tissue defects. Antibiotic can thus perfuse an infected area. Good "take" of split-thickness skin grafts is promoted by this method. The microvascular free-flap technique is an alternative, but requires microsurgical facilities and expertise. The muscle flap has wider application than the musculocutaneous flap, is easier to use and more flexible, and provides better cosmetic results. A large defect may be covered using a combined muscle and musculocutaneous flap. Muscle flaps are covered by nonexpanded mesh split-thickness skin graft. In cases of chronic osteomyelitis, sequestrectomy combined with flap coverage can provide a well-padded covering that is resistant to trauma and will promote the cure of osteomyelitis.

13–10   **Management of Failed Total Hip Arthroplasty With Muscle Flaps.** Muscle flap operations provide a possible solution in the infrequent cases of deep wound infection complicating total hip arthroplasty that are refractory to conventional measures. Phillip G. Arnold and David J. Witzke (Mayo Clinic) used this approach in 7 patients

(13–9)   J. Trauma 23:411–419, May 1983.
(13–10)   Ann. Plast. Surg. 11:474–478, December 1983.

with failed total hip arthroplasties and multimicrobial infections. Removal of the prosthesis and cement and secondary closure had failed in all. Six to 25 procedures for wound sepsis had been done since the arthroplasty. The defects had been present for a mean of 19 months before muscle transposition. The rectus femoris or vastus lateralis, or both, was used, with or without the overlying skin. Thorough debridement of the wound is essential. The vastus lateralis was used if the rectus femoris did not adequately fill the defect. Antibiotics were given during and after operation. Patients without contraindications usually started walking after 3 weeks with assistance. The muscle transposition procedure is illustrated in Figures 13–18 through 13–21.

There were no serious complications, but 1 patient required partial

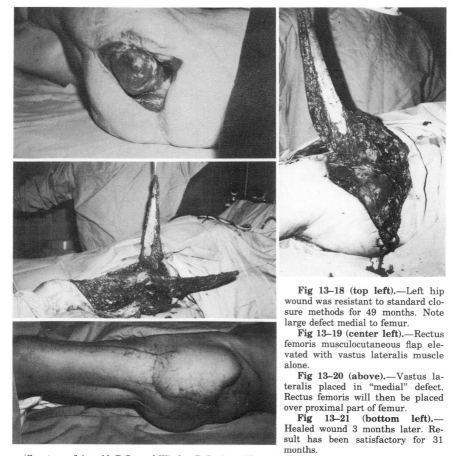

Fig 13–18 (top left).—Left hip wound was resistant to standard closure methods for 49 months. Note large defect medial to femur.

Fig 13–19 (center left).—Rectus femoris musculocutaneous flap elevated with vastus lateralis muscle alone.

Fig 13–20 (above).—Vastus lateralis placed in "medial" defect. Rectus femoris will then be placed over proximal part of femur.

Fig 13–21 (bottom left).—Healed wound 3 months later. Result has been satisfactory for 31 months.

(Courtesy of Arnold, P.G., and Witzke, D.J.: Ann. Plast. Surg. 11:474–478, December 1983.)

debridement of the transposed muscle. All the wounds were well healed at follow-up, and all the patients were able to bear weight. Three patients had been unable to bear weight preoperatively. Mean follow-up was 30 months. No patient had dysfunction related to the muscle transposition procedure.

The excellent blood supply brought into these ischemic, contaminated wounds by the transposed muscle apparently overcomes the threat of a septic situation. The muscle flap procedure has yielded favorable results in patients with recalcitrant hip wounds after total hip arthroplasty and conventional treatment.

▶ [When postoperative wound sepsis complicates total hip arthroplasty in the patient with multiple previous operations or in the patient in whom the infection has been allowed to "smolder" for many months, wound closure following excisional arthroplasty can be difficult. The scarred and fibrotic soft tissues will not obliterate the residual dead space and eventually create a sinus tract, which can become secondarily colonized leading to recurrent sepsis. In this situation, a local muscle flap has been an invaluable technique in obtaining wound closure. Frequently, a sizable portion of the greater trochanter must be excised to achieve wound closure. Prior to transposing a local muscle into the defect, the surgeon must be certain that all remaining pieces of methyl methacrylate have been removed. Retained methacrylate, especially cement plugs used for fixation of the acetabular component, can lead to recurrent sepsis.—R.H. Fitzgerald, Jr.] ◀

13–11   **Comparative Evaluation of Cefamandole and Cephalothin in Treatment of Experimental *Staphylococcus aureus* Osteomyelitis in Rabbits.** Cefamandole is a second-generation cephalosporin with excellent in vitro activity against *Staphylococcus aureus*. Jon T. Mader and Katharine J. Wilson (Univ. of Texas at Galveston) compared its efficacy with that of cephalothin in a rabbit model of *S. aureus* osteomyelitis. Osteomyelitis was produced by injecting a suspension of coagulase-positive *S. aureus* into the intramedullary cavity of the left tibial metaphysis. Treatment began 2 weeks later with either cephalothin, 50 mg/kg every 6 hours, or cefamandole, 30 mg/kg every 6 hours, for 4 weeks. The animals were killed 4 weeks after the last subcutaneous injection of antibiotic.

Bone cultures yielded *S. aureus* in all 11 control animals, 9 of 13 cefamandole-treated animals, and 7 of 15 given cephalothin. Cephalothin-treated rabbits gained more weight than did those in the other groups and had the least severe gross infections. Antibiotic concentrations in bone are compared in Figure 13–22, and growth curves in Figure 13–23. β-Lactamase inactivation of cefamandole was more evident than that of cephalothin (Fig 13–24).

The most effective cephalosporin for use in treating *S. aureus* osteomyelitis would be the one least affected by inoculum size and the one most resistant to β-lactamase. Cefamandole offers no advantage over cephalothin in the treatment of experimental *S. aureus* osteomyelitis in the rabbit. The slightly higher concentration of cefamandole than

(13–11)   J. Bone Joint Surg. [Am] 65-A:507–513, April 1983.

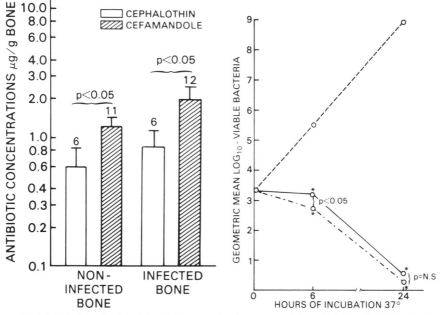

Fig 13–22 (left).—Antibiotic levels in normal and osteomyelitic bone in infected rabbits 45 minutes after a single subcutaneous injection of cephalothin, 50 mg/kg, or cefamandole, 30 mg/kg. Numbers above the half-brackets represent the number of bones assayed; the bar graph with half-brackets indicates the mean and standard errors.

Fig 13–23 (right).—Effect of cephalothin, 1 μg/ml, and of cefamandole, 2 μg/ml, on growth curves of *Staphylococcus aureus* in Mueller-Hinton broth. (- - - -) = no antibiotics; (————) = cefamandole; (— · — ·) = cephalothin; (*) = in comparison with the no-antibiotic line, $P < .01$.

(Courtesy of Mader, J.T., and Wilson, K.J.: J. Bone Joint Surg. [Am.] 65-A:507–513, April 1983.)

of cephalothin in infected bone may be offset by greater β-lactamase inactivation of cefamandole by the strain of *S. aureus* used in this study. Cephalothin was stable to both high inocula of *S. aureus* and filterable β-lactamase, and appears to be superior to cefamandole for treating osteomyelitis caused by *S. aureus*.

▶ [Antimicrobial therapy alone in the treatment of an established osteomyelitis lesion is unacceptable. This is well illustrated by failure rates of 47% in the cephalothin-treated group and 69% in the cefamandole-treated group. Although the authors conclude that cephalothin is superior to cefamandole in the treatment of experimental *Staphylococcus aureus* osteomyelitis, this conclusion is based on in vitro studies of β-lactamase inactivation of cefamandole and cefazolin. This of course is important information but does not seem justified by the results of the experimentally infected rabbits.

The authors noted increased osseous concentrations of cephalothin and cefamandole in osteomyelitic bone as compared to normal bone, utilizing a bone bioassay technique. They indicated that this observation was not the result of increased blood supply based on previous studies using an argon washout technique. Apparently in the previous study, they found that osteomyelitic bone had a decreased blood supply utilizing both strontium microspheres and dynamic ^{99m}Tc scintigraphy to quantitate

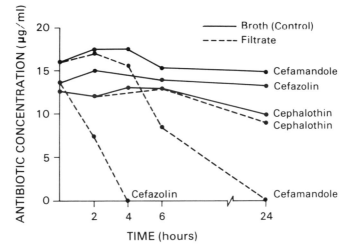

Fig 13–24.—Rate of decline in concentrations of cephalothin, cefamandole, and cefazolin when incubated at 37 degrees C in a sterile culture of a β-lactamase-producing strain of *Staphylococcus aureus* (- - - -) or a control filtrate of sterile broth (———). (Courtesy of Mader, J.T., and Wilson, K.J.: J. Bone Joint Surg. [Am.] 65-A:507–513, April 1983.)

blood flow. I suspect that the bone bioassay technique may be responsible for the differences they reported rather than an actual difference utilizing an isotopic assay. With simultaneous measurement of the interstitial fluid space, I have been able to correlate the interstitial fluid concentration of cefamandole, cephalothin, and cefazolin with the simultaneous serum concentration.

The important message in this manuscript is that cefamadole and cefazolin are subject to β-lactamase inactivation. Whether this in vitro observation is carried into the clinical situation remains to be defined. Experience with cefazolin in the treatment of osteomyelitis from which *S. aureus* has been isolated would indicate that inactivation of cefazolin is by β-lactamase producing staphylococci is not a clinical problem.

Cefamandole is a more expensive agent than either cefazolin or cephalothin. Of these three agents, cefazolin is the least expensive and is equally efficacious in the treatment of *S. aureus* osteomyelitis. Until further information is uncovered that indicates otherwise, cefazolin would appear to be the drug of choice in the treatment of this disease.—R.H. Fitzgerald, Jr.] ◄

13–12 **Pharmacokinetics of Penicillin in Osteomyelitic Canine Bone.** Osteomyelitis continues to be a difficult treatment problem, partly because of a lack of understanding of the pharmacokinetics of antibiotics in this setting. Brad B. Hall and Robert H. Fitzgerald, Jr. (Mayo Clinic and Found.), combined radionuclide methods with standard bioassay techniques to examine the pharmacokinetics of penicillin in a canine model of chronic osteomyelitis, produced by placing cotton in the medullary canal of the proximal tibial metaphysis and inoculating *Staphylococcus aureus*. The ability of benzyl penicillin to

(13–12)   J. Bone Joint Surg. [Am.] 65-A:526–532, April 1983.

penetrate the capillary membrane was determined with the use of triple-tracer indicator-dilution methods. The red blood cell space was estimated with the use of ^{99m}Tc-labeled red blood cells; the extracellular fluid space, with ^{14}C-sucrose. The volume of distribution and the interstitial fluid concentration of ^{14}C-penicillin also were determined.

Penicillin was found to cross the inflamed capillary membranes without impedance. Its passage across the vessels of osteomyelitic bone was faster than has been found previously in normal bones. The distribution of penicillin approximated the extracellular fluid space. The total concentration of penicillin in serum was directly related to that in infected osseous tissue, and the serum level of active penicillin correlated closely with the calculated interstitial fluid concentration. In contrast to the isotopic assay findings, the results of biologic assay of infected osseous tissue were inconsistent and did not correlate closely with levels of active penicillin in serum.

Penicillin crosses the capillary membranes in infected bone tissue, and it is distributed in the plasma and interstitial fluid space of osteomyelitic bone. Serum bioassay is a reproducible and relatively inexpensive means of determining the amount of penicillin in the interstitial fluid space under steady-state conditions.

▶ [The animal model in this paper shows that monitoring plasma values should bear a direct relationship to concentrations of penicillin in the interstitial fluid space of bone. This also demonstrates that there is no barrier in bone to movement of penicillin into bone.—P.J. Kelly] ◀

13–13 **Experimental Osteomyelitis: Description of a Canine Model and the Role of Depot Administration of Antibiotics in the Prevention and Treatment of Sepsis.** Osteomyelitis still is not always treated successfully, despite the many antibiotics now available. Changes in the pathogenesis of chronic osteomyelitis may be partly responsible. Robert H. Fitzgerald, Jr. (Mayo Clinic and Found.), used a canine model of subacute osteomyelitis associated with foreign body implantation to assess the chronologic roentgenographic and histologic changes and the efficacy of gentamicin, which was added to the polymethylmethacrylate cement constituting the intramedullary foreign body. Infection was produced by inoculating a suspension of *Staphylococcus aureus* around the foreign body in the tibia. The dogs were killed 1–12 weeks after surgery. Gentamicin-impregnated bone cement contained 0.5 gm of antibiotic per 40 gm of polymer.

Osteomyelitis was consistently produced in control animals. The infectious process persisted in 6 of 7 tibiae even after removal of the bone cement. The reaction was generally subacute. Involucrum formation and primary lymphocytic infiltration were noted 6 weeks postoperatively. Histologic localization of the infection was complete within 12 weeks. Antibiotic-impregnated cement prevented the devel-

(13–13)   J. Bone Joint Surg. [Am] 65-A:371–380, March 1983.

opment of infection in 9 of 10 inoculated tibiaes. The material, however, usually was ineffective in treating tibiae in which osteomyelitis was already established, despite removal of the initial intramedullary foreign body.

Osteomyelitis is consistently produced in the canine tibia by the concomitant placement of *S. aureus* and intramedullary bone cement. Sepsis did not occur in the present study when gentamicin-impregnated acrylic cement was used, but this material was ineffective in treating established infection. This model may prove useful in evaluating both newer diagnostic scanning methods and newer surgical procedures, such as local muscle flaps and free vascularized flaps.

▶ [This study provides a canine model for experimental study which in the past has centered mainly on nonmammal models. The model should be useful in testing various scanning techniques, i.e., gallium-labeled and Indium-labeled white blood cells.—P.J. Kelly] ◀

13–14 **Brucella Osteomyelitis.** The most common focal form of brucellosis is joint and bone involvement, seen in as many as 10% of patients. Maria de los A. Del Rio (Univ. of Texas, Dallas) reports a rare case of extravertebral brucella osteomyelitis.

Girl, 2, a Mexican-American, was initally seen with a limp in the left leg and an ESR of 52 mm/hr. An x-ray film obtained 2 days earlier was described as normal. The leg was swollen and tender above the ankle, but not warm or erythematous. The white blood cell count was 9,000/ml, with 22% polymorphonuclears and 14% eosinophils. A 1-cm lytic lesion without sclerosis was present in the distal left tibia. Bloody purulent material that was negative on Gram's staining was aspirated from the lesion. Cefuroxime therapy was instituted, and incision and drainage were carried out 3 days later. Chronic inflammatory tissue was reported. Cultures of the surgical specimen were negative initially, but later yielded *Brucella melitensis,* and a *Brucella* agglutinin titer of 1:80 was found. The child had eaten homemade cheese from a farm in Mexico. Trimethoprim-sulfamethoxazole therapy then was given for 6 weeks. The bone lesion was seen roentgenographically to resolve, and the ESR fell to 15 mm/hr.

Brucellosis should be considered in patients who are from an endemic area, or have a history of contact with potentially contaminated products, who present with bone lesions that develop insidiously and without generalized clinical manifestations. Focal disease due to *Brucella* can be difficult to eradicate. Both rifampin and trimethoprim-sulfamethoxazole therapy have been effective. Surgical management also is important in patients with osteomyelitis.

▶ [The article is of interest for two reasons; first, a new regime of antibiotics is offered, and second, it again emphasizes the need to obtain cultures to identify the infectious agent.—P.J. Kelly.] ◀

(13–14) Pediatr. Infect. Dis. 2:50–52, Jan.–Feb. 1983.

14. Sports

14–1 **Surgical Treatment of Exertional Compartment Syndrome in Athletes.** Exercise-related chronic compartment syndromes can interfere with an athlete's performance. C. H. Rorabeck, R. B. Bourne, and P. J. Fowler (London, Ontario) reviewed the management of 9 men and 3 women, university athletes aged 18–26 years, who were seen in 2-year period with chronic exertional compartment syndromes. Seven patients had symptoms of involvement of the anterior compartment only. All 7 had bilateral pain that subsided with rest or decreased activity. Five of the 7 patients had dysesthesia along the course of the terminal branch of the deep peroneal nerve. Three others had bilateral symptoms of involvement of the deep posterior compartment, and 2, both marathon runners, had evidence of bilateral involvement of both the anterior and posterior compartments. A slit-catheter compartment-pressure monitoring system was used for diagnosis. Electromyography and nerve conduction studies were used to exclude a nerve entrapment syndrome. Conservative measures were tried in all cases. Most patients failed to comply fully with the suggestion of complete inactivity for 4 weeks.

Bilateral fasciotomies were carried out in all 12 patients. The lateral and anterior compartments were opened in those with anterior compartment syndrome, and the superficial and deep posterior compartments in those with posterior compartment syndrome. The marathon runners underwent 4-compartment fasciotomies. All of the patients with anterior compartment involvement had complete relief of symptoms postoperatively, but 1 patient in each of the other groups had recurrent symptoms of deep posterior compartment involvement during an average follow-up of just over a year. The 2 failures appeared to result from inadequate decompression of the deep posterior compartment, a limitation of the procedure used rather than the result of faulty surgical technique.

Surgical decompression relieves the symptoms of refractory chronic exertional compartment syndrome in most patients who have elevated resting and postexercise compartment pressures. Even symptoms of deep posterior compartment syndrome should largely be relieved by a complete fasciotomy of this compartment.

(14–1) J. Bone Joint Surg. [Am] 65-A:1245–1251, December 1983.

14–2 **Results of Fasciotomy in Patients With Medial Tibial Syndrome or Chronic Anterior Compartment Syndrome.** Richard Wallensten (Stockholm) reviewed the results of fasciotomy in 9 patients with medial tibial syndrome, or shin splints, and in 8 patients with chronic anterior compartment syndrome. The respective mean ages were 26 and 21 years. The average duration of symptoms was 39 months in the medial tibial syndrome group and 30 months in the other group. Conservative measures failed in all cases. Fasciotomy was done as an outpatient procedure under general anesthesia. Patients with bilateral symptoms had both legs operated on at the same session. Intramuscular pressures were measured before and after surgery by the wick-catheter technique with the patient at rest and exercising.

Follow-up averaged 42 months in the medial tibial syndrome group and 34 months in the anterior compartment syndrome group. Compartment pressures were significantly reduced after surgery in patients with anterior tibial compartment syndrome, but in the other group, pressure in the deep posterior compartment did not change significantly. All patients with anterior compartment syndrome were free of pain, and 5 were able to train more strenuously than before surgery. Five patients with medial tibial syndrome were free of pain, and 7 considered themselves much improved. The other 2 patients believed that they were at least better than before surgery. Seven patients were able to train more than before surgery. One did not train regularly because of pregnancy.

Exercise-induced pain caused by compartment syndromes can be relieved by fasciotomy in patients with the chronic anterior compartment and medial tibial syndromes. The medial tibial syndrome can usually be managed conservatively, but fasciotomy of the deep posterior compartment may be indicated in athletes in whom conservative measures fail or recurrences are frequent. Even if pain is not completely relieved, symptoms probably will be reduced and increased activity will be possible.

▶ [The preceding two articles outline similar and appropriate approaches to the patient with exertional leg pain. In both articles, the patients with the anterior compartment syndrome were a defined group with documented pressure elevations treated by anterior compartment fasciotomy. The exercise pressure levels returned to normal, and the patients obtained good relief of their symptoms. However, the etiology of the deep posterior compartment is not clear. In the article by Wallensten, these patients did not have elevated deep posterior compartment pressures. In the second article by Rorabeck et al., the patients did have markedly elevated posterior compartment pressures preoperatively. In the first article, 4 of the 9 patients with this problem had residual pain postoperatively. In the second article 2 of 5 patients with deep posterior compartment syndromes had symptoms following fasciotomy, although their pressure values had returned to normal.

I think the points that are important in these articles are first, that the anterior

(14–2)   J. Bone Joint Surg. [Am.] 65-A:1252–1255, December 1983.

compartment syndrome seems to be a well-defined entity and treatment with fasciotomy is successful when the symptoms are documented by elevated intracompartmental pressures. Secondly, however, the deep posterior compartment syndrome may not be an isolated compartmental pressure problem, but rather, as hypothesized by Wallensten and others, may be related to fascial attachment or unnoted stress fractures.—J.R. Cass] ◄

14-3 **Another Young Athlete With Intermittent Claudication: A Case Report.** The most common cause of intermittent claudication in young athletes is external compression of the popliteal artery by an anomalous medial head of the gastrocnemius muscle. Diagnostic delay can result in loss of the extremity. S. Ward Casscells, Bruce Fellows, and Michael J. Axe (Wilmington, Del.) report a patient who lacked early signs of arterial entrapment, whose course shows the serious nature of the disorder.

Man, 19, with a long athletic career, had had progressive cramping in both calves on normal walking, and the toes had become progressively numb and turned blue on standing for a short time. Ankle and foot pain at age 14 had been interpreted as overuse syndrome, and had responded to rest, ice, and aspirin. Calf cramping during a basketball season also had resolved with limited restriction of activity. The current symptoms had begun after a long day of exercise. The toes were cool and whitish to dusky in color, and pulses were absent below the adductor canal bilaterally. Sensory loss was noted distal to the lower third of the tibia. The Doppler ultrasound ankle-arm index was 90/140. Treadmill testing and pulse volume recording were consistent with bilateral femoropopliteal stenosis, more marked on the left. Angiography showed a 4-cm occlusion on the right side and a tapering, irregular occlusion of the distal superficial femoral artery on the left; there was reconstitution only on the right side.

A left lumbar sympathectomy was followed in 3 days by a left reversed saphenous vein femoropopliteal bypass procedure with resection of an anomalous medial head of the gastrocnemius. On the right side, popliteal-popliteal bypass was done with resection of an accessory slip of the medial gastrocnemius head and subsequent lumbar sympathectomy. Clot and inflammation were present on both sides. The patient was doing well and was returning gradually to unrestricted activity when last seen.

The popliteal artery entrapment syndrome should be suspected in young athletes with intermittent claudication, and confirmed angiographically before operative treatment. Noninvasive tests such as Doppler ultrasound, treadmill testing, and pulse volume recording may be helpful, but false negative results are possible and a high degree of suspicion must be maintained.

► [The YEAR BOOK does not usually publish case reports. This is an exception—and the report speaks for itself.—Ed.] ◄

14-4 **Acute Displaced Femoral Shaft Fractures in Long-Distance Runners: Two Case Reports.** Michael A. Luchini, Alan J. Sarokhan, and Lyle J. Micheli (Children's Hosp. Med. Center, Boston) de-

(14–3) Am. J. Sports Med. 11:180–182, May–June 1983.
(14–4) J. Bone Joint Surg. [Am.] 65-A:689–691, June 1983.

scribe two well-conditioned runners who, without warning, had spontaneously displaced femoral shaft fractures requiring operative repair. Both athletes had been asymptomatic and had run long distances before the runs in which the injuries occurred.

Woman, 23, had run sporadically for about 4 years and recently had increased her weekly mileage from 10 to 15 to about 30 and had run that distance daily for 3 weeks. She missed her footing and fell after 1½ miles of a training run and experienced severe pain. Roentgenograms showed a displaced midshaft transverse femoral fracture. Skeletal traction was instituted, and closed insertion of a femoral rod was carried out 8 days after injury. The patient was able to walk with crutches 4 days after operation. Laboratory studies yielded normal results.

The other patient was a man, 38, a marathon runner, who gradually developed thigh and hip pain in the seventh mile of a marathon but who finished the race. Open insertion of an intramedullary rod was performed for the displaced femoral fracture, and the postoperative course was uneventful.

These patients apparently loaded the femur to the point of fracture in the course of a single run. The long oblique fracture that occurred in the marathon runner is characteristic of rotational stress. Transverse fractures are sometimes seen secondary to stress in the femur. Fatigue fractures of the femoral shaft have been observed in an aggressive military population, and competitive long-distance runners certainly qualify as an aggressive population. They sometimes persist in running despite severe discomfort.

▶ [The 2 cases reported by the authors are unusual in that there was no pre-existing symptoms of pain or discomfort associated with running prior to the acute displaced femoral shaft fractures. In most cases a high index of suspicion will lead to earlier diagnosis, institution of treatment, and hopefully, prevention of displacement and the necessity for surgical treatment.—F.H. Sim] ◀

14–5 **Plantar Fascia Release for Chronic Plantar Fasciitis in Runners.** Heel pain from plantar fasciitis is a frequent problem in sports medicine, and plantar fascia release has been proposed for patients who have persistent pain and disability despite vigorous conservative measures. M. P. Snider, W. G. Clancy, and A. A. McBeath (Univ. of Wisconsin, Madison) reviewed the results of 11 release operations performed on 9 serious long-distance runners between 1976 and 1981, 2 of whom had bilateral symptoms. All patients were males, with an average age of 26 years at operation. All had run at least 30 miles a week, and most had averaged 50 miles. Tenderness on deep palpation of the medial calcaneal tubercle was a constant finding. Two patients had extremely small calcaneal spurs. Corticosteroid injections were tried in all patients but 1, and many had used various orthoses. The average duration of symptoms before operation was 20.5 months. All patients had to stop running regularly.

(14–5) Am. J. Sports Med. 11:215–219, July–Aug., 1983.

The plantar fascia was incised sharply at its insertion into the calcaneus. Most patients used crutches for 2 to 3 weeks after operation. Jogging was allowed 6 to 8 weeks after operation if symptoms did not preclude it. Average follow-up was 25 months. All the feet that were operated on were improved; 10 results were rated as excellent, 1 as good. The average time to resumption of jogging was 2½ months. Eight patients returned to full training after an average of 4½ months. The final outcome was always achieved within 10 weeks after operation. The surgical specimens showed collagen degeneration and, in some cases, changes of angiofibroblastic hyperplasia and chondroid metaplasia. Calcification of degenerated matrix was seen in 1 specimen. One superficial wound infection occurred, and 2 patients had superficial wound separation.

Plantar fascia release appears to be a simple, safe treatment for patients with chronic symptoms of plantar fasciitis who fail to respond to conservative measures.

▶ [The role of operative treatment of chronic plantar fasciitis remains controversial. Certainly these authors attained satisfactory results with their operative procedure. Doctor D. Baxter from Houston also reports results such as those described in this paper, again in runners.

Traditionally, operative treatment of so-called plantar fasciitis has been fraught with many difficulties and uncertain results. It is almost as if, at least from a treatment outlook, the problem in runners is different from that of the nonrunning population. A healthy skepticism seems indicated in considering operative treatment of plantar fasciitis.—K.A. Johnson] ◀

14–6 **Athlete's Pubic Pain Syndrome (Pubialgia): Comparison of Radiologic and Scintigraphic Findings.** The puboabdominal region is a frequent site of complaints in sports medicine, particularly in soccer players, athletes, and swimmers. The complexity of this mechanical type of pathology requires rigorous diagnostic assessment from a therapeutic and prognostic point of view. The major clinical sign is pain of a mechanical nature brought on by effort, poorly systematized, involving the puboabdominal region, and frequently radiating to the internal aspect of the thighs. F. Vazelle, P. Rochcongar, J. J. Lejeune, J. Y. Herry, and A. Ramee (Rennes, France) explain the pubic pain syndrome on the basis of 2 principal mechanisms: muscle insertion tendinitis or dynamic arthropathy of the pubis.

Classification of these 2 entities is achieved by comparing radiologic and scintigraphic findings. This particular study was based on a relatively small sample of 32 case histories. The seemingly low frequency of this condition is believed to be primarily a function of lack of recognition in areas not directly related to sports medicine. In the absence of radiologic and scintigraphic findings, involvement of the symphysis proper may be excluded, and exploration may be directed toward muscular pathology, by way of echography, for example.

(14–6) J. Radiol. 63:423–428, June 1982.

Radiologic investigation is necessary: to rule out other pathologic conditions (coxofemoral, for example); to confirm the presence of pubic lesions; to establish extent of lesions; and to determine predisposing factors (hyperlordosis, asymmetrical length of lower extremities, symphyseal and sacroiliac instability).

The comparison of clinical, radiologic, and scintigraphic findings allows diagnostic evaluation of pubialgia by differentiating dynamic arthropathy of the pubis and muscle insertion tendinitis. This distinction is important since dynamic arthropathy will require prolonged rest, while tendinitis, although clinically similar but without osseous involvement, responds well to treatment and physiotherapy (analgesics, antiinflammatory agents, or ultrasound).

▶ [We have seen the same syndrome in a young football player. Recovery occurred with anti-inflammatories, but it was slow. Careful physical examination and study of the x-rays would make the diagnosis relatively simple.—M.E. Cabanela] ◀

14–7 **Mountaineering Accidents in the Sierra Nevada.** Accidents in the Sierra Nevada, with ten peaks higher than 14,000 ft, have increased markedly despite more knowledge of risks and better skills and equipment. Jon G. McLennan and John Ungersma (Bishop, Calif.) reviewed data on 201 mountain climbers who in a 5-year period sustained a total of 215 injuries while climbing on class V routes, requiring ropes for protection. The average age was 25 years. Only 43 climbers had more than 5 years of experience with class V routes. Seventy-five climbers had participated in physical fitness programs before climbing the back country. Only 31 reported knowledge of mountain medicine or first aid training. Acclimatization to altitude was practiced by only 32 subjects. More than 60% of the 90 injuries occurring during ascent were associated with acute mountain sickness. More than 10% of the 125 injuries occurring during descent were related to hypothermia. Seventeen patients died of injuries; most were head injuries. Impaired judgment was the cause of 100 injuries, as assessed by patient and partner interviews. The weather was a cause in 32 cases, and equipment failure, in 15.

All prospective climbers should have a general physical examination and participate in a comprehensive training program at least 2 months before a planned trip. Both aerobic training and isokinetic strength training are desirable. The benefits of altitude acclimatization cannot be overemphasized. Poor judgment is the most frequently cited cause of these injuries. Both acute mountain sickness and hypothermia impair judgment. Most injured climbers can be managed adequately by immobilization and evacuation by either climbing partners or a mountain rescue group. Each day's activities should be concluded before the onset of fatigue. Basic training in mountain medicine is recommended for mountain climbers.

(14–7) Am. J. Sports Med. 11:160–163, May–June 1983.

▶ [This article contains several statistical pearls, both in the introduction and the discussion. Ninety-eight percent of all outdoor accidents result from unsafe behavior or mechanical and environmental conditions. In this study, 100 of 215 accidents were the direct result of poor judgement on the part of the participants. The authors strongly reinforced the need for caution in outdoor activities, both our own as well as those of our patients outdoor adventures. They give a superficial but informative review of the diagnosis and treatment of mountain rescue operations and how it can affect the injury rate. For those involved in mountain rescue operations, their belief that 99% of the helicopter fixed wing evacuations were unnecessary and that the behavior of the rescuers from a medical standpoint was most often inappropriate are each sobering thoughts. They recommend that most of these patients should be treated by simple immobilization and land-based evacuation methods.—J.R. Cass] ◀

14–8 **Treatment of Recurrent Dislocation of Peroneal Tendons.** Recurrent dislocation of the peroneal tendons over the lateral malleolus is an uncommon injury that causes much pain and inconvenience and usually precludes participation in sports activities. Rupture of the retinaculum probably is caused by sudden supination of the foot with the knee flexed and the foot dorsiflexed. Chronic dislocations are best managed surgically. R. G. Pöll and F. Duijfjes (Leiden, The Netherlands) treated 10 posttraumatic recurrent dislocations of the peroneal tendons in 9 patients seen between 1974 and 1982. The 5 men and 4 women had an average age at operation of 25 years. Sports injuries were responsible for all initial dislocations. Only 1 patient had a past history of injury to the affected ankle. Most patients experienced daily dislocation while walking normally, usually with persistent pain. The average delay before surgery was 1 year. Two patients had signs of joint laxity on examination.

The superior peroneal retinaculum was reconstructed by transposing the calcaneofibular ligament to the lateral side of the peroneal tendons. The calcaneal insertion of the ligament was mobilized with a small bone block, reinserted in its bed after transposition, and fixed if necessary with a small spongiosa screw or a vitallium nail. If needed, the malleolar groove can be deepened subperiosteally. The ankle was immobilized in a short-leg plaster cast for 6 weeks, with weight-bearing allowed after 2 weeks. The usual findings were overstretching of the peroneal sheath and rupture of the retinaculum. The average hospital stay was 8 days. No active or passive redislocation of the peroneal tendons was apparent on follow-up after an average of 4 years. Ankle function was normal except for a slight decrease in inversion in 1 patient. There was no instability. Radiographs showed no degenerative change except in a patient with preoperative degenerative changes caused by a Pott's fracture.

Satisfactory results were thus obtained in patients with recurrent dislocation of the peroneal tendons by reconstructing the peroneal retinaculum through transposition of the calcaneofibular ligament laterally. No scarring or adhesions to the peroneal tendons develop

(14–8)   J. Bone Joint Surg. [Br.] 66-B:98–100, January 1984.

after the cancellous bone block is refixed in its original site after transposition.

▶ [The authors report on another method for repair of subluxing peroneal tendons. The procedure seems relatively simple and the results are acceptable. Some of the criticisms that the authors direct toward other methods are probably unjustified, however, as they have been reported to work equally well.—J.R. Cass] ◀

14–9 **Traumatic Dislocations of the Peroneal Tendons** are discussed by Scott R. Arrowsmith, Lamar L. Fleming, and Fred L. Allman (Emory Univ.). It has been estimated that complete peroneal tendon dislocation occurs in 0.5% of all skiing injuries and that sprain of the peroneal retinaculum occurs in 2.5% of cases. It appears that the retinaculum strips the periosteum from the lateral malleolus or avulses a thin cortical shell, while the fibrous ridge usually remains in place. A lax retinaculum after trauma or in a paralytic calcaneovalgus ankle may predispose to tendon dislocation. Violent dorsiflexion of the ankle is followed by sudden reflex contraction of the peronei and other plantar flexors that overcomes the retaining soft tissues. There usually is a snapping sensation in the posterolateral ankle and intense pain, which typically subsides rapidly. The patient often is unable to walk. Variable posterolateral swelling and ecchymosis are noted. In chronic cases a snapping or pooping sensation is noted. The avulsed cortical fragment is best seen on the mortise, or internal rotation view.

Conservative treatment remains controversial and has no role in chronic cases. Surgery includes soft tissue reconstruction or reinforcement, or both, and bony procedures for deepening the groove behind the lateral malleolus. Most bone procedures include some degree of soft tissue repair. A modification of the Evans' lateral ankle reconstruction, utilizing the peroneus brevis tendon, and a groove-deepening procedure were used to treat 3 acute and 3 chronic dislocations. All 5 patients who were followed up were free of recurrent dislocation, and all except 1 sedentary patient had returned to vigorous sports activities.

Traumatic dislocation of the peroneal tendons can become chronic if misdiagnosed as lateral ankle sprain. Conservative treatment can succeed where there is stability against dislocation following acute injury, but surgery is indicated if an inadequate or convex groove is present, and for all chronic cases. Observations of tendon fraying and rupture in chronic cases emphasize the need for early surgery when instability is demonstrated. With proper surgical treatment, even chronically affected patients usually can return to full athletic activity.

▶ [We are indebted to the authors for bringing to our attention this fairly common injury which may occur as a result of a skiing injury, and is frequently misdiagnosed.—R.N. Stauffer] ◀

(14–9)   Am. J. Sports Med. 11:142–146, May–June 1983.

Subject Index

Index to Authors